MW01199717

**ALSO BY
TODD S. PURDUM**

*Something Wonderful:
Rodgers and Hammerstein's
Broadway Revolution*

*An Idea Whose Time Has Come:
Two Presidents, Two Parties, and the
Battle for the Civil Rights Act of 1964*

DESI ARNAZ

THE MAN WHO INVENTED TELEVISION

TODD S. PURDUM

SIMON & SCHUSTER
New York Amsterdam/Antwerp London
Toronto Sydney/Melbourne New Delhi

Simon & Schuster
1230 Avenue of the Americas
New York, NY 10020

For more than 100 years, Simon & Schuster has championed authors and the stories they create. By respecting the copyright of an author's intellectual property, you enable Simon & Schuster and the author to continue publishing exceptional books for years to come. We thank you for supporting the author's copyright by purchasing an authorized edition of this book.

No amount of this book may be reproduced or stored in any format, nor may it be uploaded to any website, database, language-learning model, or other repository, retrieval, or artificial intelligence system without express permission. All rights reserved. Inquiries may be directed to Simon & Schuster, 1230 Avenue of the Americas, New York, NY 10020 or permissions@simonandschuster.com.

Copyright © 2025 by Todd S. Purdum

All rights reserved, including the right to reproduce this book or portions thereof in any form whatsoever. For information, address Simon & Schuster Subsidiary Rights Department, 1230 Avenue of the Americas, New York, NY 10020.

First Simon & Schuster hardcover edition June 2025

SIMON & SCHUSTER and colophon are registered trademarks of Simon & Schuster, LLC

Simon & Schuster strongly believes in freedom of expression and stands against censorship in all its forms. For more information, visit BooksBelong.com.

For information about special discounts for bulk purchases, please contact Simon & Schuster Special Sales at 1-866-506-1949 or business@simonandschuster.com.

The Simon & Schuster Speakers Bureau can bring authors to your live event. For more information or to book an event, contact the Simon & Schuster Speakers Bureau at 1-866-248-3049 or visit our website at www.simonspeakers.com.

Interior design by Lewelin Polanco

Manufactured in the United States of America

10 9 8 7 6 5 4 3 2 1

Library of Congress Cataloging-in-Publication Data has been applied for.

ISBN 978-1-6680-2306-8
ISBN 978-1-6680-2308-2 (ebook)

In memory of Douglas G. McGrath,
whose idea this was

Contents

DESI
ARNAZ

PROLOGUE

O n Sunday evening, October 3, 1954, Ed Sullivan, the stone-
faced New York newspaper columnist who had become perhaps the most awkward, unexpected television star, hosted a special
celebration on his popular CBS program, *Toast of the Town*: a tribute to
I Love Lucy, the network's top-rated show, which was already a national
institution on the eve of its fourth season on the air.

At a V-shaped banquet table bedecked with flowers, Sullivan had
assembled a collection of celebrities—including Dusty Rhodes, the
New York Giants outfielder who had just led his team to a World Series victory, and Howard Dietz, the lyricist of Broadway standards like
"Dancing in the Dark" and "You and the Night and the Music"—to pay
homage to the most beloved husband-and-wife team in contemporary
entertainment, Lucille Ball and Desi Arnaz.

The evening's roastmaster was a balding, avuncular, tuxedoed
character named Tex O'Rourke, a onetime Texas Ranger, Wild West

show performer, sports promoter, and boxing trainer who introduced Lucy and Desi as "two of my very favorite people, who have virtually dynamited their way into the hearts of all of us." By this point, Lucille Ball needed no introduction to anyone, but O'Rourke nonetheless fancifully celebrated her as "the worst kind of redhead." O'Rourke then turned to Arnaz, who was in fact the dominant force behind the scenes of *I Love Lucy*. "Down in the Caribbean, another hurricane was making up" one who "was born with a golden guitar in his lap, son of the *alcalde* of Santiago de Cuba, the biggest mansion in town, the biggest ranch in the hills, imported motor cars, a yacht." Then came the revolution of 1933. "He was lucky to get out of the country, got over into Miami, a refugee, penniless . . . He hooked up with a fella who supplied canaries for the local drugstore." At this, Arnaz covered his eyes in mock chagrin and demanded, "How did you find that out?" O'Rourke plowed on, "That's my job, Desi. You might say he started at the bottom because his principal job was going around in the mornings and cleaning the birdcages. But in a way it was musical. They were singing canaries."

O'Rourke then recounted Arnaz's breakout as a Latin bandleader and how he and Lucy had met when Desi went to Hollywood to repeat his role as a South American football star in the film version of the Rodgers and Hart Broadway musical *Too Many Girls*. "From the start, it was a team through rough seas and smiling skies, but always a team," O'Rourke said. "Sometimes a little bit hectic, but way down deep in their hearts they were always the kind of lovers that the whole world has got to love."

When it was her turn to speak, Ball saved her warmest words for the man who, she knew better than anyone, had been most responsible for the show's creation and for making her into one of the most famous women in the world. She and Desi had undertaken *I Love Lucy* at the lowest moment in their careers, when both had run out their string in the movies and were willing to leap into the still-untested, second-tier medium of television. Desi had persuaded a reluctant network and skeptical sponsor that the public would accept them—an unconventional, intermarried couple—as an all-American team. He had seen something in Lucy—and in the two of them together—that he knew would click with audiences. In personal terms, the show was also a determined attempt to save their marriage, after ten years of frequent career conflicts that kept Desi on the road with his band, by allowing them to work together at last. Now they had triumphed beyond their wildest expectations and seemed to have everything.

"His name escapes me at the moment," Ball deadpanned, "but this guy, who seems to be in all places at once, making like an actor, a banker, a politician—in short, a producer—gets my vote as the greatest producer of all time. And I have two little Arnazes at home to prove it." At this she cast a sexy, heavy-lidded sidelong glance at her husband, the studio audience burst into supportive laughter, and Arnaz wiped his forehead with his pocket square. "Desi, I love you," she said. "Signed, Lucy."

Arnaz rose last, with an earnest intensity not at all like his character Ricky Ricardo's so-often-exasperated mien. "Thank you, sweetheart," he began. "Thank you, Ed. You know, if it wouldn't have been for Lucy, I would have stopped trying a long time ago, because I was always the guy that didn't fit." He recounted his uphill battle to get the show on the air with himself as the costar. "Finally, one executive at CBS said, 'Well, maybe the audience would buy him, because after all they have been married . . .'" Struggling to compose himself—his shoulders hunched, looking into the middle distance and not at the camera, barely holding back tears—he went on. "We came to this country, and we didn't have a cent in our pockets. From cleaning canary cages to this night here in New York is a long ways. And I don't think there's any other country in the world that could give you that opportunity. I want to say thank you. Thank you, America. Thank you."

Arnaz sat down with his head in his hands. Sullivan—a keen judge of talent who had known Desi for years and understood better than most the crucial role he had played in his wife's success—cuffed him around the ear and drew him close in a fatherly embrace.

. . .

The gratitude that Desi Arnaz expressed that night was mutual, for against all the odds, white-bread, conformist, Eisenhower-era America had taken him and his unconventional alter ego to heart. He was adored as the man who loved Lucy, the combustible Cuban bandleader whose spluttering Spanish and long-suffering straight man's frustration at the comic antics of his crazy wife softened into a loving embrace at the end of each episode. But Desi Arnaz was so much more than Ricky Ricardo. If Ball's brilliant clowning—her beauty, her mimicry, her flexible face and fearless skill at physical comedy—was the artistic spark that animated *I Love Lucy*, Arnaz's pioneering show-business acumen was the essential driving force behind it. He was, as NPR's *Planet Money* once put it, the man who "invented television."

"There's a misconception that we—that Desi wasn't all that important to the show," Madelyn Pugh Davis, the founding cowriter of *I Love Lucy*, would recall years after his death. "And Desi was what made the show go. And he also knew that she was the tremendous talent. He knew that. But he was the driving force, and he was the one who held it together. People don't seem to realize that."

Today, nearly four decades after his death, Arnaz the performer remains a widely recognizable figure—"one of the great personalities of all time," as his friend the dancer Ann Miller once put it. Much less well understood is the seminal role he played in the nascent years of television, helping to transform its production methods, and transforming himself, a successful but second-tier Latin bandleader, and his wife, a journeyman actress in mostly forgettable B movies, into cultural icons.

It was Arnaz (and *I Love Lucy*'s head writer and producer, Jess Oppenheimer) who assembled the world-class team of Hollywood technicians who figured out how to light and film the show in front of a live studio audience, with three cameras in sync at once—a then-pathbreaking method that soon became an industry standard for situation comedies that endures to this day. It was his ability to preserve those episodes on crystalline black-and-white 35-millimeter film stock that led to the invention of the rerun and later to the syndication of long-running series to secondary markets. This innovation also made it possible for the center of network television production to move from New York to Los Angeles and created the business model that lasted unchallenged for the better part of seven decades, until the streaming era established a competing paradigm.

"*I Love Lucy* was a crucial part of entertainment in this country," said Norman Lear, the creator of the landmark situation comedy *All in the Family* and many other shows. "Lucy and Desi—I think it can be said they pretty much opened the door of Hollywood to America, and to the situation comedy. There was only one Lucy and one Desi, and between them, they knew what it took. He was a great businessman in the persona of a wonderful entertainer."

It was Arnaz's unselfconscious portrayal of the paterfamilias of an ethnically mixed family that proved a vivid contrast to the all-WASP lineup of contemporary sitcoms like *Father Knows Best* and *Leave It to Beaver*, and made him a breakthrough cultural figure in a country that would soon be transformed by growing social justice activism and a greater acceptance of diversity as a strength.

"In real life or fiction, neither Desi nor Ricky ever betrayed his Latino identity," the columnist Miguel Perez would write in the New York *Daily News* after Arnaz's death. "When Americans saw him on the screen in the 1950s, and when the world sees him now and in the future, they will not see Arnaz playing one of those criminal or drug-dealer roles usually given to Latinos. They see him as the head of an

American family who, in spite of his accent and Cuban quirks, is realizing the Latino-American dream."

Finally, it was Arnaz whose name came first in Desilu, the production company that he and Ball founded, which became the largest
producer of television content in the world in the late 1950s; provided
the studio space where many other shows, including those of Danny
Thomas and Dick Van Dyke, were staged; and eventually spawned the
global entertainment juggernauts *Mission: Impossible* and *Star Trek*.

• • •

From the start, Desi Arnaz's story is that of an unrelenting go-
getter who repeatedly defied conventional expectations and saw
creative ways forward when others did not. He was born a son of the
Cuban aristocracy, but his family lost everything and was forced to flee
in the 1933 Cuban revolution that followed the overthrow of the repressive American-backed regime of Gerardo Machado. Arnaz, seventeen years old, wound up penniless in Florida. A future that had once
envisioned college at Notre Dame and then a law degree disappeared
in favor of a high school diploma and reinvention as a self-taught musician in Miami Beach. Eventually, he formed his own band and helped
fuel the demand for Latin music that was sweeping the country, promoting the conga dance craze, first in Miami and then as a nightclub
headliner in New York.

Arnaz often attributed his willingness to take risks to this youthful
dispossession and trauma. The painful corollary was that even at the
peak of his fame and success, he would never quite fit comfortably in
either the mainstream white culture or the Mexican American community that predominated in his adopted hometown of Los Angeles.
He was a refugee, not an immigrant, and he never forgot it. "If you
feel betrayed by your own country, you're always on the run," observed
the Cuban American playwright Eduardo Machado, himself a childhood refugee, from Fidel Castro's Cuba. "And no matter how talented

you are, and no matter how many things you get, you're always being told, 'This isn't real. Our real life is in Cuba.'" He added, "You feel like a phony, because you don't know who you are. I think the more you make it, the more you feel like a phony." Even in complimenting Arnaz's business prowess, Hollywood resorted to crude stereotypes. "Yes, he's the wetback they all waited for, the wetback TV was created for," the Oscar-winning lyricist Sammy Cahn wrote for a parody roast of Arnaz to the tune of "That Old Black Magic."

Arnaz endured endless slights from an entertainment establishment that looked askance at his accent, his ethnicity, and his perpetual public image as a second banana to his superstar wife. Too many valet parking attendants and hotel clerks addressed him as "Mr. Ball." Well into the 1970s, newspapers and magazines routinely reproduced his spoken words in interviews in comically accented dialect, as if he actually were Ricky Ricardo. Network executives at first underestimated him, but they did so at their peril, because his explosive negotiating style often won out in the end. At the peak of Arnaz's power, in the late 1950s, his longtime secretary Johnny Aitchison recalled that an important business caller once complained, "'My God, I can get to the president easier than I can get to Desi Arnaz,' and I said, 'Yeah, but he's not doing a show every week, too.'"

Arnaz himself made fun of his mangled pronunciation—"He spoke no known language," his friend George Schlatter said—and his accent was almost as thick in real life as it was on the air. He proudly kept a sign in his house proclaiming ENGLISH BROKEN HERE. He was prone to malapropisms like "goosepimple pie," and once in a game of charades, trying to act out the movie title *Mildred Pierce*, he mimicked retching, hoping to summon the words "meal dread." Ricky was forever asking Lucy to "'splain" herself. "Everybody thinks of Desi as flamboyant," his longtime friend Marcella Rabwin recalled. "He wasn't flamboyant at all. He talked loud. He said funny things. But he wasn't a flamboyant man. He was a very serious, wonderful man who felt very deeply."

A 1957 profile in *Parade* magazine was typical of the condescension Arnaz faced. The author, Lloyd Shearer, found Arnaz at the Hollywood Park racetrack, recounting how he'd just turned down a multimillion-dollar offer from the Texas oil baron Clint Murchison to buy Desilu's studios because he feared relinquishing creative control. "How do you like that?" an unnamed woman in the next box sniffed. "Refusing $11 million in cash. Why, I remember when that Cuban was getting $250 a week for banging bongo drums."

But the onetime bongo player was extraordinarily prescient. "I think TV is still a child," he told the Broadway columnist Earl Wilson in the late 1950s. "Eventually, you'll have a whole wall of your house for a screen. You can have a screen as big as your house is."

Arnaz's daughter, Lucie, who has herself forged a successful fifty-year career in show business, opened unpublished private family archives—letters, telegrams, medical records, manuscripts—for this book, believing that, in life and in death, much of the Hollywood ruling class never gave her father the credit he deserved. "They kind of kicked him to the curb," she says. "Worse, they never even really gave him a place on the street to begin with."

• • •

One who consistently credited Arnaz's success was Lucille Ball herself, who by all accounts remained deeply in love with him even following their divorce in 1960.

"I had this feeling when I went into TV we were pioneering almost—no one really believed in it," Ball told an interviewer in the early 1960s, in notes for a proposed memoir she later set aside. "I enjoyed the challenge and was more surprised than anyone when *Lucy* was a success." Ball's cousin Cleo Smith once told Lucie Arnaz in an oral history, "He made it all happen, and your mother certainly was the first to give him credit for all that, no matter where the relationship went.

There just never would have been Desilu. There never would have been the production companies. There never would have been anything."

Arnaz himself acknowledged his obsessiveness as a weakness. "I got a one-track mind," he once said. "The biggest fault in my life is that I never learned moderation . . . I either work too hard or play too hard. If I drank, I drank too much. If I worked, I worked too much. I don't know. One of the greatest virtues in the world is moderation. That's the one I could never learn." Indeed, at the pinnacle of his achievement, he became a victim of his own success, the pressures of which accelerated a spiral into alcoholism and compulsive patronage of prostitutes. And in the end, the industry that Arnaz had once dominated and done so much to build passed him by.

Depending on his mood, Arnaz would sometimes claim credit for the ideas and achievements of others, or he might be self-pitying or unduly humble. He once told the composer Arthur Hamilton, "You know me, pardner. I'm no singer. As a matter of fact, I'm not a very good actor. I can't dance and I don't write. I don't do anything. But one thing I can do. I can pick people."

That he could do. Among the television talents who cut their teeth at Desilu were Jay Sandrich, who would go on to become the principal director of *The Mary Tyler Moore Show* and *The Cosby Show*; Quinn Martin, the producer who created police procedurals like *The F.B.I.* and *Barnaby Jones*; and Rod Serling, who wrote the first episode of what became *The Twilight Zone* for an installment of Arnaz's anthology series *Westinghouse Desilu Playhouse*. A lanky young actor named Aaron Spelling got his start in a bit part in *I Love Lucy* and would go on to become perhaps the most powerful television producer of the 1970s with hits like *Charlie's Angels* and *The Love Boat*.

In the nearly seventy-five years since *I Love Lucy* debuted, it has been shown in more than eighty countries, dubbed into more than twenty languages, and seen by more than a billion people. In the 1980s,

TV Guide judged that Lucille Ball's face had been seen more often, by more people, than the face of any human who ever lived. At the beginning of the twenty-first century, an episode of the show was playing every hour of every day, somewhere in the world. Its characters are as familiar as our own families, and their images appear on lunch boxes, salt and pepper shakers, tea towels, pajamas, clocks, Christmas ornaments, and the postage stamps of multiple countries. On movie and television locations to this day, the doors of the "honey wagons," the portable toilet trailers provided for the actors and crew, are not labeled "Men" and "Women" but "Desi" and "Lucy," and no one has the slightest doubt what they mean.

The singular genius of Lucille Ball has everything to do with that, of course. But so does the singular vision of Desi Arnaz.

"Because he was an outsider and a disruptor, he asked questions that people weren't asking and therefore changed the way we make TV," said Amy Poehler, who directed the 2022 documentary film *Lucy and Desi*. "And the way we make TV is very similar to how Desi first shaped it. Both he and Lucy did not look like the faces of gatekeepers in the 1950s. His story is often, at best, minimized and, at worst, like he was lucky to be on the show. And he made the show!"

How he did so is as good a story as any he ever produced. But it takes some 'splainin'.

one

ONCE ON AN ISLAND

He was a Pisces, born on an island, and for the rest of his life, in happy times and times of bad trouble, he would always return to the sea. He was an only child—a rarity in the Catholic culture of his time and place—a handsome, dark-eyed boy. In surviving formal photographs, he is sober, in his sailor suits and white linens, or in a pirate costume and painted mustache at an early birthday party. He looks mature beyond his years, and that is perhaps not surprising: From the beginning, Desiderio Alberto Arnaz y de Acha was raised as a prince.

He was born on March 2, 1917, in a spacious Spanish colonial house on Santa Lucia Street in Santiago de Cuba, the island's original capital and still its second-largest city after Havana. Not twenty years earlier, Theodore Roosevelt had stormed up the San Juan Heights, on Santiago's northeastern fringes, in the Spanish-American War. He had pronounced it a "quaint, dirty old Spanish city," though he allowed that

"it was interesting to go in once or twice, and wander through the narrow streets with their curious little shops and low houses of stained
stucco, with elaborately wrought iron trellises to the windows and cu-
riously carved balconies." Other visitors might have likened the city's
hilly, bayside topography to San Francisco's, and its polyglot, *bon temps
rouler*, music-filled atmosphere to that of New Orleans. To this day,
the region is known as *la tierra caliente*, as much for the natives' fiery
temperaments as for the high temperatures.

Situated at the head of a wide, safe harbor on the southeastern,
leeward side of the island, Santiago had been settled by the Spanish
in 1515; over the next three hundred years the city was successively
plundered by French and English forces and a rogues' gallery of pirates.
The aftermath of the slave uprising in neighboring Saint-Domingue,
now Haiti, in the 1790s brought an influx of newly freed Africans—
together with fleeing slave owners and their human chattel—that created an unusually rich demographic mix, importing African musical,
culinary, and cultural influences and establishing sugarcane—"white
gold"—as the island's dominant cash crop. Tobacco farming, copper mining, and fishing were Santiago's other industries, and in 1862
the Bacardí rum distillery was founded there, spreading its signature
sugar-based spirit across the Caribbean and the Americas.

"Something about *Oriente* invites exaggeration," the journalist Patrick Symmes wrote of the region around Santiago. "It is the hottest
part of Cuba, the most mountainous, the first settled, and the earliest to achieve glory and shame. . . . There were men present at the
founding of the city who had known Columbus himself, and the 1515
date was so early that it rooted Santiago more in the European Middle
Ages than in the new world to come. Santiago was the first capital of
Cuba, reigning for forty years before eventually losing out to Havana,
an insult never forgotten. The city served as a kind of Jerusalem to the
Americas, spreading the new faith of conquest, and the new tongue of
Castilian."

And, Symmes continued, "white or black, poor or rich, the *Santi-aguero* insisted with a straight face that fruit is riper, the sun is stronger, the women more passionate, the politics more sincere, the talk more profound, the cemeteries more grand, even the night darker, than else-where in Cuba." Residents of *Oriente* "insisted that not only was Cuban music the best music in the world, which everyone already knew, but *Oriente* was the only source of Cuban music."

By the time of Desi's birth, *la familia* Arnaz (properly pronounced Ar-NAAS, not Ar-NEZZ, as Hollywood would later Anglicize it) was firmly established as Santiago aristocracy. The matriarch, Dolores Vera y Portes, had fled Seville with her parents in the early nineteenth century when Joseph-Napoléon Bonaparte, the emperor's older brother, invaded Spain and exiled the family. The Vera family bought or was granted land in and around Santiago and built a hilltop villa on Cayo Smith, a tiny islet near the mouth of Santiago Bay. Dolores, an only child, would eventually marry Manuel Arnaz y Cobreces, the munic-ipal fire chief of Santiago, who in 1869 would be appointed the city's mayor by Queen Isabella II of Spain. (The surname *Arnaz* itself is of Basque origin, after the town of Arnaz in Spain; in France it is rendered *Arnault* and in Italy *Arnaldi*.) Manuel and Dolores's only son, Deside-rio Arnaz y Vera, the first Desi in the family line, was born in 1857. His family sent him back to Spain to study medicine at the University of Seville, and he returned to Santiago as a practicing physician. In 1884, he married Rosa Alberni y Portuondo, a member of the Cuban nobility descended from an old and illustrious Santiago family. (Her great-grandfather, the first count of Santa Inés, had also been mayor.) She would bear Dr. Arnaz seven children: three sons and four daugh-ters. One of those sons, born in 1894, was also christened Desiderio, and he would become the father of the family's third Desi, who won worldwide fame.

• • •

The first Desiderio Arnaz's growth to maturity had coincided with the rise of the movement for Cuban independence from Spain, a drive that began in 1868 when a small plantation owner, Carlos Manuel de Céspedes, freed his slaves and proclaimed Cuba a sovereign state. This sparked a ten-year war that left two hundred thousand people dead but resolved nothing—though the resulting economic disaster led for the first time to heavy American investment in Cuban real estate and agriculture. In 1886, a royal Spanish decree finally abolished slavery on the island. And in 1895, the Second War of Independence began, this time led by José Martí, a poet, journalist, and lawyer who had been an active lobbyist for the Cuban cause from his exile in the United States. Martí was killed in his first battle and is revered to this day as a national hero (both by Cubans on the island and Cubans in exile; one of the few points on which they agree). His tomb in Santiago's Santa Ifigenia Cemetery is a shrine. In 1898, spurred on by a group of neocolonialist American politicians (including Theodore Roosevelt, who was then assistant secretary of the navy, and Senator Henry Cabot Lodge of Massachusetts) and whipped into a frenzy by sensationalist press coverage of wartime Spanish atrocities and the mysterious sinking of the USS *Maine* in Havana harbor, the United States joined the Cuban rebels to repulse Spanish rule—and, not coincidentally, secure the U.S. economic stake in the island. (Many historians contend that the Cubans were already winning and did not need American intervention.) In any case, the effort was short and successful—a "splendid little war," Secretary of State John Hay called it—and climaxed in the assault on the San Juan Heights outside Santiago on July 1, 1898. That cavalry charge in turn swiftly propelled Roosevelt to the governorship of New York later that year, to the vice presidency two years later, and ultimately to the presidency upon the assassination of William McKinley, in 1901.

But Cuba's nominal independence came at a high price. The island traded its status as a Spanish colony for effective subjugation to the United States, beholden to American strategic and commercial interests. Congress passed the Platt Amendment, which was also enshrined in the new Cuban constitution, allowing the United States to intervene with military force in Cuban internal affairs as it saw fit. The next thirty years would see steadily increasing American influence and entanglement with a succession of Cuban governments, whose leadership was largely made up of veterans of the 1895–1898 war.

Arnaz family lore holds that Desiderio was attached to Roosevelt's cavalry forces at San Juan Hill, though hard evidence is lacking. What is not in dispute is that Don Desiderio achieved the rank of captain in the Liberation Army, "obtained after bloody battles in the fields of Cuba," as one of his obituaries would later put it, and the Arnaz dynasty became firmly entwined in the Cuban-American alliance. As a youth, the doctor's son Desiderio II was apparently a handful, academically capable but easily distracted and too curious and querulous for the Catholic brothers who taught him. So his parents sent him off to school in America, to the small town of Sidney, New York, near Binghamton, a destination chosen for reasons that his descendants never understood. He spoke not a word of English, lived with an American family, and had a tough time of it. His family wanted him to follow his father's career and become a physician. Instead, he eventually enrolled at the Southern College of Pharmacy in Atlanta (now part of Emory University), and in 1913 he earned the pharmacist degree that would let him style himself for the rest of his life, like his father before him, as "Dr. Arnaz." The young Desiderio returned to Santiago, opened his own drugstore, and in 1916 married Dolores de Acha y de Socias, who had been born in the neighboring Dominican Republic in 1896 and was once declared one of the twelve most beautiful women in Latin America. Dolores, known to everyone as Lolita, gave birth to their only son the next year, and the youngest Desi would grow up in an atmosphere of unquestioned privilege. Lolita's father, Alberto de Acha, had started as a Bacardí rum salesman, loading mules with as many bottles

as they could hold and hawking his load in Santiago and the surrounding countryside. He later wound up as a vice president of the company,
and when Bacardí was reorganized as a stock corporation in 1919, he
received shares valued at ten thousand dollars (nearly two hundred
thousand dollars in 2020s currency), a windfall that would benefit his
family for decades to come.

Besides running his pharmacy, the younger Dr. Arnaz operated
three farms in the countryside surrounding Santiago, one of them raising beef, another a dairy farm, and a third producing poultry and pork,
with an accompanying slaughterhouse. (A Desilu corporate press release would later claim the family's holdings amounted to one hundred thousand acres, but that may have been Hollywood hype.) These
extensive enterprises evidently did not scratch every itch, and in 1923
Desiderio II followed in his grandfather Manuel's footsteps, becoming
mayor of Santiago, at age twenty-nine the youngest in the city's history.
In his case, however, the office came not by royal appointment but after
a vigorous election campaign in which he ran on a reform platform of
improving the city's public works and infrastructure, a program that
would eventually lead to his reputation as *el alcalde modelo*, the model
mayor. Arnaz put management of his pharmacies in the hands of employees and set about remaking his hometown, which lacked a reliable
water supply, adequate sanitation, and paved streets.

He built parks and a municipal swimming spa, installed the city's
first traffic light, inaugurated the first radio telegraph service, celebrated the creation of an airfield by Pan American Airways, and greeted
a visiting Charles Lindbergh in 1929. But his crowning achievement
was the restoration of the crumbling alameda on the city's waterfront,
where he built graceful welcoming arches, a seawater swimming pool,
a wide park, and a striking clock tower, which the local chamber of
commerce dedicated in his honor. The alameda opened in 1928 with
a parade and the crowning of a queen, escorted by the eleven-year-old
Desi III, "the *simpatiquísimo* son of our Municipal Mayor, who will be

the representative of his popular father in this *simpatico* event," as one local newspaper put it.

"I don't rest," a contemporary newspaper quoted *el alcalde modelo* as saying. "I am always running at a trot." But, he added, he was ecstatic at the public's support. "I am convinced that all we need here is initiative. . . . It is possible you think me crazy, but I think to pull Santiago out of the miserable situation that exists—ruined and forgotten—we have to do some crazy acts, and I will do them."

• • •

As the only son of Santiago's most influential citizen, Desi III reaped the benefits and bore the high expectations that came with such stature. In a family scrapbook kept by Mayor Arnaz, there are pictures of little Desi, always meticulously dressed and groomed. In one, he is decked out as a swarthy buccaneer, surrounded by a gang of similarly outfitted boys and girls at his birthday party, when he appears to be about six or seven. "Desi, always social, with more friends than anyone else," his father noted in the caption. In another photograph from the same time, Desi holds a checkered starter's flag and, looking slightly frightened, stands surrounded by a raft of boys in small racing cars, ready to judge a soapbox derby in Cespedes Park, the city's central square, facing the Santiago Cathedral and city hall. Mayor Arnaz's caption combines parental pride and fatherly ego: "He was always a leader, as I taught him to be."

Indeed, young Desi was taught to take his place among the island's elite, and discipline was expected. In summers, in the country, he rose at dawn with other farmhands to milk cows and perform chores. For as long as he could remember, he rode a horse well and herded cattle; for his tenth birthday, he received a fine Tennessee walking horse. He was responsible for earning his own spending money. But from the beginning, there was also a touch of the devil in the boy, and he was more than a little spoiled. When he was four, with his family now living in a larger gray stucco colonial house in San Basilio Street, directly across from his Arnaz grandparents and about four blocks from city hall, Desi tried using the drawers of his father's bedroom chiffonier as steps "to reach a lovely pearl-handled revolver I knew he kept in the first drawer from the top, safely out of my reach, or so he thought. I was grabbing the revolver when the chiffonier tumbled forward, pinning me under and cutting a deep gash in my chin and head while simultaneously causing the revolver to fire and scaring the hell out of me." The bullet struck an antique cuckoo clock, which proceeded to chirp frantically as his nanny rushed in and extricated him and took him across the street, where his grandfather the doctor stitched him up with a needle and thread.

On San Basilio Street, his house was forbidding from the outside, with heavy wooden shutters and wrought-iron bars at the windowed facade. But the thick old walls made the home cool and shaded inside, and there was a gracious interior garden courtyard open to the sky and a front porch with rocking chairs facing the street. Mosaic tile covered the floor of the living room, which featured a plush sofa and chairs and an oil painting of Desi and his parents. Old-fashioned brass lamps shed gentle light, and a "monstrous French player piano" that no one in the family could play added an elegant touch, Arnaz's childhood friend Marco Rizo would recall. Desi would have grown up listening to the sounds of streetcars running down the middle of the cobblestoned avenues and the cries of street vendors hawking everything from peanuts to produce to household goods. He would have smelled the scent of horses, which were still a common means of daily transportation and commerce in his childhood. And, always and everywhere, he would have heard music, which streamed across the city day and night. "Music was something we both ate, drank, and bathed in from birth," Rizo recalled. Desi's uncle Eduardo de Acha played the guitar, sang, and composed songs, and another uncle, Rafael de Acha, was also musical. Somewhere along the way, Desi himself learned to play the guitar, but he never learned to read music, though he did take a few lessons from Don Alberto Limonta, an Afro-Cuban who taught many of the city's privileged sons. "No, he wasn't a prodigy who could play a Brahms concerto on an instrument by the age of four," Rizo recalled, "but he definitely stood out as an appreciator of anything musical from childhood on."

Desi's favorite place by far was his family's summer home on Cayo Smith. The *cayo*, or key, was a small island at the mouth of Santiago Bay, perched just below El Morro, the rockbound Spanish fort that guarded the entrance to the harbor. Named for the wealthy British slave trader who had once owned it, *el Cayo* rose from the blue Caribbean like "a little mountain coming out of the water," Desi would remember decades later. The island was ringed with fishing boats, crested with a white hilltop church, and dotted with wooden "bungalows"—actually, spacious vacation retreats for the city's elite. There were no cars or streets, and an energetic teenager could circle the little island's perimeter in no more than forty-five minutes on foot. Desi and his friends often swam around it instead. It was also the scene of an adolescent misadventure more embarrassing than Desi's climb up his father's dresser.

Casa Arnaz, perched on a hill and with polished hardwood floors and shuttered windows, opened onto a seventy-five-foot pier with a two-slip boathouse, berthing the sleek speedboat that took Desi's father to work at city hall each morning and Desi's own eighteen-foot, wooden Norwegian fishing skiff. It was in one of the dressing rooms of that boathouse, still ignorant of the facts of life at age twelve, that the boy undertook to learn. His co-conspirator was the same age, the daughter of his family's Black cook. "After locking the door, we began to experiment about how this thing was done," he would recall. "Neither of us had the slightest idea . . . but I was obviously anxious and noticeably ready for action and getting more and more frustrated by the minute. We had tried a number of ridiculous experiments and were working on a new one when there was a loud knock on the door. It was her mother the cook, asking her to come out. I didn't have any trouble putting on my trunks in a hurry. The small proof of my anxiety had disappeared. I wish I could have done the same."

Frantic to escape, Desi dove out a high window straight into the water below and swam as long as he could under the surface to a neighboring pier, where he heard his uncle Salvador, his father's younger brother, calling out: His mother had seen the whole tableau in pantomime. That night, Desi's father took him into his study and let him have it. "Have you ever seen me insult your mother?" Mayor Arnaz demanded. "Have you ever seen me embarrass her or make her ashamed of me? . . . You listen to me, young fellow, and listen good. Don't you ever insult your mother that way again or embarrass her as you did. Now get the hell out of here."

In an unpublished draft of his memoir decades later, Desi would reflect, "I thought in later years it was really very nice of my dad to treat the incident that way, because the wrong kind of approach at that time would have probably made me awful scared of sex and ashamed of having to find out about it. But he put it on the basis of being a gentleman and respecting your mother. If you're going to do that thing, do it privately and not in front of your house." Alas, this was a lesson that Desi, man and boy alike, seemed destined to never quite learn.

Desi's sexual education culminated three years later, at fifteen, when his uncle Salvador, who owned a small soap factory, took him to Casa Marina ("the finest whorehouse in Santiago," Desi would recall), which featured live music, elegant parlors, and an elite clientele. Desi assumed that the outing had come at the direction of his father, and there in the deluxe bordello "I learned the whole deal," as he would later put it, from "ladies of the house" who were "all young and clean and treated me very kindly, very nicely, very tenderly, and very expertly. Sometimes I wonder if perhaps it is not better to educate a young boy like that instead of letting him get into a lot of trouble trying to find out for himself."

In fact, this formative experience would cause Desi plenty of trouble in future years, because he had internalized the mixed messages about sex and gender reflected in the patriarchal, chauvinist Latin culture in which he was raised. On the one hand, sex with whores was there for the asking while nice women, respectable women—like his mother, elegant and aloof—were to be treated with courtesy extending to gallantry. On the other hand, the society of his class and time subjugated even such respected women to second-class, subordinate roles and a cruel double standard: Men could stray sexually, unpunished; women could not. Desi's grandfather Arnaz kept a *casa chica*, a second home with his mistress and multiple illegitimate children, on a small farm in El Caney north of Santiago. Marco Rizo recalled that Mayor Arnaz also "kept himself satisfied with two longstanding private relationships with women outside his marriage," a reality known to Santiago society but apparently not to Lolita. When Desi's grandfather, a non-churchgoer, was dying, his wife implored her grandson to bring a priest to pray with Dr. Arnaz. "*Ponga el corazon con Dios*" ("Put your faith in God"), the priest counseled. "*Ponga el corazon con Dios y el rabo tiezo*" ("Put your faith in God and a stiff prick"), Grandfather Arnaz replied.

Desi would struggle throughout his life to make sense of these dichotomies. "I got very mad at my father sometimes," he would recall decades later. "I was the only son, and due to his job, or whatever the hell it is, he wouldn't be home until late, and everything else, and my mother used to adore this guy and her whole life was him and I used to say to her, 'What the hell? What is this with you?' you know. 'You're like a slave to this guy. You treat him like he's a goddamn king or something.' My mother said something that I'll never forget. She said, 'Yeah, that's true, I treat him like a king.' I said, 'Why?' She said, 'That's the only way I can be a queen.'"

Indeed, by all accounts, Dolores de Acha went through life with a regal air and was a difficult, domineering woman. "Lolita came from a very privileged level of society in Cuba," Lucille Ball's cousin Cleo Smith, who came to know her in later years, would recall. "I mean, you have help by the dozens, and never lifted a finger, and never learned to cook, and you never did a bit of housework, you never did anything." The longtime Ball-Arnaz family friend Marcella Rabwin was more succinct: "Lolita was impossible for anyone to love."

Of Mayor Arnaz himself, another family member would recall, "He didn't like people that weren't sincere. He wanted everything to be just right, no deviation from the way things should be." Rabwin would remember, "There was a certain egotism in Dr. Arnaz," and after Desi III became world famous, his father "did not want Desi, in his great importance, to be more important than he had been. There was a sort of rivalry thing there. Desi didn't really feel it, but I think the father did, because he wouldn't let Desi have the last word. If they were talking and there was any slight difference of opinion, Dr. Arnaz prevailed." Decades later, Desi's daughter, Lucie, who witnessed her father's interactions with her grandparents as a young adult, would judge that Desi had lacked the deepest sort of parental nurturing and emotional support. "The mother-father strange relationship that never really was embracing, never really was loving, never was unconditional," she said. "It was always, 'You have to prove yourself. . . . You're not enough if I don't have enough,' and that'll kill you, you know."

In his own memoir, Desi would recall his father's blend of sternness and indulgence. Desi's high school was the rigorous Colegio de Dolores, led by the Jesuit order, where a decade later a boy from the provinces named Fidel Castro would also be a student. "Neither an overt rebel nor a dreamer," Marco Rizo would recall, Desi "was always a person of action." When he was a teenager, his parents gave him a car, and he drove around "with as many girls as he could fit in it," Rizo said.

In his junior year of high school, Desi realized to his chagrin that he was about to fail geometry and trigonometry and would not be able to pass his final exams—a potential crisis for a student who aspired to attend college in the United States (he and his parents often spoke of sending him to Notre Dame, a storied Catholic school and football powerhouse) and then law school. "So, what do you want from me?" Mayor Arnaz demanded when Desi gave him the news. "I'm sorry, Dad, I don't know what happened," the son explained, and the father retorted, "I know what happened. You discovered girls, and from the report I got from my soap-making brother, you didn't have any trouble learning *that* subject." Still, the mayor agreed to help out, dispatching a police sergeant on the *Palacio Municipal* detail, who was a whiz at math, to tutor Desi privately.

In March 1933, when Desi turned sixteen, his father wrote him a letter of advice that he would keep for the rest of his life. "You are now sixteen, and in my book, that means you are no longer a child; you are a man," Mayor Arnaz wrote. He warned his son that life was like the road from Santiago to the family's farm in nearby El Cobre, sometimes smooth and beautiful, sometimes ugly and rough. "Remember, good things do not come easy, and you will have your share of woe—the road is lined with pitfalls. But you will make it, if when you fail, you try and try again. Persevere. Keep swinging." It was timely advice. Desi's father might have had some inkling of just how much that counsel would be needed in the months and years ahead, because by 1933 the Cuban political and social establishment that the senior Arnaz had thrived in was falling to pieces—into violence, repression, and turmoil.

• • •

Mayor Arnaz's political career had coincided with the rise of Cuba's most powerful figure, President Gerardo Machado. One of the youngest generals in the Cuban War of Independence, Machado had aligned himself in the 1910s with liberal forces opposing the American-backed regime. He won office in 1924 as the Liberal Party candidate, campaigning on a platform of "water, roads, and schools." He pledged to serve only one term and to seek abrogation of the Platt

Amendment allowing American intervention in Cuban political affairs. He undertook an ambitious plan of public works, winning the support of local officials beholden to him. His efforts were responsible for the National Highway that stretches across the entire island and the Hotel Nacional in Havana. The hotel quickly became a deluxe destination for the American tourists who had been flooding to Cuba since the advent of Prohibition in 1920, a phenomenon celebrated by Irving Berlin in his song "I'll See You in C-U-B-A," which promised a rum-soaked paradise where "dark-eyed Stellas light their fellers' panatelas."

Sugar production thrived, American investors prospered, and Cuba became known as "the Switzerland of the Americas." But soon enough, Machado waffled on his pledge to overturn the Platt Amendment and reneged on his promise to serve just one term, running again, this time unopposed, in 1928 (with the acquiescence of President Calvin Coolidge) and forcing passage of an amendment to the Cuban Constitution through a compliant national assembly so that he could be reelected to a new, and extended, six-year presidential term. The 1929 stock market crash soon ended the boom times, and Machado led an increasingly repressive and brutal regime, backed by the United States in exchange for stability in a country now deeply entwined with American economic interests. He dealt harshly with labor unions and authorized the torture and assassination of his political opponents, who increasingly included not only leftists and university students but the country's educated elites.

"Machado was the cleverest politician ever produced by the island, greedy, revengeful and unscrupulous," wrote Ruby Hart Phillips, a distinguished American journalist of the period whose husband, James, was the *New York Times* correspondent in Havana (she would go on to assume that job herself after his death). "But he was the result of a system of government rather than the creator of a dictatorship," she added, noting that under Spanish rule, no Cuban had ever been granted governing authority. The country's post-independence leaders had all been former guerrillas, "and it was inevitable that they should follow the rule by which they had lived—that to the victor belongs the spoils." The Cuban writer and revolutionary leader Rubén Martínez Villena dubbed Machado the "*asno con garras*" (the "donkey with claws"), and the nickname stuck.

In Santiago, the Arnaz administration enforced its own measure of civic discipline. Mayor Arnaz himself undertook a kind of cultural repression against his city's signature public event. On the eve of Santiago's carnival in July 1925, the *alcalde modelo* condemned the distinctive African-derived line dance that to this day is the city's defining annual ritual. "The 'conga,' the 'rope' and other similar dances full of improper contortions and immoral gestures that do not belong to the culture of the city are not and never have been manifestations of the masquerades, and conflict with their tradition," Mayor Arnaz declared, promoting instead the more benign elements of carnival—the floats and parades and parties. "I refer to the 'conga' as that strident group of drums, frying pans and howling, to the sound of which epileptic, ragged, and semi-naked crowds run through the streets of our city. Between lubricious contortions and brutal movements, they disrespect society, offend the morals, cause a bad opinion of our customs, lower us in the eyes of the foreigners, and, most gravely, contaminate by example the minors of school age who are carried away by the heat of the display, and whom I have seen, painted and sweaty, engaging in frenetic competitions of bodily flexibility in those shameful wanton tournaments." In 1929, as violence and political unrest were growing, the mayor forbade the dances outright, banning "every kind of *comparsas* or 'parrandas' that use the music of the bongo, and other similar instruments."

In his memoir decades later, the younger Desi would not recall his father's stern injunctions. Instead he remembered the immense, convulsive power of the conga-dancing crowds as they paraded through the streets to Cespedes Park on the plaza in front of city hall. He relished the effect that the singing and dancing, the sticks and drums and clanging upside-down frying pans, had on one of his father's political advisers, Alfonso Menencier, a distinguished, middle-aged

Afro-Cuban who was always impeccably dressed in a white linen suit
and carefully knotted tie as he stood on the steps of city hall. As a raucous crowd approached the plaza one year at carnival time, Señor Menencier had more and more trouble controlling his tapping cane and
itchy feet. Finally he gave in. "He could not control himself any longer,
nobody could," Desi recalled. "His collar came open and his tie un-
done with one fuck-it-all yank. His straw hat landed on the back of his
head; with his cane high in the air, he joined them in ecstasy and so
did everyone else standing on those steps, including the mayor and the
American tourists and embassy guests of his."

Desi would claim to have had little consciousness of race until he
arrived in the United States. But in fact his father saw the conga as a
threat to civic order in part because of Santiago's complex racial dynamics. "Race mattered in Santiago, deeply," Patrick Symmes has written.
"It was the blackest city in the blackest region, the Afro-Cuba metropolis par excellence, but Santiago was still ruled by whites, who preferred
to think of Santiago as a city with 'easy' or 'warm' relations between the
races. That was only because blacks knew their separate place, and kept
to it." Country clubs, restaurants, and schools—including the Colegio
de Dolores—were all segregated, and in such elite institutions, "white
was the only color that counted."

Mayor Arnaz had a personal instrument of repressive authority
in maintaining public order: his brother Manuel, who was Santiago's
fearsome chief of police. "We had that town pretty well wrapped up,"
Desi would crack years later. While there is no evidence that Mayor
Arnaz himself was any more menacing than a local cog in the island's
political establishment—or that he was personally corrupt—the same
is not so clear for Manuel, a physically huge, forbidding figure. His
nephew George Rodon, who grew up in Santiago, remembers being
terrified of Manuel as a child, even in the 1950s. "Oh my God, it's scary,
because politics was dirty then, and Lord knows what he did," Rodon
recalled. "I don't assume Uncle Desi was dirty, but no one went into

Cuban politics and came out poor." Young Desi himself was well aware of the brutality of the Machado regime. In an unpublished draft of his memoir, he referred to Colonel Arsenio Artiz, the head of the Santiago branch of the *Porra*, the government's notorious secret police, as "a real son of a bitch, a butcher, he liked to kill."

Mayor Arnaz was at least acquiescent enough to the Machado regime to run successfully for Congress in 1932, leaving the mayoralty to join the national government in Havana. In the midst of that campaign, in the wee hours of February 3, a devastating earthquake struck Santiago, destroying about a third of the city's buildings, including city hall. Desi and his mother were alone in their house on San Basilio Street—"the big beams in the open ceiling of that huge old house were dancing around like toothpicks," he would recall—and his father, who had been at work in his office, came running home, covered with plaster and looking "like a ghost."

In the aftermath of the quake, Desi's father built the family a new house in the leafy, elegant suburb of Vista Alegre, on the city's northeastern edge, which had been developed in the 1920s with spacious mansions in the Cuban eclectic architectural style for the city's elite. The new Arnaz house—an all-wood frame, with carved columns on its front porch, the better to withstand future earthquakes—was on the neighborhood's main boulevard, the Avenida Manduley, at the edge of a circular park named for the Cuban Romantic poet José María Heredia and just across the street from an exclusive tennis club. The Arnazes moved there in late 1932. But nothing could protect them from the shock of the political earthquake that was coming.

• • •

By the summer of 1933, despite its ever-escalating campaign of torture and repression, the Machado government was collapsing. In early August, food was scarce. Across the island, conditions were growing intolerable. "Everything is paralyzed, industries shut down, stores closed, streets deserted. On the National Highway, private cars are being fired upon," Ruby Hart Phillips recorded.

In Santiago, Desi was in the new Vista Alegre house with his mother—his father was in Havana—on the afternoon of Saturday, August 12, when the phone rang with a call from his mother's brother Eduardo de Acha, a prominent lawyer. "Get your mother out of the house right away!" his uncle said. "They're coming after you!"

"Who's coming after us?" Desi asked.

"Machado has fled the country, and anyone who belonged to the Machado regime is in danger."

Indeed, the situation in Cuba had gotten so bad that the American ambassador, Sumner Welles, had given Machado an ultimatum to step down. Machado had taken a plane to Nassau in the Bahamas—taking with him, by Mayor Arnaz's later firsthand account, "five guys in pajamas," each of them "carrying two or three sacks of gold," Desi would recall.

It seemed inconceivable to the sixteen-year-old Desi that the populace of Santiago could have turned so abruptly against the *alcalde modelo*, whose election to Congress they had celebrated only the previous fall. But his uncle explained that in the chaos, a motley crew of protestors and activists were bent on revenge and wreaking havoc, with the city's Moncada military barracks in flames and the local police unable to maintain order. "Just as I hung up, I heard a rumble," Desi would recall. "I looked out and could not believe what I saw. About eight blocks away, just beginning to come over the top of the hill on our main boulevard, there was a mob of five hundred people or more carrying torches, pitchforks, guns, and God knows what else."

Together with the family's Black manservant, Bombale, Desi and his mother prepared to flee to the home of Lolita's uncle Antonio Bravo Correoso, a former senator and a leading criminal lawyer who was a political opponent of Machado. As it happens, they were driven there by Emilio Lopez, a friend who was one of the leaders of the ABC movement, an anti-Machado organization. Lopez rescued Desi and his mother when Bombale realized he had removed the battery in the Arnaz family car for repair that morning. The family hid at Lopez's house until dark, when they headed for Bravo's residence, passing *Casa Arnaz* on the way. The year-old house had been torched, though not burned to the ground, and its contents strewn all over the front garden: clothes, furniture, paintings, records, plates and glasses, sports equipment. Desi's mother's rosewood piano—which had belonged to her mother and grandmother before her—was smashed to pieces. Desi's own guitar lay in splinters like a pile of kindling.

"Civilization was stripped away in one stroke," Ruby Hart Phillips would write of that week. "Relatives of boys who had been tortured and killed started on vengeance hunts and they knew the men they were seeking." The Arnaz farms and the family house on Cayo Smith suffered similar rampages; rioters killed the livestock, leaving it to rot, and sank the family boats. At his uncle Bravo's house, Desi found himself in a state of shock. "For the next few days I walked around the house like a zombie," he would remember. "I ate and I slept, I took a bath, I talked and I thought. I thought a lot. The only thing I couldn't do was cry. I could not understand what had happened. Dad had always been loved in that town."

Mayor Arnaz was either arrested or decided to turn himself in to Havana's La Cabaña prison for protection. When Desi and his mother eventually made it to the capital themselves, conditions were if anything even worse there. "There was one sight I will never forget," Desi would recall more than forty years later. "A man's head stuck on a long pole and hung in front of his house. The rest of the body was hung two doors down in front of his father's house."

The fall of the Machado regime led to a series of short-lived governments in Havana from which a onetime army sergeant, Fulgencio Batista, eventually emerged as the dominant figure. For the next quarter century, in one strongman guise or another, Batista would remain a force in Cuban politics, ultimately ruling from 1952 on in a repressive regime whose brutality and corruption would pave the way for Fidel Castro's revolution of 1959. For Desi Arnaz, the collapse of the only social, emotional, and family universe he had ever known—at the formative age of sixteen—created psychic scars that would last a lifetime. But this youthful trauma would also be forever linked with a willingness to take bold risks—and a burning, consuming drive to succeed.

two

LA CONGA!

By January 1934, Mayor Arnaz had been languishing in Havana's La Cabaña prison for five months, without specific charges from the new government or any prospect of a hearing to resolve his fate. The family began leveraging its establishment connections to secure his release. "In my opinion as a lawyer, after studied cause, there is no charge to dictate prosecution, Desiderio," Lolita's uncle Antonio Bravo Correoso wrote the inmate. In February, Lolita's brother Eduardo de Acha argued Mayor Arnaz's cause before a judge, writing to reassure the family that Desiderio looked well, had not lost weight, and was dressed "elegantly." After some back-and-forth with state prosecutors—who seemed unwilling to accuse the mayor of any actual crime—the judge granted a writ of habeas corpus and ordered Arnaz released. Several hours later, after more anxious waiting by his family, he was finally freed.

Upon his father's release, Desi would recall years later, Mayor Arnaz was advised by Fulgencio Batista himself to go to Miami until conditions in Cuba had again stabilized. So the mayor set out alone, leaving Desi and Lolita in Havana for the time being. The clearest sign that Mayor Arnaz had not himself ultimately profited from his alliance with the Machado regime was that he arrived in the United States all but penniless and for some time did not have enough money even to afford to have his wife and son join him. Some months later, when Desi suggested to his father that it might have behooved him to himself abscond with "a couple of sacks" of the gold bars he had witnessed Machado spiriting out of the country, the son got an earful. "Money means nothing," the mayor said. "It does not create inner happiness and peace in a man. Honor and honesty does."

Finally, in May 1934, seventeen-year-old Desi traveled the ninety miles from Havana to Key West by ferry. His father had managed to scrape together only a couple of hundred dollars, so Lolita remained at her father's house in Santiago. When Desi at last made it past the glass partition of the immigration desk in Florida, he greeted his father with a long, tight, relieved *abrazo*. "*Bienvenido a los Estados Unidos de Norte América*," the mayor declared, adding that those would be the last Spanish words he'd speak to Desi until his son learned English—a challenge from the start. His father assured him that it would take some time for "your ears to get used to it and for your tongue to handle it." Decades later, Desi would confess, "My ears eventually got used to it pretty well but my tongue has been fighting a losing battle ever since."

On the bus ride to Miami, the mayor made a gesture that implied recognition of how fast Desi had grown up since they'd last met: He offered his son a cigarette. Desi had never smoked in front of him and wondered how his father knew he'd picked up the habit. "Oh, I just figured that sometime during the last nine months you probably had," the mayor replied. Their temporary home was a single bedroom in a rooming house in southwest Miami. On Desi's second night on

American soil, his father told him he'd have to get used to being on his own and sent him out to a restaurant to have dinner alone. Unable to read the menu, Desi pointed to items on four separate lines—and wound up with four bowls of different kinds of soups, "which I ate or drank or whatever the hell you call it."

Miami in 1934 was not the cosmopolitan center of Latino culture we think of today. It was still a slow, sleepy Southern town of barely a hundred thousand people, operating under the Jim Crow laws of racial segregation. It was also a winter resort for northern snowbirds fleeing the cold, and the population of Miami Beach, in particular, was increasingly Jewish. A building boom in the 1920s had promoted the barrier island of the beach as "America's Winter Playground," and the construction of the Dixie Highway south from Chicago had brought new residents and vacationers alike. Miami, like Cuba, had thrived in Prohibition, and even the Depression had not greatly diminished the tourist trade. A 1935 state law had allowed localities the option of permitting slot machines, and illegal gambling, card rooms, and casinos all thrived. But there were very few Cubans—or Spanish speakers of any stripe—in Miami. The main Cuban émigré community in Florida was then in Tampa, center of a cigar-making industry, and the great Cuban exodus that would transform the demographics of South Florida over the next forty years had not yet gathered steam. By the end of the decade, there would be some six thousand Cuban émigrés living in Miami, but when he landed in his new country, Desi would have been an outlier.

In such a bustling new environment, Mayor Arnaz knew that Desi's high school English from Santiago could not cut it in everyday life, so he arranged to send him to a Catholic summer school, St. Leo's, about forty miles north of Tampa. A niece of the deposed President Machado knew the headmaster, who gave the Arnazes a break on tuition. When Desi did not understand English—which was most of the time—he would simply say, "Yeah, yeah, okay." This occasionally led to trouble,

as when he unwittingly agreed to a boxing match with the school's experienced coach after two fellow Cuban students had claimed that Desi
was Santiago's middleweight champion. (Desi eventually took care of
the two Cubans one at a time.)

By the fall, when Desi returned to Miami, his father had joined
some other Cuban exiles in starting a business to import Mexican
tile—roof tiles, bath tiles, kitchen tiles. The Pan American Importing
and Exporting Company was capitalized with all of five hundred dollars and was operating in a small building on Third Street Southwest in
Miami. Behind the office was a forty-by-forty-foot warehouse, with a
toilet and washbasin and a smooth concrete floor. Desi suggested to his
father that they close off a portion of the warehouse as living quarters
and save the five dollars a week they had been paying the boarding-
house. The mayor just stared at Desi for a long time before replying, "I
don't want my son living in a warehouse." Eventually the elder Arnaz
relented. But living on canned pork and beans—and contending with
the vermin in the warehouse—was a trial. As Desi would later recall, "I
would get 'home' from a date and find my dad, who had been the king
of my hometown for ten years, a good-looking, still young, wonderful
guy, going around with a fucking baseball bat trying to kill the rats
before we could safely go to bed."

Mayor Arnaz's company also sought other business opportunities,
including importing bananas from Puerto Rico. The first shipment
made a promising profit, but the second arrived completely rotten, so
the idea was abandoned, and the mayor's partners gave up. All that was
left of Pan American Importing and Exporting was a pile of broken
tiles. Eventually, the mayor came up with an idea to salvage the shards:
He convinced a Miami builder that fireplace surrounds of broken tile
would be just the thing for his new apartment houses—claiming the
style was an old Santiago tradition. The scheme was such a success
that the Arnazes were soon breaking perfectly good tiles on purpose
to keep up the supply. "We were finally making enough money to eat

good," Desi would recall. "By 'good' I mean we were eating. We were still living in the warehouse. By that time, however, it wasn't too bad. We had added an easy chair, a lamp, a radio, a few necessary pieces of china and silverware, even a tablecloth. And we had won the battle of the rats."

• • •

I n March 1936 Desi turned nineteen but had not yet finished high school. His dream of college at Notre Dame now seemed far out of reach, but Mayor Arnaz was determined that his son should at least earn a high school diploma. And so in the fall of 1936, Desi enrolled at St. Patrick parish school on Garden Avenue in Miami Beach. The school had been started a decade earlier by Monsignor William Barry, an Irish-born priest, and a group of Dominican nuns and was initially housed in a cluster of former polo pony stables, though a new Spanish-style building had recently been completed. Desi entered as a senior and immediately leapt into school activities, playing basketball, joining the swim team, and earning B's in English, history, and biology and A's in Spanish. He worked out a deal in which he attended school half days so that he could earn money in the mornings from his new job: cleaning canary cages for the father of a friend who raised and sold the birds on consignment in local drugstores. The last stop on Desi's daily rounds was at a store in Miami Beach near St. Patrick. He didn't want his new schoolmates to see him doing such menial work, "so I spent a lot of time hiding behind piles of Kotex and Kleenex boxes."

"Oh, he was very polite, very manly," John Ingraham, a janitor at the school, recalled decades later in an unpublished oral history with Lucie Arnaz. Ingraham said that Desi, as one of the very few Cubans enrolled at St. Patrick, could always be recognized by his accent—"A very fine kid." Desi's best friend and basketball teammate was a stocky young boy named Al Capone Jr., the son of the infamous Chicago mobster who was serving a federal prison sentence for tax evasion

in Alcatraz. The Miami of this era was in fact a haven for the mob
and assorted raffish characters from the cities of the North. "The *real*
Miami Beach . . . was certainly the theatrical, gangster, middle-class,
New York–Chicago people," Alfred Barton, a prominent local socialite,
would recall. "They made the hotels and they created an atmosphere
here which was certainly quite different from any other town in Florida. The gangster element was so predominant here . . . that Twenty-
Third Street was the hangout for every known gangster in America."
"Sonny" Capone "was kind of on the mischievous side, too," Ingraham
recalled. Sonny's mother, Mae, would cook lunch for the boys in the
family's elegant, gated home on Palm Island in Biscayne Bay, serving
lemonade and cold drinks, and Desi and Sonny would get together
after school to sing and play the bongo drums. Sonny's uncle Ralph
Capone became a friend of Mayor Arnaz.

Desi had scraped together enough money to buy a cheap five-dollar
guitar, with a painted panorama of palm trees and girls in hula skirts
on its face, in a pawnshop. Though he never could read music, he had
learned to play the guitar as "a very young boy" in Cuba, inspired by
his uncles Eduardo and Rafael. He would later recall that "an integral
part of romancing is serenading, and for serenading, the guitar is perfect," while "you would have a hell of a time carrying a piano." His new
instrument may have been cheap, but it was perfect for beach picnics,
where "we ate and drank, sang and played, and screwed and screwed,"
he remembered. "It was fantastic."

In fact, Desi's musical talents—limited as they may have been—
soon brought an end to his cage-cleaning duties. As it happened, Alberto Barreras, the former president of the Cuban Senate, was now also
living in Miami, and he had a friend who led a small rumba band at the
Roney Plaza Hotel, one of the grand, turreted tourist destinations on
Miami Beach, its Spanish Baroque architecture mimicking the Giralda
bell tower of the Seville Cathedral. The hotel's main orchestra was led
by Buddy Rogers, a Hollywood actor and trombonist who would soon

become the third husband of the silent screen star Mary Pickford, but it was the Roney Plaza's second band that needed a guitarist and singer. The group was called "Siboney Septet," in honor of the seaside Cuban town just outside Santiago, though in truth it had only five members. Desi auditioned and was offered the job at thirty-nine dollars a week, but his father balked. "Oh, no," Mayor Arnaz decreed. "My son is not going to be a goddamn musician."

Senator Barreras lobbied on Desi's behalf, and the elder Arnaz eventually relented. The "septet" played seven nights a week and for afternoon tea dances on Sundays, but at first the band had trouble persuading customers to dance to the still-unfamiliar Latin rhythms of the rumba. So Desi, demonstrating an uncanny early instinct for showmanship, went to Buddy Rogers with an idea. He asked Rogers to end his own band's sets with a bouncy Cuban number like "The Peanut Vendor" and let the Siboney Septet's pianist take over midway as the rest of the group stepped in gradually to take up the tune. "The music will never stop," he said, "and the people will still be dancing, but they'll be dancing to our band."

The gambit worked, and within a month, with a steady income and improving prospects, Desi and his father sent for Lolita to join them at last.

. . .

A kind of cold war had persisted with Lolita for the nearly three years that she remained in Cuba, ostensibly because Desiderio could not yet afford to receive and support her in the comfort to which she had long since grown accustomed. The truth was more complex. Mayor Arnaz had begun a relationship in Miami with another woman.

She was a young widow named Ann Wilson, who had moved to Miami from New Jersey in 1934 with her three-year-old daughter, Connie. Ann had been born Anna Kropay in Schenectady, New York, where she grew up feeling she had an uncertain future as one of ten

children of Central European immigrant parents. She was newly widowed at thirty-two, after her severely mentally ill husband, an oil company executive, died in a hospital. Now she hoped for a new start and
a better life in Miami, where she had a friend who owned a winter
home. "Mother brought me to Miami because she thought it was easier to live," Connie would recall decades later. At first they stayed
with her mother's friend, then moved to an apartment in Miami
Beach. Ann met Mayor Arnaz at a social event of some sort, and before long they were an item. "The marriage of Desi's mother and his
father was broken long before they ever came to the United States,"
Connie would remember. "Because in Central and South America
divorce was frowned on, the answer was 'Just keep it quiet and each
go our own way.'" Desi's childhood Cuban friend and fellow musician
Marco Rizo said of Mayor Arnaz, "He wasn't a saint, you know? He
used to have a lot of girlfriends, and Lolita didn't like that, and that
was the beginning of the end."

It all ultimately proved too much for Lolita to accept after she arrived
in Miami, and she and Desiderio would indeed divorce in 1939. Soon
thereafter, Mayor Arnaz married Ann Wilson and adopted Connie. "He
was really the only father I ever knew," Connie would remember. "He was
a good father, on the strict side, but good. Now, looking back, he was an
excellent parent, because he instilled all the good things in me. I feel that
I'm a better person because of him."

As for young Desi, Connie recalled that he was "very nice, but we
hardly ever saw each other," given Desiderio's complicated domestic
arrangements and Desi's busy teenage life.

In his St. Patrick's 1937 senior class yearbook, the editors praised
Desi in the caption next to his formal class portrait in white cap and
gown: "We had the distinction of having an orchestra leader in our
midst for the afternoon classes this past year. . . . He possesses a splendid voice and every now and then lends it to the choir. We voted him
the politest Senior on account of his very precise Cuban mannerisms."

In fact, the raucous enthusiasm of Desi's classmates for his performance at a Roney Plaza tea dance one fateful Sunday caught the eye and ear of a visiting listener, a balding man with a pencil mustache who struck Desi as vaguely familiar. It was Xavier Cugat, the Spanish-born band-leader. Cugat had grown up and made his name in Cuba as the undis-puted king of the rumba, the sexy, syncopated step-close-step dance with swaying hips that he had popularized—often conducting with one of his tiny chihuahuas crooked in his free hand. Years later, Desi would recall Cugat's summoning him to his table with a cry of "Hey, Chico!," while Cugat would remember Desi—"a young, mild-mannered, hand-some Cuban from Santiago"—himself asking to join Cugat's band as a vocalist. Whoever asked whom first, Cugat decided that Arnaz "had a talent which matched his exuberance" and offered to hire him after an audition the following afternoon. He asked how soon Desi could come to New York, where Cugat led the house band in the elegant Sert Room at the Waldorf-Astoria Hotel. Cugat was shocked to learn that Desi had not yet graduated from high school but told him to get in touch when the academic year ended in June.

Soon enough, Desi was bound for Manhattan by bus, with one small suitcase containing a single suit and a couple of shirts and fif-teen dollars in his pocket. He was agog at the luxury of the Waldorf and quickly began rehearsals for the band's next engagement—at Billy Rose's Aquacade in Cleveland. Rose, the veteran Broadway songwriter and showman, had mounted a traveling spectacular that featured sing-ing, dancing, showgirls, and the swimming star Eleanor Holm, who was about to become his second wife. (He was previously married to the stage and radio star Fanny Brice.) The troupe performed on a giant stage adjoining a man-made lake. "Showgirls, swimmers, fantastic cos-tumes, and the Cuban birdcage cleaner," Desi would later characterize the show.

At the end of the Cleveland appearance, Cugat officially hired Desi at thirty dollars a week, nine dollars less than he'd been making with the Siboney Septet. But he was now a small part of a big-time band. There followed a whirlwind tour, starting at the Arrowhead Inn, a swanky gambling casino in Saratoga Springs, New York, during the summer Thoroughbred racing season. One evening, the club's headwaiter asked Cugat if it would be acceptable for Desi to join an admiring guest at his table, a practice generally forbidden. The guest turned out to be Bing Crosby, the most important popular singer of the day, who had revolutionized vocal crooning with his novel use of the microphone, understated conversational style, and blue-eyed sex appeal. Crosby greeted Desi in more-than-passable Spanish, praised his performance, and after a couple of shots of Añejo Bacardí rum asked what Cugat was paying him.

Crosby took up the young man's cause. "Listen, you cheap Spaniard, what do you mean paying this fine Cuban singer thirty a week?" he demanded of Cugat, in Desi's later retelling. "Give him a raise. One of these days you are going to be asking him for a job."

"Okay, okay," Cugat replied, but then turned the tables. "How about singing a song with the band, Bing?"

Crosby promptly agreed, on the condition that Cugat come through with the raise—which turned out to be to thirty-five dollars a week, with the added duty for Desi of walking the bandleader's three dogs— two chihuahuas and a big German shepherd.

Over the next six months, in appearances from Detroit to Boston to New York and every place in between, Desi absorbed hard-won lessons in showmanship and management from Cugat, who was a master of the art. Arnaz learned the importance of a crisp appearance (Cugat's band was always meticulously attired); the varieties of popular taste in music and dance; the value of commercial appeal; the intricacies of rehearsals, payroll, and personnel. But his education came at a price: He was barely getting by even on thirty-five dollars a week and had taken to stuffing celery and rolls in the billowing sleeves of his rumba shirt every time he passed through the Waldorf's kitchen. Over breakfast with Cugat, Desi told him he was quitting and was heading back to Miami to try to put together a band of his own. Cugat was skeptical but made a counter-offer. He told Arnaz he would let him bill himself as "Desi Arnaz and his Xavier Cugat Orchestra Direct from the Waldorf-Astoria Hotel in New York City." Desi was thrilled and made his own offer: He'd pay Cugat twenty-five dollars a week for the use of his name.

• • •

Cugat's secretary and Desi's fellow dog walker, Louis Nicoletti, also quit his job and agreed to accompany Arnaz to Miami as the manager of the yet-to-be-formed band. They drove south in a broken-down jalopy with just forty dollars between them and fetched up in the small two-bedroom house where Desi's parents were then still living in what must have been an uneasy truce. It was early December and the Miami Beach season wouldn't start until just before New Year's, but the boys learned that Bobby Kelly, the son of a well-known local bar owner, planned to open a little club of his own and was in the market for a Latin band. Kelly's still-unnamed club would be in the area near Twenty-Third Street, known as Miami Beach's "Rum Row" and home to such picturesque nightspots as the Ball and Chain, the French Casino, El Chico, and the Riptide Club. Posing as much bigger shots than they actually were in the Cugat organization, Arnaz and Nicoletti talked their way into being the new club's opening act—at six hundred fifty dollars a week for Desi and a five-piece ensemble, twelve weeks guaranteed. Now the trick was to get actual musicians in time for New Year's Eve, no easy order. In the end, Cugat managed to send only a motley crew—a bass player, a drummer, a pianist, a saxophonist, and a violinist—hardly the makings of a pulsing Cuban combo, which more typically included eight or ten musicians and almost certainly one trumpet and a flute.

When Desi assembled the sorry-looking group at the train station, he asked if they knew any Latin tunes at all. The answer was *not really*, so Arnaz scrambled to piece together a handful of numbers. At

10 p.m. on Thursday, December 30, 1937, Desi gave the first downbeat of his bandleading career. His players looked spiffy enough; Lolita had spent the past week sewing frilly rumba shirts, and Desi sported a red bow tie with his white linen dinner jacket. But the sound the ragtag ensemble produced was atrocious, and Bobby Kelly fired them after the first set. The musicians' union rules, however, required that Kelly had to keep the band for at least two weeks, so they got a reprieve. A local radio announcer even volunteered to feature Arnaz on a live remote broadcast. But Desi knew the pitiful sound of his new band could never cut it. The musicians had adequate skills; they just had no idea how to make a Latin sound. So before the last set of the night, Arnaz had an inspiration.

He remembered Santiago, and carnival, and the conga—the raucous, undulating dance that his father had tried to ban. His players had no plangent Chinese cornet to make the conga's signature shrill wail, no wooden claves to clack together in its defining rhythm. But Desi had a conga drum, and the little club's kitchen had a frying pan, spoons to beat it with, and a board to nail it to. So he borrowed a bottle of Bacardí from the bartender, gave his boys a few shots, and told them to follow him: "One-two-three-KICK! One-two-three-KICK!" Louis Nicoletti sprang onto the dance floor, shouting "Follow me, folks!" while Desi jumped atop the bar. Soon the whole crowd was snaking across the floor in a sinuous conga line. Desi would later call it "My Dance of Desperation."

Ever afterward, Desi would claim that on that night, he single-handedly introduced the conga to America. And while it is true that he played a crucial role in starting the conga craze that soon swept the country, it is also true that the Cuban musician Eliseo Grenet had performed the conga in 1936 in New York at a cabaret called Yumuri (later renamed Birdland) and that Desi himself had played congas with Cugat in New York in the summer and fall of 1937. What Arnaz now quickly became was the conga's brilliant popularizer and promoter—the first of many times that he would appropriate and adapt an authentic Cuban musical form to make it accessible to North American audiences. The dance's origins date to seventeenth-century Santiago, when slaves were allowed a designated time at the end of the annual sugar harvest to dance and sing in the streets in promenades known as *comparsas*. The multicultural instrumentation of an authentic conga includes bass drums (perhaps taken from Spanish military bands), *bocuses* (a portable variation of the Congolese *yuka* drum), the *corneta china* (a high-pitched trumpet brought by Chinese migrant workers in the nineteenth century), and car brake drums struck with a metal rod, which today have replaced frying pans on blocks. The act of *arrollando* rolling through city streets in a seething, pulsing human mass that mixes race and class (you might see "a cockroach dance with a cat," as one Cuban song puts it) remains seared in the memory of anyone who has ever experienced it, as Desi certainly had in his most impressionable years.

The American nightclub audiences of 1937 did not need to be experts in ethnomusicology to learn the conga's simple steps. Within a week, Bobby Kelly's new little club was jammed, with nightly conga lines spilling out into the street and around the corner, then back onto the dance floor all over again. The local press took appreciative note of the club's unique ambience and energy; one review noted, "The place is the only thing around that provides for those who like to devote themselves strictly to the rumba and tango and it's easy to forgive Band Leader Desi Arnaz when he does slip into an occasional popular dance tune because you can't keep doing those body shakers all night. Or can you?"

Dave Singer's Park Avenue Restaurant adjoined Kelly's club and provided food for patrons. "Bobby Kelly was ecstatic and told me to forget about the two weeks' notice," Desi would recall. But when Kelly suggested calling the club Desi's Place, the young bandleader demurred.

"No," he said. "Call it La Conga."

. . .

Back at the Waldorf, Cugat got wind of Desi's sudden success and dangled a golden offer: a five-year contract at two hundred dollars a week, fifty-two weeks guaranteed. Desi was torn. He asked a friend's father, Mario Mendoza, who had been a prominent lawyer in Cuba, for advice. Mendoza was dubious. "I read it," he told Desi, "and the only thing that, according to this contract, Cugat cannot do to you is fuck you—and even that is debatable because I haven't really had time to read all the small print." Mayor Arnaz, too, advised his son not to sign. "My dad told him, 'Don't do that,'" Connie Arnaz would recall. "'You won't be able to move.' He didn't know anything about show business, but he knew that."

And Desi knew himself well enough to know that he had bigger ambitions. So he turned down Cugat's offer. After the Miami winter season ended, he headed back to New York to see what he could make of himself. The initial prospects looked dim. He arrived in the city flat broke. New York in 1938 was not an especially welcoming city to an aspiring Cuban musician. To the extent that the city had a Latino population, it was overwhelmingly Puerto Rican; a 1917 act of Congress had granted United States citizenship to all Puerto Ricans. The Spanish-speaking community was concentrated in East Harlem and had yet to see the explosive growth that would follow World War II. Latin music was growing in popularity, but it was still a nightclub niche, not a ubiquitous element of popular culture. The 1939 WPA Guide to New York City listed just a single Latin American restaurant by name and airily advised that others could be found "in the vicinity of 5th Ave. and 110th St."

Desi found a home with Caesar De Franco, his bass player from Miami, and his wife at 74 Avenue O in the predominantly Italian American enclave of Bensonhurst, Brooklyn. The De Francos charged him five dollars a week rent (taking IOUs when he lacked the cash), did his laundry, and kept him nourished with pasta, cheese, bread, and jugs of red wine. He would get up at four o'clock in the morning and walk across Brooklyn and then over the Brooklyn Bridge to Manhattan, saving subway fare to buy a nickel donut and coffee, and seek work at the musicians' union headquarters.

Desi's limited musical skill was also a handicap. Working at a German restaurant in Yorkville on the Upper East Side of Manhattan, he desperately tried to hide the fact that he could not read music, playing his guitar so softly—without a pick—that he hoped it wouldn't be heard, at one point breaking his strings on purpose. His job was saved when he got even the staid Germans dancing to the conga. Eventually he picked up odd gigs here and there before landing a booking in the summer of 1938 at a lodge in Lake George. The following winter, he took the same crew back to La Conga in Miami, by now billed as "a corner of Havana in Miami Beach."

Desi's second winter in residence at La Conga picked up from where he'd left off; it was now one of Miami Beach's most popular nightspots. From the start, the club attracted celebrities: the comedian Joe E. Lewis; the Norwegian ice-skating star Sonja Henie; and Harry Richman, a now-forgotten singer and actor who was one of the highest-paid entertainers of the era and had introduced Irving Berlin's song "Puttin' On the Ritz" in an early talking picture of the same name. Richman was present one night when Desi gave a subpar performance, and he delivered an important message: "Now listen, you Cuban, you didn't go all out on that conga bit tonight. Don't you ever do that again. You don't know who might be sitting out there. You should do your best all the time, whatever you are doing."

As it happened, sitting out there one night was one of the most important figures in American show business: the lyricist Lorenz Hart. With his composing partner Richard Rodgers, Hart had been the toast of Broadway and Hollywood for fifteen years, churning out a string of hit shows and songs like "My Funny Valentine," "Where or When," and "The Lady Is a Tramp." Short, balding, brilliant, alcoholic, and gay, Hart burned his candle at both ends and loved Miami's sunshine and raffish nightlife. With his agent, Milton Bender, a former dentist generally considered to be Hart's procurer of men and known familiarly as "Doc," Hart dropped by La Conga one night. He was enraptured by Desi's palpable charisma. Some accounts suggest that Hart had developed a terrible crush on the sexy young Cuban.

Desi, not yet twenty-two, did not even realize he had been spotted. But that chance encounter would change his life.

three

————•⊰❈⊱•————

TOO MANY GIRLS

Any number of show business figures could credibly claim to have had a hand in setting Desi Arnaz on the road to stardom. Desi's own account of his big break was straightforward: In the memoir he published in his late fifties, he recounted how a man named Mario Torsatti had walked into La Conga in Miami Beach one night in the winter of 1939, admired his act, and offered him a job at a new club he was opening in New York. It was also to be called La Conga, on West 51st Street just north of Times Square, in the heart of the bustling nightclub district. Desi recalled that Torsatti had also hired "Diosa Costello, a Puerto Rican singer and dancer who had an exciting act and fitted perfectly into my conga thing. She could shake her ass better and faster than anybody I had ever seen—a great performer."

Indeed, Diosa Costello was reputed to be able to balance a glass of water on her wiggling posterior without spilling a drop. But she was much more than a tushy-twisting second banana. She was the breakout

Latina star of the era, known as "the Latin Bombshell," and her account of Desi's rise is more complicated. She was born Juana de Dios Castrello in Guayama, Puerto Rico, in 1913 and had made a name for herself in clubs from Spanish Harlem to Florida. In later years she would go on to play a replacement Bloody Mary in the original Broadway production of *South Pacific*. In the fall of 1938, when Desi was back in Miami waiting for the winter season to start again, Costello recalled, she had already been signed by Torsatti to work at La Conga in New York. In the meantime, she was fulfilling a monthlong engagement at the Five O'Clock Club in Miami Beach, a jumping joint co-owned by the brassy singer and comedienne Martha Raye, which got its name because it gave free drinks to any patrons still on their feet at 5 a.m. "Desi used to come around—I never knew the man—he used to come around with his guitar to see if he could get a job," Costello would recall decades later, in an oral history for the Smithsonian Institution's National Museum of American History. "So me, with my soft heart, I went to Martha and I said, 'Martha, this guy's looking for a job. Do you think we could do something?'" Raye told Costello that there was no money to hire Desi, but he could come around if he wanted and play for tips. So Desi would drop by after 2 a.m. "He didn't do it for the audience," Costello remembered. "But he did it for us.

"Months went by," she continued, "and he came back to New York. And he looked me up. I was at La Conga, and I went to Mario . . . and I said, 'Mario, what do you think about this guy?'" At the time, Carmen Cavallaro, known as "The Poet of the Piano," led the house Latin band at La Conga, but he was leaving to go to the Waldorf-Astoria, and Costello suggested that Desi might take his place. "So Mario says, 'Well, what does he do?' And I said, 'Well, he plays the guitar very bad. He doesn't sing so good. He doesn't play the conga so good, either. But look at him! He's gorgeous! He's gonna draw the women! What else? Who cares what else he does?'"

To put it another way, whatever it is that makes a star performer, Costello knew that Desi had it. And however it happened, Torsatti hired him, and he quickly became a phenomenon, billed as "King Conga." He drew the cream of New York society, including the season's reigning debutante, Brenda Frazier, and her frequent escort, the *New Yorker* cartoonist Peter Arno. Women he'd never met soon passed him mash notes with the keys to their apartments. Walter Winchell, the most powerful gossip columnist of his day, became a fan and a regular patron. Dorothy Kilgallen, who wrote the Hearst newspaper chain's "Voice of Broadway" column, described Desi as "a black-eyed, slim-hipped rhythm conscious young Latin on the threshold of becoming a fad."

La Conga had timbered ceilings, mirrored walls, and fake palm trees, and the press described it as a "basement place where even the bartenders shake up drinks in a one-two-three-kick tempo." It featured three shows nightly—at eight, midnight, and two thirty a.m.—and served dinner from eight to ten, starting at a dollar twenty-five. The club even published a small brochure illustrating how to do *la conga*, "the most popular dance created since dancing was first introduced because of its simplicity, grace and rhythm." Desi could barely believe his good fortune. The slim-hipped sensation drew not only the leading lights of Manhattan's haute monde but the A-listers of its underworld as well—chief among them Polly Adler, the proprietress of the most elegant, exclusive bordello in town, with four-poster beds, seventeenth-century French décor, antique mirrors, candlelight, fresh-cut flowers, and the fairest young women this side of Elysium.

Adler was a celebrity in her own right, the sort of genteelly notorious figure that a more permissive age could not have produced. She was charged at least seventeen times with maintaining ever-grander houses of prostitution and generally got off with a slap on the wrist. In her memoir, *A House Is Not a Home*, she boasted that in the late 1930s she ran a close second to Grover Whalen as New York City's official greeter, drawing her patrons not only from *Who's Who* and the *Social Register* but also from the *Almanach de Gotha*, the definitive directory of European royalty. Her clients included the playwright George S. Kaufman (who ran a tab), the actors Milton Berle and John Garfield, and the *New Yorker* writer Robert Benchley, who had selected the fine books and signed first editions that lined the shelves of Adler's establishment. ("I regret to say, as yet unread—at least by me," she would confess.) Desi became a customer after he noticed a gorgeous redhead moving past La Conga's bandstand one night—she was one of Polly's employees—and Adler invited him over for a breakfast of caviar, sturgeon, and scrambled eggs, with the redhead as a complimentary dessert.

"A man's visit to Polly's meant more than just sleeping with a woman," Adler wrote. "He expected to be amused and even informed. He knew he could count on conversation about the latest plays and the newest books; he would hear fresh and funny stories and anecdotes about the town characters. Good talk and good liquor; good-looking girls in good-looking surroundings, these were the ingredients which went into the making of a good night, and when my men said, 'Good night' (although it was usually five or six in the morning), they really meant it had been." Desi's summary of the experience was less elevated. "I've had my share of delicious sex in my life, but that redhead was something else," he recalled. "If there was anything I had not learned at Casa Marina, she taught it to me. She was insatiable."

So, it turned out, was Desi, and not just with redheads but with blondes, brunettes, and every shade in between. He would never forget the sybaritic surroundings of Polly Adler's—the crystal chandeliers, fresh flowers, deluxe breakfasts, the king-sized beds, candlelight, and strategically placed mirrors. He relished the no-questions-asked, uncritical welcome he could count on there, without getting "into any romance deals," and for the rest of his life, married or single, drunk or sober, Desi would patronize prostitutes of varying elegance or seaminess for release and relief. This fondness for quick, commitment-free sex outside of any emotional relationship would become an ingrained habit—and ultimately an obsession. More than any propensity for conventional philandering, it would bring Desi to grief. But in the short term, his patronage at Adler's paid off in a practical way: Polly sent a lot of her customers off to dance at La Conga every night.

• • •

One night after the first show at La Conga, Mario Torsatti summoned Desi to the club office.

"Do you know who wants to talk to you?" he asked his young bandleader.

"Who?" Desi responded.

"Rodgers and Hart."

"Who are they?"

Desi was surely one of the few people who didn't know. In the decade and a half since their breakthrough hit *Garrick Gaieties* in 1925, Richard Rodgers and Lorenz Hart had been the most dynamic songwriting team on Broadway, producing show after show and one enduring standard song after another. Only Irving Berlin, Cole Porter, and Jerome Kern and his various collaborators (including Oscar Hammerstein II) stood in the same rank. Torsatti advised Desi that he had better be at his most charming. It turned out that Rodgers and Hart, and their librettist George Marion Jr., were looking for a college-age Latin lad to play a South American football hero in their forthcoming musical, called *Too Many Girls*. Larry Hart told Desi he'd seen and admired him at La Conga in Miami, which was flattering, and asked if he could act.

"I don't know," Desi answered. "I did a couple of parts in small plays when I was in Cuba, and I used to be on the debating team." He said he was game to try anything. His visitors told him he'd first have to pass muster with a "Mr. Abbott," but Desi didn't know who that was either. He would soon learn.

George Abbott was an actor, director, playwright, show doctor, and all-around man of the theater who was among the most powerful figures on Broadway. He was also a skilled and passionate ballroom dancer, and he promptly came to La Conga and joined the nightly undulating line that Walter Winchell had by now dubbed "the Desi Chain." Impressed, Abbott told Desi to come audition in two days. The director's standing practice was to have actors approach their auditions cold, without preparation, so he could better judge their raw talent and their ability to follow his instructions. But so keen was Larry Hart to see Desi in the role that he and his agent pal "Doc" Bender drilled him on the part of Manuelito, the show's hot South American football prospect. When Desi arrived for his audition—at the ungodly hour of nine in the morning—he sang an old Rodgers and Hart tune (Abbott's verdict: "Well, he's loud enough"), but when he began reading his dialogue, Abbott instantly realized that he'd been coached, and badly. Desi slunk off the stage and apologized. Abbott then said that if he didn't mind working his ass off, the part was his. "How much of an actor he was, we didn't know," Abbott would recall. "But we knew he'd be good in the songs."

Diosa Costello had already been cast in the show, and once again, her recollection differed from Desi's. Abbott, a notorious ladies' man, had eyes for Costello, and so she told him, "If you don't give Desi the part, I'm not going dancing with you." Costello enjoyed this memory. "I feel success, it's a ladder," she said, "and I didn't make him a big star because you have to have a certain amount of talent. But I felt I was responsible for a few steps of that ladder."

The plot of *Too Many Girls* was wafer thin. It told the story of a madcap rich girl, Consuelo Casey, whose father sends her to his alma mater, Pottawatomie College, to keep her out of trouble, protected by four football players he secretly hires to be her bodyguards. Unwittingly, she falls in love with one of them, only to break up with him when she learns his true role, before being happily reunited by the final curtain. Marcy Westcott, a veteran of another Rodgers and Hart show, *The Boys from Syracuse*, played Consuelo, and Richard Kollmar, who would soon marry the columnist Dorothy Kilgallen, played the male lead, with comic support from Eddie Bracken, a former child vaudeville performer. Desi and Diosa were secondary characters, singing a frisky second act duet, "She Could Shake the Maracas." In the evenings after rehearsals, the *Too Many Girls* company members came to La Conga to dance, and Abbott decided they had to work a conga number into the show for Desi. So Rodgers adapted a college rally song, "Look Out," written as a march, to fit the conga beat, and it became the rousing finale to the first act.

In a pattern that would persist through the years, Desi's still shaky English meant that he did not initially get all the jokes in the show—including one about how the girls at Pottawatomie wore little beanies on their heads to signify that they were virgins. "At first I thought it might be a religious joke," he would remember, until Abbott eventually explained it to him. At the first out-of-town tryout in New Haven, Connecticut, on September 28, 1939, Desi felt like a zombie, and the first big laugh he got scared him to death. "I had never heard the sound of a theater laughing at a joke, a boffo," he remembered. "What a wonderful sound that is, and what a sensational feeling!" He felt even better when his conga number stopped the show. But by the time the play got to Boston for its next stop on the way to Broadway, Desi was in pain, with an infected toe. It appeared that his understudy—a tall, blue-eyed, freckle-faced chorus boy from Rhode Island, would have to go on in his place, with a dark wig and tan makeup. But in the end, a doctor numbed Desi's foot each night and he was able to perform—and he and the chorus boy, Van Johnson, who did not have to take his place but would soon enough become a boy-next-door movie star, remained friends for life.

Too Many Girls opened at the Imperial Theatre in New York on October 18 and was an immediate hit, running for 249 performances and making Desi an overnight star. "Humorous, fresh and exhilarating," was the verdict of the *New York Times* critic Brooks Atkinson, who praised Desi as "a good wooer of women," while Richard Watts in the *New York Herald Tribune* called it "as pleasing a girl-and-music carnival as the theatrical season is likely to offer." Desi's own summary of the play's appeal was typically succinct: "Our whole show was about college kids, football, and screwing."

Mario Torsatti and his partners at La Conga arranged to accommodate Desi by scheduling a special early show at 7:30 (which allowed him time to get to the theater before his first appearance onstage), plus the usual two late-night performances. That meant that on matinee days, Desi was doing his intense conga routine five times a day and racing between nightclub and theater to boot. "When you are young, you can do a lot of things," he would remember. The dancer Margaret Little Durante, part of Desi's circle of young performers, recalled years later what it was like to be so young and alive. The nightclubs were "all lit up, bright," she said, "and then after the shows, down to Chinatown or up to Harlem. I mean, we stayed up all night, slept all day."

• • •

Desi threw himself wholeheartedly into the show and into a theater world he knew nothing about, rehearsing the play by day while continuing to perform his three shows each night at La Conga. Around this same time, Desi was facing upheaval in his family life. His parents had finally decided to divorce, and years later he would recall how this news shocked and angered him, despite his knowing of the obvious troubles in their marriage. The divorce led to a period of serious estrangement between Desi and his father that lasted, to one degree or another, for several years. More significantly, this turn of events also meant that for the rest of his life, Desi would be saddled with the care and feeding of his mother, who by most accounts was never truly happy again.

Desi was just twenty-two years old, and he was living his best life in Manhattan, subletting a penthouse on Central Park West from the boxer Barney Ross. The neighbors included a much bigger Broadway star, Ethel Merman, and the duplex was elegant, with large windows overlooking the park. But the apartment lost much of its appeal as a bachelor pad because Lolita Arnaz came to New York to live with her son in early 1940. Desi could hardly bring a girl back to the penthouse if his mother was there.

Still, he managed. In this first flush of his fame, Desi could have had his pick of almost any woman in New York, and he struck up a passionate romance with a famous ballroom dancer, Renee De Marco, who was separated from her much older husband and dancing partner. Desi was smitten with the woman he dubbed "Freckles" and would always consider her his "first real love." But he was not so smitten that he didn't take a simultaneous detour with the young actress Betty Grable, "the most gorgeous thing I have ever seen in my life," who was making her Broadway debut in Cole Porter's musical *Du Barry Was a Lady* alongside Ethel Merman and Bert Lahr. De Marco was understanding, realizing that Desi was "a young guy in his first big hit on Broadway, enjoying every minute of life and drinking everything that was sweet to drink."

Desi had become a darling of the press as well. The *Boston Post*'s esteemed drama critic Elliot Norton proclaimed him "New York's newest glamour man, pet of the Park Avenue proletariat and candidate to succeed Rudolph Valentino in the hearts of the nation's ever-loving ladies." Dorothy Kilgallen allowed, "It takes no well-oiled crystal ball to predict that the days when Desi may stroll down Broadway unmolested by feminine throngs are numbered. He is a lad destined to belong to the stage door Susies." The United Press said Desi would have a hard time "living down his reputation as the darling of the debutantes." But a sympathetic piece in the *Miami Herald* came much closer to summing up how Desi preferred to see himself, noting that he would like to be known as "The Cuban Mickey Rooney," Metro-Goldwyn-Mayer's triple-threat young performer and that year's number one worldwide box-office star. "I do not want to be seen as a glamour boy or an oomph boy," Desi said. "I don't like it. It doesn't fit any man."

Indeed, Desi did not easily fit in any category. Elliot Norton's judgment notwithstanding, he was not really the seductive Latin lover type, and he never would be—at least not on the stage or screen. Nor did he fit the other prevailing Latin archetypes, the swarthy villain or the sleepy-eyed comic bumbler. Instead, he *was* a bit like Mickey Rooney—handsome, earnest, sincere, clean-cut, slightly mischievous, and surprisingly skilled at comedy, music, and drama alike. It was not surprising that Hollywood quickly came calling on the new Broadway sensation.

• • •

The first feeler came from 20th Century-Fox, which wanted Desi to star with Alice Faye in a Technicolor musical, *Down Argentine Way*. The studio offered him a contract at fifteen hundred dollars a week for forty weeks (thirty-three thousand dollars a week in 2024 dollars). George Abbott told him that Rodgers and Hart wouldn't stand in his way in the face of such a big break, but Desi decided he still had a lot to learn about performing and should stick with *Too Many Girls*. Don Ameche took the part instead, and in one of those show business twists that no one could make up, Alice Faye got pregnant, and Desi's sometime girlfriend Betty Grable won that role, her first big break in the movies—and the first step toward her eventual dethronement of Faye as the reigning diva of Fox musicals.

Soon enough, a more clear-cut opportunity presented itself: RKO Radio Pictures bought the film rights to *Too Many Girls*, hired George Abbott to direct it, and he signed Desi to reprise his role in the movie. With his former theater dresser, now employed as his personal valet, in tow, Arnaz headed to Hollywood, stopping in Detroit on the way to pick up a brand-new Buick Roadmaster convertible, which he bought wholesale through the father of an old Miami girlfriend whose company manufactured the upholstery for General Motors vehicles. Lolita had gone back to Cuba to get her permanent U.S. resident papers, so Arnaz and the valet checked into the Hollywood Roosevelt, and the next morning, with the valet, Richard, doubling as chauffeur, made their way down to RKO on Melrose Avenue and rolled through the main gate of the studio, which abutted the much larger Paramount Pictures lot next door.

RKO was not the biggest or the richest studio in Hollywood, but it was one of the so-called Big Five and had carved a classy niche for itself as the home of the elegant musicals of Ginger Rogers and Fred Astaire. RKO had also made *King Kong, Gunga Din, The Hunchback of Notre Dame, Little Women*, and *Bringing Up Baby*; Katharine Hepburn, Cary Grant, and Carole Lombard were all RKO stars. The very same week that *Too Many Girls* began shooting in late June 1940, Orson Welles began principal photography on another RKO project called *Citizen Kane*. It was almost too much for Desi to process as he gathered with fellow cast members in the studio's Little Theatre, where Ginger Rogers's mother, Lela, held acting classes for young studio recruits. Van Johnson and Eddie Bracken had also been hired from the Broadway cast, but most of the *Too Many Girls* performers were new to the show, including Richard Carlson in the male lead and Ann Miller (a bubbly tap dancer about as non-Latina as you could get) in Diosa Costello's part. The role of Connie Casey, the female lead, went to a twenty-nine-year-old contract player at RKO who had already made sixty movies. Her name was Lucille Ball.

Desi's first glimpse of her was not promising. She walked in from another soundstage, where she had been filming a vicious catfight with Maureen O'Hara in a backstage melodrama called *Dance, Girl, Dance*. Ball was playing Bubbles, a gold-digging burlesque dancer vying with O'Hara, a chaste aspiring ballerina, for the affections of a drunken playboy. When she walked into the Little Theatre, she sported a black eye, a bandaged leg, a clawed back, and a torn dress. She looked, Desi would recall, "like a two-dollar whore who had been badly beaten by her pimp." Desi did not understand how she could possibly play the dewy-eyed ingenue in *Too Many Girls*.

A few hours later the company reconvened for a musical rehearsal. Desi was at the piano, running through "She Could Shake the Maracas," when a striking woman he did not recognize walked into the room in a snug pair of beige slacks and yellow sweater, with blond hair and huge, luminous blue eyes.

"Man, that is a hunk of a woman," Desi told the accompanist.

"You met her today," the piano player replied.

"I've never seen her before," Desi answered.

"That's Lucille Ball."

four

————— ·❖· —————

ENTER LUCY

If Desi Arnaz had lived a privileged existence until 1933, Lucille Ball's childhood was colored by privation, trauma, and dislocation almost from the start. "I wasn't an unloved or an unwanted child," she wrote in middle age. "But I was moved around a lot, and then death and cruel circumstances brought many painful separations."

Lucille Desiree Ball was born August 6, 1911, in Jamestown, New York, the first child and only daughter of Henry Durell Ball and the former Desiree Eveline Hunt. Her father, known as Had, was a slim, blue-eyed electrical lineman, and her mother, a force of nature with a porcelain complexion and auburn hair, was known to all as DeDe. The family moved around on account of Had's job, living at times in Anaconda, Montana, and Trenton, New Jersey, before settling in Wyandotte, Michigan, where Henry worked for Michigan Bell. There, in February 1915, he died of typhoid fever—apparently after eating a bowl of unpasteurized ice cream. He was just twenty-seven years old, and Lucille was just three and a half. DeDe, three months pregnant, returned to her family's home in Jamestown—about ninety miles south of Buffalo on the southern edge of Lake Chautauqua in western New York—where that July she gave birth to their son, Fred.

From that moment on, Lucille's home life was a series of disruptions that would have left any child uncertain of her place in the world. "I think that people who have known her, and who love to talk about her, are people who have not realized the depth of her suffering in her life," her childhood friend Pauline Lopus would recall. "They have taken it for granted that she was always a clown—and, I mean, they haven't studied clowns, they don't know that clowns, generally, have a very bad personal life—there's always big, big holes in it. And there certainly was in Lucille's life."

DeDe's parents, Fred and Flora Belle Hunt, were loving presences in little Lucille's world, but after baby Fred's birth the family splintered. The Hunts sent DeDe, probably suffering from postpartum depression, off to California for a rest and kept the infant Fred with them, but they farmed Lucille out to the nearby home of their younger married daughter, Lola Mandicos. DeDe eventually returned to Jamestown and in 1919 married Edward Peterson, a metal polisher who Lucille hoped would become a new father to her. But on their wedding day, when Lucille asked, "Are you our new daddy?" Peterson just replied, "Call me Ed." "Ed was never mean or abusive, but his presence in the house was shadowy," Lucille recalled. Ed and DeDe soon decamped to Detroit in search of work, sending Lucille to live with Ed's strict Swedish Lutheran parents in another house in Jamestown. The Petersons banned mirrors from their home, except for a single one over the bathroom sink, and chastised Lucille for vanity when she was caught admiring herself in it. She credited their cold, unyielding ways for instilling her own perfectionist work ethic and her impeccable housecleaning skills.

Finally, by about 1921 or early 1922, the extended family was reunited in a modest wood-frame house that Fred Hunt, a skilled furniture maker in Jamestown's leading industry, had bought for two thousand dollars at 59 Eighth Street in the village of Celoron, a lakeside community just west of Jamestown. It was the closest thing to an anchor that ten-year-old Lucille had ever had, and she would spend the rest of her life trying to re-create it. In July 1922, Lucille's beloved grandmother Flora Belle died of uterine cancer, and from that point on, a total of seven people crowded into the little house. There were three small bedrooms under the sloping eaves of the second floor: DeDe and Ed Peterson shared one; Grandpa Hunt and young Fred took up another; and Lucy and her cousin Cleo, Aunt Lola's toddler daughter (whom Lucy always regarded as a younger sister), were in the third, overlooking Grandpa's large vegetable garden and a row of lilac bushes in the backyard. Lola, now divorced, probably slept in the curtained-off parlor that had been Flora Belle's sickroom. The house, with a single bathroom and no heat on the second floor, was cramped but charming, with quarter-sawn oak woodwork, an upright piano, and a claw-foot bathtub. For better or worse, there was love. The three grandchildren all knew Fred Hunt as their Daddy, and in his backyard workshop he built them small toys and toboggans for winter sledding. "Wintertime was Currier and Ives, and the summertime it was Norman Rockwell," Cleo would remember.

Though the family lived near Celoron Park, a lakeside amusement venue with carnival rides, daily life was a slog. Asked decades later what he and Lucille had done for play, Fred Ball would recall, "Probably the most important thing in that respect would be the fact that we didn't play. We worked." DeDe herself worked as a hat saleswoman while Lucy was responsible for cleaning the house and prepping for the meals DeDe cooked each night. Fred helped Grandpa with his small garden truck farm, selling berries and produce and grinding wild horseradish.

Cleo would recall that Lucille was a "very willful and determined young lady." Her brother Fred was less decorous in his description. "Oh, she was full of hell all the time," he said. "She was always a goer, she was the head of whatever group she was in. She was the head. She was in charge." Tall and slender, she was a good basketball player, with bobbed brunette hair. And in the disapproving shorthand of the day, she was fast. By age fourteen she was dating the twenty-one-year-old Johnny DaVita, the son of a local businessman whose enterprises were not all legitimate. Lucille would recall the handsome Johnny as having "a John Garfield build" with "finely chiseled" features, but others remembered him as a small-time hood, engaged in both bookmaking and bootlegging. (Johnny's father, Louis, would eventually be shot dead, arguing in Italian with his assailant in the street after coming out of church.)

It seems likely that Lucille's first theatrical forays occurred in the small entry hall foyer of the Celoron house, which served as a makeshift stage blocked off from the parlor by a curtain hung on a wooden rod. And so sometime in late 1926 or early 1927—perhaps to get Lucille away from Johnny, and certainly in recognition of her daughter's restless discontent—DeDe agreed to send her daughter off to Manhattan, a six-hour train ride away, to attend the Robert Minton–John Murray Anderson School of Drama. Lucille was just fifteen and no match for the refined thespian academy, where the star student, eighteen-year-old Ruth Elizabeth Davis—soon to be known as Bette—left Lucille tongue-tied. Her teachers told DeDe that Lucille was wasting her time, and she slunk back home. "All I learned in drama school was how to be frightened," she would recall.

It was on the Fourth of July weekend in 1927—with Lucille apparently in New York City—that a tragedy occurred that would change the family forever. As an early present for Fred's twelfth birthday, Grandpa Hunt had given him a .22-caliber rifle, and on that Sunday afternoon Fred, Cleo, and two neighbor children were in the backyard taking target practice. Joanna Ottinger, a friend of Fred's, was holding the gun when Warner Erickson, their eight-year-old next-door neighbor, heard his mother call him home. He jumped up and ran into the line of fire just as the bullet discharged, severing his spinal cord and paralyzing him. He fell into a lilac bush screaming in pain. Warner's family sued Fred Hunt for negligence in failing to properly supervise the children, and he was forced to serve a year's house arrest before eventually losing his home to satisfy the judgment. (Warner would die of his wound five years later.)

In her posthumously published memoir, *Love, Lucy*, Lucille would recall the shooting as if she had been present, and indeed it was such a wrenching trauma that she could be forgiven for thinking she'd lived through it herself. "It ruined Celoron for us," she wrote. "It destroyed our life together there." The family moved into an apartment in Jamestown, and it was around this time that Lucille began running away—to Buffalo, Cleveland, Chicago—any place to which she could afford bus fare or bum a ride. Over the next five years, she went back and forth to New York City so many times that nearly a century later it's impossible to track her movements precisely.

In Manhattan she auditioned for acting jobs, styling herself as Diane Belmont of Butte, Montana, because she thought it sounded more exotic. (After she became famous, she would register under the name Diane Belmont in hospitals and hotels to protect her privacy.) Eventually she was hired as a model for the fashion designer Hattie Carnegie, in whose posh shop on East 49th Street she would live-model clothes for sophisticated society customers. With her hair dyed platinum blond, she bore an uncanny resemblance to Constance Bennett, the reigning movie queen of the moment, and often made thirty to forty outfit changes a day. But she was lonely and unhappy, and she returned to Jamestown and high school. That summer she was cast in a local theater company's production of *Within the Law*, a melodrama about a shopgirl who turns to a life of crime. Lucille played Agnes

Lynch, the petty criminal girlfriend of a guy not unlike Johnny DaVita, and when the production was reprised at the Chautauqua Institution, a renowned cultural retreat north of Jamestown, Lucille won a rave from the *Chautauquan Daily*, which judged that "she lived the part of the underworld girl with as much realism as if it were her regular existence." That gave her confidence enough to go back to New York.

Lucille auditioned for more acting parts, but it was a modeling job in the spring of 1933 that provided her big break. She posed as a "poster girl" in an advertisement for Chesterfield cigarettes, in a blue chiffon dress with a pair of Russian wolfhounds, and the broadside was plastered all over Manhattan. In mid-July, outside the Palace Theater on Broadway, she ran into an agent named Gloria Hahlo, who recognized her from the glamorous ad, and told her that the comedian Eddie Cantor needed another chorus girl for Samuel Goldwyn's musical film *Roman Scandals*. And though she could really neither sing nor dance, Lucille was soon on the train to Hollywood.

. . .

Soon after her arrival in California, Lucille gathered her dispersed family around her once more. She summoned DeDe (by now divorced from Ed Peterson), brother Fred, Grandpa Hunt, and Cleo to join her in a rented Georgian frame house at 1344 North Ogden Drive in Hollywood. A new friend, the actress Ann Sothern, helped her paint and decorate. The Goldwyn job had led to a short-lived contract at Columbia Pictures, but in the fall of 1934 she was laid off. Luckily, she learned that RKO was casting the Jerome Kern–Otto Harbach musical *Roberta*, starring Irene Dunne and the still-new team of Fred Astaire and Ginger Rogers, and needed actresses who could model clothes, since the film was set in a fashion house. Lucille was hired as a contract player for $75 a week. She was on her way. The studio was a graduate school for Lucille, who came under the wing of Lela Rogers, the den mother of contract players, who saw in Lucille the talent of a natural comedienne. At first Lucille won small parts in big movies (like Astaire and Rogers's *Top Hat*), then bigger parts in smaller movies, and finally strong parts in A pictures, like 1937's *Stage Door*, George S. Kaufman and Edna Ferber's tale of actresses in a Broadway rooming house, with a standout cast that included Ginger Rogers, Katharine Hepburn, Ann Miller, and Eve Arden.

Lucille earned that role in part by virtue of her relationship with Pandro Berman, one of RKO's most prominent producers, who was married but so besotted with Lucille that he would meet her for trysts in a hideaway apartment. She eventually broke off the affair, but she had an active love life through this period. Through her friend Carole Lombard, she met and dated the actor Mack "Killer" Gray, so nicknamed by Lombard for the gangster parts he played. She had a tempestuous romance (and even a brief engagement) with the boozy, heavy-browed young actor Broderick Crawford, who sent her impassioned telegrams bragging about being on the wagon. She went on a double date with Ginger Rogers and a couple of fledgling actors, James Stewart and Henry Fonda, who was Lucille's escort but thought her makeup too heavy.

In later years Ball would hint that she was no more immune to the predations of the casting couch than any other young actress of the era. But as her daughter Lucie recalled, "She wouldn't be specific. She wouldn't talk straight about it. It's become clear that in those days, everybody who got off the train, if you wanted to get anywhere, you had to sleep with somebody, not because you liked them."

Eventually Lucille settled into a serious romantic relationship with Alexander Hall, a journeyman director whose career in Hollywood had begun as an actor in silent pictures. He had directed Shirley Temple in *Little Miss Marker*, had many friends in town, and owned a turkey ranch in the San Fernando Valley. It was Hall who introduced

Lucille to a couple—Marc and Marcella Rabwin—who would become her close friends for life. Marc Rabwin, a prominent physician, was Al Hall's doctor and would go on to be chief of staff at Cedars of Lebanon Hospital and caregiver to many movie stars. His wife was the executive assistant to David O. Selznick, the brilliant, mercurial producer who was about to make *Gone with the Wind*.

"I think that he was a very important source of security to her," Marcella Rabwin said of Al Hall. But Lucille didn't love him. "He came into her life at a very opportune time. She needed the father figure." Ball and Hall were discreetly living together when she walked into that RKO music rehearsal and Desi Arnaz's eyes opened wide.

• • •

Unbeknownst to Desi, Lucille had actually seen *him* before—on Broadway, in *Too Many Girls*. "I couldn't take my eyes off this Desi Arnaz," she would write years later. "A striped football jersey hugged his big shoulders and chest, while those narrow hips in tight football pants swayed to the catchy rhythms of the bongo drum he was carrying. I recognized the kind of electric charm that can never be faked: star quality." Now in their first encounter on the RKO lot, she played fresh, answering his tentative "Miss Ball?" by replying, "Why don't you call me Lucille and I'll call you Dizzy?"

"Okay, Lucille, but it's not Dizzy," he replied.

"Oh, how do you say it? Daisy?" she countered.

"No, Daisy is a flower. It's Desi—D-E-S-I." (In fact, in years to come, Lucille would take pains in private and public to pronounce Desi's name in the correct Spanish way as "DESS-y.")

Having cleared that up, the next words out of Desi's mouth were the corniest kind of come-on: "Do you know how to rumba?" Lucille did not, but she promptly agreed to join Desi and the rest of the cast for dancing that night at El Zarape, a Mexican restaurant on Sunset Boulevard. "And when they got there, they ordered a table for two," George

Abbott recalled. "And I said, 'Oh, come on over and join us now.' And the word came back, never mind, they were all seated. They stayed there. And they stayed there for the rest of the run."

There is a moment early in the film version of *Too Many Girls* that captures something of the intense chemistry Lucille and Desi must have felt in real life. His Manuelito, not yet having signed up to play football, is working as a waiter at an inn in Maine when a radiant Lucille as Connie Casey emerges from her limousine, pauses, then fixes a quizzical but appreciative gaze on him. He is thunderstruck, sliding down a pillar into a heap on the inn's front porch. "Will someone please come?" Connie says. "There's a waiter fainted out here." Their first evening together at El Zarape, Desi didn't faint, but he was bewitched, and he and Lucille danced all night and "got loaded," in his recollection. He took her home and said a chaste good night because there was a complication: his ostensible girlfriend, Renee De Marco, was arriving in town. That weekend, Desi took Freckles to Eddie Bracken's rented beach house in Malibu, where he spotted Lucille. She patted the sand beside her and asked him to sit down. "I sat down and never went back to Freckles," Desi recalled. The pair spent that night together in Lucille's apartment. The next day, Lucille called Al Hall to tell him she would have someone collect her belongings from his house, and Desi called De Marco to confess that he couldn't explain it but had fallen in love with Lucille. She had fallen just as hard and fast for him. "When you fall in love immediately, and violently, as we did," Lucille told an interviewer years later, "you fall in love with your senses—sense of sight and sound and touch and smell. Seems a funny thing to say and I don't quite know how to say it except that, well, heck—the way Desi smells, like soap, like a baby, that clean hair smell or something, was a factor in my falling in love with him, and a factor in my staying in love with him."

Their romance thrived in the hothouse atmosphere of the movie they were making. Abbott was a demanding boss, insisting on repeated retakes. "That's no good," he would say. "You'll have to do it over again.

And get more expression this time." Lucille was already experienced enough in film technique to know that Abbott's direction was lacking, because he was thinking in terms of the stage. He was "shooting a picture with a Kodak in a hotel room," she said. "He'd been so used to that proscenium arch" of a live theater, "and he used the camera as a fourth wall," with the static viewpoint of someone sitting in the audience, not the fluid motion that film allowed. Once, after filming a close-up shot, she asked Abbott—who had already told her to change her clothes— if he didn't need a matching close-up of her costar Richard Carlson. Abbott told her to go to lunch and forget about it. "I said, 'Would you like to bet me, George, that before the picture is over, they're going to ask you for the matching shot when they start cutting?'" she remembered years later. "It was my first bit of knowledge that I ever remember speaking up about. . . . And by God, they did. And he said, 'Yes, I'll bet you.' He bet me fifty dollars, and I still have the check."

Abbott himself would confess that *Too Many Girls* wound up being "a lousy movie," but Desi would say he never again made a picture in which everyone had so much fun. And the film's dramatic finale—in which Desi barrels into the scene beating a conga drum two-thirds the size of his body, sashaying to and fro in torchlight as Ann Miller taps up a storm—captures his sexual magnetism. And over that summer, as filming ended, he and Lucille embarked on a tempestuous courtship whose highs and lows would foreshadow the rest of their lives together. Even in the first flush of their romance, Lucille had doubts about Desi's fidelity in a climate where starlets and civilian women alike threw themselves at him. "I don't remember a time that wasn't tough," their friend Marcella Rabwin would recall. "By that I mean his indiscretions were always disturbing."

Desi's perennial explanation—his perpetual excuse—was that he was simply exercising his birthright as a Latin man. In an infamous 1936 *Esquire* article, "Latins Are Lousy Lovers," the writer Helen Lawrenson contended that Cuban men were notable not so much for their technical prowess in the feathers as for their self-absorption. "God knows, the Cuban man spends enough time on the subject of sex," she wrote. "He devotes his life to it. He talks it, dreams it, reads it, sings, dances it, eats it, sleeps it—does everything but do it. That last is not literally true, but it is fact that they spend far more time in words than in action." Desi spent plenty of time in action, of course, but the rest of Lawrenson's analysis fit him. "A smart American who makes an appointment with a Cuban at a café always makes the Cuban sit with his back to the street; because if he does not, the Cuban will eye every woman who passes, and, like as not, at a crucial point in the business transaction, will interrupt to make anatomical comments on some pretty who is just going by. They telephone each other at their offices during business hours to describe in minute detail a new conquest. According to them, they always had their first affair at the age of two."

Lucille was not naive when she and Desi met. She was wise in the ways of love and sex and in years to come would deflect a reporter's query about Desi's reputation as a ladies' man with her own show of bravado: "I like to play games, too." In fact, she was neither so bold nor so insouciant. She was just crazy about him. Lucille's friends warned her against the match, she would recall, but, she said, "I had flipped." Romantic getaways to Palm Springs and Big Bear Lake (where a waitress asked if Desi was Native American because she wasn't allowed to serve liquor to Indians) alternated with jealous outbursts and bitter arguments. When filming was finished on *Too Many Girls*, Desi had to go to Chicago to appear in the national company tour of the show, in which Van Johnson now had the lead. Lucy remained in Hollywood, where she was shooting *A Girl, a Guy, and a Gob* with George Murphy and Edmond O'Brien. She went to Chicago for a visit, and Desi came to Los Angeles at the beginning of October for the *Too Many Girls* premiere. The reviews were not what he might have hoped for. Bosley Crowther of the *New York Times* dismissed Desi as "a noisy, black-haired Latin whose face, unfortunately, lacks expression and whose performance is devoid of grace."

But that pan was nothing compared to the scathing review Lucille delivered when she found out that Desi had taken out Betty Grable one night while she was busy.

When she got wind of this, she drove to the house he now shared with his mother on Wilcox Avenue in Hollywood, barged past Lolita at the front door, and excoriated Desi, who was still in bed, as a two-timing bastard—all with Lolita in earshot. Decades later, in unpublished notes for his memoir, Desi would wonder whether such an outburst should have been a clue that he and Lucille were simply unsuited for each other, that her jealousy (even if it was justified) would smother him. But in the short term, the fighting—and the inevitable making up— only seemed to draw them closer. Desi had to go to New York to fulfill an engagement at the posh Versailles nightclub on the East Side. When he'd try to call Lucille in Hollywood from his hotel in New York, she'd let the phone ring unanswered simply to annoy him. When she did pick up, she'd answer his worried queries about where she'd been with a nonchalant "Here and there." She accused him of "laying every god-damned one of those chorus girls" at the Versailles, while he suspected her of having an affair with the handsome mayor of Milwaukee when her scheduled one-day promotional appearance there for *Dance, Girl, Dance* was extended to a week. Her long-distance phone bill topped a hundred dollars a week (two thousand dollars in 2024 money), and she claimed that Desi's was twice as much. Their daily, sometimes hourly, telegrams were just as impassioned, if less costly.

By late November, unbeknownst to Lucille, Desi had decided that they should get married—despite the fact that their RKO contracts contained clauses forbidding either of them from tying the knot. Desi now had a deal at RKO for three pictures at ten thousand dollars each, he was doing five live shows a day with his band at the Roxy Theater in New York, and he felt secure enough to hold his own in the relation-ship. Lucille arrived in Manhattan on Friday, November 29, after her week in Milwaukee, and spent the afternoon in her hotel room with a fan magazine writer, Eleanor Harris, who was working on an article tentatively titled "Why Lucille Ball Prefers to Remain a Bachelor Girl." Between shows, Desi repeatedly burst in to try to propose but had to wait until he finally found Lucille alone. When he asked, she wavered but agreed.

Desi had arranged for the ceremony to take place the following day in Greenwich, Connecticut—with plans to be back in Manhattan in time for his 11 a.m. show at the Roxy. The couple left the Pierre Hotel before dawn, with Doc Bender, by now Desi's agent, and Deke Magaziner, his business manager, in tow. But Desi hadn't counted on the time needed for the required blood test, or a judge's waiver of the normal five-day waiting period, or a last-minute trip to Woolworth's for a cheap ring, which would grow thinner and greener with the passing years, though Lucille kept wearing it faithfully. Justice of the Peace John P. O'Brien decreed that his office was not an elegant enough setting for a wedding, so the party regrouped at the Byram River Beagle Club for the noontime ceremony. With a motorcycle escort back to Manhattan, they made it to the Roxy in time for the second show, and Desi carried his new bride across the threshold to his dressing room. Then he introduced her to the audience in the seven-thousand-seat theater, who showered the newlyweds with rice. Years later, Lucille would confess to her trepidations about the match. Her friends had warned her against it, listing their arguments: She had always dated older men; Desi was a playboy; she was six years older than he. But her family accepted him. "We really all of us were taken with his charm immediately," Cousin Cleo recalled. For her part, Lucille would recall, "I sensed in Desi a great need. Beneath that dazzling charm was a homeless boy who had no one to care for him, worry about him, love him. And I wanted him and only him as the father of my children."

Desi was so happy about the marriage that he overcame his bad feelings for his father and cabled Mayor Arnaz, who he thought was back in Santiago: DEAR POP I JUST WANT YOU TO KNOW THAT YOU

HAVE ACQUIRED A DAUGHTER AS I GOT MARRIED . . . TO LUCILLE BALL THE MOST WONDERFUL GIRL IN THE WORLD. Nearly a week later the senior Arnaz replied by telegram, apparently from Miami: MY HEART-IEST CONGRATULATION WISH YOU BOTH ALL KIND OF HAPPINESS AND GOOD UNDERSTANDING FOR A HAPPY FUTURE IN YOUR MARRIED LIFE . . . SORRY COULD NOT CONGRATULATE SOONER YOUR ADDRESS UNKNOWN TO ME. LOVE AND KISSES TO YOU AND LUCILLE YOUR DAD.

That Saturday night Desi arranged a white-tie wedding party at El Morocco, the fashionable blue-and-white zebra-striped nightclub on East 54th Street, for their friends, including Rodgers and Hart and George Schaeffer, the president of RKO. They'd been drinking champagne all day and didn't get to bed until six o'clock Sunday morning. Waking with a thirst, Desi slapped Lucille's behind and asked her to get him some ice water. She complied, but when she woke up again a few hours later, she told him he could get his own water. It was an omen: In their marriage, Desi adopted the Latin husband's dominant domestic attitude—and for a long time, Lucille would let him.

After his Roxy engagement was done, Desi showered Lucille with tenderness on their honeymoon trip back to Hollywood. He combined two sleeping compartments on the Santa Fe Super Chief into one rolling suite and filled them with red and white carnations. Lucille's favorite flowers were actually lilacs, but carnations would become Desi's signature gift bloom for the rest of their lives. When he sat quietly strumming his guitar and humming to himself, Lucille worried that he might already be bored until he emerged from his reverie with a love song he'd composed just for her:

> *When I looked into your eyes*
> *And then you softly said, "I do"*
> *I suddenly realized I had a new world*
> *A world with you*
> *A world where life is worth living*

A world that is so new to me
A world of taking and giving
Like God meant the world to be
Where good times will find two to greet
Where hard times will find two to beat
I found my new world with you, darling
When you softly said, "I do."

To go with his ballad Desi had adopted a new name for his new wife, a soft, Spanish-sounding diminutive that reflected his unique pride of place in her affections. Other men had loved Lucille. He alone would love *Lucy*.

five

DESILU

By getting married, Desi had pledged himself not only to Lucy but also to Hollywood, resolving to make a go of it in the movies, with his RKO contract in hand. But translating his Broadway and nightclub success to steady work in films would prove a frustrating challenge, as he struggled to find his footing in a business in which Lucy was already a well-established figure, if not an A-list star.

To be sure, Hollywood's welcome was warm enough at first. In October 1940, just before he married Lucy, the syndicated International News Service columnist Inez Robb, one of the highest-paid female reporters in the country, set out to determine whether Desi "really carries a baseball bat to fend off his feminine following." Noting that Broadway journalists had built Arnaz up "as a Cuban composite of Romeo, Casanova and Rhett Butler," Robb wrote that she "expected something considerably older, more sinister and devastating than Arnaz turned out to be."

"Don't misunderstand," she continued. "He is certainly bound to make millions of us gals feel that the nation's good neighbor policy is worthwhile. But he doesn't seem to be so much a successor of Valentino as the masculine version of another Hollywood original: Clara Bow," the sexy silent movie star who personified the Roaring Twenties. "What young Mr. Arnaz has is *it*—and make no mistake. He also has a nice assortment of dese, dems, deys and dose in the way of huge, snapping black eyes, sleek black hair and flashing white teeth. He is the universally understandable Latin answer to a maiden's prayer. Despite the fact that his name has been connected with every Hollywood honey except Edna May Oliver and every Broadway belle except Katharine Cornell, Arnaz insisted his charms have been greatly exaggerated.

"In Cuba, I look just like everyone else," he said in reference to his much-publicized pan. "There's nothing custom-built about my kind in Cuba."

In one sense, as 1940 ended, Desi was ideally suited to take advantage of what amounted to a national love affair with all things Latin. In 1934, President Franklin Roosevelt had abrogated the Platt Amendment—abandoning America's proclaimed right to intervene with force in Cuban politics if it saw fit and pledging support for a broad policy of self-determination and nonintervention in Latin American affairs. Six years later, with the European continent now at war, Roosevelt's "Good Neighbor" policy was doing what it could to build hemispheric solidarity on the western side of the Atlantic. Moreover, Hollywood was avoiding stories set in Europe—except, of course, for war movies—in favor of frothier musical and comedy fare in Latin locales. Desi himself had helped spawn the national craze for the conga, which soon swept Hollywood. Judy Garland and Mickey Rooney would dance the conga in *Strike Up the Band* in 1940, Barbara Stanwyck would do the same in *Ball of Fire* in 1941, and Desi's old flame Betty Grable would offer her own version in *Moon Over Miami* the same year.

Yet Desi's Latin heritage also all but guaranteed that, as a performer, he would be marginalized and pigeonholed into a very slender niche of entertainment—and that, as a citizen of Southern California, he would be vulnerable to prejudice in a society where Mexican Americans still held distinctly second-class status. As we have already seen, Desi's complexion sometimes led him to be mistaken for a Native American, and he tanned deeply with the slightest exposure to sun. That—and his thick accent—made him stand out in an overwhelmingly white, Anglo environment. In the 1940 national census, the entire Latino population of the country was lumped into the tiny four-tenths of 1 percent of the United States that was not categorized as either Black or white. Latino culture was in no sense ubiquitous, and even in Los Angeles, Latin American food was a comparatively exotic specialty. Restrictive real estate covenants limited where Mexican Americans could live, and restaurants often had signs reading *se sirve solamente a raza blanca* ("WE SERVE WHITES ONLY"). The police routinely harassed Latino youths, and in 1942, nine young Mexican Americans were convicted of murder on flimsy evidence in the so-called Sleepy Lagoon case. Their convictions were ultimately overturned, but in 1943 a mob of some three thousand Anglos inflamed by the case, many of them servicemen, set upon Latinos and Blacks on downtown streets and sidewalks, as the police stood idly by, in the infamous Zoot Suit Riots. As a Cuban, with elite status in the town's leading industry, Desi would presumably have been insulated from the worst of such prejudice, but he could not have been unaware of it or emotionally unaffected by it.

Desi's first film outing after his marriage was *Four Jacks and a Jill*, a forgettable B picture, barely an hour long, that also starred Ray Bolger and June Havoc and had a convoluted plot involving a nightclub singer, minor royalty, and mistaken identity. Desi played a cabdriver who posed as a king. The movie sank without a trace. A more promising prospect was *Father Takes a Wife*, which starred Gloria Swanson, the onetime top-rank silent star who was making a return to the screen after a seven-year absence. The story, by the veteran brother-sister

Broadway team of Dorothy and Herbert Fields, was amusing enough. A rich shipping magnate in his second childhood, played by the dapper, mustachioed Adolphe Menjou, marries a younger Broadway actress (Swanson) only to see her become infatuated with a dashing Latin opera singer, Carlos Bardez (Arnaz), who has stowed away on their honeymoon cruise.

Desi is at his charming best, with a mouthful of the sort of malaprops that a decade later would become a national phenomenon. He is first seen in a rough beard and sunglasses, to shield his eyes from the light after hiding in a shipboard cubby, then in the full flower of his clean-shaven youth, swanning around in a silk bathrobe practicing his aria. "He doesn't need that voice," the veteran character actress Helen Broderick declares at one point. "When you have a face like that, all you need is a face like that!" The same was not quite true for Desi, because the picture was also a textbook example of the ways in which Arnaz couldn't seem to catch a break in Hollywood, despite his handsome mug. He had been cast after the new head of RKO, Charles Koerner, had heard him sing the gentle Latin ballad "Perfidia" at a benefit and liked his voice. But since his character was supposed to be an opera singer, the number was dubbed in the film by an Italian tenor.

• • •

Desi and Lucy had better luck finding a place to set up housekeeping together. At first they lived in her apartment on Laurel Avenue in Hollywood, but they wanted a home to call their own. So they investigated the not-yet-suburban San Fernando Valley, where Lucy's old boyfriend Al Hall had his turkey farm, where Carole Lombard and Clark Gable also lived on a working ranch, and where acres of orange groves were still common. Lucy's friend Jack Oakie had a house in Chatsworth, about twenty-five miles northwest of Hollywood, and introduced them to a developer who was subdividing tracts to build homes on little *ranchitos*. They fell in love with a partially built ranch house, ringed by a white wooden fence on five acres, at 19700 Devonshire Boulevard. It was designed by the prolific African American architect Paul Revere Williams, who created homes and commercial structures all over Los Angeles for celebrities and ordinary citizens alike. The developer wanted $14,500, which the Arnazes did not have at the ready, but he settled for a $1,500 down payment and a ten-year note.

The house had a combined living-dining area on its north side, with sixteen-foot-high floor-to-ceiling windows facing the Santa Susana Mountains. Desi soon set about making improvements, building a backyard Cuban-style *bohío* thatched-roof hut and renting a bulldozer to dig a swimming pool, rimmed with rocks to make it look like a natural pond. Lucy furnished the house in secondhand pieces from local thrift shops—"Early Victorian and Bastard American," she called her style—and decorated it with cabbage-rose wallpaper in contrasting pinks and reds. There were some two hundred orange seedlings, plus plum and avocado trees, and the Arnazes planted a large garden, featuring Lucy's favorite vegetable, Swiss chard. Eventually, the *ranchito* would be home to more than two dozen chickens, Harold the hummingbird, Felicity the cat, three cocker spaniels—Tommy, Pinto, and Dandy—plus a 2,200-pound black-and-white Holstein cow they dubbed the Duchess of Devonshire.

As often as not, the menagerie included both their mothers, a pattern that would continue throughout the Arnazes' marriage. DeDe and Lolita were frequent houseguests and an inevitable presence at the newlyweds' festive parties—an arrangement that seems to have chafed on Desi more than Lucy, who clung fiercely to the mother from whom she had been separated in childhood. For his part, Desi was unswervingly loyal to Lolita, but her imperious ways (and her steadfast refusal to learn much English) sometimes made her company a chore. "He felt very obligated," Desi's friend Marge Durante recalled. "He did say that 'I will always take care of my mother, 'cause my father mistreated her.'"

Befitting their newly minted status as a Hollywood couple, Lucy and Desi sought an appropriate name for their new spread. Other married pairs had combined their names to christen their homes—Douglas Fairbanks and Mary Pickford had Pickfair in Beverly Hills, but "Arball" did not roll trippingly off the tongue. Instead, they landed on "Desilu," a euphonious coinage that the playwright Thornton Wilder told Desi sounded like the past participle of a French verb.

"It was the most hospitable, warm, happy house," Van Johnson would recall. "Every hour there was a new tray of something," including Lucy's signature hors d'oeuvres—potato chips with a dressing recipe from Carole Lombard or saltine crackers topped with salty cottage cheese and sweet strawberry jam. "She was out in that garden, digging and hoeing and working those vegetables and fruit every day. She was a real earth woman," Johnson said. Lucy had learned such skills from Grandpa Hunt, but she would confess that her cultivation was not cost-effective, joking that every serving of vegetables ran about $9. Still, Desi was the star at Desilu. He loved cooking his Cuban specialties—black beans and rice, arroz con pollo, picadillo—and grilling on the elaborate stone barbecue he had built. "He had a magic touch with food," Marcella Rabwin said. On Lucy's thirtieth birthday, August 6, 1941, Desi threw her a surprise party with forty guests, a Latin combo, and a carpet of white gardenias floating in the pool.

Yet the ranch's distance from Hollywood and the RKO studio—thirty-five to forty minutes on heavily trafficked roads in the years before freeways—was a sign of the couple's second-tier status. "It meant," the actor Jackie Cooper noted, "that you couldn't afford to live in Beverly Hills or Bel Air or Brentwood."

From the start, Lucy and Desi fought fiercely. One night not long after they were married, they had a huge fight, and Lucy took a hammer and smashed every window in their new station wagon, later telling her business manager Andrew Hickox to have it fixed and send the bill to her. Lucy also complained that Desi lost everything she gave him—coats, rings, watches—and that while he was a good cook, he left the kitchen in shambles. She called Desi "the *mañana* boy," a procrastinator who tended to chores when the spirit moved him; she was annoyed that he managed to accomplish "just as much in his easygoing way as she did in her intense one." For his part, Desi would call Lela Rogers to ask how he could make Lucy happy, while Lucy called her mother, who was careful never to take sides but sometimes privately referred to Desi in exasperation as "that Spic." Years later, in dictated notes for his memoir, Desi would wonder, "Why didn't I ever feel really comfortable with Lucy? Was it her family always being there—kind of making our home their home? Her mother, in particular. My mother was treated as a visitor and not as a part of it. Always felt like a visiting guest. DeDe was nice enough, or seemed nice enough, but I never felt comfortable with her."

And yet, as Lucy would recall, "in those early years, our fights were a kind of lovemaking. Desi and I enjoyed them, but they exhausted our friends and family, I'm afraid." She added, "My usual complaint was that Desi only worked at marriage in spurts. I don't believe he ever really intended to settle down and become a good, steady, faithful husband. He said I was much too jealous, and so the arguments rolled on and on. But we remained very deeply and passionately in love." Sometimes that love had a strange way of expressing itself. Marcella Rabwin would recall how one cozy night after dinner, Desi had begun playing guitar in front of the fireplace when Lucy left the room and returned with a tray of little red votive candles and placed them in a semicircle around him as if they were footlights. "He was so upset with her and screamed, in front of these people just screamed, and the epithets and everything. She just sat there and looked at him. She loved him so much she would take it." Jackie Cooper said that Desi sometimes seemed self-conscious about the age difference between him and Lucy. "He had a concern about being a little younger than Lucy," Cooper said. "He had a big concern that everybody was looking at him because he was younger and that it might not be true love from him to Lucy because she was older, maybe making more money, which she was, and he had a big concern about that. And at the same time, very warm in talking about Lucy's trying to talk him out of that feeling."

The couple's relationship was not improved at the premiere of De-si's film *Father Takes a Wife* in October 1941. Desi had spent the day proudly polishing his Buick Roadmaster for the gala. But when he and Lucy left the Pantages Theater in Hollywood that night, a valet called out, "Lucille Ball's car, please!" Half a block from the theater, Desi turned to Lucy and insisted, "That does it! I'm getting out of this god-damn town and get a job. . . . There's no way I'm going to stay here and become Mr. Ball." Lucy urged him to be patient, but he chafed. He re-called every slight about his subordinate status to his wife. The previous January, when he was playing a limited engagement with Lucy at the Rumba Casino in Miami Beach, newspaper ads touted "Desi Arnaz and His Movieland Bride Lucille Ball," as if Lucy were the main attraction.

"Desi was a little concerned about his accent and making it as an actor," recalled Cooper. "Lucy felt he could do it. She felt he had a lot of personality, a lot of energy, and indeed he did. But the studio heads in those days were very concerned if you had an accent, from a foreign country especially—bad enough if you had a Southern accent. But from a foreign country, they were very concerned, so Desi was afraid of being typed, of playing things that might be degrading his nationality, and he felt he really belonged in nightclubs, where he really enjoyed himself."

• • •

Soon enough, Desi would indeed be back on the road, though not quite in the way he had imagined. The Japanese attack on Pearl Harbor in December 1941 sparked a patriotic fervor, and celebrities were enlisted in the cause. One spectacular early effort was the Holly-wood Victory Caravan, a traveling all-star cavalcade to sell govern-ment war bonds. The troupe set off in April 1942 and included Charles Boyer, James Cagney, Claudette Colbert, Bing Crosby, Cary Grant, Olivia de Havilland, Bob Hope, Bert Lahr, Laurel and Hardy, Groucho

Marx, and an assortment of lesser lights. Desi was asked to lend his musical talents to the proceedings, which kicked off in Washington, D.C., with Oliver Hardy and Stan Laurel at the wheel of a Jeep and Desi sharing the back seat with the dancer Eleanor Powell. Eleanor Roosevelt hosted a tea for the company at the White House, followed by a meeting with the president himself, and the *Washington Post* declared of the three-hour show at Constitution Hall that "the scope and variety of the bill was such as to stagger the most intrepid showman." Indeed, one journalist estimated that it would have cost $4 million a night to put on a show with such star power. The revue was staged by Mark Sandrich, who had directed most of the Astaire-Rogers musicals, and featured sketches by the Broadway playwrights George S. Kaufman and Moss Hart and music by Jerome Kern, Johnny Mercer, and Frank Loesser. The conductor was Alfred Newman, the music director of 20th Century-Fox.

The show went on to play Boston, Philadelphia, Detroit, Cleveland, St. Paul, St. Louis, Des Moines, Houston, and Dallas, where even standing-room tickets cost $2.20, at a time when it cost just a quarter to see a movie. The Santa Fe Railroad provided a special train for the tour, with two dining cars, a club car, and seven cars with drawing rooms and sleepers for the stars. For Desi, decidedly among the most junior members of the troupe at age twenty-five, the experience was overwhelming. "I think there has never been a show like this in the history of show business," he would recall decades later. Arnaz's novice status didn't keep him from being incensed when Bing Crosby joined the tour in Chicago and briefly bumped him out of the lineup. "Crosby came in and they took Desi out of his spot and put Crosby in," Bob Hope remembered. "Oh, my God, he carried on." Apparently the good turn that Crosby did in getting Desi a raise in pay from Xavier Cugat five years earlier had passed its expiration date.

Crosby, a punctilious performer, had expected a jerry-built enterprise but instead found "a show that ran as smoothly as if it were being presented on ball bearings, everyone having fun, everyone with first class material and playing to capacity business in the biggest theatre in town wherever we went." Bert Lahr, the blustery Cowardly Lion of *The Wizard of Oz*, called the outing "a caravan of love," and the company formed a tight bond on the rollicking three-week trip—in Desi's case, a little too tight.

"Only one passenger sparked real enmity," Crosby's biographer Gary Giddins would write, noting that Desi had "boarded with his bongo drums while his uninvited wife, Lucille Ball, remained indignantly at home." He recounted that Desi "attempted to personify the Good Neighbor policy by seducing every eligible woman on and off the caravan, offending other passengers who might have been as ardent but practiced discretion. Audiences admired his enthusiastic drumming and dancing, and charm, but he did himself no favors as tales of his incessant lechery beat the train back to Los Angeles."

The chief critic with whom Desi did himself no favors, of course, was Lucy, who was undergoing career struggles of her own. She was still earning $3,500 a week from RKO, but an Audience Research Institute survey found that only a third of moviegoers could identify her photograph, and she seemed destined to toil forever as "Queen of the B's," the second-tier movies that rounded out the demand for double features in theaters. Still, she managed to snag a role that she would always regard as the best of her film career, the spoiled, paralyzed Gloria Lyons in Damon Runyon's *The Big Street*. Her character abuses the hapless busboy who adores her, played by her onetime date Henry Fonda. The critics took note, with James Agee of *Time* declaring that Lucy "was born for the parts Ginger Rogers sweats over" and "tackles her 'emotional' role as if it were sirloin and she didn't care who was looking." But the film was a box-office bust, and Lucy sensed that her days at RKO were coming to a close.

Desi himself had just one more movie under his RKO contract, *The Navy Comes Through*, a respectable melodrama in which sailors on an American freighter commandeer a German U-boat supply ship and rig its torpedoes to blow up the submarines to which they're being delivered. The film stars Pat O'Brien and George Murphy, and Arnaz plays the extravagantly named Patricio San Francisco Eduardo de la Vega Tarriba, a Cuban volunteer who signs up to fight the Nazis.

"Tell me," O'Brien's character demands at one point, "how is it a Cuban hotfoot like you comes all the way over here to join the United States Navy?"

"Well," Tarriba replies, "the United States helped to make Cuba free so I come here to free the United States."

Arnaz's character is subjected to the usual malaprops-for-laughs routine, at one point worrying, when shipmates are trying to rig up a makeshift radio, "Suppose we get a short circus here?" But he also has a couple of lovely, tender moments, playing the guitar and singing "Masabi," a Cuban son—a distinctive Afro-Spanish song form—to cheer his shipmates at one point and inspiring them by reciting, first in Spanish and then in English, some lines from the Cuban national anthem: "Don't be afraid of a glorious death, 'cause to die for your country is to live." But the critics were unimpressed. The New York Times judged that the film "floundered on the treacherous shoals of banality."

• • •

With his movie career not going much of anywhere, Desi was happy to be hired by Ken Murray, a comedian and former vaudeville and burlesque performer, for his Blackouts of 1942, a racy, old-fashioned stage revue in Hollywood that featured songs, sketches, and variety acts. The show would ultimately run (under various annual titles) for eight years, racking up more than 3,800 performances with various lineups of acts. Desi sang and beat his heart out on the conga, but the most salient feature of his time in the show was a backstage encounter one night with Louis B. Mayer, the boss of bosses at MGM. Mayer summoned Arnaz the next day to his palatial office, with its white leather walls, on the studio lot in Culver City and delivered a strange, backhanded compliment: "When I saw your show last night, you reminded me of Busher."

Arnaz was enough of a horse-racing fan to know that Busher was one of Mayer's prized Thoroughbreds, so he asked politely for an explanation. "Well," Mayer explained, "Busher looks very common when he's around the barn, but when they put a saddle on him and he goes out to the track, you know he's a champion. The same thing happens to you when you hang that drum around your shoulder. Up to that point, you're just another Mexican." After Desi corrected him as to his nationality, Mayer offered a contract at five hundred dollars a week; Desi talked him up to six-fifty. He first had to fulfill a commitment to a USO tour of the Caribbean—the only time he would ever return to Cuba, squeezing in a quick visit with his mother's parents in Santiago during a stop at the nearby U.S. naval base at Guantánamo Bay. When he returned to Los Angeles, he was cast in MGM's *Bataan*, the most prestigious, and probably the best, film he would ever make.

With a top-notch cast led by Robert Taylor, the film tells the World War II story of a baker's dozen of American soldiers assigned to hold a ridge in the Philippines so that General Douglas MacArthur and American and Filipino forces can make their retreat. The group is an ethnic and racial mélange of "typical" American types, the kind of ensemble so common in war movies over the decades. Desi plays Private "Fell-ix Ramirez," as he introduces himself, a National Guardsman from "Cal-ee-fornia" who has a home-built jalopy and loves Tommy Dorsey's big band swing sound. "Oh, he sends me, Sarge," Ramirez tells his commanding officer at one point. "He makes me lace up my boots!" The Americans are gradually picked off by the Japanese one by one, but Ramirez contracts malaria and expires in a feverish haze. "Jitterbug kid, shakin' himself to death," Robert Taylor's character says in sympathy. Racked with hallucinations, Ramirez recites a Catholic prayer of confession. It was Desi's suggestion to the director Tay Garnett that he say the confiteor not in Spanish (as the script dictated) but in the schoolboy Latin he'd learned at the Colegio de Dolores. A fellow soldier translates as Desi softly murmurs: "I confess that I have sinned exceedingly, in thought, word, and deed, through my fault, through my fault, through my most grievous fault." Taylor reaches down to close the private's eyelids as a muted "Taps" plays softly on the soundtrack. The *New York Times'* Bosley Crowther found Desi "convincing" as a soldier and the film a faithful depiction of the "true and ugly detail" of war, though the death scene struck him as "maudlin." *Photoplay*, the Hollywood fan magazine, gave Desi its citation for "Performance of the Month" in June 1943. "It wasn't the Academy Award," he would recall, "but damn good enough for me."

The previous month, the "jitterbug kid" had been drafted into actual American military service. A year and a half earlier, in the wake of Pearl Harbor, Desi was commissioned as a lieutenant in the Cuban army, but he decided he'd rather volunteer for the U.S. Navy. The rub: He was not yet an American citizen, and noncitizens could be drafted but could not volunteer. But now Uncle Sam had caught up with him, and his draft notice had, in fact, arrived. He applied for the Army Air Corps and was set to go to bombardier school when he tore the cartilage in his knee playing baseball at an army intake center and wound up fighting the Battle of Southern California at a series of camps in the greater Los Angeles area, ultimately arranging entertainment for the troops as a staff sergeant at Birmingham Hospital in the San Fernando Valley. There Lucy helped him recruit starlets to restore the morale of troops suffering battle fatigue. "Desi is doing a big job," she told the Hollywood press. "His job is to take the 3,000 boys under him, all boys who are back from Bataan, Corregidor, Tarawa, and see to it that every kind of entertainment is at their fingertips . . . all kinds of shows . . . movies, too, of course. He helps them with their letters. He sees to it that they have fruit and candy and cigarettes in their rooms."

Desi finally became a naturalized citizen on October 1, 1943. He was stationed close enough to come home on breaks, but he did not always do so, and the separation did nothing for his marriage—or for Lucy's increasingly frustrated hopes to start a family. In the scrapbooks she kept faithfully, she had taken to pasting pictures of babies' faces from Johnson's baby products ads. "I don't see any pictures of me in this book—and this is your third year—quit kiddin'!" she wrote in 1943, and on the next page added plaintively, "And <u>this</u> being your <u>fourth</u> year—You realize, of course, that there will now have to be <u>two</u> [double-underlined] of us. Please hurry before we get too old to care. Love, Susan and Desi Jr."—the two names Lucy had already picked out for their prospective children.

Both Desi and Lucy were jealous—she with much greater cause— and they exchanged forlorn love letters, each beseeching the other to keep the faith. "Lucy, sweetheart, you have no idea how happy you've made me—really and fully happy," Desi wrote at one point. "You're a wonderful baby and I adore you. I don't mistrust you, baby, but I am jealous. I can't deny that." Lucy replied: "My baby, you called about an hour or so ago. I'm kind of lonesome tonight. Kind of lost again. Desi, darling, please don't worry about me. Believe me, I wouldn't do anything to make you unhappy. If you are going to do the right thing as conscientiously as I am we have nothing to worry about. Please believe that. All my love forever."

But the static continued. Desi got drunk at a Birmingham Hospital picnic and called his superior officer names (just what discipline this would have provoked is unclear). His solo nightlife also had Hollywood gossips talking about the starlets he lured to perform at the base and a weekend in Palm Springs he had reportedly spent with another woman. By the summer of 1944, he had stopped coming home. "I closed my eyes, put blinders on, and ignored what was too painful to think about," Lucy would recall. By September, she'd had enough. She served Desi notice that she was divorcing him. Thirty years later, working on his memoir, he called her to ask why. Her answer was succinct: "You were screwing everybody at Birmingham Hospital." He denied it but would confess in his memoir, "If she had caught me in bed with a girl, unless it was right in the middle of the act, I would have jumped out and demanded to know how that girl got in there."

After filing for the divorce, Lucy escaped from the loneliness of the ranch for a time. Incredible as it may seem, she went to live with Desi's old girlfriend, Renee De Marco—the "Freckles" he'd been dating when Lucy and Desi met. De Marco, by now remarried to Jody Hutchinson, another dancer, was living in Hollywood and had become a friend of Lucy's.

That November, the day before Lucy was to appear in divorce court seeking her interlocutory decree, Desi called and asked what she was doing that night. "Nothing particular," she replied. He took her to a farewell dinner in Beverly Hills, where they talked over their problems and agreed that they would behave with more understanding in their next marriages. Apparently it was a very heartfelt conversation, because they returned to an apartment that Lucille had borrowed for the night and wound up in bed.

At seven thirty the next morning she bounded up, announcing, "Oh, my God, I'm late."

"Where are you going?" Desi asked.

"I told you, I'm divorcing you this morning," Lucy replied. "I gotta go through with it. All the newspaper people are down there. I got a new suit and a new hat." She went to court, got the divorce decree from the judge, and came right back and joined Desi in bed again—thus invalidating the breakup under California law, which had a one-year period banning cohabitation after a provisional decree. Cuddled together, they read the afternoon papers announcing their split.

After that, they went back to their Desilu ranch—and Desi started coming home on the weekends.

six

NECESSITY'S INVENTION

W hile Desi was in the midst of his army service, he was still receiving two hundred to three hundred admiring letters a week. "When Desi comes back, I don't believe there is any doubt but what MGM will realize that in him, they have one of the biggest bets in the business," Lucy told the Hollywood fan magazine writer Gladys Hall. That may have been wishful thinking, corporate loyalty, or some combination of the two. Because in late summer 1942, around the time Louis B. Mayer hired Desi, Lucy had left RKO and also gone to MGM, which was the gold standard of the still-thriving studio system, turning out the equivalent of a new movie every week.

   Lucy's initial experience at MGM was so intimidating as to be overwhelming. The image makers at the biggest, richest, starriest studio of all fussed and fretted, poked and prodded, with advice about her wardrobe, her figure, her style. But her MGM years would prove crucial—in ways not immediately apparent—to her emergence as a distinctive entertainment personality, her development as a comic performer, and her ultimate status as a Hollywood power player. For starters, it was MGM that made her a redhead. "When she arrived at MGM, her hair was medium brown," recalled Sydney Guilaroff, the studio's master hairstylist. "I would not say that it was dull, but it was not interesting. I thought there were enough successful blondes, so why not a redhead?" Guilaroff and his stylists ultimately arrived at a color that Lucy called Tango Red, but she judged that "actually it was as orange as a piece of fruit hanging on a tree." Makeup artists applied coral-orange lipstick and feathery false eyelashes and sketched thicker eyebrows than she'd had before, all the better to photograph her in her first Technicolor picture. And her first role at the new studio was glamorous indeed: the lead in *Du Barry Was a Lady*, the part that Ethel Merman had originated on Broadway (and a show in which Desi's sometime girlfriend Betty Grable performed), in a cast that also featured Red Skelton, Gene Kelly, Tommy Dorsey, and Zero Mostel, in his film debut. Lucy also got to work with the Academy Award–winning cinematographer Karl Freund, who not only photographed her beautifully but impressed her with his technical skill and attention to detail.

The Cole Porter score was bowdlerized for a middle-American audience, and Lucy's singing was dubbed by Martha Mears, but she looked sexy and spectacular in towering white powdered wigs and rainbow silk and satin gowns. She plays a nightclub singer and Skelton the coat-check attendant who falls in love with her. When he quaffs a spiked drink, he dreams he is King Louis XV and Lucy is Madame Du Barry. Under the guidance of the inventive choreographer Charles Walters, the two dance on a king-sized bed that turns out to be a trampoline. The film was a box-office success, too, bringing in nearly triple its cost in ticket sales upon its release in August 1943.

Lucy's second feature for MGM was another adaptation of a Broadway musical, *Best Foot Forward*, in which she plays herself, invited to a military school dance by a lovesick cadet who never dreams that she'll show up. When she does arrive—in a publicity gambit—she has to pretend to be another woman, the cadet's real girlfriend, to avoid ejection by the snooty dance committee. The film's not-so-funny running joke is that Lucy is only recognizable to the boys when she appears in a bathing suit or skimpy cheesecake outfit. Backed by a cast that included Nancy Walker, June Allyson, and Gloria DeHaven, the film was another hit. Its director was Edward Buzzell, a veteran vaudeville performer who had attended bubbly parties at the Desilu ranch and seen Lucy's easy clowning at home. He now discerned in her a marked natural gift for comedy and "saw the potential in me for humor and pathos I didn't even know I had," she would recall.

So did two other important figures who would become her teachers and mentors. The first was Buster Keaton, the legendary silent film comedian. Keaton was no longer the bankable star he had been a decade or two earlier and had taken a kind of consolation job at MGM to help devise gags and bits of comic business for other actors. It was he who first counseled Lucy to understand and master the use of props as "priceless friends" in comedy. The second mentor was Edward Sedgwick, who had also been working in Hollywood since the silent era and had directed some of Keaton's films. He had first met Lucy when she arrived in Hollywood and was working for Goldwyn, and had seen in her limpid blue eyes and expressive face something that evoked the great silent comedienne Mabel Normand, who could convey a singular mix of laughter and tears in her close-ups. He told Lucy that she could be the greatest clown in show business, but she dismissed him with a sardonic look that made him think he was right. Lucy had come to know him and his wife, Ebba, well when she was dating Al Hall, and they became something like surrogate parental figures for her, especially after the death of her grandfather Fred Hunt in 1944. Sedgwick, who had also watched Lucy closely at her informal parties at the Desilu ranch, saw that her humor was innately physical. If she tried to tell a conventional joke, she got tangled in the tale and forgot the punchline.

But if she picked up the slightest ordinary object, she could improvise a brilliant scene.

Lucy needed such supportive friendship. With Desi away at Birmingham Hospital—and faithful only in his fashion—she had often found herself lonely at the ranch, in dungarees with her flock of "decrepit chickens" and still longing to start a family. She had gone on her own sixteen-city war bond tour in 1943, alongside Fred Astaire, Greer Garson, Mickey Rooney, Harpo Marx, and other stars. But the studio often shunted her around without allowing her to spread her comedic wings, giving her a tiny part in *The Ziegfeld Follies*, a big musical extravaganza, and a supporting role in *Without Love*, one of Spencer Tracy and Katharine Hepburn's lesser efforts. "It was a strange, lonely, unreal kind of life," she would remember.

By the winter of 1945, Lucille was once more filming a picture— again directed, like *Best Foot Forward*, by the sympathetic Eddie Buzzell—that played to her strengths. *Easy to Wed* was a remake of *Libeled Lady*, a 1936 Jean Harlow vehicle. It starred Van Johnson and MGM's musical swimming star Esther Williams. The convoluted plot involves a socialite (Williams) who sues a newspaper for libel after it claims she caused the breakup of a marriage. To moot the suit, the paper has its handsome star reporter (Johnson) temporarily marry a beautiful but dim showgirl (Ball) so that she can sue Williams's character for alienation of affection when Williams and the reporter are caught in a clutch. Lucy has a bravura, eye-rolling drunk scene with Johnson, and Bosley Crowther in the *New York Times* praised her "exceptionally keen comedy sense." The film made a healthy profit, and Lucy now expected a string of more good roles. Instead, MGM quickly put her into a forgettable turkey called *Two Smart People*. Years later, she would say that the powerful MGM producer Arthur Freed, the head of its blockbuster musicals unit, kept putting his own red-haired mistress, Lucille Bremer, into the kinds of roles Lucy thought she had been hired to do. "Whatever they had in mind for me kind of went down the tube."

• • •

As for Desi, he was discharged from the army on November 16, 1945, and looked forward to getting back to work, especially since he was thirty thousand dollars in debt, mostly in back taxes, which he paid off by taking a loan from Lucy. This lapse, presumably a result of wartime dislocations, was atypical. Desi—and the Arnazes' business manager, Andrew Hickox—usually kept a close eye on finances (and in future years, Desi would veto a proposed *I Love Lucy* plot in which Ricky fudged on his taxes, on the grounds that no good American would do so). Finding a job would not be so easy as paying his debt. With stepped-up raises that had taken effect in his absence, his MGM salary was now a thousand dollars a week, but the studio had no projects to offer him. He'd heard of a forthcoming musical starring Esther Williams as a would-be female bullfighter with a twin brother who *is* a bullfighter but wants to be a composer. Desi thought it was just the kind of part he had been hired for, but while he was in the army, a new face had appeared in town: Ricardo Montalban, a Mexican-born actor and singer who had grown up in Los Angeles but then returned to his native country, where he'd become a hit in Spanish-language films. MGM cast Montalban in *Fiesta*, and his star quickly rose. He took up all the available oxygen for Latin roles—and, indeed, would for decades take the kinds of varied parts that Desi would have liked to play in film and television. In truth, Desi was not cut out to play a stereotypical Latin lover—and he never really did. He was a *caballero*, not an *enamorado*, radiating a sweetness and wholesomeness more than any sense of danger or dark romance. He was exotic in his own way but never threatening. "It was quite a heartbreaker for me," Arnaz recalled. "I guess it was out of sight, out of mind. I had been gone two and a half years and they had forgotten what they hired me for . . . musical comedies."

Desi went to Benny Thau, MGM's honcho of business affairs, and asked to be released from his contract. The studio agreed, and Desi booked an eight-week engagement at Ciro's nightclub on the Sunset Strip with a twenty-two-piece orchestra and a new comic named Larry Storch. This was the last golden gasp of the nightclub era, before television helped put an end to the business, and celebrities and ordinary couples alike would take in a nightclub floor show with dinner in an elegant, black-tie atmosphere—or drop by for a drink and some dancing after a movie. It was around this time that Desi introduced into his repertoire a pulsing, throbbing, wailing Afro-Cuban number that would henceforth become his signature song: "Babalú."

The number was written in the 1930s by the Cuban composer Margarita Lecuona and was first recorded by Miguelito Valdés, a deeply talented Cuban musician who had worked with Xavier Cugat in the early 1940s, after Desi. Told in dialect, the song is a hymn to Babalú-Aye, the Santería religion's patron saint of sickness, who suffers from a stew of debilitating illnesses and thus understands the suffering of others. Santería is a pantheistic Afro-Cuban religion that also includes some elements of traditional Catholic belief. The number tells of a bembe, a drum-infused religious ceremony, to Babalú, and it incorporates a frenetic, jazz-inflected call-and-response section that, in Desi's hands, brings to mind the comparable ritual in an American Black church. "It was lighthearted, rhythmically graceful, and extremely catchy—in short, it was a great song, especially when Miguelito sang it," the writer Ned Sublette explained. Depending on one's perspective, Desi's version, recorded first for RCA Victor, was a sanded-down homage or a blatant lift of Valdés's more authentic hit—and it landed with white, postwar American listeners as an exotic, exciting novelty. "He appropriated Miguelito's persona pretty much wholesale, necessarily replacing Miguelito's musical talent with his comedic talent and his considerable showman's skills, which were becoming better all the time as he learned in close proximity to the best in the business," Sublette wrote. Just as he had earlier done with the conga—and just as Elvis Presley would soon do by channeling Black musical forms for enthusiastic white listeners—Desi was once again popularizing an authentic Afro-Cuban musical idiom for mainstream American audiences, and he proved a sensation.

George Schlatter, who booked the acts at Ciro's, summed up Desi's appeal: "His act was not the best, but he had a great close in 'Babalú.'" By the early summer of 1946, Desi had even cracked the Emerald City of nightclubs in New York, the Copacabana, on East 60th Street, just off Fifth Avenue, where he and his band were booked for a run of three shows a night, at 8:30, midnight, and 2:30 a.m. The Hearst columnist Lee Mortimer gave Desi and his band a rave in the *Daily Mirror*. "Now he is one of the most entertaining fellows and leaders you've ever seen, doing everything well—singing, hoofing, clowning, emceeing." Desi's appearance featured the comedian Peter Lind Hayes and a young vocalist destined for a long cabaret career, Julie Wilson, who introduced "The Coffee Song" ("They've got an awful lot of coffee in Brazil").

Arnaz sought to capitalize on this new popularity by making *Cuban Pete*, a cheap, quickie, hour-long comedy for Universal Studios. Chock-full of Latin numbers, it's more a proto–music video than a feature film. It opened that July, and the *Hollywood Reporter* was scathing. "Just to give a quick notion of the depths to which *Cuban Pete* dips for laughs, you might as well know right now that the chief comic in the show is a parrot, a Cuban parrot that is," the trade paper reported. "The whole thought behind making this film musical was to cash in on the growing popularity of Desi Arnaz, now clicking on both coasts." The reviewer complained that the film failed "to do right by the Arnaz talents."

With Desi back on the road again, and the couple reliant once more on long-distance telephone calls to hold their marriage together, Lucy and Desi resumed their pattern of ferocious battling and making up. In New York, Desi would see a newspaper clipping of Lucy out on the town in Hollywood and accuse her of the worst; she'd see a report about him and the Copa chorus girls and do the same. Desi tried to tell himself that his casual dalliances didn't mean anything to Lucy. "I must admit that I was an old-fashioned Latin, raised observing and believing in the classic double standard," he would write years later. "Your wife is your wife and you want to know that you can trust her and be secure in that knowledge. Your fooling around can in no way affect your love for her. That relationship is sacred, and a few peccadilloes mean nothing. Lucy knew this." But she did not—not really, not ever—and his infidelity hurt her more and more deeply as time went on. "*Too Many Girls* is the story of your life!" she would bellow when they fought.

. . .

I n part to keep him closer to home, Lucy suggested to Bob Hope that he hire Desi as the house bandleader for his popular weekly radio show, which was recorded in front of a live audience in Hollywood, with occasional out-of-town shows when the peripatetic Hope happened to be on the road. Hope hired Desi, though Hope's stable of joke writers found the Cuban's comic talents lacking. "I'd say, 'Give him a line,'" Hope remembered. "And the writers would say, 'He doesn't know how to read a line.' I said, 'Give him a line, what's the difference?' And he'd walk up and a guacamole would fall out." Desi was forced to agree. "Not only couldn't I say them well, I didn't understand the jokes."

In a way that makes for cringeworthy listening, Desi was all too often the butt of the "jokes" he was given. On the air, Hope referred to Desi as "San Fernando's reject" and variously called the band "Desi Arnaz and his banana boat symphony" or "Desi Arnaz and his thirty-two musical relatives." When the singer Martha Tilton appeared on one show, Hope asked her how she took care of her voice, in anticipation that her advice might help Desi. "Oh, Bob," Tilton replied, "all singers take good care of their voices. They spray their throats and that sort of thing."

"Oh, Desi tried that," Hope replied. "The chili got through all right, but the beans always clogged up his atomizer."

The working relationship with Hope was not always easy. Early in their time together, the *Hollywood Reporter* recounted that friction between Desi and Bob "has become really acute in recent weeks" but also that their differences had "been ironed out." In time, though, just as he had done earlier with Xavier Cugat and George Abbott, Desi knew to look, listen, and learn. "I was going to the best college anyone could hope to find to learn the art of comedy as taught by its leading professor," he would recall of his time with Bob Hope. As the show's musical director, Desi would attend the first weekly meeting with Hope's stable of a dozen writers, each of whom was responsible for drafting a script. Hope would then spread the different versions out on the floor of his office, editing the various strands into the best possible version and selecting a diverting mix of tunes and tempos for the musical numbers. Then, the day before the broadcast, Desi would watch Hope "rehearse the entire show, supervise the music, the costumes, the props, the sets," and finally, on the night of the show, "take over that audience, as no one else but Bob can."

Meantime, Lucy's movie career was stalled once more. In 1946 she had turned thirty-five—then, as now, a dangerously mature age for a leading actress in Hollywood—and had walked away from an extension of her MGM contract rather than accept a pay cut. It now seemed all but certain that she would never become a front-rank movie star. She made *Lured*, a noir melodrama, for Universal, costarring the suave British actor George Sanders, who would later win an Oscar playing the acid-tongued drama critic Addison DeWitt in *All About Eve*. During the shooting, she may well have conducted an affair with Sanders, who was calm, smooth, soothing, and attentive—all the things Desi was not. To the end of her life, Lucy would deny that she and Sanders were ever more than costars, but Desi believed they had been, and so did the next of Sanders's four wives, Zsa Zsa Gabor.

A far more important undertaking for Lucy was her decision to appear in a live stage play for the first time since coming to Hollywood more than a decade earlier. She agreed to tour in Elmer Rice's *Dream Girl*, a romantic comedy in which a shy bookstore clerk imagines herself in all manner of adventures. It was a long, demanding part—by some estimates with nearly as much dialogue for the lead character as *Hamlet*—and Lucy would be onstage in every scene. *Dream Girl* had been a success for Rice's wife, Betty Field, on Broadway in 1945, and the playwright himself would say that Lucy was the only other actress who ever "really delighted me" in the role. The tour opened at the McCarter Theatre in Princeton, New Jersey, and ended in Los Angeles, where the *Los Angeles Times* critic Edwin Schallert recognized qualities in Lucy's performance that she had seldom been allowed to display in films. "She has efficiency as a comedienne," he wrote. "She can tinge a scene delicately with pathos. She has a special facility in dealing with sharp-edged repartee. She apparently never overdoes the sentimental side of a role."

On a night in July 1947, when Lucy was performing *Dream Girl* in Detroit, Desi narrowly avoided disaster. His band had played a gig in Madison, Wisconsin, and was next due in Akron, Ohio, so instead of joining the rest of the musicians on their bus, he flew to Michigan to see Lucy's performance. Meantime, the bus driver fell asleep at high speed on a highway in Indiana and crashed into a truck in front of him, sending half a dozen players to the hospital. The concertmaster Charlie Harris lost an eye. Tommy Dorsey, Xavier Cugat, and Duke Ellington all dispatched players to help fulfill the band's next engagement.

On this tour, the band—usually about sixteen members—played live stage shows at movie houses in midsize towns like Indianapolis; Omaha; Brownsville, Texas; and Canton, Ohio; but also big cities like Chicago and New York. In Chicago, the columnist Irv Kupcinet reported—in a typically stereotyped summary—how Desi raced back from a show at the Chicago theater to the Ambassador East hotel to prepare a "Latin lunch—chicken and rice, Cuba's favorite meal," for the press. "The wary critics, taking no chances, brought their own bicarbonate," he couldn't resist adding.

Desi put up with the rough road conditions, condescending columnists, and one-night stands because he needed the work. His road manager was Lucy's brother, Fred Ball, who had his hands full managing hotels, travel, logistics, and payroll—plus navigating the love lives of various band members, some of whom had remarried without bothering to divorce their first wife, and babysitting his brother-in-law after the last show. From the start, Fred told Desi he had two conditions: Desi could not ever involve him in his relationship with Lucy, and he could not yell at him. Desi tested both propositions.

"He couldn't be awakened in the morning except right on the minute," Fred Ball recalled. "I couldn't be five minutes ahead, it couldn't be five minutes late. It had to be right on the minute, and I had to time how long it took him to get out of bed and get dressed and get him on the elevator and over to the theater, because he was always, you know, right there. Just at the last minute . . . I had to shepherd him all night because we were up half the night, you know, boozing or whatever, which I couldn't do, because I couldn't handle the booze and him and the job at the same time."

Still, Desi was making the most of the moment when big bands still had broad appeal. "In spite of his limited musical training, Desi had an extraordinary ear and a precise concept of how he wanted his orchestra to sound," his childhood friend Marco Rizo recalled. The band he assembled featured a powerful rhythm section, sharp punctuation by the brass, and a "clarity" and "naturalness" of sound, Rizo said. Desi was also a savvy showman, with a keen understanding of public taste, good business sense, and "an outstanding presence," Fred Ball said. "He knew enough about music to know how to hire good arrangers and musicians, and he let them do the work. He'd give them the idea, the direction, what he wanted to accomplish, but he'd let them

do it. Desi would not get in and struggle to accomplish a musical objective." And, Fred noted, Desi had another objective that had never
left him: keeping up with a wife whose career—whatever its highs and
lows—had always been more successful than his: "She was growing,
and he had to grow. He had to work to make his end match. He always
had that feeling."

• • •

Lucy herself was about to grow in two important ways. The first
was in a medium where she had not yet performed: network
radio. She had appeared on national broadcasts, of course, but usually
to promote one of her films or in one-off dramatic or comedy roles—
not in an ongoing series. At the same time, she would fully embrace
and hone her talent for slapstick physical comedy on film. For fifteen
years, she had played almost every kind of role in the movies: blond
showgirl, wised-up dame, red-haired glamour queen, and a wide array
of supporting parts. Now she would finally flourish in the genre for
which she seems to have been destined all along. As Ball's biographer
Kathleen Brady wrote, watching Lucy in this moment was "like standing before a photographer's developing tray and seeing a photograph
of Lucy Ricardo emerge."

The catalyst for these career developments was a new agent, Don
Sharpe, who was making a specialty of packaging movie stars whose
box-office receipts had slipped, into partnership with radio networks
and sponsors in ways that could revive their careers. Sharpe approached
CBS about a vehicle for Lucy, based on a popular book by Isabel Scott
Rorick, *Mr. and Mrs. Cugat: The Record of a Happy Marriage*. By the
fall of 1948, this concept had been developed into a weekly series for
Lucy called *My Favorite Husband*. The main characters' names soon
changed after the show had been on the air a while to George and Liz
Cooper, to make them sound less exotic and more middle-American

(and to not risk summoning the inevitable suave shade of the world's best-known Cugat—Xavier). Richard Denning, a smooth, blond, square-jawed actor, was hired to play Lucy's husband, a bank vice president. The series premise was "two people who live together and like it," and each episode typically featured some kind of minor domestic crisis, usually caused by one of the wife's harebrained schemes.

The writing team was led by a pair of young CBS staff writers who had been working on the comedian Steve Allen's show—Madelyn Pugh and Bob Carroll Jr. They were soon joined by a more experienced head writer, producer, and director named Jess Oppenheimer. Like Desi and Lucy, they had come of age in the Great Depression and were looking for success in the changing world of popular entertainment following World War II. Madelyn Pugh grew up in Indianapolis, where she cut her teeth working on her high school newspaper with her classmate Kurt Vonnegut. She moved to Los Angeles with her widowed mother after college and got a job as a writer at NBC Radio, in part because of a shortage of male staffers during the war. After a short stint writing musical revues and sketches, she moved to CBS, where she met Bob Carroll, a Floridian who had begun his Hollywood career as the front desk clerk checking celebrities into the studio. They eventually became a writing team—and even dated from time to time—and found they shared an easy comic sensibility as they sat facing each other with two lamps and two typewriters. Over the years they went through a total of four weddings (none of them to each other), three divorces, two children, and nearly a thousand scripts for radio and television. Jess Oppenheimer, born in San Francisco, was a brainy child who later went to Stanford and made his way to Hollywood, writing for stars like Fred Astaire, Jack Benny, and Al Jolson. His biggest writing credit in radio was *The Baby Snooks Show*, starring the legendary comedian and singer Fanny Brice, so he had experience dealing with a strong female performer like Lucille Ball. Oppenheimer had a vision for shaping the character of Liz that fit Lucy's strengths. "She would be a stage-struck schemer with an overactive imagination that got her into embarrassing situations," Oppenheimer wrote years later. "This would give me an excuse to engage Lucy in some broad slapstick comedy."

The show struggled at first, but by the end of 1948 *My Favorite Husband* had emerged as a staple of CBS's Monday night radio lineup, eventually sponsored by Jell-O. The show was performed in evening clothes in front of a live audience at the network's studios on Sunset Boulevard in Hollywood, but Oppenheimer found he was having a hard time getting Ball to loosen up and fully exploit the comic possibilities of the scripts in this environment. So he gave her two tickets to Jack Benny's show so she could see how that master of timing played off his audience to enhance the laughs. Ball was thrilled. "Oh, my God, Jess," she told him. "I didn't realize."

At the same time, Ball was still making movies and honing this very same comic skill set. Her mentors Buster Keaton and Ed Sedgwick had left MGM and were now at Columbia Pictures, and in early 1949 Lucy signed a contract at the studio from which she had been so demoralizingly fired fifteen years earlier. Together, Keaton and Sedgwick schooled her—drilled her, really—in the subtleties of comic timing, which depended first on laser-like attention and listening, then *reaction*, and then and only then taking an action of her own. She promptly had the chance to put their tutorials to use in *Miss Grant Takes Richmond*, a comedy with the rising Hollywood star William Holden. Lucy plays the dimmest graduate of a secretarial school, hired by Holden, who is using his realty company as a front for illegal gambling and figures she'll never catch wise. Instead, Lucy's character takes the job seriously and embarks on a campaign to build low-cost postwar housing that ultimately succeeds (as does an unexpected romance with Holden).

Next came *The Fuller Brush Girl*, a zany caper with Eddie Albert that amounted to an old-fashioned silent slapstick comedy but with sound. Lucy plays a would-be door-to-door cosmetics saleswoman in a plot that involves corporate corruption, murder, mistaken identity, and romance as she gamely plunges into one physical stunt after another. She gets a face full of bath powder, bounces on a clothesline, dips into the smokestack of a steamship, rolls around its deck in a barrel, tries to plug a leaking wine cask by drinking from the hole, and in the climax hangs from a whole bunch of bananas and slithers around on the peels. Along the way, she blows up a telephone switchboard, administers home permanents that leave her clients bald, and impersonates a stripper displaying mile-long gaudy false eyelashes and her own still-flawless showgirl's legs. Her eyes bulge, her mouth puckers, but all she really wants is marriage and a modest little nest with her fiancé. She delivers laughs and pathos in equal portion.

. . .

While Lucy was starting to flourish with these new roles, nothing much was happening for Desi. In a chronology prepared for him when he was writing his memoir in the early 1970s, the year 1948 has just a single notation: a question mark. He was thirty-one years old and making a decent living—clearing a hundred thousand dollars a year with the band, more than 1.3 million in 2024 dollars—but his late-night work schedule and continued travel did nothing at all for his marriage. He and Lucy grew accustomed to a ritual where they greeted each other at dawn as their cars passed on Ventura Boulevard—she on her way to an early call at the studio, he on the way home from a late night at a club—or at dusk at the crest of Coldwater Canyon in similar circumstances. There was still no sign of the hoped-for baby that Lucy believed might cement their union.

Desi's mother, Lolita, was adamant that the reason for their childlessness was their civil marriage, and so on June 19, 1949, in a classic reflection of hope over experience, they renewed their vows in a small Catholic ceremony in Our Lady of the Valley in Canoga Park. Ed Sedgwick gave away the bride, who wore a soft Alice Blue dress, while Desi looked elegant as always in a white suit. "It was a beautiful ceremony, and I believed in it," Lucy would recall, adding that, at the time, "I seriously intended to become a Catholic." For his part, Desi said, "When I saw her coming down the aisle with her bouquet and wedding dress and hat, I got as much of a thrill as the first time, perhaps even more." The coolness with Mayor Arnaz remained. "As much as I would love with all my heart to be with you both on this great day of your happy life," he telegraphed from Miami, "due to your short notice it is impossible for me to be there because of a special important appointment already made. People flew from Cuba to see me and this requires my permanent [sic] here this weekend."

Six months later, like clockwork, Lucy was delighted to learn that she was pregnant. The joy did not last long, as she had a miscarriage. There was a sliver of good news, though: Her doctor discovered that in treating her for an earlier miscarriage at the start of her marriage, physicians had inadvertently closed a fallopian tube. He reversed this procedure and advised her to try again after three months. Though Lucy was now thirty-eight years old, she had renewed hope that she would soon be a mother.

Desi made one last film in this period, also for Columbia. *Holiday in Havana* is not well remembered, but it deserves to be, both because Desi's performance as Carlos Estrada, a Cuban busboy turned bandleader and composer, is charming and because it deftly presages his persona as Ricky Ricardo. The film is just seventy-three minutes long and chock-full of music (it includes stock footage of a real Cuban carnival and floats), and Desi plays Carlos as a well-mannered, sweet-tempered Latin lover, not a menace. "He is a comic caballero, a somewhat ridiculous Don Juan," the Cuban American writer and poet Gustavo Pérez Firmat explained. When Carlos has to spend the night with Lolita Valdes, the girlfriend he is still just pretending to be married to—in her own parents' house—he is chaste and respectful, singing her a tender goodnight bolero but then retreating to sleep on a porch, which collapses under his weight. "Desi is the Latin-lover-next-door, the one who won't abduct you unless he marries you first," Pérez Firmat added. "No wonder Lolita's implacable mother calls him 'a corny Casanova.'"

At this point, with Lucy and Desi apparently having gone as far in Hollywood as the industry would let them, the imperative for both of them—certainly the goal for Lucy—became to find a way to work together, a way that would keep Desi at home and off the road, away from temptation. In part for tax reasons, they had incorporated a company, Desilu Productions, with the idea of making movies of their own in partnership with Sedgwick, in whom Lucy placed such trust. This effort didn't go anywhere at first, but another prospect soon presented itself. Lucy's success as the star of a radio show had come just at the moment the commercial power of the medium was beginning to give way to television. In 1947, only 179,000 television sets had been sold in the United States; by 1949, the figure was two million. The radio networks saw the writing on the wall and had established television divisions, which needed programming to attract viewers and advertisers. CBS began pressing to transfer *My Favorite Husband* from radio to television, but Lucy was adamant that she would consent to this only if Desi could play her husband. The network rejected this idea, and Desi himself acknowledged it was unrealistic in the context of the show, in which George Cooper was the very American "fifth vice president" of a bank. "There was no way I could play that guy," Desi said.

So between them, Don Sharpe and Desi came up with a strategy to persuade CBS that audiences would accept the Arnazes as a couple who could be the focus of a new television comedy. After all, they had actually *been* a couple for almost ten years. And the entire rationale for creating a television show in which they would costar was so that they could manage to live and work together in the same town, on the same schedule. It is no exaggeration to say that what became *I Love Lucy* was born as a means of saving their marriage. "Let's try it this way," Desi proposed to Lucy. "We'll get an act together, and this summer you come with me on my theater tour and let's see what the American people think of us working as a team." Desi holed up in a suite at the Hotel del Coronado, across the bay from San Diego, with an old friend, Pepito Perez, "Pepito the Spanish Clown," the onetime court jester to King Alfonso XIII of Spain, whom Desi had known in his New York days. Perez was a master of pantomime, and he worked with Lucy to develop a routine using a beat-up cello and a xylophone.

Bob Carroll and Madelyn Pugh worked up some sketches and dialogue, and in the summer of 1950 the Arnazes went on the road. Desi and his band, as they always had, performed a live stage show before movie screenings in large houses. But now, in the middle of the musical performance, Lucy would come striding down the aisle in a baggy coat and smashed felt hat, demanding, "Where is Dizzy Arnazy?" She would go on to say she wanted to join the band, swinging her cello case and knocking over music stands as she took the stage. Desi would insist, "Wait a minute . . . I have to see your credentials." At this, he recalled, "she would then do a big take, look shocked and cross her arms over her bosom." Lucy imitated a barking seal, sliding along on her belly. Desi sang "Cuban Pete," and Lucy came out to join him, dressed as a floozy, singing of Sally Sweet, "the Queen of Delancey Street." Another sketch dealt with their own real-life difficulties in getting together.

The Arnazes' act opened at the Roxy in New York on June 9, 1950, the scene of their wedding day celebration almost ten years before, and the theater staff gave them an early anniversary party. The critics were delighted with what *Variety*, in its showbiz slang, declared "a sock new act." The *Hollywood Reporter*'s Broadway columnist, Radie Harris, pronounced the act "by far the best show of its kind that I've ever seen" and said that any other Hollywood stars planning to make personal appearance tours should emulate Desi and Lucy. "Instead of relying on just coming out in an act hastily put together, their entire spot shows the thoughtful preparation and originality that adds up to entertainment plus," Harris said. "No wonder that Lucille and Desi, who created most of their own material, were also smart enough to package this act themselves for their own company, Desilu Productions."

And the *New York Times*' A. H. Weiler, with a clearer crystal ball than anyone could have imagined, wrote simply that Desi and Lucy were "a couple who bid fair to become the busiest husband and wife team extant."

seven

———•⊰❖⊱•———

GETTING AIRBORNE

At the end of the 1940s, television was still a curiosity, looked down on as déclassé by the elite of the entertainment establishment. In *All About Eve*, Joseph L. Mankiewicz's scathing 1950 film about the Broadway theater, a young Marilyn Monroe, playing a frightened showgirl, has just thrown up after a failed audition.

"Now what?" she asks in exhaustion.

George Sanders, playing the malevolent theater critic who is exploiting her ambitions to demand her affections, answers drily: "Your next move, it seems to me, should be towards television."

"Tell me this," Monroe demands, "do they have auditions in television?"

"That's, uh, all television is, my dear," Sanders answers. "Nothing *but* auditions."

Lucy and Desi had reached enough of a dead end in their film careers that they were willing to audition. Lucy's friend, the lanky comic actress Virginia O'Brien, appearing on Ed Wynn's *Camel Comedy Caravan* program one night, peered up at the balcony of the CBS studio in Los Angeles and saw the Arnazes perched there, gazing down—studying the actors, the cameras, the technology. And on Christmas Eve 1949, Lucy and Desi themselves made their television debut on Wynn's show.

Wynn was a beloved vaudeville and Broadway clown, but even a casual viewing of the program explains why early television was seen as unserious by serious artists. The production values were sketchy, the picture quality poor, and the writing on par with that of a collegiate comedy troupe. After Desi introduces himself in a fusillade of friendly Spanish, Wynn deadpans, "Desi doesn't speak English, *does he*?" before going on to acknowledge, "These are the kind of jokes, you know, that will eventually ruin this medium!" As usual, Desi is subjected to ridicule about his command of English—or more precisely, his lack thereof. To help translate, Wynn summons a comely showgirl in a bathing suit, introducing her as "Lolita Pepita Chiquita Pepita Carmenita Mesquita" as Desi struggles to keep from breaking up.

Later on, after Desi, dapper in a blazer and light-colored slacks, sings "Straw Hat Song," Wynn praises him.

"*Muchas gracias!*" Desi says.

"And Sepulveda Boulevard to you, too!" Wynn replies.

Lucy then joins Wynn for a sketch lampooning silent movies, vamping in the style of the 1920s silent film star Theda Bara, and there's a running gag in which whatever Wynn does Desi keeps banging his conga drum. "You'll ruin the whole show!" Wynn complains. "It only lasts a half hour. You play those drums, they think it's some African show!" By this point, Desi is silently laughing so hard, his shoulders shaking, that Wynn says, "Look at the way he's laughing there. . . . He should buy a ticket!"

Their appearance was amateurish, but the Arnazes' presence showed just how much they were willing to risk to break into television.

On tour the following year, their exhausting schedule and Lucy's vigorous physical stunts also jeopardized their other great off-screen hope: having a baby. In June 1950, during the New York run of their vaudeville show, Lucy was relaxing in her dressing room between shows listening to Walter Winchell's radio broadcast when she heard him announce she was "infanticipating," the columnist's lingo for "pregnant." He'd been tipped off by a medical lab informant before the Arnazes themselves had learned the news. Even after Desi and Lucy trimmed the planned length of the tour, Lucy did not cut back on her onstage seal-bellyflop antics, and though it's not clear that had anything to do with what happened just weeks later back home in Chatsworth, she suffered yet another miscarriage.

Desi was still keeping his father at arm's length, but they were in touch from a distance. Mayor Arnaz was now involved in the cigar importing business in Miami. "Do not worry or give up," he wrote Lucy in somewhat broken English, "because now it show positive that we will have what you promise me: Desi IIII. This always happens in most of every woman with the first child, but that do not mean anything is wrong. I am positive sure you will have in a very short time—about two or three month—another baby and it will be for sure, because the surgens, I am almost sure, have done to you what you needed, so it will never happen again. . . . With all my love and kisses to you both."

As Lucy and Desi plotted with their agent, Don Sharpe, about the future, they must have felt deep ambivalence along with their grief. Going into television was a risk—and a major concession. "It meant . . . you were washed up in pictures," Jackie Cooper said. "Lucy, certainly no agent would have let her go into television if she were a star at the time. Things had faded and faded and they didn't know what to do in movies with a lady that might be thirty or thirty-five years old." Lucy was actually on the cusp of forty, and she would recall just how much the Hollywood establishment regarded television as the enemy. "So terrified was Hollywood of this medium, movie people were afraid to make even guest appearances," she would remember. "If I undertook a weekly television show and it flopped, I might never work in movies again."

· · ·

Selling the idea of their own television show would prove a high hurdle for the Arnazes. So far, Desilu Productions had produced nothing much but their vaudeville tour. Desi had made a few commercials, starring the bandleader Lionel Hampton and others, but securing a weekly TV comedy show was an altogether more challenging task. General Foods—the maker of Jell-O—sponsored *My Favorite Husband*, and their sponsorship money could determine whether or not such a new show would be financed. General Foods' advertising agency, Young & Rubicam, told the Arnazes that their best bet was to produce an audition show—the television term "pilot" had not yet been coined—and try to sell it to a network. Jess Oppenheimer, Madelyn Pugh, and Bob Carroll could not work on a spec script because they were under exclusive contract to CBS, so Lucy and Desi commissioned various other writers to draft a script, but most of their ideas did not click. One concept, though, had Lucy and Desi effectively playing themselves—a bandleader and his movie star wife—whose plans for a quiet anniversary celebration are ruined by *Life* magazine. That idea did pique the interest of NBC, which in turn finally got CBS's attention.

By this point, Harry Ackerman, the CBS radio executive who had overseen *My Favorite Husband*, had been promoted to vice president in charge of the network's West Coast radio and television programming. In the late fall of 1950, Ackerman began working with Don Sharpe and Oppenheimer to refine the idea of a CBS show for Desi and Lucy. The network was still deeply skeptical about the idea of Desi costarring with Lucy in a weekly series but was also so determined to keep Lucy happy that it agreed to put Desi under contract for a modest radio show of his own. Still, the prospects looked dim, especially at the top levels of the network, up to and including the company's founder and CEO, William S. Paley. "Bill said he was completely opposed to the idea of Lucille and Desi trying to do a television series together and sent word . . . that I should drop any such plans," Ackerman would recall.

In the end, a stopgap solution was devised. CBS had planned to broadcast an unsponsored Sunday afternoon radio quiz show called *Earn Your Vacation*, which was reconceived as a vehicle for Desi to demonstrate his capacity to draw a network audience. The title was changed to *Your Tropical Trip*—with the prize giveaway a Caribbean vacation—and Desi debuted as the host on January 21, 1951, from the Columbia Square Playhouse on Sunset Boulevard. The CBS house orchestra became Desi's on-air band.

Opening a typical show a few weeks later, on Easter Sunday, the announcer Johnny Jacobs enthuses, "Yes! That young man who in such a short time has become a sensational star in nightclubs and theaters and on records, our Latin-American ambassador of goodwill and great music of all the Americas, Desi Arnaz!" Desi takes the mic with a cheery flood of greetings in Spanglish before landing on an ebullient "Happy Easter!"

"Ladies and gentlemen, it's really a great pleasure to a-grain—again! *Agrain*? *Agrain*? What is that?" Arnaz asks aloud, before correcting himself. "Again! Bring you some music, have you meet some nice people, and to fly somebody on a tropical trip south of the border." That day's prize destination was Santiago de Chile, courtesy of a Braniff Airlines DC-6 sleeper plane, and Desi celebrates the city in song, "In Santiago, Chile, it ain't chilly at all!"

His first contestant is a housewife from Inglewood, just south of Los Angeles. He asks her a quiz question: "If you were traveling, and someone gave you a *mantilla*, what would you do with it? Would you put it on your lap and play it, would you roll it on a stick and fry it, would you give it to your mother-in-law to wear it, or would you take it to a shop and stuff it?"

"I don't know what *you'd* do with it," she replies saucily, referring to the distinctive Spanish-style head-and-shoulders shawl, "but I'd wear it," and she wins a Westinghouse electric refrigerator in the bargain.

The next contestant is a retired mailman. "Well, shake hands with a re-treaded musician," Desi says gamely.

Your Tropical Trip never did attract a sponsor, but it kept Desi anchored in Los Angeles, where he and the band simultaneously played a stand at the Biltmore Bowl in the elegant Biltmore hotel downtown.

"Lucy had that kind of power even then," Ackerman recalled. "CBS didn't want to lose her. Even though it wasn't certain that she and Desi would be right together on a television series, the network wanted to make it clear that it respected Desi, too." Lucy had always been acutely sensitive to Desi's tender ego. "I'm proud to be called Mrs. Arnaz," she had told an interviewer during the vaudeville tour. "But I warn you Desi doesn't appreciate wiseacres who call him Mr. Ball. That's when he sees red and I don't blame him. We've been married ten wonderful years this month. He's the boss in this combination."

Lucy had also insisted on 50 percent ownership with the network of any television show and said she would only do it if Oppenheimer, with whom she had grown comfortable and confident on *My Favorite Husband*, was hired as the producer and head writer. In Ackerman's memory, Lucy and Desi's initial idea was to do the show as themselves, with movie star friends dropping in for talk and songs. "Knowing that such a show would quickly go down the toilet so to speak, I made an impassioned speech in favor of their playing fictional characters in a fictional series," he recalled. In any case, Ackerman tasked Oppenheimer with finding the right idea.

Brainstorming together one day, Oppenheimer asked Ackerman, "Why don't we do a show about a middle-class working stiff who works very hard at his job as a bandleader and likes nothing better than to come home at night and relax with his wife, who doesn't like staying at home and is dying to get into show business herself?" Lucy liked this basic premise. Because Oppenheimer's contract granted him a participation interest in future projects, CBS offered him 20 percent ownership of the new show—a provision that, if it was conveyed to the Arnazes, did not register at the time.

. . .

There was a happy complication: Lucy had become pregnant again in the fall of 1950, and by the late winter of 1951 she was beginning to show visibly. Jess Oppenheimer, Bob Carroll, and Madelyn Pugh considered this in writing the audition episode to create scenarios in which Lucy could be draped in loose-fitting clothes. (Now that the show was being developed by CBS, Bob and Madelyn could be brought back on board under Jess's leadership to handle the writing.) The plot drew heavily from their work on the Arnazes' vaudeville act, and it would also include an appearance by Pepito the Clown. The lead characters' proposed names were Lucy and Larry Lopez, but those names wouldn't last. There was a popular bandleader named Vincent Lopez at the time, and so to avoid any confusion, Lucy and Ricky Ricardo were born. Another hurdle was the name of the show, which was needed for the title cards to be used in the audition film. Oppenheimer's working notion had been to call it simply "*Lucy*, starring Lucille Ball and Desi Arnaz." But Desi wanted top billing, and even after Oppenheimer thought he had convinced him that the gallant approach would be to let Lucy go first, Desi came back proposing alphabetical order. In the end, the title Jess kept returning to was *I Love Lucy*—in which, he realized, Desi actually got "first-place billing after all."

The audition was set for March 2, 1951, Desi's thirty-fourth birthday, and it was performed before a live audience at the network's studio complex on Sunset Boulevard, Columbia Square's Studio A. The show would be captured over a closed-circuit television hookup and then filmed from a video monitor so it could be shown to prospective sponsors, producing what was called a kinescope (videotape had not yet been invented). Still, the performance almost did not happen. The Arnazes were still negotiating over details of their agreement with CBS, and just before curtain time that night a network executive, Hal Hudson, told Desi that the test could not proceed without a signed contract. Incensed, and already confident he and Lucy had a valuable property in hand, Desi demanded to know how much it would cost to produce the show. Told the figure was nineteen thousand dollars, he yelled, "Okay, I'll pay for it myself, and it will belong to us," before CBS finally relented and agreed to foot the bill.

That same day, Oppenheimer himself realized that he, too, was still working without a contract and decided he'd better register his brain-child with the Writers Guild of America. So he typed up a précis, paid his one-dollar fee, and laid claim to "I LOVE LUCY, Created by Jess Oppenheimer," in which the lead characters "are happily married and very much in love" and "the only bone of contention between them is her desire to get into show business and his equally strong desire to keep her out of it." He filed the stamped carbon copy away. That was a wise move, one that would grant Oppenheimer important leverage in the future.

The test show begins with a stock shot of the Manhattan skyline, looking eastward along 57th Street, as the announcer, Bob LeMond, explains, "In this city live Lucy and Ricky Ricardo . . . where they laugh, love, and thoroughly enjoy life." A hand slides into the frame and re-moves a chunk of a model-sized apartment building—as if pulling out a puzzle piece—and the camera glides in to reveal Lucy and Ricky asleep in twin beds, as LeMond announces, "It's eleven o'clock now. They should be getting up."

The sets are flimsy, the doors shake, and the painted muslin walls billow as if they are sails in the breeze. But from the first frames, the recognizable ecosystem of *I Love Lucy* emerges in miniature. Ricky awakens fresh as a daisy, in pajamas with a picture of a snorting bull on the back. A groggy Lucy gazes aghast at herself in the mirror, contorts her countenance into one of its seemingly infinite expressions, and asks, "I wonder whatever happened to my type?" As Ricky shaves, she sits beside him, mirroring each twist of his face. He accuses her of "tizzing" him, but she insists that she is not. The plot is simple and will be repeated with endless variety in the years to come: Ricky has a big audition for a television program, and Lucy wants a part in the show.

"You'll never be a success on television, anyway," she pouts.

"What do you mean?" Ricky demands.

"You don't have a pretty girl in the act," she says.

But Ricky is insistent: "I want a wife who is just a wife. All you gotta do is clean the house for me, hand me my pipe when I come home at night, cook for me, and be the mama for my children."

"You don't smoke a pipe," Lucy replies without missing a beat.

In a vain effort to persuade Ricky to give her a chance, Lucy sashays like a showgirl with an upside-down lampshade on her head and wearing a blanket to hide her real-life pregnancy, but Ricky is not biting. To keep her away from the audition, he sends her downtown to deliver copies of their wills to their lawyer while he goes off to the nightclub to work on the act with his friend Pepito the Clown. But Pepito falls off a bicycle in the middle of rehearsal, and Ricky sends him back to their apartment to rest, where Lucy, returned from the lawyer's office, sees him and asks him to demonstrate the bike-riding routine, and this time he really injures himself. So Lucy arrives at the club in baggy coat and pants with her beat-up cello—just as she had done in the Arnazes' real nightclub act—demanding to see "Ricky Risker-dough."

"Do you play that thin?" Ricky asks, going along with the joke, but once again struggling to keep a straight face.

"What thin?" Lucy says.

"Never mind making fun of my English!" Ricky replies.

"That's English?"

In the episode, Desi performs three musical numbers: snippets of "Babalú" and "Granada," and a song called "Cuban Cabby." But of course it is Lucy who scores such a big hit—mugging, romping, once again flopping around like a seal despite her pregnancy as she toots a xylophone made of horns—that *she* gets offered the television contract. The episode ends with Ricky in a sulk and with Lucy in an apron holding a broom agreeing to be the stay-at-home wife her husband wants, having baked his favorite pie before the final kiss.

. . .

With the test in the can, the next task was to find a sponsor. CBS remained dubious, and Desi was part of the reason why. One network executive, the programming chief Hubbell Robinson, asked Oppenheimer, "How can I possibly sell that?" In those days, commercial sponsors had enormous power over what the networks put on their air. They not only bought and paid for airtime, they exercised considerable creative input—and typically had a veto—over the casting, concept, and writing of a show, which they normally sponsored in its entirety. Young & Rubicam, whose client General Foods sponsored *My Favorite Husband*, showed some initial enthusiasm, but by early April, CBS still had not lined up a buyer for *I Love Lucy*. Part of the problem was that the pilot episode, with its clown acts and musical numbers, was almost as much a variety show as it was a situation comedy. There was clearly lingering skepticism about Desi, and on April 16 CBS circulated a promotional prospectus to potential advertisers that went out of its way to tout him and his talents, however untested the network actually thought he was. "Desi Arnaz shows that his newly-discovered aptitude for comedy is on the same high par as his better-known singing ability," the three-page pitch read, even though just such an aptitude remained unproven in the network's eyes. "His characterization of a harassed husband is far more than a foil for Lucille Ball's zany wife; it's a skillful interpretation by a polished comedian."

There was one adman who had all along expressed more interest than the others: Milton Biow, the proprietor of a large, independent agency that billed more than $50 million a year at its peak, whom the *New York Times* would describe as one of the originators of the modern Madison Avenue school of advertising. Biow's clients included Pepsi-Cola, Bulova Watch, and the giant tobacco company Philip Morris. Biow thought that *I Love Lucy* had potential, so he arranged for Philip Morris's top public relations consultant, Benjamin Sonnenberg, then one of the nation's leading PR men and a bon vivant, to hold a private screening in the elegant, chintz-covered, fifty-person screening room on the top floor of his Gramercy Park town house in Manhattan. One of the test viewers was Biow's good friend Oscar Hammerstein II, who with his composing and producing partner Richard Rodgers then stood at the pinnacle of their power, with *The King and I* having just opened on Broadway.

"Keep the redhead but ditch the Cuban" was Hammerstein's critical verdict, according to Oppenheimer's later telling.

"He's her husband," Biow explained. "It's a package deal. To get her, we have to take him."

"Well, then, for God's sake, don't let him sing," Hammerstein supposedly replied. "No one will understand him."

In his own memoir—written years later, after *I Love Lucy* had achieved iconic status and virtually every executive in New York and Hollywood was only too eager to take credit for having had a hand in the show's success—Biow offered what was surely an embellished account of his own influence, insisting that it was he and Hammerstein who envisioned something other than "a routine vaudeville show, with a comedy couple, a guest star, and a band."

"Oscar Hammerstein sat in to watch it with me one day," Biow wrote. "We began to talk, and it was he who developed the idea of a warm, human story, built around a wholesome, lovable, dizzy couple who would engage the viewers' affections. He predicted, 'This should be a smash hit.'" No one could top Oscar Hammerstein's skill when it came to warm, human stories, but there is no reason to believe that Jess Oppenheimer, Bob Carroll, and Madelyn Pugh were not already committed to just such a course—since it was, after all, the very kind of show they'd created in *My Favorite Husband*.

In the end, Philip Morris bought the show for a projected budget of roughly twenty thousand dollars an episode and ordered a weekly series, thirty-nine episodes, for the 1951–52 television season. There were two zingers in the company's proposal. The first reflected the enduring ambivalence about Desi. The contract with Philip Morris stipulated that "in each program the major emphasis shall be placed on the basic situations arising out of the fictional marriage, and that the orchestra will furnish only incidental or background music except where an *occasional* script shall require a vocal number by Desi Arnaz *as part of the story line*." The second caveat was the thirty-nine episodes, which represented a disappointment for Lucy. She had hoped to produce a show only every other week, which she thought might allow her to at least keep one toe in the movies. A weekly schedule would mean abandoning that. Don Sharpe went to the Desilu ranch to give the Arnazes the news. Lucy told him that the couple wanted to work together more than anything, and that if Desi was willing to give up taking the band on the road, she was willing to give up seeking film roles. Desi agreed, saying, "We'll gamble everything on this show."

· · ·

The full extent of "everything" soon became apparent. Milton Biow telephoned one day to ask when the Arnazes and the writing team would be moving to New York, which was then the undisputed center of live television production. Lucy was seven months pregnant at the time, and Desi was thunderstruck. He was in the process of building a nursery wing onto the Desilu ranch—at twenty-three thousand dollars, half again the original cost of the house—and the whole point of doing the new show was to keep the family together in Los Angeles. Oppenheimer, with a newborn baby himself, was just as stunned.

But Biow was adamant. "Jess," he told Oppenheimer, "I bought a show that's going to be done from New York. I am not about to put on a program where 15 percent of the audience see it clearly and 85 percent see it through a piece of cheesecloth." Biow was referring to the standard process by which television shows were broadcast live to Eastern and Midwestern states (85 percent of the U.S. viewing population), but viewers in the West had to content themselves with watching a blurry "kinescope" version, shot off of a TV screen, usually on nontheater-grade 16-millimeter film, and shipped by air for delayed broadcast a week or more later. There was, as yet, no coaxial cable to carry television transmissions coast-to-coast. With the vast bulk of the viewing audience living in the East and Midwest, only a very few programs—like Ed Wynn's—originated in Los Angeles, and were filmed from a television monitor for later airing. The picture quality of kinescopes was poor, in part because of the differential between the speed of film and the flickering video images on the monitor, and nothing could improve it. "There are only two shades on the Wynn show—black and white," wrote John Crosby, the *New York Herald Tribune*'s television critic. "There's nothing in between. Also the film jerks unexpectedly in spots. Or else Ed Wynn has arthritis."

The Hollywood trade papers reported on the standoff. CLIENT NIXES KINE ON LUCI AND DESI, *Variety*'s headline blared. Biow sent a subordinate to Hollywood to negotiate, but Philip Morris held fast: *I Love Lucy* either had to be broadcast live from New York or *filmed* in Los Angeles—that is, captured on high-quality film for later broadcast rather than being shown live. It wasn't an unheard-of demand. CBS's popular show *Amos 'n Andy* was already in the process of being produced on film, but no one was yet sure how well the system would work. On top of everything else, the technical requirements of shooting on standard theatrical 35-millimeter film—the editing, post-production, and all the other requirements of what would amount to making a short motion picture—would cost more, about 25 percent more, in fact, or an extra five thousand dollars an episode. CBS and Philip Morris reluctantly agreed to put up two thousand dollars each. That still left a thousand-dollar shortfall. Desi and Lucy were to be paid a total of five thousand dollars between them per episode, plus 50 percent ownership of the show. Desi agreed that they would take a one-thousand-dollar-a-week pay cut to defray the cost of filming the show. In the Arnazes' high-income marginal tax bracket of roughly 90 percent, he figured, that was not really such a sacrifice. In after-tax dollars, a pay cut of thirty-nine thousand across the season's thirty-nine episodes would really amount to a loss of at most four or five thousand dollars in income.

But Desi had one important condition: He wanted to own 100 percent of the rights to the resulting films. This had implications that neither party quite realized at the time, but it turned out to be hugely important. At this point in television's development, there was no such thing as a rerun. Programs were broadcast once, then typically disappeared forever. The best evidence suggests that Desi might have had some notion that he could resell the *I Love Lucy* films in foreign markets. But CBS was focused on the short-term costs and saw little risk in acceding to Desi's demand. "They did not think that filming the shows the way we wanted to do them was going to work," Desi recalled. "So, what the hell? they probably thought." As for Desi himself, he acknowledged, "I had made them all believe that I knew what I was talking about, when in reality I didn't have the first clue."

eight

———·❖·———

LIGHTNING IN A BOTTLE

It was no accident that in 1951 television programming was almost
totally live. Instantaneous transmission of picture and sound over
the spectrum of the airwaves was, after all, the whole point of the new
medium—*the magic of television*. But the preference for live broadcasts
dated back to the earliest days of radio, and there were philosophical,
practical, and commercial reasons for it. In the 1920s, sound recording
equipment was bulky and unreliable. Network executives like CBS's
founder, William S. Paley, contended that live broadcasts provided the
extra dimension that only radio could supply: coverage of real-world
events as they were happening. But Paley and his fellow network executives also had a business motive. If recorded broadcasts were permitted, singers and comedians could produce and sell their own programs
to local independent stations, cutting the radio networks out of the
loop—and the profits.

Musicians and music publishers also feared that radio itself might cut into the sales of records and sheet music, since the medium gave away their tunes for free. Ultimately, of course, radio became the leading means of promoting the sale of records—and a mix of live and recorded programming became the norm.

In the years following World War II, the motion picture industry saw a similar threat in television. The major movie studios were already reeling from a 1948 Justice Department consent decree that had forced them to divest themselves of their ownership of theater chains—and thus of a captive market for their films. Studio executives feared that television could spell disaster if broadcasters could provide visual entertainment for free. In response, a sharp and clear divide between film and television emerged, in which film remained the home for long-form uninterrupted dramas, comedies, and musicals (often in color, or later in special wide-screen and novelty formats, like 3-D and CinemaScope). By contrast, television was the new place to see shorter, lower-budget fare: skits and musical acts, in the form of variety shows and half-hour situation comedies (and, eventually, of course, old movies on *The Late, Late Show*). Moreover, because television was a sponsor-driven medium, production was anchored in New York, the headquarters of the major national advertising agencies, not in Hollywood.

"It is only a network which can provide on a nationwide basis the real magic of television—its real vitality," CBS president Frank Stanton would insist, "the live program, seen by the nation just *as* it happens and just *when* it happens."

But there was a problem with this logic in the era before the advent of the coast-to-coast coaxial cable—a metal-shielded copper bundle of wires designed to block signal interference—made possible the live carriage of programs nationwide. Viewers who happened to live outside the broadcast range of a transmitter where a program was being performed live (typically in New York) could not actually *see* it live, but, as explained, depended on the use of kinescopes filmed off a monitor and delayed for broadcast. This generally meant households in the Western states, since most shows still originated in New York. Years later, Desi himself would acknowledge that he had not really had any clear idea of the eventual value of recording each episode of *I Love Lucy* on film and of owning the negatives. "I just knew that we could do a better show on film," he recalled. "Lucy would be better photographed, and whatever mistakes we made during filming could be corrected by retakes." But it was Desi's insistence on doing so that carried the day. The West Coast CBS executive Martin Leeds had initially rejected Desi's demand to own the filmed shows and had warned him that Desilu would never be able to afford to produce the series on its own. So Desi appealed to a higher-ranking executive, Hubbell Robinson, of the network's business affairs division in New York, who finally agreed.

The consequence was that after each episode's initial broadcast, Desilu—not CBS—would control the rights to the show. The network was not yet thinking about the potential value of those rights, but instinctively Desi knew that film would produce a superior product. His innovation represented the beginning of a shift in power from the networks and sponsors to the studios and producers. At a stroke, Desi had effectively given birth to the business model that would become the industry standard. If a television program could be shown again and again, it could be sold again and again—and soon enough, that is exactly what began happening. Producers, advertisers, and audiences all came to accept the new reality as mutually beneficial (even if reruns eventually became the source of occasional boredom), and to one degree or another, the practice persists to this day on television of all kinds.

But the immediate question was more practical: how to film the new show. And that quickly became an even more complex question, because Harry Ackerman of CBS, Jess Oppenheimer, and the Arnazes knew from their experience making *My Favorite Husband* that Lucy's comedy was most effective in the presence of a live audience. Ackerman, especially, feared that Ball's brilliant spontaneity would be lost on film, especially if a soundtrack of recorded laughter had to be added later. So at a meeting on the terrace of the Beverly Hills Hotel in that summer of 1951, Ackerman told the Desilu team that they would not only have to find a way to film the new program but to do so in front of real live people. "I'm afraid I increased the size of the bombshell when I announced that, film or not, *I Love Lucy* was going to be done before an audience," he recalled years later. "There was a thunderstruck silence. Then the babble of objections began, with even Desi trying to dissuade me from my stand."

Ackerman's prescription would mean filming the show in order, in continuity, like a play—rather than piecemeal, in separate scenes that would later be stitched together, like a film. Nothing quite like that had ever been done before, and certainly not in front of a live audience. Since the dawn of the movie business, feature films had been shot almost entirely with a single camera for each sequence. Except in long shots in which the whole scene is visible, the process requires separate camera setups for each action and reaction, and in the case of close-ups one actor and one face at a time; watching it happen is about as exciting as watching paint dry. Moreover, a motion picture soundstage is a working factory floor, with heavy equipment, white-hot lights, miles of electrical cable, and severe fire hazards all around. Cramming an audience of perhaps three hundred people into that enclosed space would violate numerous safety codes and regulations.

To help solve the first problem, Desi, Jess, and the production team soon decided that they wanted to use three separate cameras to record the actors simultaneously from different angles (or sometimes in close-up). That way there would be no need to record separate reaction shots, which would preserve the comic pacing. Having three cameras going at once would also allow the dialogue and audience laughter to be synchronized, further capturing the energy of the live performance.

From the start, Desi had only one cameraman in mind to create and oversee such a setup: Karl Freund, the Academy Award–winning cinematographer he and Lucy had met at MGM when she was making *Du Barry Was a Lady*. Jess Oppenheimer called Freund "a giant in the movie industry," though he was also "not an easy man to get along with." But when Desi telephoned Freund to ask his advice, the expert cameraman's answer was emphatic.

"You cannot do it," Freund declared.

If anyone should have known that, it was Freund, a large and imposing man (he was said to weigh 360 pounds) beloved by two generations of actors, who fondly called him "Papa." Born in Austria-Hungary in 1890, he emigrated to Berlin with his family just after the turn of the twentieth century and got his start in films as a projectionist. He was a veteran of German expressionist cinema, having worked with directors like F. W. Murnau and Fritz Lang. Freund had photographed Lang's landmark science-fiction masterwork *Metropolis* in 1927, creating the film's multi-exposure sequences live on the set, not in a lab. He is credited with pioneering the use of the "unchained camera," in which for the first time the movie camera was unleashed from a static tripod and moved around a scene, on a dolly track, a crane, and sometimes even on Freund's own protuberant belly. He had also pioneered the "process shot," in which a simple rear projection was used to provide the background for a scene shot in the studio—a staple of the industry in the days when on-location filming was expensive and rare. Its modern counterpart is the "green-screen" digital technology in which backgrounds are added after shooting, so that Spider-Man can swing from tall buildings and Harry Potter can perform untold feats of wizardry. Freund came to the United States in 1929 and photographed the Oscar-winning Best Picture *All Quiet on the Western Front* the following year. He directed Bela Lugosi's *Dracula* and won his own Academy Award for cinematography on *The Good Earth* in 1937. He was also rich, having invented an innovative light-exposure meter that became widely used in the industry. To market his discovery, Freund borrowed against his life insurance and mortgaged his home to found the Motion Picture Research Corporation, started in his garage. "It was a hobby," he liked to say. "Now it's my annuity."

Freund was nothing if not practical. In the 1940s, when the director Richard Brooks was preparing to shoot his first film, Freund had offered some unsolicited advice, sending Brooks home one day with two brown paper bags filled with rolls of 16-millimeter film, instructing him to watch them. Brooks was stunned to see that they were crude pornographic movies from the 1920s. "What's it got to do with directing?" Brooks asked the master the next day. "Lesson number one," Freund replied. "Many times you will be wondering, do you put the camera up here or down here? Maybe you make the scene a little bigger, a little smaller. You say, 'What do I do?' Did you watch these pictures closely?"

"Yes," Brooks replied.

"Okay," Freund explained. "Lesson number one: Get to the fucking point."

Despite his skepticism, Freund was intrigued by Arnaz's challenge and agreed to take the job. He bestrode his sets, invariably carrying a thermos full of martinis and giving orders in a German accent but never appearing drunk. "He was a kind and brilliant man," Desi would later recall. But now Freund was telling Desi that the notion of using multiple 35-millimeter cameras to film all the action at once was quite impossible. Why?

"Because, my dear boy," Freund explained, "you must light for the master shot one way, light for the medium shot another way, and light for the close-up in yet another way. You can't photograph all three angles at the same time and get any kind of good film quality. On top of that you want to do it in front of an audience." Just to make the prospect even less attractive, Desi told Freund he could only pay him union scale to start. But Freund seemed energized by the challenge. He spent a week in New York watching how television cameras might be moved around a set without impeding an audience's view of the action and was unimpressed. "There are no rules for our kind of show," he said, "so we'll make up our own."

· · ·

In fact, using multiple cameras at once was not a completely new idea. As early as the silent era, directors including Cecil B. DeMille had sometimes used multiple cameras running simultaneously to record action. The advent of sound had made doing so more complicated because cameras made distracting noise, and the practice fell away. But as it happened, in that summer of 1951 there were a handful of people in Hollywood who had fresh expertise in varying aspects of what Ackerman, Oppenheimer, Freund, and Desi wanted to do. In 1947 and 1948, Jerry Fairbanks, the head of NBC television's small film division in Los Angeles, had begun using three 16-millimeter cameras at once to film several shows—including vehicles for the ventriloquist Edgar Bergen and the singer Dennis Day—though not in front of a live audience.

In April 1950, Fairbanks adapted this technique for Ralph Edwards, the producer of the popular radio game show *Truth or Consequences*, which was making the transition to television. The program was performed in front of a live audience, though not all the cameras always ran at once. Some months later, another production executive named Al Simon joined the Edwards operation, upgrading the filming to 35-millimeter stock and creating an intercom system that allowed technicians to talk to each other during the shooting. Though *Truth or Consequences* was a game show and not a miniature play with characters and a plot, Eddie Feldman, Milton Biow's representative on both that show and *Lucy*, knew that Simon's technique could be just what Desilu needed. Feldman suggested that Desi call Simon and then did so himself, and Desi quickly hired him as production manager.

Decades later, when Desi published his memoir and was eager to claim the credit for *I Love Lucy*'s success that he believed the industry had denied him over the years, he relegated Simon to the status of a supporting player. But in a draft manuscript for the book, he was much more effusive, saying of Simon, "I am sure we could not have done it without Al." Desi added: "I know I'm not the easiest guy in the world to work with, but that never seemed to bother him at all. If I wanted to stay in the office until midnight trying to find the answer to something which we hadn't been able to find as yet and I would get upset and discouraged, he would always say, 'Let's go home, have a good night's rest. Tomorrow we'll look around and I'm sure we'll come up with the answer to that problem.'"

One of the many problems Arnaz now had to solve was where to film the show, and he took the lead in figuring that out. "Desi quickly proved to have great and unexpected talents as an organizer," Harry Ackerman recalled. Desi and Karl Freund scouted a number of locations, including nightclubs and theaters in the greater Los Angeles area. Each option had its problems. Nightclubs had obstructed sightlines, while the proscenium stages at most theaters were too small to hold three or four standing sets at once, which is what the team wanted to provide—high production values instead of the flimsy sets then prevailing on TV. Eventually, a friend of Al Simon's suggested that the *Lucy* team look at General Service Studios on Las Palmas Avenue, in the heart of old Hollywood. It had been a center of film production since the days of silent movies, and its stages echoed with the ghosts of performers from Harold Lloyd to Shirley Temple. But the brothers who owned it, Jimmy and George Nasser, were going broke and about to lose the property to their creditors. Desi realized the location would work, and CBS agreed to loan the funds to help finance a lease. Desilu soon began renovations, knocking down walls to create a bigger space on Stage 2 and installing more soundproofing to keep from disturbing residential neighbors. To satisfy Los Angeles Fire Department regulations that required an exit door to the street for any venue with an audience, Arnaz arranged to open a double-wide entrance at 6333 Romaine Street, on the south side of the stage. This created what was promptly dubbed "the Desilu Playhouse," with sleek Art Deco–style lettering. The company proudly advertised the venue in the trade press as "the nation's first television film-theatre." The *Hollywood Reporter* announced that the audience would sit in an "amphitheater," but the reality was more prosaic: Herb Browar, the stage manager, came up with the idea of wood-and-metal bleachers that could seat three hundred spectators, raised high enough above the rolling cameras to be able to see the action.

Another task was to find a director. Desi and Lucy's first choice was Eddie Buzzell, who had been so supportive of Lucy's talents at MGM. "I turned it down, like a fool," Buzzell recalled years later. "I didn't want to do it. Television was nothing then. I was at Metro, getting a big salary and anything I wanted. If I didn't like a story or a picture, I'd turn it back. And they accepted it. Why should I leave Metro to go with this?" Instead, Desi and Jess Oppenheimer turned to Marc Daniels, a young director who had done both theater and live television with multiple cameras in New York. Daniels had worked as assistant stage manager on the Broadway production of *Dead End*, and during World War II he had toured with Irving Berlin's all-soldier musical revue, *This Is the Army*. His wife, Emily, worked as his camera coordinator, calling the shots as shows unfolded.

Meantime, Karl Freund was designing a system of "flat" overhead lighting that would allow simultaneous photography of long, medium, and close-up shots (and keep the lights out of the way of the cameras), along with a system of silent rolling dollies that could move each of the three cameras wherever it was needed. Stage 2's rough old wooden floor was resurfaced with a composite material previously used by the May Company for its department stores so there would be no bumps or jolts in the camera movements. As the construction and technical work continued, word of mouth was beginning to build for the new venture.

In June, CBS screened the *I Love Lucy* pilot for the press in an empty storefront next to its network complex in Hollywood, tacking a sheet to the wall and placing the projector on an orange crate. Dan Jenkins of the *Hollywood Reporter* was enthused. "We saw the audition kine of CBS's *I Love Lucy* yesterday," he reported on June 28, "and are happy to predict the immediate ascendancy of Lucille Ball and Desi Arnaz to TV stardom come airing of the first filmed show in the fall. And by stardom, we mean in the top five of everybody's rating system in every area. Keep your eyes peeled for this one. It's a honey."

Just before the long-term lease for the General Services stages was signed, one last contractual hurdle nearly derailed the whole project. In Desi's negotiations with CBS, the network had apparently not told him of its commitment to give Jess Oppenheimer a 20 percent ownership stake in the show. When Desi learned of this provision in a conversation with Jess, he exploded, and in Jess's recollection told Lucy the show was off. Oppenheimer was unrelenting—despite tearful pleas from Lucy—and ultimately the Arnazes, who by now had everything to lose if the show did not go on, finally gave in. Oppenheimer then told Desi that he thought Bob Carroll and Madelyn Pugh should also have a piece of the action, but Desi flatly refused. So Jess gave his cowriters 5 percent out of his share, leaving himself with a 15 percent ownership stake.

• • •

All the while, Jess and Bob and Madelyn had been working hard to get a batch of scripts in the can. The audition episode had focused solely on the characters of Lucy and Ricky, but the creators wanted to round out the show with additional regular characters who could serve as foils for the Ricardos. That had been the case with *My Favorite Husband*, in which the character actors Gale Gordon and Bea Benaderet had played George Cooper's boss and his wife. For *I Love Lucy*, the writers came up with a novel conceit. Typically in comedy—certainly in

musical comedy—the secondary characters are younger than the leading lovers, but in this case, Oppenheimer and his colleagues were drawn
to the idea of an older couple as a contrast to the Ricardos. Lucy believed
that Gordon and Benadaret would be ideal for the parts, but neither was
available. The lovably snarling character actor James Gleason—one of
Lucy's costars in *Miss Grant Takes Richmond*—priced himself out of contention, asking for a salary of $3,500 a week when Lucy and Desi were
only going to make $4,000 together.

Like so many casting decisions that come to seem inevitable,
the choice of performers to play Fred and Ethel Mertz, the Ricardos'
neighbors, landlords, and friends, was anything but foreordained.
Lucy would later remember that she had received the first feeler from
the veteran character actor William Frawley, whom she'd known from
their shared days in Hollywood, to play Fred Mertz; for his part, Desi
recalled in his memoir that Frawley had telephoned him. Whatever
the case, Frawley needed the job. Sixty-four years old, Frawley had
been a successful vaudeville performer who had toured with the likes
of Jack Haley and Bert Lahr. He was among the first performers to
popularize the standards "Carolina in the Morning" and "My Mel-
ancholy Baby" and had played the press agent Owen O'Malley in the
original Broadway production of Ben Hecht and Charles MacArthur's
Twentieth Century. He had appeared in more than a hundred movies,
beginning in silent pictures in 1916. Frawley's face—if not his name—
was warmly familiar to a generation of moviegoers. He had played the
Duke to Mickey Rooney's Huck Finn, the music publisher who takes
a flier "Swinging on a Star" in Bing Crosby's *Going My Way*, and the
wise political boss who instructs the flustered judge in *Miracle on 34th
Street* to accept Edmund Gwenn as the real Santa Claus.

But Frawley had also earned an unfortunate reputation around
Hollywood as a curmudgeon and an unreliable drunk. John Stephens,
who would work with Frawley in later years on the sitcom *My Three
Sons*, attested to his prodigious consumption: breakfast with three or

four gin fizzes; by 11 a.m., a couple of Bloody Marys; a highball or two before lunch, with bourbon after; then pre-dinner martinis. "I've never in my life—and I've seen a lot of drinkers—known anyone who could drink as much as he could in one day," Stephens recalled. "And that's not to mention the different types of drinks."

Before offering Frawley the role of Fred Mertz, Desi, no slouch in the drinks department himself, took him to lunch at Nickodell, a popular Hollywood restaurant, and laid it on the line. "Okay, Bill, I'll tell you what I'll do with you," Desi recalled telling him. "The first time you are not able to do your job, I'll try to work around you for that day. The second time, I'll try to manage again. But if you do it three times, you are through, and I mean through, not only on our show, but you'll never work in this town again as long as you live. Is that fair enough?"

Frawley agreed and sealed the deal by ordering another drink: "Hey, waiter, what the hell is this, the Sahara Desert? We are thirsty. Okay, Cuban, we have a deal, and we'll show all them bastards how wrong they are."

It took longer to hire an actress to play Ethel Mertz. Marc Daniels remembered a performer he knew from his days in New York theater, an actress he had directed in summer stock productions. In late July he dragooned Jess and Desi to a show at the La Jolla Playhouse just north of San Diego to see this actress, Vivian Vance, in a revival of John van Druten's *The Voice of the Turtle*, a World War II sex comedy about two actresses competing for the affections of the same soldier on leave in Manhattan.

Vance had played this role to raves a few years earlier in the national tour, and by her own account she had no interest in television, which she called "a silly new third entity that attracted little attention." She would later recall that "it had been hard enough to come out of hiding and play *Voice of the Turtle*. Take on a full-time job in a medium that didn't amount to anything? The strain involved wasn't worth it. Besides, what could it lead to? No series anything like this *I Love*

Lucy had been successful so far." Vance, forty-two years old, had been Ethel Merman's understudy in the original 1934 Broadway production of Cole Porter's *Anything Goes*, followed by a series of brassy roles in other musicals with stars from Bob Hope to Danny Kaye. She had lost out on one plum role, as Mrs. Mullin, the merry-go-round owner in Rodgers and Hammerstein's *Carousel*, believing that the choreographer Agnes de Mille had blackballed her by unfairly blaming Vance for misbehavior by chorus girls in an earlier show, *Hooray for What*.

At the La Jolla Playhouse, Desi found himself completely charmed by Vance's performance in *Voice of the Turtle*. "She was such a wonderful actress, so honest," he would recall. "Every line, every reaction, every move she made was just perfect." Jess and Desi went backstage afterward and offered her the part of Ethel on the spot, only for Desi to panic on the way home that Lucy might not like her. Indeed, Lucy's first reaction was "Who the hell is she?" She would learn soon enough.

• • •

I n the midst of all this, on July 17, 1951, Lucy gave birth to a baby girl, two weeks late, delivered by cesarean section because she was breech. Desi had finished the addition to the ranch—two new bedrooms, plus a nursery kitchen paneled in white tile and fitted with sterilizing, cooking, and laundry equipment. Lucy had spent the final weeks of her pregnancy doing nothing more vigorous than knitting, while Desi, who usually drove like a demon, had wheeled his yellow convertible "as conservatively as an old lady," Lucy recalled. Years later, Lucy would remember the times just before and after the baby's birth as the best year of their marriage, with Desi at home and apparently faithful and "attentive to every need." "This was the way I'd always hoped our marriage would be," she wrote. Thrilled to be a mother at last, Lucy asked to see the newborn the moment her anesthesia wore off. "I want to see Susan!" she told the nurse, using the name she believed that she and Desi had agreed on if the baby was a girl, after

Lucy's good friend, the young actress Susan Peters, who had been paralyzed from the waist down in a duck-shooting accident. "You mean
Lucie?" the nurse replied. Without consulting her, Desi had already
written Lucie Desiree on the birth certificate, naming the little girl for
her mother and maternal grandmother. Lucy was surprised but didn't
make a fuss. The name was, after all, a compliment she could hardly
resist (and it didn't hurt that Desiree just happened to be the feminine
French version of Desiderio). Lucy was in pain from the cesarean in-
cision, and she struggled to hold the baby's first bottle and Lucie at the
same time, but she was thrilled. "This is our baby," she kept repeating.
For his part, Desi was smitten as only a father can be with a daughter.
He stayed up all night composing a tune to celebrate the new arrival,
and the lyricist Eddie Maxwell wrote the words that Desi would sing
on the next episode of *Tropical Trip*:

> *There's a brand-new baby at our house*
> *She's twice as sweet as honey from the comb.*
> *She's the image of my spouse,*
> *She's the tricky Mickey Mouse,*
> *Who has changed our happy house to a home.*

Desi was a warm, playful, and hands-on presence in a way that his
own parents may not have been capable of. "I tried to get home as early
as I could every evening from the studio just to be able to hold my little
girl in my lap in a rocking chair I had in the nursery," he would recall.
Lucy would keep the baby awake until Desi could get home. "I would
hold little Lucie on my chest, with her cheek next to mine, and rock
her back and forth. When I did that she would coo and laugh and play
with my ears, my nose, and my lips, pull my hair, and stick her finger
in my eye."

Lucie's own first memory of her father is of his leaning over her
crib, reaching toward something above her. Only years later, when

comparing notes with her mother, did she learn what he was reaching for: the Arnazes had hung a ticking plastic Kit-Cat Klock, with a swishing tail and shifting eyes keeping the time, over her bed, and Desi would stretch his arms to set it. What she remembers most, always, is her father as a "very touchy-feely, grab, jump in the pool with you, carry you on his back" kind of parent. From the beginning, Lucy had a pricklier relationship with parenthood. Delighted as she was to have a baby at last, Lucy had given birth just twenty days before her fortieth birthday, and she was long used to her own routines and rhythms. She insisted from the start that mothers should not let children run their lives, and during the workday, the baby was cared for by a newly hired nurse.

Just six weeks later, amid the sound of hammers and saws at General Service Studios, Lucy went back to work full-time. Karl Freund had refined his lighting system, with dimmable lights mounted on the bottom of camera dollies and above each lens, and directional microphones (to capture audience reaction) and loudspeakers hung from the ceiling of the soundstage. A control booth had been built at the rear of the bleachers, with a panoramic view of the action. Two weeks before the first scheduled filming, Desi got a hard lesson in the risks and burdens of entrepreneurial ownership: Desilu's start-up costs for the show were running higher than expected, and he went to Martin Leeds, the CBS business affairs executive, to report that the company had run out of money. Leeds advanced sixty thousand dollars against future expenses and loaned some of CBS's lighting equipment.

At this point, Desi's to-do list ranged down to the smallest details, including finding a head janitor for his new playhouse. The special new floors "had to be really clean and smooth," he would remember, because "it is unbelievable, the jump in the film when a camera rolls over a little matchstick." He found his man in Lou Jacoby, a jack-of-all-trades, who not only kept the floors clean but made sure the watercoolers were filled and there was coffee and donuts on hand for the crew. Because he could hardly play Ricky and conduct his band at the same time, Desi also needed to hire a music director—not to mention a whole raft of technicians.

The filming of the first episode was set for Saturday, September 8. After the camera rehearsal on Friday evening, Desi cooked up a batch of arroz con pollo in his bungalow on the lot and Lucy tended bar while they and the key production personnel huddled in conference to critique the show. Early Saturday evening, as the final sets were being finished, Al Simon's secretary was supervising the placing of multicolored cushions on the metal bleachers. The floor crew and CBS executives were given red carnation boutonnieres for good luck, and a line of spectators was queuing up on Romaine Street outside the new entrance. Suddenly a final crisis loomed. A city health inspector urgently buttonholed Desi to say the show could not go on. The inspector had just realized that while there was a public men's room accessible to the audience as required by city code, there was no comparable convenience for female spectators.

Lucy assured the nervous inspector that she would be happy to share the bathroom attached to her dressing room. "That's no problem," she gamely said. "Tell the ladies to be my guests." Crisis averted, the filming could proceed.

In a ritual that would last as long as the show itself, Desi's and Lucy's mothers took their seats in a place of honor in the stands. (Desilu veterans would say that DeDe Ball's distinctive laugh could be heard on television for decades, because other situation comedies would eventually cannibalize I Love Lucy's live recorded laughter.) To placate an audience that had been waiting longer than expected for the show to start, Jess Oppenheimer suggested that Desi go out and warm up the crowd.

Onstage by himself, Desi was his most charming, drawing on his years of experience as the front man and spokesman for his various big bands. He assured the audience that the cameras would never interrupt their line of vision, then motioned all three floor cameras to close in around him to completely hide him from view. "You see what I mean?" he deadpanned. "At no time will the camera interrupt your line of vision." He then launched into a long shaggy-dog story in which a beautiful teenage girl sees a turtle perched on a rock. The turtle explains that he used to be an army sergeant till someone put a curse on him, but he assures the girl, "If you take me home and let me sleep in your bed under your pillow, by tomorrow morning I'll be an army sergeant again." The girl does so, and the next morning, her mother comes into the room to wake her up for school and finds a handsome, six-foot-two-inch soldier in bed with her. "And do you know," Desi concluded, "to this very day that little girl's mother doesn't believe the story about the turtle?" He then introduced Vivian Vance and Bill Frawley, after which the conductor, Wilbur Hatch, launched into the new *I Love Lucy* theme song. Desi cried out, "Here's my favorite wife, the mother of my child, the vice president of Desilu Productions—*I* am the president— my favorite redhead, the girl who plays Lucy, Lucille Ball!" Lucy emerged in a pale blue, fur-trimmed negligee robe, her brilliant blue eyes shining in the lights, running from one end of the stage to the other taking bows as the audience exploded.

And with that, the cast launched into the first episode, "Lucy Thinks Ricky Is Trying to Murder Her," a cascading series of comic misunderstandings. The show starts with Lucy engrossed in reading a murder mystery, *The Mockingbird Murder Mystery*, which terrifies her, but she can't stop reading. Meantime, Ethel is experimenting with amateur fortune-telling and predicts Lucy's death. Then Lucy overhears a conversation between Ricky and his agent, Jerry, and mistakes their recitation of the female names of dogs in a planned nightclub act for a string of women Desi may be courting. When Jerry asks Ricky what he's going to do about a singer under contract, Lucy only hears Ricky say, "I've decided to get rid of her," and thinks he's going to bump her off. She then arms herself with a skillet tied across her stomach as a bulletproof vest (which couldn't have been very comfortable because Ball was still sore from her C-section) and heads to the Tropicana Club to confront Ricky with a gun. She sees the dog act, realizes her mistake, and all ends well.

The episode is full of the touches that would soon become familiar to viewers: Lucy's saucer-eyed expressions of surprise, Desi's bug-eyed, exaggerated irritation. At one point, frustrated that Lucy's obsession with the mystery novel is keeping him awake, he acts out a step-by-step demonstration of just how a husband might kill his wife, trying a gun and a knife before finally settling on strangulation. Still, there were a few glitches. At one point, a camera cuts away too far, revealing a false half wall between the Ricardos' living room and bedroom, letting the viewer see both at once. And because the production team was uncertain whether the studio audience would tolerate breaks for costume changes without getting bored, the performers wore multiple bulky layers of clothing that they could quickly shed as needed.

There was a small party onstage after filming ended. Desi felt good. "How smoothly everything went that night, mechanically and performance-wise, was hard to believe," he would recall many years later. "It all seemed effortless, which only goes to prove that it takes a lot of effort to make something look effortless."

In perhaps the strangest twist of the whole creation of *I Love Lucy*, it turned out that all the technical innovation and risk-taking that had led to that Saturday night's initial filming need never have happened at all. Only four days before, on September 4, President Harry Truman had addressed the United Nations conference in San Francisco in a speech that was carried simultaneously live in New York. AT&T had at last made transcontinental transmission of live broadcast signals possible for the first time, bridging its nearly completed coast-to-coast coaxial cable with microwave relays. By the end of September, *The Colgate Comedy Hour*, hosted by the comedian Eddie Cantor and others, was originating from Los Angeles, "removing the very problem that had caused us to abandon our original plan to telecast the series live from Hollywood," Oppenheimer would recall. "That change in plans had been the catalyst for all the technical innovations that would contribute so much to the success of *I Love Lucy*, the growth of the Desilu empire, and the eventual shift of the center of television production from New York to Hollywood."

. . .

There remained a big task: to assemble the vivid chunks of film into a cohesive narrative—a miniature motion picture. For that, Jess and Desi were betting on Dann Cahn, a twenty-eight-year-old film editor, for their new experiment. Cahn's father and uncle were both veteran film editors, and Dann himself had edited army training films in World War II and done some work at Republic Studios, a maker of low-budget Westerns. He was having trouble finding a job but hit it off with Jess right away. "I was adaptable, and I wasn't threatening to them like some of the forty- or fifty-year-old editors of the time, with very definite positions," he would recall. "They already had the whole crew set, except for the film editor. And this was to be the definitive first use of multiple cameras in a situation comedy, a story that would be edited."

Cahn found himself with perhaps two hours' worth of film that he would have to cut to the length of a half-hour episode, leaving time for commercials. The three cameras had all rolled in synchronization with the sound, but each film magazine held only ten minutes. Moreover, the production team had actually used four cameras for the first filming, worried about getting adequate coverage. Assembling all these bits on a traditional Moviola—the editor's tool of the trade, a motorized, rear-lighted viewer through which film could be run reel by reel—would prove incredibly time-consuming. "With three usable angles of every shot it just took us too long to view each of them, one after another," Oppenheimer explained. But Al Simon knew a guy named George Fox, who had commissioned the Moviola company to build a three-headed version of the machine in which three reels of film could be locked and projected simultaneously. A fourth head held the soundtrack. Fox had been hired by Desilu as "film operations manager" because he had devised a way of syncing sound and picture electronically that turned out not to work. So Oppenheimer let him go and Fox took the editing machine with him, keeping it in his own workspace across the street from General Service. Dann Cahn still had a key and snuck in to use what quickly became known as the "three-headed monster." Fox found out and threatened to sue until Jess brokered a settlement that led to Desilu itself buying the machine and, eventually, fabricating and selling copies of the contraption, which became the industry standard. After that, the work went quickly.

By Friday, September 14, as the cast was deep in preparation for filming the next episode, Cahn had assembled a rough cut. "The whole mob headed for a projection room," he recalled. "The director, Jess, Al Simon, the Biow Agency, and the whole high brass from CBS . . . The first time anyone saw the picture was that afternoon in the projection room, and you can be sure I was pretty tense. . . . Desi was very quiet. Picture's over and the silence was incredible. You could have heard a pin drop on the floor—or in our case, a paper clip. Nobody said a word. The silence seemed an eternity to me. Lucy was sitting directly behind me, and she put her hands on my shoulders and said, 'Danny, it's a good cutting job.' That broke the tension and everyone started talking—'Oh, yeah, it's gonna be a hit, it's gonna be wonderful, it's gonna be fine.'"

CBS began airing promotional spots for the new show, with Lucy and Desi peering out from a cutout that mimicked CBS's eye-shaped logo.

"Hey!" Lucy said. "We're on TV now. Watch for *I Love Lucy*."

Desi chimed in, "With Lucille Ball."

"And Desi Arnaz," Lucy added. "He's my husband."

"Typecasting, I calls it," Desi rejoined.

Meantime, the second episode was being filmed. As soon as it was assembled, Desi took the first two episodes to a sneak preview at a movie theater in nearby Riverside, California, where the audience reaction was so loud it drowned out the laughter on the soundtrack. Desi was thrilled. Because of what the team considered technical imperfections in the first episode—chiefly the flawed sound-and-picture synchronization—the decision was made to air the second filmed episode first, and the premiere had long been set for Monday, October 15, at 9 p.m.—just after Arthur Godfrey's top-rated program on CBS. Finished film prints of the debut show now had to be shipped to local CBS stations across the country, where they could be projected via a special mirror into a television camera for simultaneous broadcast over the airwaves in each region.

By the time that Monday rolled around, the show's stars and staff were at General Service conducting a read-through for yet another episode when they suddenly realized airtime was approaching and the Arnazes would not have time to get home to Chatsworth to see the show. Emily and Marc Daniels, who lived in nearby Laurel Canyon, invited the whole crew to come watch at their house and have dinner.

The opening credits are a charming cartoon—produced by the animators William Hanna and Joseph Barbara, creators of Tom and Jerry, in which stick figures of Lucy and Desi scamper atop a giant cigarette pack. (The now-familiar satiny heart logo would appear only years later, in reruns.) The announcer Johnny Jacobs intones, "Philip Morris, America's finest cigarette, presents the Lucille Ball–Desi Arnaz show," as blinds on the cigarette pack open to reveal, one word at a time in sync with the announcer's voice, "I . . . Love . . . Lucy." The episode's title was "The Girls Want to Go to a Nightclub," and it involves a disagreement between Fred and Ethel over how to celebrate their wedding anniversary. Fred wants to go to the fights, while Ethel wants to dance at the Copacabana. Lucy and Ethel ultimately tell their husbands they will go to the nightclub without them—and intend to arrange dates for themselves to boot. Desi calls a singer friend to find dates for him and Fred so they can go to the Copa to check up on their wives. But when Lucy calls the *same* mutual friend and learns of the plan, she and Ethel decide to disguise themselves as country bumpkins and show up at the Ricardos' apartment as the boys' blind dates. Of course, it all gets sorted out in the end, and everyone heads off to watch boxing.

In Laurel Canyon, Cahn recalled, the whole group "crowded around this little television set" at the Danielses' house, and the only person who laughed out loud was Vivian Vance's husband, the actor Philip Ober, which just irritated everyone else. Then halfway through the program, the sound went out completely. "I thought Desi's eyes would pop out of his head," Cahn remembered. "Then it came back on, but now we had two soundtracks. It sounded like a football field where you hear it from both speakers and one is behind the other, so it had a reverb and an echo to it. Desi looked at me, and I said, 'What do I know?'"

It turned out to be a problem only at the local CBS station. As was standard practice, technicians had set up a second, fail-safe projector in the control room, which was supposed to run silently in sync with the main one, whose sound and image were being beamed over the air by the television signal, in case that failed. But both had somehow switched on at once. As the show ended, Desi, Lucy, Jess, and the team were relieved but still didn't know just what they had created. That would have to await the verdict of viewers and critics out there in the dark.

nine

IT'S A HIT!

On Tuesday morning, October 16, there was bad news from one very important viewer: O. Parker McComas, the president of Philip Morris. McComas, a former banker, socially polished Princeton graduate, and Silver Star winner in World War I, called the Biow Agency to ask what it would cost to cancel his company's contract for the show. He pronounced it "unfunny, silly, and totally boring," though he liked the commercials. Terry Clyne, Biow's vice president of television, and Eddie Feldman, of the agency's West Coast office, begged him to hold off. It was wise advice, and McComas reluctantly agreed. By Wednesday, *Variety* had pronounced *I Love Lucy* "one of the slickest TV entertainment shows to date" and, moreover, predicted that it would establish "films' secure place in the video sweepstakes."

"For here is a film that has all the Grade A qualities of major studio production, achieving a depth and visual values that pertain to theatre presentation, yet encompassing the desired intimacy for TV," the reviewer continued. "It's a slick blending of Hollywood and TV show-manship." Dan Jenkins of the *Hollywood Reporter* raved: "Every once in a rare great while a new TV show comes along that fulfills, in its own particular niche, every promise of the often-harassed new medium. Such a show, it is a genuine pleasure to report, is *I Love Lucy*." Jenkins said the "outstanding pertinent fact" about the new show was its estab-lishment of Lucille Ball as "America's No. 1 comedienne" but added: "Half a step behind her comes her husband, Desi Arnaz, the perfect foil for her screwball antics and possessing comic abilities of his own more than sufficient to make this a genuine comedy team rather than the one-woman tour de force it almost becomes."

And when the Nielsen ratings—the surveys that measured audi-ence size—came out at the end of the week, *Lucy* placed among the top ten programs on the air. For their part in that achievement, Lucy and Desi instantly took their place alongside the leading pioneer talents of television, including Milton Berle, Arthur Godfrey, Jack Benny, Red Skelton, Dean Martin, and Jerry Lewis.

In fact, while Lucy's evident brilliance was the outstanding visible element of the new show, Desi's work—not only as a performer but as the behind-the-scenes force who had led the drive to get the show off the ground—was just as important. Desi (with Jess Oppenheimer, who had created the Lucy character in Ball's own image) had assem-bled the creative team, including Madelyn and Bob, and had hired the perfect cast in Bill Frawley and Viv Vance. He had helped to recruit Al Simon, Karl Freund, Dann Cahn, and the rest to surmount formida-ble technical, logistical, and financial obstacles. From the beginning, Desi's management style involved delegation to capable and carefully chosen subordinates, but he had done as much as anyone to make the show an immediate hit.

Desi's work in front of the camera was proving just as resource-ful, and Oppenheimer was not the only one forced to reassess his first impressions. Desi became the first Latino to costar in a national

English-language prime-time network show (and to this day, one of the few). "When we started *I Love Lucy*, I thought of Desi as a big question mark," Jess would recall. "Neither he nor anyone else knew whether he could really do this kind of thing at all. But Desi was a quick study and considerably brighter than many people gave him credit for. He was conscientious and worked extremely hard to prove his doubters wrong. In the end, to everyone's delight, Desi proved himself to be a skillful farceur and fine actor, providing Lucy with a charming foil and giving the show an added dimension." Madelyn Pugh was just as emphatic on the point. "We needn't have worried about whether Desi was funny or not," she recalled. "He learned comedy very quickly."

A perfect example was the famous episode filmed at the end of that first season (and aired at the beginning of the second): "Job Switching," in which Lucy and Ethel and Ricky and Fred bet that neither the boys nor the girls can do each other's jobs—in the home or in the workplace. The women take an assignment in a candy factory, and the side-splitting sequence in which they cannot keep up with chocolates speeding down an assembly line would prove to be one of the best-loved moments in the entire series. Less remembered, but almost as funny, is the corresponding sequence in which Ricky and Fred attempt to cook dinner. Belying Desi's actual skill as an excellent cook, Ricky sets out to make arroz con pollo for four, starting with a pound of raw rice per person. When the bubbling pot overflows the stove like a miniature volcano, Desi scrambles frantically in his frilly apron to clean it up. "They had never done the scene with real rice until the actual filming, and nobody realized how slick rice gets when you step on it," Madelyn Pugh remembered. "Desi accidentally slipped and fell flat but acted like it was part of the scene. He then managed to slip 'accidentally' to get two more laughs before the scene was over."

Gone was the nervous, self-conscious breaking of character that had marked Desi's early television and radio appearances. He swiftly developed into a straight man's straight man, with a photographic memory for dialogue. In another early episode, "Be a Pal," Lucy is afraid their marriage has gone stale because Ricky is ignoring her. To get his attention at breakfast, she catapults a piece of toast from the toaster his way, and he catches it one-handed without looking up from his newspaper or missing a beat, then kisses her proffered grapefruit-half goodbye. When Lucy tries to join Ricky and Fred's poker game and is so ignorant that she calls the chips "little round things," Arnaz stays sober as a judge but is also really steamed. And when she decorates their apartment with palm trees, a live burro, and chickens in an effort to remind him of the Cuba she thinks he misses, he is convincingly annoyed, confused, and not amused. "Lucy, darling," he says tenderly at the episode's end, "if I'd wanted things Cuban, I'd've stayed in Havana. That's the reason I married you—because you're so different from any-one I'd known in Cuba!"

· · ·

From the very beginning, Lucy and Desi established the Ricardos as a genuine married couple—two people who really fought and then really made up, with all the connection that implied. They kissed, and kissed like they meant it—on the lips. This amounted to a rev-olutionary posture in the safe and generally sexless terrain of 1950s sitcoms. Ricky "tolerated his wife's foibles good-naturedly, but he could only be pushed so far," Lucy recalled in her memoir. "The audience had to believe that I lived in fear and trembling of my husband's wrath, and with Desi, they could. There was also a chemistry, a strong mutual attraction between us, which always came through." By the end of the first season, Hearst's *American Magazine* could analyze their appeal. "The captivating thing about Lucy and Ricky is, we think, the fact that they hold a mirror up to every married couple in America. Not a regu-lation mirror that reflects truth, nor a magic mirror that portrays fan-tasy. But a Coney Island mirror that distorts, exaggerates and makes vastly amusing every little incident, foible, and idiosyncrasy of married life." *Look* magazine's Laura Bergquist would write with particular insight about Ricky's character: "It's dazzling to find one TV show in which a husband isn't portrayed as a perfect boob or a grown-up child."

Despite his accent and Cuban identity, Desi had indeed established Ricky as a quintessentially masculine American man, a steady husband, a solid breadwinner, the grounded force that anchors Lucy's flights of fancy. This stood in sharp contrast to another real-life bandleader, Ozzie Nelson, who made the transition to television about the same time. Working with his wife, Harriet, and their two sons, David and Ricky, Nelson was nominally a paternal authority but actually a bumbling figure whose family ran laps around him. The other two most famous TV dads of the era—Hugh Beaumont as Ward Cleaver on *Leave It to Beaver* and Robert Young on *Father Knows Best*—were also comparative milquetoasts with humdrum office jobs, leading some social critics to complain that television had softened and feminized the American man. There was never the slightest such suggestion with Desi, even if he did, in an apparent concession to vanity, wear lifts on the heels of his shoes, manicure his nails, and, as time went on, rinse his graying hair black for each show.

Ricky Ricardo's work in the Tropicana nightclub is portrayed not as elitist or exotic but simply as a natural reflection of his personality and talents. Because the network's initial contract had required that Desi perform musical numbers only when they were central to the plot, Jess Oppenheimer recalled that in the beginning, the writers intentionally took care to make sure there were plenty of such storylines. After the show was a hit, no one cared, and Ricky sang and drummed away whenever it seemed appropriate, and the contractual restriction was lifted. Indeed, there was sometimes so much music in a given episode that it amounted to a kind of mini musical comedy, and Desi's orchestra, filled with his usual complement of skilled players, performed live in front of the studio audience, just like the actors.

"The revelation of *I Love Lucy* was Desi," wrote Lucy's biographer

Kathleen Brady. "When they watched the shows, Jess, Bob, Madelyn and Marc realized he really was as good a comic actor as Lucy had insisted." Brady added that Desi soon relaxed into the role of Lucy's foil and "gave each show a dash of sex and was the only one of her leading men to mute her strength. In her films, she had never been really feminine or vulnerable, but Desi's presence brought out those qualities in her. He also got laughs on his own account, especially for his mispronunciations, which provided any number of comic possibilities."

From the start, in fact, Lucy's writers turned the very thing that had so limited Desi's career in the movies—his thick Cuban accent—into a unique and unmistakable asset. But they quickly learned that it had to be treated with subtlety and sensitivity so that the audience was laughing with Desi and his struggles with English, not at him. "The audience resented it if we had anyone make fun of his English besides Lucy," Madelyn recalled. "Apparently other people making fun of his English was insulting, but she could do it because it was done in a loving manner." Desi's real accent was, in fact, just about as thick as Ricky's, and Madelyn once compiled a catalog of Arnaz's pronunciation patterns. He dropped his "ex" prefixes, hence "'splain" for explain, "'zaggerate" for exaggerate, and "'spensive" for expensive. He had trouble with the long *O* vowel—hence "hat" for hot, "hohney" for honey, "dunt" for don't, "wunt" for won't. He slurred his consonants—"parmen" for apartment, "mushin picturs" for motion pictures, "awar" for award—and transposed his *J*s and *Y*s ("yob" for job) and *T*s and *D*s—"ret" for red and "het" for head, so "favorite ret-het." The writers—to Desi they were "Rubert" and "Mallen"—also learned never to write the accent into the script. Arnaz's natural pronunciation for "Take it easy" was "Take a tizzy," but if they wrote "Take a tizzy" into the script, Arnaz would clearly say "Take it easy."

Desi was the first to admit he didn't always understand American idioms or jokes—he didn't know that giving someone a gold watch meant putting them out to pasture, for example—but he never questioned the writers' judgment on this point. If they thought something was funny, he did too. They would play off his accent in subtle ways. In an episode in the second season, "Redecorating," Lucy and Ethel scheme to win a free home makeover and have to wait around so as not to miss the all-important telephone call they must answer in order to win. But Ricky has tickets to the new Rodgers and Hammerstein show and decides to arrange a phony call to tell the girls they've won. He asks Fred to make the call because he knows Lucy will instantly recognize his accent if he tries to do so. Frawley deadpans: "You're gonna use an accent?" The line is a reflection of the fact that Ricky is an accepted part of the club—a joke, yes, but one that reflects his friends' loving appreciation of him.

Arnaz also put his Spanish to regular subversive use in Ricky's explosions of irritation at some mayhem wrought by Lucy. It is a sign of Desi's daring—and also presumably of the CBS censors' condescending certainty that audiences wouldn't understand him—that Ricky is allowed to unleash invective in Spanish that no character could ever utter in English on American television in the 1950s. At one point, Ricky mutters, "*Dios mío, pero que cosas tiene la mujer esta?*" (loosely the equivalent of "My God, can you believe this dame?"), while at another he explodes: "*Mira que jode la mujer esta!*" ("Look how this woman screws with me!").

At least one critic, John Crosby of the *New York Herald Tribune*, complained that *I Love Lucy* had reduced "the role of husband to roughly that of the male spider, and I wouldn't be at all surprised if at the end of the season, Miss Ball ate him." Crosby judged that Arnaz's principal duties "are the expression of pained exasperation at some of his wife's crazy antics and crazier utterances." But that seems more a reflection of Crosby's own misogyny than of Ricky's actual function in the show—or Desi's role in its production. In fact, Ricky's posture was never so passive, and Desi's role in the weekly production routine was central from the start. Jess Oppenheimer may have been producer and head writer (what today would be called the showrunner), but after all it was Desi (and Lucy) who owned the show, and Desi flexed that muscle whenever he needed to. In doing so, he effectively became not only the first Latino television star, but the first Latino television executive.

• • •

P roduction quickly settled into a disciplined routine. In preparing for the show to be filmed live on Friday night, the Day One drill began with a table read of that week's script at 10:00 Tuesday morning. (In the fall of 1953, filming would shift to Thursdays, so the whole routine began a day earlier, on Mondays.) Those initial readings always marked the first time that Lucy and Desi would see the script, and Desi's first reactions were inevitably sharper than his wife's. "Desi was always much better than Lucy at these first read-throughs," Oppenheimer remembered. "He would understand the material as soon as he saw it and give a good reading the first time through. His performance would be exactly the same, never any better or worse, four days later." By contrast, Lucy needed rehearsals and time to play the script over in her mind to refine the details of her performance, which would rise to the heights by week's end. Her first reactions were often negative and undiplomatic. "She would say, 'This doesn't work,' and our hearts would sink," Madelyn Pugh recalled. "Desi would start, 'Oh, this is pure gold, but a few little things.' . . . He just had that instinct for what worked and what didn't." Bob Carroll agreed, noting that Desi "had a great sense of comedy which his wife did not have. Lucy did not know what was funny in concept. When she did it, she was the greatest in the world. But she didn't know." Desi was also a good script doctor. "He said, 'There's something here in the end that's not quite working out,'" Carroll said. "He wouldn't know why it didn't work, and he was always right. We'd say, 'Oh, let's go fix it. The old Cuban knows what he's doing.'"

Bill Asher, who replaced Marc Daniels as the show's director at the end of the first season, agreed. "At the readings, Desi would really control the table," Asher said. "He would make most of the suggestions, and most of them were right." The first day's work would usually last until 6 p.m. or so, after which Bob and Madelyn would go to their office to grapple with a draft of the next week's episode.

Day Two's task was to get the week's episode up on its feet, blocking on the set from roughly 10 a.m. to 6 p.m., with the expectation that the actors would have memorized forty to forty-five pages of dialogue from the day before and would be off script. Bill Frawley was notorious for just tearing out and learning his own pages, with the result that he often did not initially understand the punchlines he was called on to deliver. In one famous example, he did not grasp why it was supposed to be funny when he entered the Ricardos' apartment and said, "Hello, Ethel." The setup, established on the prior pages, was that Ethel was clad in the hindquarters of a horse costume, her face away from Fred, who nevertheless instantly recognizes her and says, "Hello, Ethel." (Frawley and Vance's on-screen feuding was more than echoed in their real-life unhappy relationship: Vance resented having to play wife to the much older Frawley, and Frawley, the old vaudeville trouper, turned up his nose at Vance's singing, among other sources of tension.) At 4:30 p.m., there would be a full run-through without cameras but with Karl Freund watching and making notes for lighting and camera cues and Jess Oppenheimer giving line readings and critiques.

On Day Three, Freund would start lighting the set and working out camera action, while the cast rehearsed again until 6. At 7, there would be a full-dress rehearsal, followed by a long notes session that could run as late as 1 a.m., with discussions of plot, props, lines, logic, and so on. "Sometimes there were heated arguments," Madelyn Pugh recalled, "since everyone cared a lot about the show. Vivian was rather vocal and Frawley would doze off."

Day Four proceeded on two tracks. First was the writers' private plotting day, in which Madelyn and Bob would have breakfast together at the old Schwab's Pharmacy on Sunset Boulevard, working on some one-line ideas for the show two weeks hence. They jotted their ideas in spiral notebooks and would meet later with Jess to flesh out a full story idea and structure. "We usually tried to have a small physical comedy routine for Lucy in the first act and a larger one for the ending of the show," Madelyn recalled. Jess liked to have the finished script for the following week over the weekend, and sometimes the writers would drop off their second draft (he had already marked up the first) at his house in Brentwood as late as 3 a.m. on Saturday so he could do a re-write. Jess thought it was important to keep a tight hold on the feel of the show with one voice but was forced to acknowledge that his writers never really liked his changes. Once, after he gave them a detailed memo explaining the reasons for his edits line by line, their verdict was blunt: "We still think you screwed the whole thing up."

Meantime, the second track of Day Four began at 9 a.m. with camera blocking using stand-ins. Lucy would arrive around 1 p.m. for hair-dressing, with a final dress rehearsal at four o'clock followed by camera notes from Freund and dinner at six. Shooting began at 8 p.m., always in order, with as few retakes as possible, and only after the audience had left. Once the three-headed monster was up and running, Cahn could do a rough cut in as little as a day.

The weekly routine was an unending grind for the writers especially. Forty episodes of *I Love Lucy* were filmed that first season, with thirty-five of them aired—the rest were saved for the start of season two. Madelyn would recall that they were always hoping President Truman would speak on a Monday night to preempt the show and let them get a week ahead on their work. But the effort paid off. By the end of 1951, the show ranked in seventh place, according to the ratings, and in January 1952 only *Arthur Godfrey's Talent Scouts* was drawing a bigger audience. By the spring of 1952, the show's weekly audience was approaching thirty-one million viewers—more than double the total number of people who saw an average first-run Hollywood movie.

· · ·

For Desi, the show was also an exercise in entrepreneurialism. He had long managed his traveling band, of course, but the scale of this new weekly enterprise was altogether different. "Playing Ricky was the least of my problems," he remembered. "After a while, I could have phoned Ricky in." In the start-up business that was Desilu—without its own accounting or legal departments at first—Desi wore many hats. He was forced to deploy all that he had learned from Xavier Cugat, George Abbott, and Bob Hope about both showmanship and the nitty-gritty of the business of entertainment. An early lesson involved the difference between operating and capital budgeting—the difference between recurring weekly costs (like salaries) and onetime expenses (like sets and equipment). At first Desi charged nonrecurring expenses as they popped up, which quickly broke the agreed-on weekly budget of some $24,500. He simply paid each bill as it came along, with the result that by his accounting, the first episode had cost $95,000. By the fourth episode, the show was in the neighborhood of a quarter million dollars over budget, and since Desilu's contract called for CBS to pay any overage, network executives were growing understandably nervous. Desi soon realized his mistake and made a point of keeping expense categories separate, and eventually the per-episode cost averaged between $12,000 and $18,000, and the first thirty-nine episodes as a whole went only about $9,500 over budget.

The Desilu method of shooting the show with three cameras live on film was also drawing wide attention in the industry. By February, *Newsweek* reported that Bing Crosby, Rosalind Russell, Danny Thomas, and Frank Sinatra had all toured the Desilu soundstages at General Service with an eye to developing programming produced in a similar way. And that spring, Desi acquired Desilu's second show—*Our*

Miss Brooks, starring Lucy's old *Stage Door* costar Eve Arden. The series about a beloved high school teacher had debuted on CBS radio, and the network had planned to transfer it to the brand-new CBS Television City complex in the Fairfax District.

Arden wanted to produce her show the way *I Love Lucy* was done and asked Desi to help. He quickly realized that Desilu's cameras and equipment were being used only two days a week and thus had excess capacity. In late January, *I Love Lucy* shot one of its episodes a day early so its usual crew could film the *Our Miss Brooks* pilot. When Desilu negotiated its second-season contract with CBS, the network agreed to buy a 25 percent stake in Desilu Productions for $1 million, and Desilu acquired equipment—including the lights CBS had advanced it for the first shows. Desi then created a separate production entity—Zanra, "Arnaz" spelled backward—and sold the new shell company the equipment Desilu had been using, including the three-headed monster and Freund's lights. Zanra then turned around and rented the equipment back to Desilu, which passed the cost along to *Our Miss Brooks*, which was owned by CBS. It was a profitable bit of vertical integration, and CBS business executives initially objected. But the company's chairman, William Paley, was forced to acknowledge that Desi had simply made a savvy deal, because his company alone controlled the requisite suite of equipment for efficiently filming shows live.

Desilu also began producing commercials for Philip Morris and General Foods, which allowed Desi to address a personal pet peeve: the way the screen went to black when a commercial came on, with an awkward pause of dead air. Instead, he worked with Dann Cahn to bridge the gap with music for a seamless transition, with *I Love Lucy*'s own commercials the first test case. Other shows and sponsors soon asked for help. "We were the first company that ever required that commercials be integrated," recalled the Desilu executive Ed Holly. "He made it an entity. You didn't see a break or hear a break between show and commercial. No one had the guts to try it and no one else really had the clout to do it. And Desi, operating as he did, he never backed away from something that he knew was right, and if it just happened that we could make a buck in doing it right, that made it all the better."

Desi was also insistent that *I Love Lucy*'s laughter should always be recorded live, not added from a canned track after filming. In fact, Desilu's live filming technique was so effective that some Hollywood skeptics assumed that the laughter could not all be real. After the first two episodes had been shot, Oppenheimer took pains to explain to the trade press that the show was, in fact, all recorded on a single master track and that the only exceptions occurred during the rare retakes, after the studio audience had left, to tie up loose ends or missed shots. "If a retake with dialogue occurs at a spot where a laugh is going on," Jess said, "we must leave the master track, and this results in a sudden cutting off of the audience laughter. We must bridge this in the dubbing to bring it under the retake dialogue and make it sound natural. Except for a few instances like this, at the most five or six times during a show, and allowing for a few special problems now and then, at least 90 percent of the laughs you hear on the air are exactly as they occurred when the show was filmed."

The reality was slightly more complicated. Cahn and the postproduction staff told Desi that some laughs would have to be added from time to time to create the correct rhythm. But Desi insisted that all the laughs should come from actual *I Love Lucy* audiences, so James G. Stewart of Glen Glenn Sound went through recordings of past shows "cataloguing and arranging them—a twitter here, a giggle there, and the occasional guffaw. Each got a number, starting with L-1." In this way, an audio track containing laughs of Lolita Arnaz, DeDe Ball, and Bob Carroll's father were preserved in sitcoms far into the future.

Even so, despite Desi's many skills—and Desilu's swift successes—he remained a distinct second banana in the public eye. He, more than anyone, understood Lucy's unique talent. But he also had growing ambitions of his own.

ten

Baby Mogul

For all of *I Love Lucy*'s success, tensions were building behind the scenes. Lucy had long been attuned to Desi's exquisite sensitivity about his standing in Hollywood relative to hers and had gone out of her way to give him public credit and praise whenever she could. With that in mind, in rehearsal one day Lucy asked Al Simon to suggest to Desi that he should become executive producer. Not long afterward, Desi went to see Jess Oppenheimer in his office. "Jess," he said, "you and I know that after this show goes off the air, I'm not going to get a lot of other acting jobs. What I really want to do is produce, but I need to build a reputation as a producer. How would you feel about letting me take executive producer credit on the show?"

Oppenheimer's contract with CBS specified that he had creative control and that any disputes with Desi were to be put to a three-way vote, with Lucy holding the effective veto. He worried that Desi's taking the executive producer title might sow doubts about his own authority, as he was also working to build up his reputation in Hollywood. He suggested alternatives—"executive in charge of production" or "co-producer"—but Desi wouldn't bite. They agreed to discuss the matter again after thinking it over. On March 2, 1952, Desi turned thirty-five, and in the middle of his birthday party he again approached Jess about taking the title. Desi's timing was opportune. By this point, Oppenheimer would recall years later, he was so exhausted by his multiple duties as producer and head writer that he had been considering quitting the show altogether. So he was willing to be relieved of some of the business-related decisions that came with his job, and when Desi assured him that his executive producer title would come after Oppenheimer's in the roll of on-screen credits and would not affect his producing powers, they agreed that the new arrangement would start in April.

With the episode that aired on Monday, April 7, *I Love Lucy* became the first program in the history of television to reach ten million homes, or 63.2 percent of all the television sets in America. With an average of 2.9 viewers on each set, that meant that more than thirty million people, including seven million children—nearly one-fifth of the country's population—were watching the show. Later that month, the A.C. Nielsen rating service officially pronounced *I Love Lucy* the number one show on television. At a party to celebrate that milestone, Desi gave Jess a small trophy of a baseball player in mid-swing with the inscription JESS OPPENHEIMER THE MAN BEHIND THE BALL. The production team seemed united in triumph.

But a few days later Jess was shocked to get a call from Eddie Feldman at the Biow Agency, urgently telling him to get hold of a copy of the *Hollywood Reporter*. Dan Jenkins, one of the Arnazes' favorite reporters, had the scoop on Desi's new title. He apportioned credit for the show's success to many hands—including Oppenheimer's—but "above all to Desi Arnaz, the crazy Cuban whom Oppenheimer insists has been the real producer all along and who in two weeks reluctantly starts taking screen credit as producer." Jess was stunned and stormed angrily into Desi's office, demanding to know how Desi could have put such words in his mouth.

"It's like I told you, amigo," Desi replied calmly, "I need to build a rep as a producer." Oppenheimer instantly realized that he couldn't correct the record without hurting the show—*and* the Arnazes' marriage—so he and Desi worked out an uneasy détente. "He started to get into the various areas of production and postproduction," Dann Cahn said of Desi, "and he was a quick study and he did grab it all, and there was a certain creative conflict between him and Jess as to who was running the show." In effect, Desi now vied with Jess for the role of showrunner, once again becoming the first Latino to lay claim to such an assignment—a job he would eventually take on undisputed before the end of the show's run. Bill Asher, the director, added: "It kind of became a wedge between them. They never really got along after that."

Jess was still smarting nearly twenty-five years later, when Desi published his memoir and failed to acknowledge that *I Love Lucy* had ever had any producer other than himself. Desi had become so used to being underestimated and taken for granted that when it was finally his turn to control the narrative, he sometimes took too much credit. That's a shame, but it shouldn't detract from the indispensable contributions he had made from the start. After all, he and Lucy owned the show, and Lucy never left any doubt that it was Desi who controlled the purse strings—a reality also always reflected by Bob Carroll and Madelyn Pugh.

"Bob and I have always attributed a great deal of the success of *I Love Lucy* to the fact that Lucy would do absolutely anything we could dream up and Desi would pay for it," Pugh recalled. "It gave us marvelous creative freedom. Nothing was impossible. If it was funny, we could do it."

. . .

I n May 1952, just as the first season's shooting was winding down, Lucy came to Desi with a bulletin. They adored little Lucie, and were still adapting to parenthood, but they had always envisioned a bigger family. "Hey, Father," she told him, "I've got news for you. I'm pregnant again." Just nine months after the birth of Lucie, this was indeed a bombshell—and perhaps a death knell for *I Love Lucy*. It seemed impossible that a pregnant woman would appear on the air.

"Oh, my God. What are we going to do?" Jess Oppenheimer exclaimed after hearing the news.

"What do you mean, what are we going to do? She's going to have a baby," Desi responded. "What about Lucy Ricardo having a baby as part of our shows this year?"

"They'll never let you do that," Jess immediately retorted.

That was Desi's recollection. A much more credible account—offered by both Jess and Lucy—is that Desi came to Jess with the news, visibly worried and swallowing hard.

"How long will we have to be off the air?" he asked.

In a flash, without thinking, it was Jess who took Desi's hand and pumped it—with a brainstorm that would make television history. "Congratulations, this is wonderful!" Oppenheimer said. "This is just what we need to give us excitement in our second season. Lucy Ricardo will have a baby too!"

Whoever had the idea, what is not in dispute is that the notion of a pregnant Lucy Ricardo faced a steep and immediate uphill battle in the corporate suites of CBS and Philip Morris. While there was no codified ban on pregnancy on television, it was a mass-market medium, dependent on the blandest possible, inoffensive, middle-of-the-road appeal to the maximum number of viewers. And the act that produced pregnancy—that is, sex—was all but nonexistent on television, where even married couples typically slept in twin beds. It may be hard to imagine, but in 1952 pregnancy was still regarded as such a debilitating (or vaguely embarrassing) condition that expectant mothers were routinely dismissed from their jobs. The network and sponsor suggested alternatives: hide Lucy behind furniture (impossible, since Ball ballooned dramatically in her pregnancies); devote only one or two shows to the plotline; avoid showing the pregnancy at all costs. But Oppenheimer insisted that the story could be done in good taste, and Desi was adamant that an effective narrative arc required half a dozen or more episodes to track the progress from the first word of the pregnancy to the actual birth. Still, they got nowhere. Desperate, Desi appealed to the ultimate authority, the chairman of Philip Morris, Alfred E. Lyon. Desi wrote him a remarkable letter, laying it all on the line:

> Mr. Lyon, I guess it all comes down to you. You are the man who is paying the money for this show and I guess we will have to do whatever you decide. There's only one thing I want to make certain that you understand. We have given you the number-one show in the country and, up till now, the creative decisions have been in our hands. Your people are now telling us we cannot do this, so the only thing I want from you, if you agree with them, is that you must inform them that we will not accept them telling us what not to do unless, in the future, they will also tell us what to do.
>
> At that point, and if this is your decision, we will cease to be responsible to you for the show being the number-one show on television, and you will have to look to your people, to the network and to the Biow Agency for that responsibility.
>
> Thank you very much for all you have done for us in the past.

Within a week or so, opposition to the pregnancy plot suddenly faded. Desi would claim he only learned why a couple of years later, on a visit to Lyon's office in New York, when the chairman's secretary surreptitiously showed him the memo the chairman had sent to his staff at the time. "Don't fuck around with the Cuban!" it read.

To assure that Lucy Ricardo's pregnancy was handled as tastefully and as inoffensively as possible, Desi and Jess sought the advice of Cardinal James McIntyre, the Roman Catholic archbishop of Los Angeles; Rabbi Edgar Magnin of the Wilshire Boulevard Temple (the rabbi to many Jewish studio heads and movie stars); and Reverend Clifton Moore of the Hollywood Presbyterian Church. In the end, Moore wound up as script consultant to Bob and Madelyn, as did two other clergymen, Rabbi Alfred Wolf of Wilshire Temple and Monsignor John Devlin of St. Victor's Catholic Church. The three of them carefully reviewed every episode's storyline for any moral objections.

Devlin's church was just off the Sunset Strip in West Hollywood, and his famous parishioners included Ricardo Montalban, Cesar Romero, and Loretta Young. He was also head of the Legion of Decency, the national Catholic hierarchy's censorship board, which held powerful sway over movie content from the 1930s until well into the 1960s. He had served as an adviser to religious-themed movies like *Going My Way* and *The Bells of St. Mary's*, whose star Bing Crosby summed him up as "a very serious, quite humorless, but nice man." The religious consultants "were with us four days a week to see the rehearsals and filming," Desi recalled. "They used to have lunch and dinner together and became very good friends," but in the end they had no objection to anything the writers dreamed up.

The production team also faced a logistical issue. With the baby due in January, Desi did not want Lucy to have to work from about the end of October until mid-March. This would require some rejiggering of the work schedule, because Desilu was required to deliver a season of thirty-nine episodes to CBS. There were already five episodes in the can that had been filmed the prior spring, but other accommodations would be needed, including ending the summer hiatus a month early, in July. After some discussion, CBS agreed to rerun ten episodes from the previous season—a most unusual concession—if the *I Love Lucy* team could produce a new opening scene for each, essentially turning them into flashbacks in which the Ricardos and Mertzes reminisce about the past as they contemplate the impending birth. Since hardly any filmed television programs (the essential ingredient for a high-quality repeat broadcast) existed in 1952, this development also amounted to a Desilu innovation—one that would be repeatedly employed in sitcoms in the decades to come. The pregnancy shows would be filmed in September and October, when word of Lucy's condition had become public.

The planned schedule gave the cast and writers time to explore aspects of pregnancy in all its comic possibilities, including several that gave Desi a special opportunity to shine. In one episode, Ricky experiences sympathetic, psychosomatic labor pains—with priceless expressions of illness by Desi—while Lucy indulges in weird food cravings like pistachio ice cream drenched in hot fudge and sardines. In yet another scenario, Lucy is so determined that their child speak proper English that she hires a fussy tutor, a professor whose real ambition is to perform at Ricky's nightclub. This episode allows Desi a brilliant turn critiquing the vexing inconsistencies of English, in which Ricky tries to read a children's book aloud and stumbles on a series of words ending in "o-u-g-h" that are variously pronounced with *oo*, *ow*, and *uff* sounds. Eventually he promises to get the professor an audition with "every record company in town" if he will embrace Ricky's mispronunciations. The professor sings a rousing snippet of "Babalú," and Lucy admits defeat.

But the triumph of the pregnancy shows—and probably the most moving episode of the entire series—was titled "Lucy Is *Enceinte*," the French word for pregnant, chosen as a private dig at the network censors, who had banned use of the term, though the religious advisers had expressed no objection to it. (The titles were for the production team only; they were not announced to the public.) In this episode, Lucy, feeling inexplicably tired and gaining weight, visits her doctor and, after she learns her happy news, spends the day in vain trying to tell Ricky in a private, tender way but is constantly interrupted. Finally, she goes to the Tropicana and passes the maître d' a note, which Ricky reads aloud, without knowing who sent the note:

"Oh, isn't this sweet. Listen. 'Dear Mr. Ricardo: My husband and I are going to have a blessed event. I just found out about it today and haven't told him yet. I heard you sing a number called 'We're Having a Baby, My Baby and Me.' If you will sing it for us now, it will be my way of breaking the news to him.'" At this, Ricky strolls around the club, singing the opening bars of "Rock-a-bye Baby," asking couple after couple if they are the parents to be—including an elegant, silver-haired matron who blushes as the audience laughs. Meantime, Lucy has quietly taken a seat at a ringside table, and when Ricky passes, he silently points and nods as if to ask her—"as if it's a big joke," the script reads—whether she's the lucky one. At that, the scene cuts to a close-up of a misty-eyed Lucy nodding yes. Desi continues his stroll and song before coming to a dead stop and doing a stunned double-take, his mouth agape and his Adam's apple bobbing. Lucy again nods and he slides across the floor on his knees to her table.

"Honey, honey, no!" he says.

"Yes."

"Really?"

"Yes."

"Why didn't you tell me?"

"You didn't give me a chance," Lucy protests, tearing up.

At this Ricky leaps to his feet. "It's me!" he shouts. "I'm gonna be a father. How 'bout that? I want you to meet my mother! I mean my wife!"

By this point, Lucy and Desi's real emotions—as they remembered

all the years of trying so hard to have one baby, much less two—
suddenly suffuse their performances, and the Arnazes and Ricardos are
magically as one in a moment of pure emotion that no acting could ever
equal. Ricky gently takes Lucy's arm and glides her to the dance floor as
several members of the band, concerned that Arnaz was so overcome
he had forgotten his next music cue, shout, "Sing the baby song!" Ricky
launches into an old song made popular by Eddie Cantor, exulting:

> *He'll have toys, baby clothes*
> *He'll know he's come to the right house*
> *Bye and bye, when he grows,*
> *Maybe he'll live in the White House.*

Ricky tells Lucy, "I bet he's gonna look just like you," and she de-
murs, "Oh, I hope not!"

> *We're having a baby . . .*

"I'll bet she'll speak with an accent, like you," Lucy says.
"She?" Ricky asks.

> *We're havin' a baby,*
> *my baby and me . . .*

Ricky nuzzles his wife, and Lucy, tremulous once more, bites her
lip and starts to kiss him before breaking out in a radiant smile and
tucking her head against his.

By this point the studio audience and the whole cast and crew were
crying. Desi had flubbed part of the lyric to "Rock-a-bye Baby" at the
start of the scene, and up in the control booth, the director Bill Asher,
himself in tears, called for a retake, but the audience shouted in protest.
Asher shot the scene again but nothing could equal the spontaneity

and emotion of the first try, and the raw scene was used in the episode that aired on December 8. John Crosby in the *New York Herald Tribune* reported that "the news that Lucille Ball was about to have a baby was whispered demurely into roughly 12,000,000 homes."

The combined pregnancies—real and imaginary—riveted public attention. A Cleveland newspaper even started a contest to predict the exact day and time Lucy would deliver.

Because Lucie Arnaz had been delivered by cesarean section, and the obstetric practice of the day mandated a cesarean birth for all subsequent pregnancies, the Arnazes were able to fix the date of their baby's arrival. Lucy's doctor, Joseph Harris, performed his operations on Mondays, which meant that absent some emergency, Monday, January 19, 1953, was set as the big day. Though Lucy and Desi did not know the real baby's sex, they had already decided that the Ricardos' offspring would be a boy—in part so that little Lucie would come to understand that the television baby was just make-believe and that she and her sibling were the family's only actual children.

On the evening of Sunday, January 18, Lucy checked into Cedars of Lebanon to find a wire from a friend: "Well, don't just lie there, do something!" At 8:20 the next morning, through the swinging doors of the delivery room, Desi and James Bacon, of the Associated Press, the sole reporter waiting with him, heard Lucy shout through her spinal anesthetic, "It's a boy!" Within minutes, the news of the birth of the eight-pound, nine-ounce Desiderio Alberto Arnaz y Ball (the fourth of the name, but henceforth known to the world as Desi Jr.) was on the radio and wire services all over the world. That afternoon, Lucy and Desi read the first of some seven thousand letters and one thousand telegrams to arrive. (The congratulatory messages would eventually top one million.) Desi went to the Brown Derby, a show business hangout in Los Angeles, threw his hands to the ceiling, and exulted, "Now we have everythin'!"

That evening, forty-four million Americans tuned in to CBS to watch the brilliant episode in which Little Ricky Ricardo is born. The plot has Lucy, Ricky, Fred, and Ethel working out a tightly choreographed division of labor for heading to the hospital—with one in charge of the phone, another Lucy's overcoat, another the suitcase—but when the actual moment of truth arrives, only Lucy stays calm while Ricky and the Mertzes collapse into chaos and Ricky is so distraught that he arrives at the hospital in a wheelchair. When he finally sees his new little boy, the proud father faints. The broadcast ended with an announcer intoning, "To Lucy, to Ricky, and to the new baby, love and kisses from Philip Morris and from all America." The next morning, only about two-thirds as many Americans tuned in to watch the inauguration of the new president, Dwight D. Eisenhower. (Years later, when Ike ran into Desi Jr. at the El Dorado Country Club in Palm Springs, he demanded, "Is this the little fellow who knocked me off the front pages?" and bought the boy a banana split.)

· · ·

I ndeed, it *did* seem that the Arnazes had everythin'. Less than a month after Desi Jr.'s birth, they signed a fat $250,000 contract with their old studio, MGM, to make a comedy called *The Long, Long Trailer*, based on a memoir by Clinton Twiss about a couple who set out on married life in a brontosaurus-sized yellow trailer home that they haul across the picturesque mountain landscape of California. The producer was Lucy's old lover from her RKO days, Pandro Berman, who acknowledged that the film was made "entirely, entirely" because of the stunning success of *I Love Lucy*. "I conceived the idea of putting Lucy and Desi in a picture, and the Metro people in New York were appalled," Berman recalled. "They said, 'You can't sell anything that they're giving away for nothing.' And I said, 'I think you can. I think we can make a picture in color on a big screen, with people who are getting marvelous publicity every week and becoming more engraved in the hearts of the public.' It was enough different from what they were doing."

Just barely enough. The Arnazes play Nicky and Tacy Collini, whose relationship bears an uncanny resemblance to Ricky and Lucy Ricardo's, and the film's comic slapstick highlight—Tacy's flailing attempt to cook dinner in a moving trailer—amounts to an extended Technicolor sequence straight out of *I Love Lucy*. And with a screenplay by the renowned team of Frances Goodrich and Albert Hackett, and the skilled guidance of Vincente Minnelli, one of the studio's most prestigious directors, it was a first-class production all the way. When filming began in June 1953, the Arnazes were welcomed back to the studio in Culver City with a big banner at the gate proclaiming, WE LOVE LUCY. But it was Desi who drove a hard bargain with the MGM executive Benny Thau. The terms were effectively a wager on the couple's box-office power: If the picture did not gross as much as MGM's champion comedy, Minnelli's charming *Father of the Bride*, Desi and Lucy would return twenty-five thousand dollars of their joint salary; if it grossed more, the studio would owe them a bonus of fifty thousand dollars, for a total of three hundred thousand—"which tripled the combined salaries we'd received for a whole year," Desi recalled, referring to their pay when they were under contract to the studio in the 1940s. It would prove to be a wise bet. At the film's first preview, at the Picwood Theatre in Los Angeles that August, 134 out of 171 review cards rated the movie "outstanding, excellent or very good," with one audience member writing, "Great picture. Let's have some more movies with Lucy and Desi." But another astute viewer saw the venture for what it was: "It appears as if the picture was written specifically to take advantage of the stars' TV publicity. I am glad the studio did not hurt other actors by having them play these parts."

At the same time, Desilu had signed a record new eight-million-dollar contract with CBS and Philip Morris—the largest in television history to date—to continue *I Love Lucy* for two more years (with Philip Morris paying three million to CBS for the airtime and five million to

Desilu for production). Simultaneously, the film-recording revolution that Desilu had started was well underway. In the 1952–53 season just ended, forty-seven network shows had been filmed. Production of *I Love Lucy* and *Our Miss Brooks*, which had outgrown General Service Studios, was moved to the roomier Motion Picture Center lot on Cahuenga Boulevard in Hollywood. And Desi's recording of "There's a Brand New Baby (At Our House)," which he had written when Lucie was born but had been featured in an episode after Little Ricky's birth, made it to the Top 5 on the singles chart. On April 3, the first-ever issue of *TV Guide* featured Desi Jr. on the cover, with the headline LUCY'S $50,000,0000 BABY. To cap it all off, Desi made the best-dressed list with such famous clotheshorses as Dwight Eisenhower, Ezio Pinza, Rex Harrison, and Danny Kaye.

It all must have seemed too good to be true.

It was.

• • •

On Sunday, September 6, 1953, Desi was playing poker with the producer Irving Briskin in a rented beach house in Del Mar, where the Arnazes had been vacationing down the way from their old friends the Rabwins. It was a place that Desi had come to love, where he felt safe to relax, the way he had on Cayo Smith years before. But on this lazy Sunday evening, a big storm blew in, via a phone call to Desi from Kenny Morgan, Cousin Cleo's husband and Desilu's PR chief, who reported that Walter Winchell had just delivered a blind gossip item on his popular national radio broadcast, asking "What top redheaded television comedienne has been confronted with her membership in the Communist Party?" Lucy, listening at home in Chatsworth, thought that Winchell might have been referring to Imogene Coca, the zany costar of Sid Caesar's *Your Show of Shows* on NBC. But Desi knew instantly that Winchell was referring to Lucy, and he raced home to the ranch.

Just two days earlier, on September 4, Lucy had met in Los Angeles with an investigator for the House Un-American Activities Committee, who questioned her about why she had signed a California voter registration card in 1936 that listed her party affiliation as Communist. It was not the first time that she had drawn the committee's scrutiny. A year and a half earlier, she had been questioned in a closed session about the same issue—and she had testified that she had simply been trying to mollify her iconoclastic Grandpa Fred Hunt, who during the Great Depression had urged the whole family to register Communist. Lucy had told the committee's investigator, William Wheeler, that she had "never been too civic-minded and certainly never political-minded" and had simply sought to please her grandfather. "In those days that was not a big, terrible thing to do. It was almost as terrible to be a Republican in those days," she had testified with rueful humor. No word of that earlier testimony had leaked out, but now it clearly had. Desi and Ken Morgan and Howard Strickling, the powerful head of publicity for MGM, which had yet to release *The Long, Long Trailer*, gathered at the Arnazes' house to decide how and whether to respond.

The stakes were terrifically high. In the wake of Soviet aggression in Eastern Europe in the aftermath of World War II, anti-Communist hysteria had swept the United States, and Hollywood made a fat target for right-wing politicians. Screenwriters, directors, and actors who had supported left-wing causes in the 1930s—or had been early opponents of Adolf Hitler—were suddenly accused of the Orwellian offense of "premature anti-Fascism." Some of these figures had indeed joined the Communist Party—as Lucy noted, something less than a grave sin in the tumultuous climate of the Depression and the war years, when the Soviets were allies of the United States against the Nazis. But with the dawn of the Cold War, such associations had taken on a sinister tinge, and in November 1947 the Hollywood studio chiefs, bowing to political pressure, had agreed in a meeting at the Waldorf-Astoria in New York that they would not "knowingly" employ any Communist.

The result was a sweeping employment blacklist that spread throughout film, television, and radio, destroying careers and sending many of
those who refused to testify to Congress to jail for contempt.

Winchell's report could therefore amount to a career-ending crisis
for Lucy, even though she had never actually joined the Communist
Party and had never voted the Communist line. Desi, who had known
Winchell since his days in Miami, was puzzled at why the columnist
had not simply called him to clear things up. Even so, the Arnaz team's
initial decision was for Desi to stay silent and hope the whole thing
would blow over. And for a few days all seemed quiet, but on the following Friday, Lucy saw two reporters in fedoras standing near the
orchard in Chatsworth, and Desi recalled waking up to the sight of a
photographer outside their bedroom window. The news had broken
into the wider media via a front-page splash in an extra edition of the
afternoon *Los Angeles Herald-Express*, complete with a headline in red
ink: LUCILLE BALL NAMED RED.

In this moment, Desi's combative instincts, years of show business
experience, and fierce determination to protect the brand that he and
Lucy had built shone bright. His first move was to call the *Herald-
Express*'s battle-axe of a city editor, Agness Underwood—known for
carrying a gun in her newsroom and firing blanks to get her staff's
attention—to demand that she order her reporters off the Desilu
grounds. His next step was to rush to the studio and begin working
the phones. He called J. Edgar Hoover, whom he'd known from the
FBI director's yearly trips to the Del Mar racetrack, and asked if the
bureau had any grounds for concern about Lucy. "Absolutely nothing!"
Hoover replied in Desi's later telling. "She's one hundred percent clear
as far as we are concerned."

Then Arnaz called Frank Stanton, the president of CBS, and told
him that he and Lucy were determined to fight the smear. If Philip
Morris declined to air the following Monday night's show, Desi insisted
that Desilu would pay the thirty-thousand-dollar bill for the time slot

so he and Lucy could go on the air to defend themselves. He called Alfred Lyon at Philip Morris, who agreed to stand by them. To top it all
off, the first newly filmed episode of the 1953–54 schedule (the season
premiere, shot the previous spring, was already in the can) was to be
filmed that very Friday night in the new quarters at Motion Picture
Center. Lucy was a wreck, unsure if the show should go on.

Desi finally reached Congressman Donald Jackson of California,
a former Marine Corps colonel who had taken Richard Nixon's old
seat on the Un-American Activities Committee, and insisted he hold
a news conference that same evening. Jackson professed ignorance of
the source of the leak and said that the committee had no beef with
Lucy. He agreed to summon the press to the Statler Hotel in downtown Los Angeles. Desi then called a friendly reporter, Jim Bacon of
the Associated Press, and asked him to telephone him the minute the
news conference was over. Moments before Desi headed out to warm
up the audience for that night's filming, Bacon called the studio to assure him, "You'll be having nothing but beautiful headlines tomorrow
morning."

Thus fortified, and speaking into a small handheld microphone,
Desi asked the studio audience to reserve judgment until they read
the next day's accounts. He struggled in vain to hold back tears, and
at one point, his voice broke completely. "Lucy is as American as Bernard Baruch and Ike Eisenhower," he said. "By the way, we both voted
for Eisenhower. So ladies and gentlemen, don't judge too soon. Read
for yourselves." The audience responded with applause. He then introduced "my favorite redhead—that's the only thing about her that's
red, and even *that* is not legitimate . . . the girl who plays Lucy—Lucille
Ball!" Bill Frawley and Vivian Vance had tears in their eyes, Lucy
sobbed, and the audience rose as one, hollering, "We love you, Lucy."
DeDe called out from the top of the bleachers, "You're doing great,
honey!" The cast proceeded with a hilarious episode in which Lucy
and Ethel buy a dress shop only to find that they are each other's sole

customers. A line in the script must have echoed Desi's mood. "It's this crazy business that's getting me down," Ricky says after Lucy complains that he is in a "Cuban funk." "There's no sense to show business. Every day is a tough day."

And the next day's headlines were heartening indeed. JACKSON SAYS: NO PROOF "LUCY" WAS COMMUNIST the Los Angeles *Daily News* reported. LUCILLE BALL WAS NEVER A COMMIE, JACKSON DECLARES, was the *Mirror*'s headline. That afternoon, the Arnazes summoned reporters to the ranch for drinks and snacks. Seated in a green canvas chair with a highball and cigarette, and dressed in pink toreador slacks and a white blouse, Lucy calmly answered questions in the ninety-degree heat. At the end of the session, Dan Jenkins, the Arnazes' friendly scribe at the *Hollywood Reporter*, announced: "Ladies and gentlemen of the press, I think perhaps you will agree with me that we all owe Lucy an apology."

Elite liberal opinion discerned a broader lesson about McCarthyism in the whole sorry mess. Jack Gould, the *New York Times*'s highly respected television critic, said that what happened to Lucy was a reason why the practice of blacklisting mere suspected Communists should end. "One cannot help but wonder if the fear of boycotts is not largely in the minds of those who subscribe to the use of blacklists and private loyalty files of dubious reliability," he wrote. Winchell himself apologized, in his fashion, on his Sunday radio program, declaring, "Tonight, Mr. Lincoln is drying his tears for making her go through this," while failing to acknowledge that he himself had started the flood.

And feelings still ran high in some quarters. Hedda Hopper, the virulently anti-Communist Hollywood columnist, was a longtime friend of the Arnazes and had supported Lucy through the ordeal. But her inbox filled with hate mail. "So—so—so she did it just to make her dear old grand-pappy feel good," one unsigned postcard read. "And for Grand Pappy's 'peace of mind' she turned traitor to her country?!!! Awake, Hedda." M. S. Maloney of Los Angeles wrote Hopper to say, "In behalf of the Gold Star Mothers: MY SON DIDN'T VOTE RED TO PLEASE HIS GRANDPA—BUT HE DID DIE IN KOREA FOR HIS UNCLE SAM!"

The following week *Lucy* remained number one in the ratings by a comfortable margin, and two months later, the Arnazes received a ringing endorsement from the highest-possible authority. On November 23, they topped the bill with Richard Rodgers and Oscar Hammerstein II, Ethel Merman, Helen Hayes, Bill Frawley, Vivian Vance, and other stars at a tribute to President Eisenhower hosted by the Anti-Defamation League of B'Nai B'rith. The glittering audience at the Mayflower Hotel in Washington included the Joint Chiefs of Staff, Attorney General Herbert Brownell, and J. Edgar Hoover himself.

"If we are going to continue to be proud that we are Americans, there must be no weakening of the code by which we have lived," the president told his audience. "By the right to meet your accuser face to face, if you have one; by your right to go to the church or the synagogue or even the mosque of your own choosing; by your right to speak your mind and be protected in it."

For Lucy, the experience was scarring. For the rest of her life, she never so much as cast a ballot. For Desi, it was a bittersweet victory. With discipline, calmness, good humor, and courage under fire, he had defused a potential disaster. But as he faced mounting business burdens and creative pressures, personal demons emerged that would make it hard for him ever again to rise to the occasion with quite such grace and skill.

eleven

———·◆·———

"It's Only a Show"

By the start of its third season, *I Love Lucy* was not just the number one show on television but a national institution. On Monday nights at 9 p.m. Eastern, the country would grind to a halt. In Chicago, in the 8 p.m. Central time slot, the municipal water system experienced an unusual drop in pressure at a quarter past the hour, as viewers flushed their toilets in unison during the commercial break, and the Marshall Field department store posted a notice declaring, WE LOVE LUCY, TOO, SO FROM NOW ON WE WILL BE OPEN THURSDAY NIGHT INSTEAD OF MONDAY. Hedda Hopper told the Arnazes that Colonel Robert R. McCormick, the formidable conservative publisher of the *Chicago Tribune*, enforced a policy of absolute silence in his home when the show was on. In the fall of 1952, the weekly bulletin of Immaculate Heart of Mary Roman Catholic Church in Indianapolis invited parishioners to a Monday night prayer service for the "boys in Korea" by promising, "You will still get home in time for two-thirds of 'I Love Lucy.'"

Now, in the fall of 1953, a newly minted graduate of the University of Southern California named Rosalind Wyman, running to become the youngest-ever member of the Los Angeles City Council, went canvassing door-to-door on Monday nights because she knew voters would be at home watching *I Love Lucy*. (She won.) On Tuesday mornings, people in offices all over the country asked each other, "Did you see the show?" without having to name it.

The weekly adventures in the Ricardos' apartment at 623 East 68th Street—a made-up address that would actually have put the building in the middle of the East River—amounted to what a later generation of network promoters would call "Must-See TV." As they worked to write each episode, Bob Carroll and Madelyn Pugh posted a sign in their office in an effort to keep themselves grounded: IT'S ONLY A SHOW.

But it was not. It was a burgeoning empire.

In 1953, Desilu was valued at ten million dollars, with gross annual revenues of six million that resulted in a net profit for Lucy and Desi of six hundred thousand dollars before taxes. On top of that, they earned some five hundred thousand in marketing tie-in agreements for merchandise—quickly dubbed "Desiloot" by the press. The products ranged from his-and-hers pajamas to bedspreads, furniture, hairnets, potty seats, and an *"I Love Lucy* Baby Doll" retailing for $9.98 that "drinks, wets, blows bubbles, can be bathed, [and] cries with real tears." Executives of the American Character Doll Company told toy buyers that the doll's rollout would be "one of the most outstanding promotions ever to be announced by a doll manufacturer." Altogether, the Arnazes' annual income topped $1 million at this point ($11 million in current value), at a time when the median income of men was about $3,200 a year.

Jack Gould, the *New York Times*'s pioneering television critic, wrote an article for the newspaper's Sunday magazine that attempted to sum up the show's enormous appeal, which he judged to be partly a fusion of the stars' actual lives and their television alter egos and partly "the product of inspired press agentry which has made a national legend of a couple which two years ago was on the Hollywood sidelines." But fundamentally, Gould wrote, it was the show's "extraordinary discipline and intuitive understanding of farce that gives 'I Love Lucy' its engaging lilt and lift." While Gould, like everyone else, considered Lucy the heart of the show, he allowed that Desi was "a success story in himself," observing that the very qualities that had previously hampered Desi's career now worked in his favor.

"His rather marked accent and his unprofessional style of performing were wisely left alone," Gould wrote. "The result was a leading man far removed from the usual stereotyped stage husband. It was a case of awkwardness being recognized as an asset. Today—after two seasons in his role—Mr. Arnaz is rapidly becoming a competent actor." Indeed, in an episode titled "Ricky Minds the Baby," filmed in December 1953 and aired a month later, Arnaz gave what may well have been his best performance of the entire series. The plot has Lucy complaining that Ricky doesn't spend enough time with the baby, so he rearranges his entire week's vacation, while the Tropicana club is being painted, to care for Little Ricky at home. In a remarkable scene that lasts nearly five full minutes, Ricky recites a bedtime story, "*Caperucita Roja*"—"Little Red Riding Hood"—in a bubbling mix of Spanish and English, complete with fearsome imitations of *el lobo*—the wolf. In his charming telling, Red Riding Hood is carrying a basket to Grandma, filled with "*frijoles, tortillas y vino,*" because Grandma is "feeling lousy." As Lucy, Fred, and Ethel eavesdrop, enchanted, at the bedroom door, Ricky skips around the room telling the tale, which culminates in a rapid-fire flood of Spanish capped by the inevitable English conclusion: "happily ever after!"

Alas, the Arnazes' own domestic situation was not quite as peaceful. To be sure, they had plenty to be happy about—two beautiful children, incredible career success, bounteous material blessings—and on the surface, they celebrated. On November 30, 1953, Desi surprised Lucy with an elegant thirteenth anniversary party for forty guests at

Mocambo, one of the swankiest nightclubs on the Sunset Strip, when she had expected only a quiet dinner with Vincente Minnelli. Bob and Madelyn composed some doggerel for the occasion:

> *The couple exhibited real wedded bliss*
> *Desi turned to Lucy and said with a kiss,*
> *"These thirteen years my love's grown stronger."*
> *"The way you say it," she said, "it sounds longer."*

Three months later, on a promotional trip to New York for the Radio City Music Hall premiere of *The Long, Long Trailer*, they took in some Broadway shows and were stunned when the audience at one performance rose and applauded as they returned to their seats after intermission. Lucy told Desi that Eleanor Roosevelt must be in the theater before realizing that the ovation was for *them*. As for *The Long, Long Trailer*, critics liked the picture, with *Newsweek* pronouncing it a good example of how movies and television "can be of mutual help" and *Time* trumpeting that it "brings a gifted Hollywood chicken home to roost. Lucille Ball, whom movie people in 1951 declared a has-been, went into television with Desi Arnaz and won herself a top rating." Bosley Crowther of the *New York Times* was slightly less impressed, sniffing that "any resemblance to human beings is purely coincidental, you may be sure," and adding that the film was "an almost exact reproduction of the spirit of their TV shows."

The actual trailer used in the film was deposited in the Arnazes' backyard, where the actress June Havoc lived in it for a time. But there at the ranch, the mood could now be tense, not carefree. Most weekends Desi took off for his new boat, a cabin cruiser he called (naturally) the *Desilu*, docked on Balboa Island at Newport Beach, while Lucy stayed home with the children in Chatsworth, painting watercolors or compulsively cleaning the house, her longtime means of relieving tension or stress. Since his youth on Cayo Smith, Desi had always been at home and relaxed on the water, and he often invited a cadre of carousing male companions aboard, including Kenny Morgan, Cousin Cleo's husband. Whatever marital constancy—and quieting of rumors—Desi had managed in his role as proud new paterfamilias had apparently faded by now. Kenny's penchant for drinking and straying from his spouse equaled Desi's own. Lucy was all too aware that more than fishing was usually afoot on such cruises. "Lucy used to phone Desi at the dock and say, 'You and Kenny get into trouble, but as long as you're with Danny I know you're all right,'" the still-unmarried Dann Cahn recalled. "He wasn't. We got into a lot of trouble."

The paradox is that, having created *I Love Lucy* so they could be together, the Arnazes found they now needed more and more time apart. Desi had hired the CBS business affairs executive Martin Leeds as his executive vice president in early 1953 to take day-to-day charge of Desilu. Leeds summed up the couple's challenge: "If you're trying to create the most perfect world for people to work and live in and be together for twenty-four hours a day, night and day, at work or at play, forget it. It just can't happen." But he noted that Lucy was all too aware of Desi's ongoing extracurricular activities, an awkward situation for employees pledged to serve them both: "The problem we had with Desi was that we knew she knew, and that hurt."

When Desi lost his temper, Lucy could often defuse the situation. "As a calming wifely stratagem, Lucille may grab him about the waist, kiss him behind an ear, and break into a hootchy-kootchy dance," Laura Bergquist wrote in *Look* magazine. But sometimes Lucy felt more like socking Desi in the jaw, and there were open fights at the studio. When Desi's mother showed up one day in a sable coat, Lucy lit into Desi. Her makeup man, Hal King, recalled Lucy yelling, "Where the hell did your mother get that sable coat?" When Desi confessed that he had bought it for Lolita, Lucy promptly bought a comparable one for DeDe from the separate account she still kept. Desi remained insistent that Lucy should accept his use of prostitutes and transitory indiscretions as a Latin man's meaningless *droit du seigneur* and sulked when she could not. "What is she excited about?" he would ask friends. "They're only hookers!" At other times he chose to see himself as unfairly henpecked. After an argument or misunderstanding in which he lamented Lucy's unwillingness to forgive him for some unspecified conduct (though it is easy enough to imagine what kind), he jotted a self-pitying note to himself in April 1954: "I have come to the terrible realization that my wife doesn't love me."

Around this time, Lucy apparently shared at least some of her anxieties about the marriage with the Reverend Norman Vincent Peale, the celebrated pastor of the Marble Collegiate Church in New York and the author of the best-selling self-help book *The Power of Positive Thinking*. Lucy had met Peale during the publicity tour for *The Long, Long Trailer*. "In my judgment, God is using you both to bring relaxation and happiness to millions of people, and certainly to do that is God's work," Peale wrote her. "The Lord knows the great ability you and your husband possess, and He has given you this great success because you are spiritually worthy of it, and therefore know how to handle it with humility and thanksgiving, as you are so well demonstrating." Juxtaposed against the public adoration of a presumably happy couple, the Arnazes' private strains must have weighed all the more heavily.

Desi was also still apparently at odds with his father, and a coolness that did not quite amount to an estrangement persisted. Six months after the birth of Desi Jr. and more than two years after Lucie's arrival, Mayor Arnaz had yet to meet either child. In July 1953, he wrote to Desi and Lucy, thanking them for the invitation to spend time with them at Del Mar but begging off with an unconvincing excuse. "At the present time we are very busy with the house in Coral Gables," he wrote. "I am in the worst part of building; putting concrete in the tie-beams to get ready for the roof."

• • •

B ut if Desi and Lucy were struggling, Desilu itself was thriving. Plans to repackage the pregnancy episodes into a feature film called *Lucy Has a Baby* never materialized. Still, with Martin Leeds now executive vice president in charge of day-to-day management, helping to professionalize the operations of the company and working eighteen-hour days, Desilu began expanding. On the same night that Desi defused the scare over Lucy's old Communist voter registration, the cast had filmed its first episode in the new, much larger quarters at the Motion Picture Center studios on Cahuenga Boulevard—having taken a ten-year lease on a lot where half a dozen more soundstages would be available for conversion to bleacher-equipped playhouses suitable for filming before live audiences. *Our Miss Brooks* had also moved to the new location, and Desi had for the first time invested Desilu's own funds in a show other than *Lucy*, acquiring a half interest in *December Bride*, another CBS radio series. That gave him potentially valuable leverage with the network in a property that was also making the transition to television. The show starred Spring Byington, a beloved character actress who had played innumerable tenderhearted mothers in the movies, as a widow of a certain age on the lookout for a new man. It, too, would be shot at Motion Picture Center. Desi then promptly parlayed his investment into something better, trading half of Desilu's 50 percent interest in the series back to CBS in exchange for the network's commitment to air the show right after *I Love Lucy*, at 9:30 on Monday. In that slot, *December Bride* consistently ranked in the top ten shows on the air, making Desi's 25 percent interest more valuable than a 50 percent interest in a middling show would have been. *December Bride* ultimately ran for five seasons, and Desi would consider it the company's second most successful show. Because it was so well equipped for shooting on film with a live audience, Desilu also now became the landlord for other shows, renting out its studio space to other companies' productions, including Danny Thomas's *Make Room for Daddy* and *The Loretta Young Show*, a Sunday night drama anthology starring the glamorous 1930s and '40s movie queen. Under Desi's direction, the studio also worked to develop other shows of its own: *Willy*, with June Havoc, about a small-town New England lawyer, and *The Ray Bolger Show*, for which a new plot and concept were grafted onto the less-than-successful ABC series *Where's Raymond?* Both lasted just a single season, in 1954–55. All this expansion added to the burdens on Desi, who was, after all, still costarring in his own show.

I Love Lucy remained the engine that fueled the company. In March 1954, CBS signed on for another two years of original prime-time episodes, and for the first time scheduled regular reruns, too. The repeat episodes ran on Sunday afternoons—under various names, including *The Sunday Lucy Show*—and provided a nice profit for the company. Episodes that had cost about twenty-four thousand dollars each to produce were now leased by the network for thirty thousand dollars each. "It was a Camelot," Martin Leeds recalled. "It just seemed to be that nothing we could do would go down the wrong way."

Indeed, the company was going from strength to strength. Desi's secretary, Johnny Aitchison, impressed with the way his boss attacked the mountains of paperwork that demanded his attention and decision-making, invoked a nautical metaphor. "He would have this pile of stuff on the desk and he would say, 'Well, Johnny, it's simple— just one wave at a time. We won't worry about all the waves. We work one, one, one, and then we get to the end of the others, we're out of the ocean.'" The annual company picnic, which had started as an echo of the old Desilu ranch parties with a dozen kids and fifteen couples in 1952, was expanding each year. It had begun as a true family affair, blending Desi's expansive Cuban hospitality with Lucy's love for plain, old-fashioned fare like potato salad, baked beans, and watermelon. The paternalistic tradition featured barbecued hot dogs and hamburgers and carnival games—sack races, three-legged races, softball, live entertainment—with Lucie and Desi Jr. invariably dressed in spiffy party togs or cowboy costumes. The picnic eventually took over Sunland Park in the San Fernando Valley, growing to a total of some 250 couples and perhaps a thousand children before Lucy and Desi decided it had simply become too big to continue.

At Motion Picture Center, the Arnazes also fitted out a four-room bungalow apartment with two dressing rooms, a living and dining area, and a fully equipped kitchen that gave them an in-town home away from home. And later in 1954, when word came that Harry Cohn of Columbia Pictures was trying to buy Motion Picture Center and thus become Desilu's landlord, Desi arranged for Desilu to buy a majority interest in the facility instead. He considered this a coup, but Lucy, already worried about the growing pressures on Desi, was not pleased. "You just bought yourself another coffin," she told him.

• • •

Despite the show's overwhelming popularity, by 1953 some critics dared to suggest that the plots of *I Love Lucy* were starting to seem repetitious. "The Lucy shows—let's face it—are beginning to sound an awful lot alike," wrote John Crosby of the *New York Herald Tribune*. "Miss Ball is always trying to bust out of the house. Arnaz is trying to keep her in apron strings. The variations on the theme are infinite but it's the same theme and I'm a mite tired of it." As it happened, Jess Oppenheimer and the production team were feeling the same way, and by the summer of 1954 they had devised a solution: They would send the Ricardos and the Mertzes on a cross-country road trip—to Hollywood. This not only created a fresh crop of comic possibilities but opened the way for what would become a staple of Lucille Ball's promotional strategy for the rest of her sitcom career: the importation of big-name guest stars.

The basic premise was simple enough: Ricky would be offered a screen test for a movie role as Don Juan. But the trip allowed all manner of storylines: buying a car; encountering obstacles along the route; stopping in Ethel's hometown of Albuquerque (where Vivian Vance had actually spent some of her formative years); and finally arriving in Hollywood, where Lucy would encounter Rock Hudson, Richard Widmark, Harpo Marx, Hedda Hopper, Cornel Wilde, Van Johnson, John Wayne, and William Holden—all playing themselves.

Lucy had costarred with William Holden in the film *Miss Grant Takes Richmond* back in 1949, and they had stayed friends. But now, having won an Oscar for his performance in *Stalag 17*, Holden was just about the hottest male star in Hollywood. He agreed to appear on *I Love Lucy*—like all the other stars, for union scale—as a good sport to help promote his new picture, *The Country Girl*, costarring Bing Crosby and Grace Kelly, which Paramount would release in December 1954.

The storyline involves Lucy first spotting Holden at the Brown Derby restaurant, only to cause a tray of desserts to spill all over him. Ricky runs into Holden later that day at MGM, and Holden offers to drive him back to the Ricardos' hotel, where Ricky knows Lucy will be thrilled to meet the big movie star. Instead Lucy is terrified that Holden will recognize her and disguises herself with librarian's glasses and a long putty nose—which Holden accidentally sets on fire while attempting to light her cigarette. Lucy calmly extinguishes the blaze by blowing it out, then dunking her nose in a coffee cup, and Holden gallantly keeps their previous disastrous meeting a secret from Ricky. The sequence is a tour de force and a testament to Ball's fearlessness as a performer. The putty nose was not really on fire (though a small wick at the end of it was). Jack Benny was so impressed with the episode that he made his writing staff watch it as a master class in comedy writing.

The Hollywood episodes, which took up most of the 1954–55 season and the beginning of the 1955–56 season, marked more milestones in Desilu's "firsts" in television production. In what would later be called "product placement," General Motors loaned the show a brand-new 1955 Pontiac convertible to convey the Ricardos and Mertzes cross-country. The Desilu film editor Dann Cahn filmed the car crossing the George Washington Bridge from Manhattan to New Jersey, scenes along the road in Ohio and Tennessee, and finally its arrival in Los Angeles. In the bargain, he created the first-ever "process shot" for television, in which Lucy, Ricky, Fred, and Ethel were filmed singing "California, Here I Come" against projected footage of the bridge and roadway that Cahn had shot from the rear of a moving station wagon. As part of its promotional deal, Pontiac even gave Jess Oppenheimer, Madelyn Pugh, and Bob Carroll a series of new model cars to drive for the season.

One of the Hollywood episodes involved a visit to glamorous Palm Springs, the movie colony's favored desert getaway, where Lucy meets a hunky Rock Hudson poolside. Meantime, the Arnazes had built their own Palm Springs retreat, a low-slung, one-story, mid-century modern beige stone house in the nearby area that would come to be known as Rancho Mirage, designed again by Paul R. Williams, the prominent Black Los Angeles architect to stars and gentry alike. The house was situated in a prime location overlooking the seventeenth fairway of the Thunderbird Country Club, a lot that Desi had won in a poker game. At more than four thousand square feet, and with six bedrooms, six baths, a sinuous irregular-shaped swimming pool, and indoor-outdoor tropical plantings, the $150,000 "California-Hawaiian-style" house had a large stone fireplace in the living room, a matching hooded fireplace in the kitchen, and stunning views of Mount San Jacinto, capped with snow during the crystal-clear winter months. The Arnazes moved in in November 1954 and began making the commute there with the children most weekends.

But it turned out that the Thunderbird Country Club refused membership to actors and Cubans (among other groups), which meant that Desi could live within sight of its manicured fairways and greens, and could even play golf there, but could not join. That rankled the onetime son of Cuban aristocracy, so Desi would ultimately build his own hotel nearby—and make it open to all.

Desi's growing fame and success brought other unwelcome attention to activities he would have preferred to keep quiet. In December 1954, he became the target of *Confidential*, the scurrilous scandal-sheet magazine that made a specialty of exposing drug use, infidelity, and "sex perversion"—aka homosexuality—in Hollywood, Washington, and New York. "Does Desi Really Love Lucy?" the cover story asked. "Behind the scenes, Arnaz is a Latin Lothario who loves Lucy most of the time but by no means all the time. He has, in fact, sprinkled his affections all over Los Angeles for a number of years. And quite a bit of it has been bestowed on vice dollies who were paid handsomely for loving Desi briefly but, presumably, as effectively as Lucy." The article detailed an incident from the previous August when Desi and "a male relative"—presumably the incorrigible Kenny Morgan—had huddled at a bungalow at the Beverly Hills Hotel and ordered "two cuties, medium rare" from "one of Hollywood's best door-to-door dame services." The story cited chapter and verse of other incidents, dating back to Desi's amorous wartime exploits in the army—the very betrayals that had led Lucy to file for divorce.

After Lucy asked a Desilu staffer to buy her a copy of the magazine, Desi attempted to put a brave face on the situation, openly waving a copy of the issue on the set and exclaiming, "Look what those SOBs are saying about me now." Lucy's reaction to this protestation went unrecorded, but around this time, the Arnazes were hosting a dinner at their home in Rancho Mirage with the comic musical star Danny Kaye and his wife, Sylvia Fine; the French-born opera star Lily Pons; and Martin Leeds, among others. In the middle of dinner, Kaye, who had begun his career in the no-holds-barred world of the Borscht Belt, needled Arnaz. As Leeds would later recall the scene: "Danny says to Desi, 'I see you made *Confidential.*' And Lily Pons says, '*Qu'est-ce que c'est*

La Confidential?' and Danny looks at her and says, 'A magazine about fucking.' Two little bright spots on Lucy's face. Nothing from Desi."

For Lucy, the feeling of private betrayal was hardly new. The red flush of public humiliation was. It would get worse.

. . .

These deepening tensions in the Arnazes' marriage came against the backdrop of increasing obligations to their families. Lucy felt responsible for DeDe and Fred's financial security (she would repeatedly employ her brother in a series of jobs). And Lolita remained an enduring burden for Desi. His friend Marge Durante said that Desi's mother treated him more as a replacement for her husband than as a son and insisted that he buy her things, including a car that she could not even drive. "I thought she was very domineering," Durante recalled, "and she just demanded that Desi would take care of her." Martin Leeds saw her as "a standoffish, big, powerful, ineffectual woman." In the flush of Desilu's success, Desi bought Lolita a house in Beverly Hills and furnished it with fine china, silver, monogrammed linens, and other items in an attempt to re-create the elegant house in Vista Alegre in Santiago. When he surprised her with the grand gift one Christmas, she opened package after carefully chosen package and finally sighed, "Everything for the house?" Of course, Desi had intended everything for *her*, but she could not see it that way.

Not only did both Lucy and Desi effectively remain caregivers and financial providers to their mothers, but they also had a growing duty to their own children, who were no longer babies and had independent needs. Having tried so long and so hard to have children, the Arnazes just did the best they could when their kids finally arrived—with mixed results as parents. "Within the home, Desi was the permissive parent and Lucy was the martinet," Marcella Rabwin would remember. "He had greater tolerance for the antics of kids." Lucy had become a mother on the cusp of forty, quite a late age to do so in the 1950s, and she found herself frustrated and guilt-stricken that the routine work of child-rearing could be so draining—and boring. DeDe Ball had certainly not let the young Lucille dominate her own life, and it was a poignant twist that the mother who had been absent for such a crucial part of Lucille's own upbringing now took crucial responsibility for helping to raise her grandchildren. "DeDe was the real linchpin that held that family together," taking the children shopping, to doctor's appointments, and later to church, Lucy's friend Robert Osborne, the onetime actor and future Turner Classic Movies host, would remember. DeDe was aided in this task by the family's warmly maternal Black nanny, Willie Mae Barker, an "extraordinarily compassionate" woman in Desi Jr.'s memory, and her husband, George, who functioned as a kind of butler. "We were raised by a Black woman, let's face it," Desi Jr. would say matter-of-factly years later. Desi himself gave his children his brief but undivided attention, usually before heading off to work in the mornings. "I don't have any kind of strain about the people who raised me," Desi Jr. would say. "Yes, there were things going on that were mostly between them."

Lucie's lasting impression of Desi is of a warm, ebullient presence, "singing, playing the guitar, cooking." Desi Jr. would remember his father's childlike sense of appreciation, his teaching him to swim and body surf and fish—and to play the conga drum. "My father had this amazing sense of wonder at the miracle of nature," he recalled. "And he'd just take your hand and walk you around and say things to you about, you know, 'Look at that sunset . . . God really outdid himself.'"

By contrast, Lucie remembered that her mother could impose a kind of emotional banishment—and silent treatment—if the children displeased, angered, or disappointed her. "She always took it personally, and one of the things I had to learn as a parent . . ." Lucie recalled, pausing and picking up a different thought, "My father was not like that. He would get really angry and blow his stack, and be loud, but then he'd be done and it would be like it never happened. Like a storm just passed. The storm never said, 'I'm sorry,' the storm never left a note saying, 'I'm sorry, that wasn't your fault.' But it stopped, right? My mother would get personally offended by childhood behavior or what you said, because you should have known not to say that somehow, even though no one's taught you what to say. And she would emotionally separate from you for however long she wanted to. And it would be sometimes days, sometimes weeks." Marcella Rabwin, the close family friend, would remember of Lucy: "I thought she was a loving parent, but very, very despotic."

The children attended the weekly shooting of *I Love Lucy* "from the time we were babies," Lucie remembers, eventually settling into a Thursday night routine. Willie Mae would take them dressed in their best to the studio, where they would sit in the bleachers with their two grandmothers. "Dad would do the warm-up, and he would introduce us in the audience, and my brother would stand up and do this perfect little bow like that. And then he'd go, 'My daughter, Lucie,' and I was gone. I'd hide under the bleacher. I never wanted to be introduced." Eventually, Desi Jr. would join his father in the audience warm-up. "I was very much embracing the whole thing," he would recall. By contrast, in so many pictures from her childhood, lovingly preserved in her mother's scrapbooks, Lucie looks sad—dressed in cowgirl finery at a Desilu company picnic, standing in Rancho Mirage at Easter, in candid shots and posed publicity photographs alike. She says today that she doesn't remember specifically why she might have felt sad but readily acknowledges that the photos show her looking that way. "I do, I almost always do." On one birthday, when Lucy had planned an elaborate party at the beach, she forced Lucie into a scratchy, frilly party dress that she hated wearing in the heat. Lucy wouldn't let her come out unless she kept it on, so she locked herself in a bathroom and missed her own party.

Maury Thompson, *I Love Lucy*'s camera coordinator, recalled that Lucy could display almost a split personality when it came to the children. "She didn't have much time as a mother at home, and the kids missed that," he said. "But she was so enraptured with them. If anything happened at the studio, '*What's wrong?* Something wrong with my kids?' We got all that big scene. 'Oh, my kids, my kids.' But when she's with them, she's jerking them around." Thompson recalled home movies in which Lucy is holding her daughter tight on her lap, and all the little girl wanted to do was squirm away.

The Arnazes did their best to perpetuate the fiction that they were an ordinary American family, but of course they were not. Johnny Aitchison, Desi's secretary, was struck one day to see Lucie and Desi playing with paper dolls—of their own parents. "And it was the most natural thing in the world to watch these kids playing with that, just your normal kids having a good time, but playing with paper dolls of their parents."

Desi may have been indulgent, but like his father before him, he felt proprietary about his children, and he expected their devotion and obedience in an old-fashioned patriarchal way. Years later, the film director William Friedkin would recall having met Desi when he himself was young and just starting out in Hollywood. "You got kids?" Desi asked him. Friedkin replied that he did not, and Desi told him, "I got two kids. I tell them, 'You got problems, come to me. You don't come to me, change your name to Lopez, change your name to Gomez, no more Arnaz.'"

twelve

AN EMPIRE OF THEIR OWN

Sometime in the winter or early spring of 1955, with Desi shoul-dering more responsibilities than ever at the office, he initiated a long talk with Lucy about their future. "We have two alternatives," he recalled telling her. "We can sell four years of the *I Love Lucy* shows we have done for Philip Morris for at least three million dollars, I'm sure. After we give Uncle Sam his cut, we'll invest the rest safely and conservatively, which should bring us at least one hundred and fifty thousand dollars a year in income, without touching the capital." They could do occasional specials, keep supervising the other shows they produced, and manage the studio's paying tenants. "I would still have to run Desilu, produce our other shows, and supervise the ones we'd film for others," Arnaz recalled saying, "but without having to spend fifty hours a week on *I Love Lucy*. It would be a breeze."

The alternative was sobering. As early as 1952, Desi told the Hol-lywood columnist Hal Humphrey that if and when the major studios moved into television production, an independent operation like Desilu would be unable to compete. Now that very thing was happening. In March 1955, Warner Bros. launched a television division, partnering with ABC on a weekly hour-long series that alternated episodes based on the studio's vintage films *Casablanca* and *Kings Row*, and then creating *Cheyenne*, an original Western series starring Clint Walker. MCA, the giant talent agency, had launched its Revue Productions television arm, which produced *Alfred Hitchcock Presents* and would eventually become Universal Television after MCA's 1958 purchase of Universal Studios. MGM devised its own weaker offering, the short-lived *MGM Parade*, a promotional anthology series featuring clips from its greatest hits.

The point is, the studios had decided they could not beat TV but must join it, and that was bad news for Desilu, which faced the perennial challenge of any start-up when more established, richer companies recognize the appeal of its model. Desi told Lucy that simply to stay in the game, Desilu would have to grow: "We must get to be as big as MGM, Twentieth Century Fox, Warner Brothers, Paramount, Columbia or any of the other big studios. That means hiring a lot more people, top creative people if I can get them, to help carry the load, and rent or buy a bigger studio." In Desi's telling, Lucy expressed concern about what would happen to Desilu employees if they retired, and he assured her that the top-flight talent they'd assembled would be in high demand.

But Lucy was not on board with the "sell and step back" approach. Her most consistent lifelong means of relaxation was hard work, and so she told her husband, "I don't want to quit."

"Okay, then," Desi replied, "we'll just have to get bigger or lose the whole ball of wax."

What was left unsaid in these conversations was that the Arnazes' private time together was becoming less and less enjoyable. If Desi was unable to keep from straying, Lucy was unable to relax. Even when they went to Palm Springs for the weekend, they pursued separate activities, with Desi playing golf or propping up the bar and Lucy at home in the pool with the kids. Lucy herself acknowledged the stress that Desilu's success had brought, even if she seemed unable to do much to lessen it. "It is overwhelming—and sometimes terrifying, but we don't expect to stay on top, career-wise, forever," she told the Hollywood columnist May Mann in a joint interview with Desi. No matter how much she may have privately chafed at her husband's behavior, or worried about the toll the business was taking on his health and their marriage, for public consumption she insisted that he was the boss. "We try to do everything together," she said. "Whether it is the discipline of our children, problems in our home, or our hobbies, we both believe you have to give a little, take a little to make a go of it." She added, "I have always believed that a husband and wife partnership is a 75–25 affair. With the woman on the 75 percent side." In the same interview, Desi insisted that their biggest arguments were over the temperature of their bedroom at night.

. . .

I n the spring of 1955, the Arnazes got a new bedroom in a much bigger house. Taking yet another step that confirmed their status as Hollywood A-listers, they moved to Beverly Hills. The long commute from Chatsworth had grown more and more impractical as Desi's obligations at the studio increased. Lucy had found a big white brick Georgian house at the corner of Roxbury Drive and Lexington Road for eighty-five thousand dollars. The next-door neighbor was Jack Benny, and Jimmy Stewart lived two doors down. Rosemary Clooney and her husband, José Ferrer, were just up the block, as was the lyricist Ira Gershwin and the actress Agnes Moorehead. "They came by Ciro's the night they bought the house," George Schlatter, their friend, the Ciro's nightclub booker, recalled. "And Lucille says, 'We've just bought a house on *Roxbury*.' It was Lucy moving into the upper echelon of Beverly Hills, the upper echelon of superstars." But for both Lucy and Desi, the move was an emotional wrench, even as they acknowledged it was the practical thing to do. It meant giving up the sweet little *ranchito* they had so lovingly built together and turning the page on the happiest days of their marriage. Lucy ordered new furniture from factories in her hometown in Jamestown—flown to Los Angeles by chartered plane—and spent weeks renovating the house before the family moved in. Fred Ball was dispatched to oversee the remodeling work, including installation of state-of-the-art film projection and stereo equipment. Manufacturers provided a range of free or discounted products—sliding steel doors, patio furniture, mattresses and box springs, kitchen equipment, and glassware—in exchange for Desilu's agreement to feature their wares in magazine spreads about the new house (and sometimes complained if they did not think the requisite publicity was forthcoming).

When the big day arrived in May, Desi carried Lucy across the threshold, then stopped cold. Overnight, some water pipes in the house had broken, and the carpet was soaked, the new wallpaper ruined, and freshly plastered walls dissolving. "Desi really flipped," Lucy would recall. "As the children huddled against me in terror, he ranted, raged, stormed, kicked the walls, and then began tearing them down with his bare hands. 'Come, dears,' DeDe told the babies, 'your father is rehearsing,' and she bundled them out of the place." For Lucy, it was frightening, tangible proof of how the strain of managing their growing empire—the multiple shows, the dynamics of a changing industry, the egos of the talent he had to manage—was weighing on Desi.

His top executives agreed that it was around this time that Desi began drinking more and more heavily, not just at parties after work but starting every morning. "Desi would want 7-Up in the morning and that was not 7-Up," his secretary Johnny Aitchison recalled. "Looked like 7-Up but it wasn't 7-Up." Martin Leeds said things progressed to the point where Arnaz needed "a wake-up drink that straightened him out." "He'd come in at 9, 9:15, he'd have a daiquiri at 10:30. His blood sugar was so high that he was drunk at 11. And my instructions to the personnel were, 'Anyone of you wants to talk to Desi, you can go do it. Talk to him as close to 9 as you can. Don't talk to him later 'cause it'll create problems for you.'" Maury Thompson, a Desilu staffer, recalled, "We knew that if he asked for tomato soup in the morning we were in trouble."

Both Lucy and Desi knew that things were getting out of hand. So what did they do? They plunged ever deeper into work, giving up part of their summer vacation to make another movie for MGM.

. . .

Having sparked, and then dominated, the revolution in filmed television, Desi now had visions of branching out into feature film production. In November 1954 he signed a deal with MGM to produce two movies under the Zanra corporate banner. What's more, he proposed to shoot them with Desilu cameras and technicians at Motion Picture Center, not on the venerable MGM lot. Martin Leeds recalled the reaction of the veteran MGM business executives Benny Thau and Eddie Mannix when he and Desi floated this idea. "Mr. Mannix looked down his nose at me saying, 'What makes you think that your people can make a motion picture in the fine quality of the MGM tradition?'" Leeds remembered. "'Simple,' I said to him. 'Of the 2,300 employees we have, 2,200 are ex-MGM employees.' This was true. Television had come on so fast that the motion picture studios were hurting, and since we could employ people year-round rather than sporadically, we were able to get the best, and did."

What soon emerged, though, was trouble. The problem was that the script for the first movie to be produced was subpar. The screenplay had been kicking around MGM for years, first as a vehicle for William Powell and Myrna Loy, then for Spencer Tracy and Katharine Hepburn. Now titled *Forever, Darling*, it told the story of a research chemist, played by Desi, who is so obsessed with his work on a new mosquito repellent formula that he takes his new wife for granted.

Their marriage is ultimately saved by a guardian angel who helps them see the error of their ways during a camping trip full of slapstick misadventures. The plot was a warmed-over version not only of *I Love Lucy* but also of *The Long, Long Trailer*, which gave the whole project a cut-rate feel despite its 1.4-million-dollar Technicolor budget. Lucy and Desi had wanted Cary Grant to play the part of the angel but settled for the debonair James Mason, and to direct Lucy turned to her old boyfriend Al Hall, whose career was in marked decline. (It would be the last film he ever made.)

Despite the warning signs around the production, Desi was chuffed to think of himself as a would-be mogul, proudly telling MGM executives on the first official day of shooting in June that the production was already two days ahead of schedule because the crew had used color tests with the cast to film actual scenes that had turned out fine. Dann Cahn edited the daily rushes, sometimes working in the Arnazes' garage. But Desi also seems to have recognized the inherent weakness in the script and hired Bob Carroll and Madelyn Pugh to pump up the final scene, in which Lucy punctures a rubber raft in Yosemite National Park.

The script also included what must surely have been an uncomfortable echo for its husband-and-wife costars of the Arnazes' all-too-real marital problems. "You and Larry are drifting apart," James Mason tells Lucy's character at one point. "You started together a few years ago and then you started to travel along different paths. You're going one way and Larry's going another, and from here on, you can get further and further apart. And being apart, little quarrels take on importance and one thing leads to another until two people who really belong together are separate for good. And for the rest of their lives, they wonder how it happened, how anything so vague and mixed up could have culminated in a separation so definite. . . . Sometimes things have to get worse before they can get better. Some people don't notice the clock on the wall till it stops ticking."

• • •

Off the *Forever, Darling* set, the clock had already run down on one of Desilu's most important relationships: Philip Morris announced in the spring of 1955 that it was dropping its sponsorship of *I Love Lucy*. Since the fall of 1954, it had been splitting the burden with Procter & Gamble as *Lucy*'s ratings stalled a bit, falling into the middle of the top ten programs on the air before the Hollywood-themed episodes revived the show. *Variety* reported an unspecified "conflict" between the tobacco company and Desilu, but in truth there were cold financial calculations at play. The company believed that the high cost of sponsoring such a top-rated show was not spurring adequate sales of its cigarettes, and some analysts suggested that the program's viewers were not heavy cigarette smokers. In fact, Philip Morris's sales had been flagging since the early 1950s, and surveys by rival companies showed consumers believed its cigarettes had a "musty" taste. Eddie Feldman of the Biow Agency may have put his finger on some larger problems: the Federal Trade Commission's order forcing Philip Morris to stop claiming that doctors had found its cigarettes less irritating than other brands and a 1954 *Reader's Digest* story that publicized the dangers of smoking and its potential link to cancer. (Eventually, Philip Morris's introduction of its filtered Marlboro would revive sales.) General Foods immediately picked up Philip Morris's share of the program, but it was nevertheless one more headache for Desi.

Desilu also lost key members of its production team. Bill Asher, who had done so much to shape the show since he filmed the famous candy-making episode at the end of the first season, also took his leave in the spring of 1955, after shooting an episode in which Lucy scales the garden wall of the actor Richard Widmark's house to steal a souvenir grapefruit. (The exterior of the Arnazes' new Roxbury Drive home appeared in a few background shots.) "I left the show because I felt I had no creative growth anymore," Asher recalled. "I was very frustrated, even though all the 'Hollywood' shows were fun to do. Also, there was enough dissension on the stage that I just didn't enjoy going to work." Asher would be replaced first by James Kern, then Jerry Thorpe, and finally, at the series' end, by Desi himself.

Indeed, Lucy and Desi now sometimes fought openly on the set as they rehearsed episodes and worked out blocking. If Lucy disagreed with some business Desi suggested, she would mark it, delivering a half-hearted reading.

"You god-damned, redhead sonofabitch, if you're going to try it, you got to try it, but you're going to do it as good as you can do it, and I know what that is!" Desi would yell.

"You sonofabitch, you noticed," Lucy would retort.

"You're god-damned right I noticed," Desi fumed.

Maury Thompson, the camera coordinator, recalled how the mood had changed from the show's early days. He said that Lucy "just couldn't hold back embarrassing [Desi] in front of people. The end result was always bad. What brought it on you never knew. He stooped over once and she meant to kick him higher but she didn't and she kicked him lower and the poor man just folded. He limped around for days, just days, it was awful."

In the fall of 1955, when production resumed on *I Love Lucy* after *Forever, Darling* wrapped, Jess hired two new writers: Bob Schiller and Bob Weiskopf, who had been working for Danny Thomas. Bob Carroll and Madelyn Pugh were thrilled to have reinforcements, but the arrival of the new team heralded a more unsettling change: Jess Oppenheimer himself announced that he would be leaving at the end of the coming season. *I Love Lucy* was a well-oiled machine by now, and the challenge was not so much to keep it running but to keep it fresh. To that end, the writers devised yet another novel storyline: The Ricardos and the Mertzes would take a trip to Europe—as so many Americans were starting to do amid the prosperity of the 1950s.

This storyline, like the trip to Hollywood, offered almost infinite comic possibilities as Ricky's band tours European capitals. Lucy has trouble producing her birth certificate to get a passport; she misses the boat to England because she runs down the gangplank to kiss Little Ricky goodbye and has to be flown aboard by helicopter; she gets her head stuck in a porthole; she is arrested for using counterfeit francs in Paris; and she encounters that suavest of French-born movie stars, Charles Boyer, playing himself. Desi, too, has his winning moments, especially in a Scottish dream sequence in which a kilted Ricky manages to blend a Caledonian burr with his Cuban accent. But the unforgettable highlight is Lucy's grape-stomping in an Italian winery as she soaks up local color in an attempt to get a part in a movie called *Bitter Grapes*, only to learn too late that the title is merely metaphoric.

Desi dispatched Ed Hamilton, the head of Desilu's New York office—and the point person for its product marketing tie-ins—to see if a steamship company would help underwrite the added costs of constructing an ocean liner set back in Hollywood. Hamilton negotiated with American Export Lines, whose luxury ocean liners plied the route between New York and the Mediterranean, and the company agreed to pay twelve thousand dollars toward the creation of a replica of part of the USS *Constitution*. The episodes seemed so realistic that a British company cabled Desilu to learn when the *Constitution* would be arriving in Southampton, even though its actual route was to Genoa and Naples.

Far less enthusiastic was the reception for *Forever, Darling*. When the film opened in February 1956, MGM arranged for a massive publicity rollout—Santa Fe to Chicago, Detroit, Dallas, Cleveland, Pittsburgh, and Philadelphia—that topped what had been done for *The Long, Long Trailer*, including appearances on *The Ed Sullivan Show* and the CBS game show *What's My Line?* and a helicopter arrival in snow-covered Jamestown, New York. Lucy and Desi made a sentimental trip back to Grandpa Hunt's little house in Celoron, and Lucy fingered the curtain rod in the front hall that had held the drapes for her early drama performances. Desi planted a smacker on the lips of the newly crowned Miss Jamestown, beat out an impromptu performance on a conga drum, and serenaded a gala crowd with the *Forever, Darling* theme song, written by the Hollywood composer Bronislau Kaper and the master lyricist Sammy Cahn:

> *While other hearts go wand'ring,*
> *you'll find mine as faithful as can be . . .*
> *I made this promise, and willingly I'll keep it,*
> *Forever, forever, darling, you will find me true . . .*

The song became an Arnaz family favorite at important occasions, even if Desi could not live up to the lyrics. Neither, alas, could the movie. Radio City Music Hall judged it not up to its standards, so the New York premiere was at Loew's State. The critics were brutal. "Lucy and Desi are engaging people, but 'Forever, Darling' is every bit as terrible as it sounds," wrote William K. Zinsser in the *New York Herald Tribune*. "The script is heavy and the jokes are bad. This is quite a switch on the entertainment pattern of the day—the two stars devote their best energies to television and toss off a quickie for the movies. Movie fans deserve a better break—there are still quite a few of us."

The film lost almost two hundred thousand dollars. Its failure effectively ended Desi's aspirations to be a theatrical film producer, and MGM canceled the second movie project on the Arnazes' two-picture contract. "I haven't been in many flops in my life," Lucy herself would recall, "but this one was pretty bad."

• • •

Despite the setback, Desilu itself was still going gangbusters. Its various enterprises employed more than 3,300 people, carrying a payroll of five million dollars (close to sixty million in 2020s dollars), and had produced a total of 295 half-hour television programs during 1955, including twenty-six episodes of *I Love Lucy*, along with a summer replacement series, *Those Whiting Girls*, starring the singer Margaret Whiting and her sister, Barbara. Desilu had also filmed *High Tor*, a ninety-minute musical version of a Maxwell Anderson play, starring Bing Crosby and a twenty-year-old Julie Andrews, fresh from her Broadway debut in *The Boy Friend*.

In the spring of 1956, after filming the last of the Europe episodes, Jess Oppenheimer left Desilu. Karl Freund, the brilliant cameraman who had done so much to make the show possible, also announced that he was leaving. The company was losing its family-size start-up feeling and had become a big business. Desi took pains to tell the trade press that Oppenheimer's departure would not damage the franchise and that he himself would now become the show's producer, though not directly involved in its writing.

"I hate to see Jess go, but his leaving won't interfere in the slightest with whatever plans we make for the show," Desi said. Tensions between Jess and Desi had never really abated, and Jess was ready for a change from life with the Ricardos. "We had already taken them to Hollywood, and then Europe," he recalled. "Where were we going to take them next—to the moon?" There were tears and warm feelings when the Arnazes threw Oppenheimer an emotional farewell party under a big striped tent in the backyard of Roxbury Drive in April.

At the evening's end, Desi walked Jess and his wife down the driveway and put his hand on Oppenheimer's shoulder. "Pardner," he said, "you know, if you change your mind, and you can see it in your heart to do it, I wish you'd come back."

"I'll think about it, Desi," Jess responded, "but I don't think I will."

Oppenheimer went to NBC under an ambitious deal to develop new programming for the network, but in the end he would not match his achievements from his time on *I Love Lucy*. Oppenheimer's collaboration with Desi, fraught as it sometimes was, would remain the highlight of his career. Though he produced several live specials and would later produce successfully for other networks, he would ultimately leave NBC without getting a single series on the air.

• • •

As early as the fall of 1955, Desi had approached CBS about scaling back *I Love Lucy* from a weekly half-hour series to a monthly hour-long series, in color, that could alternate with other Desilu shows. He told the Hollywood trade press that he believed the industry trend was moving toward sixty- and ninety-minute programming. More important was the fact that he and Lucy were worn out by the weekly grind—and that *I Love Lucy* had briefly fallen to third place in the weekly ratings, behind *The Ed Sullivan Show* and the quiz show *The $64,000 Question*. But as the year ended Lucy bounced back to number one, and CBS told Desi that the longer shows would have less appeal as reruns, which the network was using to help fill gaps in its own broadcast schedule. Desi dropped the idea for the time being, but he did not forget it. In the spring of 1956, CBS announced that *Lucy* would return to the fall 1956–57 season lineup at sixty thousand dollars per episode, two and a half times the first season's cost, again cosponsored by Procter & Gamble and General Foods.

At the start of the sixth season, in the fall of 1956, the production team decided to jump little Ricky's age to make him a kindergartener so that parenthood and its challenges could become more a part of the series' plot. Up to then, Little Ricky was really a nonspeaking role played by the twin brothers Joseph and Michael Mayer. Now the Ricardos' son would have his own personality. Casting was relatively straightforward. One night while watching the orchestra leader Horace Heidt's amateur television talent show, Desi and Lucy were impressed by a pint-size drummer, barely five years old, named Keith Thibodeaux, from Lafayette, Louisiana. They instantly agreed that he would make a perfect Little Ricky. Thibodeaux's father joined Kenny Morgan in the Desilu PR department and little Keith himself (rechristened by Desi with the stage name Richard Keith) joined Lucie and Desi Jr. as a playmate and semi-sibling on the weekends and during the show's summer break.

In yet another bid to keep the aging show fresh, the writers decided that the Ricardos and the Mertzes would move to the suburbs, specifically to the fictional town of Danfield, Connecticut. This allowed for a much bigger, more elegant main set: a country living room with beamed ceiling, a large fireplace, and early-American-style furniture not unlike the pieces that had decorated the Desilu ranch. The move would allow for all manner of new plot points: buying the house, dealing with Ricky's school, meeting new neighbors, getting involved in local civic affairs.

But before leaving Manhattan, the Ricardos would have interactions with two big guest stars: Bob Hope and Orson Welles. These shows, filmed in the early summer of 1956 and aired that fall, reflected a sea change in the ethos of the show. By now, not only had Lucille Ball become the nation's leading television star, but Lucy Ricardo had become a pop culture personage in her own right. The plotlines of the Hope and Welles shows presume that the world knows that Lucy Ricardo is almost as famous as Lucille Ball herself, and infamous for getting celebrities in trouble when they cross her path. The show was by now so universally familiar that it could effectively make references to its own greatest hits. In the Bob Hope episode, Lucy is attending a baseball game at Yankee Stadium when Hope sits down nearby, and she realizes that it's the perfect opportunity to buttonhole him about appearing at Ricky's fancy new nightclub, Club Babalú (a development that itself reflected Desi's own growing status in real life). Lucy is persuaded that Hope hasn't called Ricky back about a possible engagement because she's a jinx. "You don't suppose Bob heard about me and that's the reason he didn't call you?" she asks, worrying that she has become "the scourge of two continents" following her European misadventures. And in the Orson Welles episode, Lucy has visions of performing Shakespeare with the famous actor-director, while he simply wants her help as assistant for his magician's act for a benefit at the nightclub. When Ricky tries to persuade Welles that he doesn't want to get onstage with Lucy at all, he asks incredulously, "You mean she really did all those things in Europe and Hollywood? And they call me a character!"

(Welles was indeed a character. In early June, around the same time he shot the *I Love Lucy* episode, Desilu also filmed a pilot for an anthology series to star Welles, who bunked in the Arnazes' guesthouse on Roxbury, ran up a huge expense account, and turned a stay that was supposed to last three weeks into three months.)

Even in its sixth season, *I Love Lucy* remained a powerhouse. On October 2, 1956, no less a fan than J. Edgar Hoover wrote with praise for the new season. "Dear Lucy: I tuned in last evening and caught your first broadcast of the new season," the FBI director wrote. "You, Desi and Bob Hope were simply great, but all three of you had better watch out because I think little Ricky will soon be stealing the show."

But there was a much bigger development afoot that fall. In the 1955–56 and 1956–57 seasons combined, Desilu's total output of content was 691 half hours, not counting pilots. The lineup of its own shows included *I Love Lucy*, *Our Miss Brooks*, *December Bride*, plus *Whirlybirds*, a new drama about helicopter pilots, and *Sheriff of Cochise*, a Western. The shows that rented Desilu space included the programs of Danny Thomas, Red Skelton, and Betty White. But with size had come ever-larger financial commitments, and cash flow and flexibility were becoming a concern.

And so in October 1956 the Arnazes took a momentous step: they agreed to sell back to CBS the first 179 episodes of *I Love Lucy* for $4.5 million. The language of the sale agreement conveyed its sweeping scope, in which Desilu surrendered to CBS "all right, title and interest of every kind and nature whatsoever in and to the literary, artistic and intellectual property known as 'I LOVE LUCY.' " The Arnazes also received an additional one million dollars from the network in exchange for an exclusive contract for their services for another ten years (some sources say until 1970). Part of the total windfall (about one million dollars) went back to CBS to repurchase the 25 percent share of Desilu that Desi had sold to the network at the beginning of *I Love Lucy*—giving the Arnazes full ownership of their company—but the remainder was bounteous enough. For its part, CBS was glad to be rid of its partial ownership of Desilu, thus ending its corporate entanglement with Desi, who was increasingly portrayed by Martin Leeds as unreliable because of his drinking and episodic inattention to company affairs.

When seen over a longer time horizon, the deal would turn out to be a great bargain for CBS. But at the time it made good sense for the Arnazes. There was not yet a prime-time syndication market for rerun television programming, nor had anyone envisioned rerunning *I Love Lucy* episodes in the comparatively dead daytime hours—which would make the show famous to future generations. "We extrapolated out the number of shows that would have to be sold in markets untold to come up to net the company—and Lucy and Desi—the amount CBS was willing to pay," recalled Ed Holly, Desilu's chief financial officer, explaining how the hard-cash dollar figure dangled by CBS contrasted with what amounted to a blue-sky fantasy of potential future returns. "As it turns out, it was probably the worst deal ever made," at least for Lucy and Desi. "But mathematically, it was the only way to go. Because there was no market." After all, Desilu's lawyer Art Manella took pains to point out that the company could not have exploited the shows on its own, because the distribution rights belonged to CBS.

But at least one person on the creative team had a different view. "I had a hunch that repeats of *I Love Lucy* would be around longer than most people expected," Jess Oppenheimer recalled. "So when CBS offered to buy out my ownership interest as well, I told them I wasn't interested. I had been lucky enough to be part of a once-in-a-lifetime phenomenon, and my instincts told me to let it ride." His family is letting it ride to this day.

• • •

The new episodes that aired starting in January 1957 chronicled the Ricardos' move to Connecticut. These shows detail the usual travails of moving: sorting out furniture, bidding farewell to East 68th Street, and missing the Mertzes—who would soon join Lucy and Ricky in their suburban adventures, moving into their guesthouse. The set for the new Connecticut house was dressed with furniture contributed by the manufacturer as a promotional move, and at first the position of the living room fireplace stymied the crew's attempts to arrange the new pieces until Desi himself suggested placing two sofas back to back. Plot points echoed the Arnazes' past agrarian experiences at the Desilu ranch, as when the Ricardos and the Mertzes decide to raise chickens to save money on eggs. Soon they are so overwhelmed by the rapid growth of their flock that they exchange five hundred chicks for two hundred laying hens. Just as Lucy's real-life farming efforts had cost more than they saved, the "Mertz-cardo" egg hatchery yields disappointing results: six eggs in the first two weeks, at a cost of eighteen dollars per egg. "I should have raised something that I knew about—like sugarcane," Ricky exclaims, threatening to sell the whole flock. Aiming to give their birds a boost, and salvage their husbands' friendship, Lucy and Ethel purchase five dozen store-bought eggs, with plans to put them in the nests and let Fred and Ricky find them. But the girls are forced to hide the contraband in their blouses instead because Fred is chopping wood near the hen house, and then Ricky turns out to be home unexpectedly, wanting to practice the tango for Little Ricky's school PTA benefit. Lucy manages to elude his grasp until the dance's final clinch, when the raw eggs smash catastrophically. This scene produced the series' single-longest laugh—sixty-five seconds. Jay Sandrich recalled that that played as an eternity in the finished film, and editors actually had to shorten it before broadcast.

On April 4, 1957, the crew filmed the last of the season's episodes,

"The Ricardos Dedicate a Statue," in which Lucy accidentally destroys a Minuteman statue for Yankee Doodle Day in Danfield and has to pose frozen as the sculpture herself. Desi Jr. played a child in a crowd scene—the only time he appeared on the show. But this episode was more significant because it marked the final thirty-minute episode of *I Love Lucy*. Desi had gone to New York to tell Bill Paley once again that he and Lucy definitely wanted to stop doing the half hours. "What are you talking about?" Paley demanded. But on April 8, CBS announced that the half-hour series would end, though there was still no word on what might come for the fall season. Desi had at least a degree of self-awareness of the toll his job was taking on him. "I was working much too hard," he would recall years later. "My health was beginning to deteriorate. I knew something would have to give." He went to the trusted Dr. Marc Rabwin for a checkup—and told the doctor the partial truth about his situation. "I'm at the studio at seven or seven thirty AM, don't get home until after dinner," he remembered saying, "then I have a lot of paperwork to take care of. I hardly ever see my children unless it's just before they go to school and, if I'm lucky, during some weekends. I'm all tied up in a knot most of the time, and in order to untie it and keep going I'm beginning to drink too much at times."

Desi brought Ed Holly, the company's finance chief, along to the doctor's office at Cedars of Lebanon to hear his verdict—which included fear of possible liver damage owing to Desi's drinking. "And he was doing it, I think, to just help reinforce the word, and to provide more pressure on himself to try to do what he was being told that he had to do," Holly recalled. Rabwin told Arnaz that his colon was full of diverticuli—small pouches that can form in the wall of the intestine—and that he was headed for a colostomy bag if he did not change his ways. He recommended a relaxing summer off, in the usual rented house in Del Mar where the Rabwins themselves had a beach place. But Desi angrily resisted acknowledging the full depth and nature of his problem, exploding when Ed Holly urged him to read the

"Big Book" of Alcoholics Anonymous. "I remember putting a brown paper wrapper around the cover so that when I took it to his office, no one would see what I had," Holly said. "As soon as I mentioned the word AA, in his usual Cuban, demonstrative way, 'What are you talking about? I don't have a problem! You've got the problem!' et cetera, you know. So that's as far as it got. It's obvious there was no point in saying, 'Here, you read the book.'"

In 1957, Alcoholics Anonymous was not yet the mass-culture institution it would later become. There were no celebrity-studded rehabilitation hospitals and no ritual of public media confession and redemption. Yes, some films and plays—like *The Lost Weekend* and *Come Back, Little Sheba*—had presented alcoholism sympathetically and compassionately and had made the case for its status as a disease in need of medical treatment like any other. But to much—if not most—of America, alcoholism was still seen as a deeply stigmatizing moral failure. Even if Desi's macho self-image would have allowed him the introspection and self-knowledge needed to get better, he would have faced a high bar in seeking treatment for his drinking. So he did nothing. Indeed, years later, Desi Jr., after his own long experience with sobriety, would suggest: "That's when he realized the emptiness—at the crest of his success. He didn't stop drinking. He didn't know what the real poison was. This is a temporary life."

CBS eventually assented to the Arnazes' insistence on making *I Love Lucy* an occasional hour-long show—for what would end up being five episodes in the 1957–58 season—interspersed with a variety of other Monday night programming of the network's choice. The Ford Motor Company agreed to sponsor the new version for two hundred thousand dollars an episode, to introduce its new 1958 models, including the company's heavily promoted new centerpiece line: the Edsel. That would turn out to have been an ominous sign.

Desiderio Alberto Arnaz y de Acha was raised as a prince in prerevolutionary Cuba, with every conceivable childhood privilege. *Lucille Ball and Desi Arnaz Papers, Music Division, Library of Congress. Photo used by permission from the Estate of Desi Arnaz III*

From the beginning, young Desi (in sailor hat) appeared at public events and ceremonies, like this Soap Box Derby race in Santiago de Cuba's main square. *Lucille Ball and Desi Arnaz Papers, Music Division, Library of Congress. Photo used by permission from the Estate of Desi Arnaz III*

As mayor of Santiago, Desi's father modernized the city and built major public works, like this grand alameda on the waterfront.

DESIDERIO ARNAZ

We had the distinction of having an orchestra leader in our midst for the afternoon classes this past year. Desi hails from Santiago de Cuba, although he had to pull out a map to prove it. He possesses a splendid voice and every now and then lends it to the choir. We voted him the politest Senior on account of his very precise Cuban mannerisms.

As a high school senior in Miami, Desi was already noted for his musical abilities, as well as for his Latin charm. *Photo used by permission from the Estate of Desi Arnaz III*

The popular bandleader Xavier Cugat, the "King of the Rumba," was a crucial early career mentor, teaching Desi skills of showmanship and management. *Lucille Ball and Desi Arnaz Papers, Music Division, Library of Congress. Photo used by permission from the Estate of Desi Arnaz III*

In nightclubs in Miami and New York, Desi helped make the conga into a popular dance craze, and drew the cream of celebrity clientele—including the movie star Errol Flynn (in white dinner jacket at left). *Bettmann/Getty Images*

Polly Adler was the most notorious madam in Depression-era New York, running a brothel that drew the elites of show business and society alike. Desi became a regular customer. *New York Daily News Archive via Getty Images*

Desi, with his costar Diosa Costello, became an overnight Broadway sensation in Rodgers and Hart's *Too Many Girls* in 1939. *Used by permission. All rights reserved, Playbill Inc.*

Desi soon went to Hollywood to make the movie version of the musical, where he met his costar and future wife, Lucille Ball.

By the time she met Desi, Lucille had already made more than sixty films—but was not yet a redhead. Desi thought she was "a hunk of a woman." *Photo by Gene Lester/Archive Photos/ Getty Images*

Desi and Lucy were thunderstruck at first sight, and their whirlwind courtship was passionate and tempestuous from the start. *mptvimages.com*

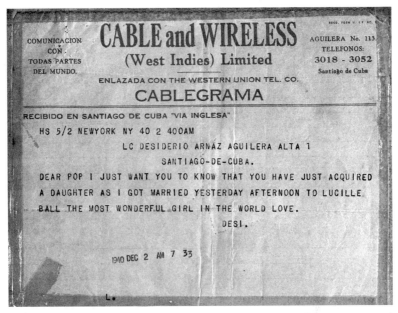

The Arnazes eloped to Greenwich, Connecticut, on November 30, 1940, and an elated Desi shared the happy news with his father. *Lucille Ball and Desi Arnaz Papers, Music Division, Library of Congress*

The newlyweds christened their San Fernando Valley ranch "Desilu," where they raised livestock and vegetables and filled the cozy house with family, friends, and happy times. *mptvimages.com*

Desi joined Hollywood's biggest stars to sell war bonds on the "Victory Caravan" in 1942, but prompted ill will on the road with his relentless philandering. *Bettmann/Getty Images*

Desi struggled to win good roles in Hollywood, but his compelling performance in *Bataan* for MGM in 1943 was one of his best. *Courtesy of Everett Collection*

Ball-Arnaz Collection,
Library of Congress

To keep him at home in Los Angeles, Lucy helped Desi get a job as musical director of Bob Hope's popular network radio show, where he was often the butt of cringeworthy ethnic humor.

Courtesy of Special Collections and Archives, Georgia State University Library

For all of their adult lives, Lucy and Desi both had financial and emotional responsibility for the care of their mothers, Desiree Eveline "DeDe" Ball and Dolores "Lolita" Arnaz, which sometimes caused tension in their marriage. *Photo used by permission from the Estate of Desi Arnaz III*

https://commons.wikimedia.org/wiki/ File:Lucille_Ball_and_Desi_Arnaz_ with_mothers_1952.jpg

To persuade a skeptical CBS that the public would accept him and Lucy as a performing team, Desi arranged an old-fashioned vaudeville tour with his band in movie houses in big cities around the country. *Osvaldo Salas*

Desilu proudly introduced the cast and crew of *I Love Lucy* in full-page advertisements in the Hollywood trade papers, and the Arnazes soon had a hit on their hands.

WELCOME ABOARD

The LUCILLE BALL–DESI ARNAZ SHOW

S.S. DESILU

"I LOVE LUCY"

CBS-TV MONDAY
OCTOBER 15, 1951
INITIAL SHOW

Presented by
PHILIP MORRIS
America's
Finest Cigarette

with VIVIAN VANCE ● WILLIAM FRAWLEY
and the DESI ARNAZ Orchestra

Producer
JESS OPPENHEIMER

Director
MARC DANIELS

Writers
J. OPPENHEIMER
MADELYN PUGH
BOB CARROLL, JR.

Director Photography
KARL FREUND, A.S.C.

Production Manager
AL SIMON

Art Director
LARRY CUNEO

Film Operations Manager
GEORGE FOX
(Filmed with the George Fox "Q" Track System)

Music
WILBUR HATCH
(Conducting the Desi Arnaz Orchestra)

Casting
MERCEDES MANZANARES

Sound
GLEN GLENN

Stage Manager
HERB BROWAR

Choreography
LEE SCOTT

Wardrobe
DELLA FOX

Announcer
JOHNNY JACOBS

Makeup
HAL KING
(Courtesy of Max Factor)

Production Assistant
EMILY DANIELS

Office Manager
FELICE GREENE

Script Clerk
MAURY THOMPSON

A DESILU PRODUCTION *

DESI ARNAZ — President
ANDREW G. HICKOX — Secretary Treasurer

LUCILLE BALL — Vice President
KEN MORGAN — Public Relations Director

Exclusive Representation — DON W. SHARPE
* Other Productions in preparation

The Desilu Playhouse
6633 Romaine St.
Hollywood 38, Calif.

Production Office
General Service Studios
1040 N. Las Palmas Ave.
Hollywood 38, Calif.

Business Office
7046 Hollywood Blvd.
Hollywood 38, Calif.

Our thanks to James Nasser of General Service Studios for his cooperation in converting a Hollywo
Sound Stage into the NATION'S FIRST TELEVISION FILM-THEATRE.

The show's head writer and producer, Jess Oppenheimer, and his colleagues Madelyn Pugh and Bob Carroll Jr. created the adventures of Lucy and Ricky Ricardo each week.
mptvimages.com

The Academy Award–winning cinematographer Karl Freund devised a revolutionary system of overhead "flat" lighting that allowed for filming of the show with three cameras at once. *mptv_DA_2: © Ruth Orkin/mptvimages.com*

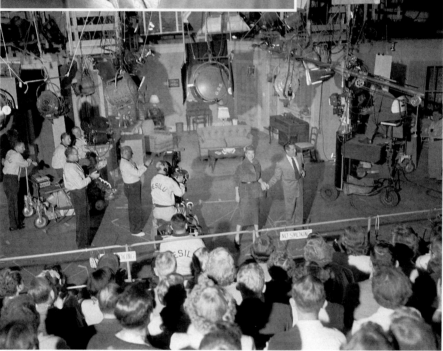

Desi arranged to film the show in sequence, like a play, in front of a live audience arrayed on wood-and-metal bleachers on a cavernous Hollywood soundstage. *mptv_DA_3: © Sid Avery/mptvimages.com*

The show's original opening credits featured cartoon stick figures of Lucy and Desi (created by the animation team of William Hanna and Joseph Barbera) advertising the program's sole sponsor: Philip Morris cigarettes. *Photo stills from* I Love Lucy *courtesy of CBS Broadcasting Inc.*

LIFE

STALIN'S GHASTLY SECRETS
HOW HE WON AND HELD ABSOLUTE POWER
BY AN EX-GENERAL OF DREADED N. K. V. D.

ALSO—12 GREAT AMERICAN PREACHERS

TV'S FIRST FAMILY
LUCILLE BALL, DESI ARNAZ
DESI IV, LUCY DESIREE

20 CENTS

APRIL 6, 1953

REG. U. S. PAT. OFF.

The birth of Desi Arnaz IV on January 19, 1953, was front-page news worldwide, and *LIFE* magazine, America's biggest picture window onto the news, eventually got the first intimate portrait of television's first family. *Copyright © 1953 Shutterstock*

Lucy and Desi met reporters in a news conference at their ranch to answer questions about Lucy's long-ago Communist Party voter registration, defusing the biggest crisis of their careers. *mptvimages.com*

The president of Desilu Productions at work in his office, where his growing responsibilities in the expanding company went hand in hand with Desi's increasing and debilitating dependence on alcohol. *Leonard McCombe/The LIFE Picture Collection/Shutterstock*

Desi's relationship with his father endured a long period of estrangement following his parents' divorce, but the two grew close again in later years. Here three generations of Desiderios posed proudly together. *Photo used by permission from the Estate of Desi Arnaz III*

Desilu's purchase of RKO Pictures' studios made it the largest motion picture plant in Hollywood, and the largest producer of television content in the world. *mptvimages.com*

Despite the troubled state of their marriage, Lucy and Desi still had palpable onscreen chemistry as performers, as shown in this drum dialogue in the debut of the hour-long *The Lucille Ball-Desi Arnaz Show* in 1957. *Photo stills from* I Love Lucy *courtesy of CBS Broadcasting Inc.*

A tipsy Tallulah Bankhead's guest appearance on the new show's second episode was a fraught experience in rehearsal, but a success on the air. *mptvimages.com*

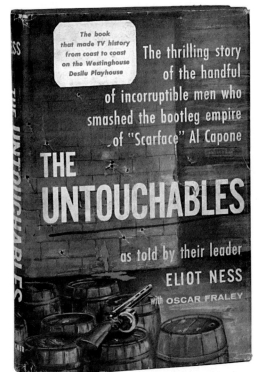

The Untouchables sparked the ire of Italian Americans and J. Edgar Hoover—and the first serious debate about violence on television—but it was a ratings smash and commercial success for Desilu.

In his forced retirement, Desi still enjoyed relaxing and fishing with close friends like his Del Mar, California, neighbor Jimmy Durante. *Leonard McCombe/The LIFE Picture Collection/Shutterstock*

Desi's last decades brought many personal and professional disappointments and a spiral into addiction and depression, but he kept up a gallant front and a spirit of *cubanidad*.
National Comedy Center Archives, Jamestown, NY

thirteen

CATASTROPHIC SUCCESS

Desi had fought hard to persuade CBS to allow the new hour-long format. In the spring of 1957 the network had offered Desilu eighty thousand dollars per new episode, and thirty thousand dollars per rerun, if he and Lucy would maintain the half-hour show—this at a time when the average cost of a top-quality sitcom was around forty-eight thousand dollars per episode. "When I turned that down," Desi remembered, "they finally realized I wasn't kidding." But he also realized the stakes at play with the new venture. "They not only have to be good," he said of the hour-long shows, "they have to be great."

Still, Desi was firm in his conviction that it was time to shake things up. "You've got to change in this business," he insisted. "You can't afford to sit still. I would rather make a big change while we are still ahead. It would be ridiculous for us to wait until people got sick and tired of the regular half hour every Monday night. We have been the luckiest show on the air, but we've worked for it. I can honestly say we have never done a really bad show in six years and one hundred and eighty shows. We threw out only two scripts that whole time and started again. What other program ever had writers with a record like that?"

Desi had high ambitions for the hour-long shows, bolstered by the Ford Motor Company's investment of $2.5 million. The new programs would still be shot with multiple cameras, but sometimes on more than one soundstage and not always completely in front of a live audience in continuity, to allow for more complex, feature film–like scenarios. The actors and crew would sometimes go on location and film outdoors, with higher production values that would open up the limited scope of the soundstage. "We'll be able to move around more and won't have to keep up with that weekly continuity," Desi explained. "Each show can be a complete and different story without having to be in that apartment every week or in a home or all that." The new episodes would also continue the half-hour series' recent practice of welcoming big-name guest stars.

At the same time, business was booming at Desilu. By early 1957, the company was producing or renting soundstages for a total of seventeen series and had to lease additional studio space at Pathe, Paramount, and Fox-Western. That same spring Desilu sold *The Walter Winchell File*, an anthology series of the columnist's adventures, to ABC—despite Lucy's objections to doing business with the man who had caused her such heartache just a few years before. The only bit of bad news came in March, when *I Love Lucy* was bumped from its number one Nielsen ranking by the quiz show *Twenty-One*, then enjoying the winning run of Columbia University's Charles Van Doren, whose answers would turn out to have been coached in a major scandal for the industry.

As if Desi were not busy enough, at the end of March he opened the Desi Arnaz Western Hills Hotel in Indian Wells, outside Palm Springs. He had built the hotel as a retort to the Thunderbird Country Club's restrictive admissions policies. He arranged a preview party

that flew the press from Hollywood to Palm Springs and then by helicopter to the Indian Wells Country Club adjoining the hotel. Each
of its forty-two rooms had its own television, "refrigerated air condi-
tioning," a built-in cocktail bar, and a private patio, the *Daily Enterprise* of Riverside reported. Built in an angular mid-century modern
style, the hotel featured a cocktail lounge with a sunken bar and a
stage above (a bit like the arrangement at the old La Conga in Miami
Beach), along with two swimming pools, one for children and the
other for adults. The total cost was $850,000, or about $20,000 per
room. It would be managed by Frank Bogert, the former manager of
both Thunderbird and the Racquet Club, a favored Hollywood retreat
in Palm Springs. "We won't discriminate against Gentiles, Jews, or
Cubans," Desi promised. The bar specialized in cocktails drawn from
Desi's personal Cuban recipes, and the house orchestra was filled with
players from his own band. This was Desi's first real-estate venture
(though not his last), and his lack of expertise in the field—and eventually his inattention—would combine to make the hotel a mixed bag
as a business proposition.

But his core business was humming. The first episode of the new
hour-long series that would now be called *The Lucille Ball–Desi Arnaz
Show* (later renamed *The Lucy–Desi Comedy Hour* in reruns) was shot
in June 1957. Its premise was to tell the story of how the Ricardos met
and fell in love. The higher budget was immediately apparent on-
screen, with elaborate and realistic sets and period costumes. A fourth
camera was added to deal with complexities. The show begins with
the Arnazes' real-life friend, the Hollywood columnist Hedda Hopper, arriving at the Ricardos' house in Connecticut to interview them
about how their romance started. The tale then unfolds in an extended
flashback from 1940, as the young Lucille McGillicuddy, a stenogra-
pher, takes a cruise to Havana with a colleague played by Ann Sothern
(Lucy's real-life old pal). The two have embarked on their trip in hopes
of meeting men when they run into a pair of honeymooners, Fred and

Ethel Mertz (with Bill Frawley sporting a hilarious, bushy toupee), on-board. The other passengers include the crooner Rudy Vallee, playing himself. When the girls land in Havana, they meet two Cubans who run a tourist sightseeing service—Ricky Ricardo and Carlos Garcia, the latter played by the veteran Latin movie star Cesar Romero. Ricky's real ambition is to become a musician in America, and Lucy success-fully persuades Vallee to give him a job in his band. Predictable mis-adventures follow, but Lucy and Ricky are happily paired up by the episode's end.

Whatever the state of the Arnazes' real marriage, their chemis-try in the episode is palpable. "You know, you're very cute when you smile," Ricky says as he buys Lucy a bouquet of violets from a strolling vender in the nightclub where he has taken her. In a sexy, charming scene, they flirt by pounding drums to each other in a kind of percus-sive call-and-response conversation, Ricky with a conga strapped over his shoulder and Lucy at a big round drum that doubles as a cabaret table. Ricky loosens his tie and moves in for a kiss, which Lucy mod-estly evades, before the drumming gets more and more intense until she finally demands, "What did we say, what did we say?"

When the episode was edited, it clocked in at seventy-five minutes, and Desi didn't want to cut it. CBS told him in no uncertain terms that the network did not air shows lasting one hour and fifteen minutes and that *The United States Steel Hour* had to start at ten o'clock. Going over the heads of CBS executives, Desi called U.S. Steel. He assured them how well their program would do with the strong lead-in from *The Lucille Ball–Desi Arnaz Show*. To everyone's surprise, U.S. Steel agreed, provided that Ford paid for the extra fifteen minutes. Desi promised to appear at the 10:14 mark and urge viewers to stay tuned. Ford even gave him one of its spiffy new Thunderbird convertibles in the bargain. "Where else could it happen except in America that a former Cuban bandleader could get U.S. Steel to move back 15 minutes!" one indus-try magazine exclaimed.

. . .

For the second hour-long episode, initially envisioned to be shot early that summer, Desi took aim at a much bigger-name guest star: Lucille's onetime drama school classmate Bette Davis, who at that point had appeared in only one or two television programs. Davis insisted on rich terms: twenty thousand dollars for a twelve-day rehearsal period plus the filming—and equal billing with Desi and Lucy themselves. Lucy was thrilled, and the Arnazes agreed, even acceding to Davis's demand that Desilu pay her airfare back to her house in Maine if she left Los Angeles within ten days of finishing the episode. But in late June, Davis fell and cracked a vertebra at her rented home in Brentwood and was then thrown from a horse and broke an arm. She was forced to drop out, and filming was postponed.

The fallback choice for the guest-star role was another diva of stage and screen, Tallulah Bankhead, who had originated the role of Regina Giddens in Lillian Hellman's *The Little Foxes* on Broadway—the part Davis later immortalized in the film version. Bankhead was a sexually omnivorous, alcoholic, exhibitionistic, larger-than-life character with a deep, distinctive Alabama drawl that the playwright and actor Emlyn Williams described as "steeped as deep in sex as the human voice can go without drowning." She was the daughter of a onetime speaker of the House of Representatives and had left a trail of lovers of both genders from New York to Hollywood. She described herself as "seething with personality," and the lyricist Howard Dietz once quipped that "a day away from Tallulah is like a month in the country."

The plot of the new episode had Bankhead playing herself, moving in next door to the Ricardos and the Mertzes in Danfield. Lucy eventually cons her into appearing in the local PTA benefit play, which Bankhead takes over, playing an Elizabethan "quin," as Ricky pronounces it. Lucy is so jealous that Tallulah has stolen her thunder that she has Ethel feed her strawberry sauce, which causes the queen to break out in hives and the play to collapse in comic chaos. The Arnazes were delighted to have snared Bankhead but were less enchanted when she showed up for the start of rehearsals on September 15.

"Tallulah was half-crocked all through that whole week of rehearsals and would never give us a good rehearsal," Desi would recall. Bankhead herself was blasé to the point of affected incoherence. "They had this plot," she told the press. "They were living in Connecticut, or *somewhere*, and rehearsing a play for the PTA, *whatever* that is."

After the dress rehearsal, there was a production conference. "We all assembled in Desi's office for notes, and the big topic was going to be, 'What are we going to do about Tallulah?'" Madelyn Pugh recalled. "Guest stars weren't invited. We all took our seats, and just as we were about to start, in came Tallulah, saying brightly, 'You didn't invite me, but I'm coming anyway.'" There was an awkward pause, which Lucy sought to fill by admiring Bankhead's cardigan sweater, which had fake pearls and gold beads running down the front. Tallulah promptly took it off and handed it to Lucy, at which point Vivian Vance cracked, "I'm glad you didn't admire the slacks," whereupon Bankhead shed those, too. Accounts differ on whether Bankhead was wearing anything else but a short teddy that left nothing to the imagination. "I have blacked out on what happened next," Madelyn recalled. "I do remember that to everyone's relief, Tallulah was wearing lace-edged panties, and I think Desi said we didn't need to have a note session after all."

In the middle of all this excitement, an issue much bigger than Bankhead's underwear was in play. For some time, with seventeen shows now in production, Desilu had been running out of space and had been forced to rent soundstages to accommodate the demand. Back in May, Desi had begun tentative negotiations to solve that problem in a dramatic way: by buying RKO Pictures' studios, the very place where he and Lucy had met and fallen in love as contract players seventeen years before. In the years since, RKO had undergone a shifting series of owners (including the reclusive tycoon Howard Hughes) and several reversals of fortune. It was now owned by the General Tire and Rubber Company, which was looking to sell. The package included not only the company's main studio, adjoining the Paramount Pictures lot on Melrose Avenue in Hollywood, but also a satellite location, the old Selznick Studios in Culver City, with its famous forty-acre backlot where *Gone with the Wind*, *King Kong*, and other classics had been filmed. All of RKO's physical assets—props, sets, office furniture, equipment, everything but its film library and the rights to unproduced projects—were up for grabs. The price: $6.5 million.

In September, Dan O'Shea, the former longtime Selznick executive who was now managing the RKO assets, called Desi to report that there was pressure to close the deal by year's end for tax reasons. So in the midst of dealing with their mercurial guest star, Desi, Martin Leeds, Ed Holly, and other top Desilu executives began frantic discussions to see if they could swing the deal. Desilu had about five hundred thousand dollars in cash on hand from the sale of *I Love Lucy* to CBS and had paid off its loan for the purchase of Motion Picture Center. Eventually, O'Shea said that RKO would sell for a two-million-dollar down payment, with the balance on credit. He gave Desi an exclusive twenty-four-hour window before he would solicit other buyers.

With the clock ticking, Desi secured the promise of a two-million-dollar loan from Desilu's regular creditor, the Bank of America, and talked O'Shea down to a purchase price of $6,150,000. Desi and his colleagues felt confident that Desilu could quickly recoup the purchase price in soundstage rentals. This seemed just the opportunity for the growth that Desilu needed. At 9 p.m. on September 27, the Arnazes were between the second and third acts of shooting the Bankhead episode when O'Shea called to say that RKO had approved the deal.

Accounts differ on whether it was Ed Holly or Desi, still in his Elizabethan knee breeches and plumed hat, who came onto the set to tell Lucy the news. She had not been kept abreast of the deepening negotiations. Ed Holly recalled that, at the last moment, Desi asked him to explain the deal to Lucy. Holly took her aside in the middle of a scene with Vivian and pulled her into her dressing room. "She understood, asked a lot of the right questions," Holly said. "She finally said, 'Is this your recommendation?' I said yes. She said, 'Then go do it.'" Jay Sandrich, by now the show's assistant director, said that when Desi gave Lucy the final word that their offer had been accepted, "Her reaction was pretty much, 'What do you need this for?' I never understood if Lucy was unhappy with the economics of it, or that Desi would be working so hard. I did have the feeling that here was a man who was proud of his accomplishment and didn't get much satisfaction from it."

For his part, Ed Holly said simply: "Lucy was stunned. I think that the initial reaction was shock. She knew what she was doing. There was no question about that, but when we said, 'It's done, you own it,' she didn't quite know how to react. She was happy, but she was really frightened. But Desi was so great with his ability to put his arm around her and say, 'Hey, babe, it's going to be great. Don't worry about it.'"

In the filming that night, Bankhead delivered a letter-perfect performance, never missing a line, and "was nothing short of magnificent," Desi remembered. But Tallulah had so unnerved the rest of the company with her week's antics that Lucy herself stumbled a time or two, her anxiety doubtless compounded by the huge decision she and Desi had just made.

When added to Motion Picture Center, the deal gave Desilu three separate lots, thirty-six soundstages, and more than four hundred and fifty offices—a million square feet of space over sixty-three acres in three locations—more than Paramount, Warner Bros., Fox, or MGM, making it the largest motion picture and television production plant in the world. "We didn't get as big," Desi recalled, "we got the biggest." Indeed, the deal comported with Desi's unshakable conviction that the company had to grow to survive and with his vision that TV's future was unlimited. Since that night in Miami when he hammered a motley crew of musicians into a conga band, his experience had shown him that risk would be rewarded, and he was now taking his biggest risk of all. Yes, the purchase would stretch Desilu's resources, but Desi had no doubt that it was a good investment. If worse came to worst, Desi had a backup plan. He knew that Jules Roth, the owner of the adjoining Hollywood Memorial Park cemetery, was running out of space for graves, and Desilu could always sell some of its real estate to him.

The next day, the Arnazes toured their new domain. "Desi was a delight when he bought RKO," Vivian Vance remembered. "He behaved like a child who'd been given a playhouse overflowing with toys." Lucy was daunted by the dust and decay on the old lot but fascinated by the warehouses full of props, including the miniature model that had come to life in stop-motion animation to make *King Kong*, and she was awestruck to find that the wardrobe department still held gowns worn by her old friend and idol Carole Lombard—and even a couple of her own from *Roberta* and *The Big Street*. Now Lucy herself was the biggest star on the RKO lot, and she claimed the old RKO dressing room bungalow that had belonged to Ginger Rogers in their days there together twenty years before; she painted the interior yellow and white.

As for Desi, he may now have become the master of a vast real estate and creative empire. But he could never forget for a moment that the company's single most precious asset was his wife. One day not long after the Arnazes bought RKO, Lucy slipped on some cables on the soundstage during a rehearsal, and as Desi helped her up unhurt, he turned to his worried production staff and warned, "Amigos, if anything happens to her, we're all in the shrimp business."

The business pages were full of Desilu's exploits, but the television critics were not overly impressed with the new hour-long format of the *Lucy* show, which debuted on November 6. The *Hollywood Reporter* summed up the prevailing reaction to the seventy-five-minute Cuba episode: "Maybe we were expecting too much but this is still painfully thin situation comedy with much studio laughter made over thin jokes and fancy mugging." Critical reaction to the Bankhead episode, which aired a month later, was similarly muted, but it still ranked as the fourth-highest-rated program of December.

The fourth episode, featuring Desi's old fling Betty Grable and her husband, the bandleader Harry James, fared no better with the critics. "Might it not be better to first write a solid comedy script punching up the Ball-Arnaz talents and then hire star guests (if needed) for added impact?" the *Hollywood Reporter* asked. But it, too, was a ratings smash—the second-highest-ranked show on the air that whole month.

Yet the move to the hour-long *Lucy* format had done nothing at all to ease the Arnazes' feeling of burnout—especially not Desi's. In fact, he was busier than ever behind the scenes and had his hands full managing the implications of the RKO acquisition. Lucy's brother, Fred Ball, had joined Desilu in 1954 to manage the operations of the Motion Picture Center property, and now he assumed responsibility for the much larger RKO lot on Gower Street as well. "There's a lot of work to be done, because Desilu was growing by way of taking on companies who wanted studio space," he recalled. "And we were providing not only studio space but a service—a budgeting service, a management service, and so forth. The offices at RKO were a disaster. Every office needed refurbishing—every stairway, every parking lot, everything in the studio needed work."

In December, Mayor Arnaz wrote to "My dearest Lucille," insisting that he loved her "like my own daughter" but going on to deliver a lecture on the pressures his son was under: "The responsibility that Desi is carrying on his shoulders and all the new business he is undertaking reminds me of my youth when I had great responsibility to the people of my own country, and in this instance is when a man has to be very careful of every movement, even in his private life (it happened to me). When you are down, no one knows you, but when you get to the top there are a lot of selfish, envious people that try to break you. That is why you have to be very careful of what you do, as the world has their eyes on you, waiting for an opportunity to destroy all your work and sacrifice."

. . .

Mayor Arnaz's letter landed soon after a period of emotional introspection in the Arnazes' marriage, coming just as the RKO deal was negotiated and concluded. Earlier that fall or late summer, Lucy had traveled to New York to see her sometime marriage counselor, Norman Vincent Peale. He had introduced her to his longtime colleague, the improbably named psychiatrist Dr. Smiley Blanton, with whom he had founded the American Foundation of Religion and Psychiatry, an organization that blended Christian doctrine with psychoanalytic theory. In their 1940 book, *Faith Is the Answer,* Peale and Blanton wrote alternating chapters, and Blanton's chapter on "Love and Marriage" made "the distinction between 'pure' and 'sexual' love," which he wrote "may easily give rise to serious maladjustment in marriage. It may prevent a healthy satisfaction in both the physical and spiritual life by driving a wedge between them." For his part, Peale advised, "It cannot be overstressed that the important factor in a happy marriage is the determination to make it work. This means that both parties must be psychologically inclined toward a positive attitude in their marriage. Their mental slant, the entire drift of their personalities must be toward success, not failure."

Lucy spent several sessions with Blanton—who had been analyzed by Sigmund Freud himself—and apparently found him helpful. And it became clear to her and her analyst that despite nearly seventeen years of marriage, she and Desi had achieved nothing close to such equilibrium or commonality of purpose. In a letter published here for the first time, Blanton wrote to Desi on September 16.

Dear Mr. Arnaz: I had some very constructive talks with
Miss Lucy and the deepest impression that remains with
me is that she is devoted to you. . . . It has been my experi-
ence in fifty years of counselling that many people, when
they reach the age of forty, feel a sense of dissatisfaction
with things and, strangely enough, the more successful the
person, the more he has achieved, the deeper the feeling of
dissatisfaction. This is because there is some inner goal or
idea that he has failed to achieve, or thinks he has failed
to achieve. Through talking it out with someone who is
experienced and whom one likes and trusts, a great deal
can be done in changing these feelings and thoughts.

During her counseling, Lucy had taken up temporary residence
with her cousin Cleo in an apartment in the Hampshire House on
Central Park South. In October Desi joined her there for some intense
sessions with Blanton. One day the psychiatrist arrived at 9 a.m. and
left after 6 p.m. "I was grateful that Desi was finally facing some of our
personal issues," Lucy would later recall. "It was like old times at the
ranch, both of us pacing up and down the hotel room yelling at the
top of our voices, then doubling over with laughter, kicking chair legs
and throwing pillows. The discussion was simply great; we both felt
so much better by dinnertime. We left the apartment arm in arm and
went on to have a perfectly marvelous evening, while Dr. Blanton went
home to have a good long rest."

On October 13, Blanton wrote again to Desi, whom he now addressed fondly by his first name.

First, we must start where we are now—with all our prob-
lems, weaknesses, difficulties and frailties. We have to get
some of the feeling of St. Paul when he said, "Wherever I
am, therewith I am content." . . . When we reach the age

of forty we must have a positive philosophy of faith that
will enable us to act wisely and effectively in all situations
if we are to lead a satisfactory life. . . . What is needed is a
deeper faith in yourself and in Lucy; a clearer realization
of your inherent powers for creation—for help—for your
living; a turning of the attention from self to others; and a
reaching out for more self-knowledge and love.

Eight days later came another letter from Blanton. He had sent Desi's Rorschach test out for analysis by Dr. Zygmunt Piotrowski, a leading expert on the test, in which subjects are asked to interpret a series of inkblots, a process that supposedly reveals personality traits. Blanton reported that Arnaz's test was complex, and Piotrowski's interpretation was not complete. But he offered a partial report:

He said you had an unusually brilliant mind, with an
I.Q. much higher than most men in your successful po-
sition. He also said that because you were an only child,
you had a rather deep dependence on the mother image
and from time to time you have, from the depths of your
unconscious, feelings of depression that you are not
quite conscious of but which make you feel on edge.

Blanton noted that he had been practicing his golf game in anticipation of playing with Desi in Palm Springs and looked forward to seeing him the following month. But there, the correspondence in Lucie Arnaz's family archive trails off. "Desi saw Dr. Blanton a few times after that" initial period, Lucy wrote years later, "but he never really warmed to analysis and he refused to admit that he had any problem." What is worse, after Desi bought the television rights to *Bernadette of Lourdes*, a 1939 book about the French saint written by Blanton's wife, Margaret, Lucy would accuse him "of buying Blanton's support."

• • •

Back in Hollywood, Desi took advantage of the contraction underway in the movie industry to hire George Murphy, his onetime
costar, who had lost his latest job in the MGM publicity department,
to assume similar duties at Desilu. He also brought on Johnny Green,
the composer, conductor, and arranger who had long headed MGM's
music department but had recently left his job as part of the studio's
cost cutting. One of Green's first assignments at Desilu was to write
the title theme for Desi's next great project: *The Desilu Playhouse*. This
was to be yet another variation on a theme—the most ambitious one to
date—in which Desi proposed that the hour-long *Lucy-Desi* episodes
would alternate with a dramatic anthology series, starting in the fall of
1958.

Desi pitched the idea to CBS in the winter of 1957–58—before he
even had a sponsor lined up. Ford, beset by the swift failure of the
Edsel line and a national recession, was not interested in extending its
costly sponsorship of the hour-long format. Ultimately, Desi reached a
two-year deal with the Westinghouse Electric Corporation, the maker
of consumer appliances, that called for a total of nearly fifty episodes—
eight of them *Lucy* shows. Lucy and Desi would also appear in Westinghouse advertisements and a promotional film for the company's
dealers. The new contract—for twelve million dollars—once again
broke a record as the largest in television history, and Desi sold the
programs sight unseen—"all without a single test film, no scripts, no
guest stars—just the Desilu track record," as *TV Guide* reported. Yet
again Desi was leveraging not only Lucy's extraordinary appeal and
popularity but his own entrepreneurial success and reputation for
quality. And yet again he was taking a risk consistent with his belief
that television was an economic powerhouse.

But it *was* a risk, and Desi's own neck was part of the collateral for
the deal. He had promised Mark Cresap, the president of Westinghouse,

that he would double the ratings for Westinghouse's current, under-performing television offering, *Studio One*, with the new show.

"What happens if I get approval of this contract and you don't do what you said you would?" Cresap asked him.

"Very simple," Desi replied. "I'll just go back to Cuba."

"Don't go without calling me," Cresap assured him. "I'll have to go with you."

Desi hired Bert Granet, a veteran screenwriter and film producer, to run the new *Playhouse* project and to live up to the new venture's ambitions. "We want our stories to 'move,'" a Desilu memo said. "It is essential that we clutch the viewers' interest quickly, that we give them no opportunity to relinquish that interest." The series would seek modern stories, especially love stories. But it would avoid costume drama and any plots with the "aberration of neurotics or psychotics." Politics and race relations were also touchy subjects. "We all should avoid stories that reflect unfavorably on any section of the country," the memo read, and here Desi crossed out in red pencil the last phrase, "especially the South."

• • •

By July 1958 *Variety* had proclaimed Desilu the number one TV producer, with thirty-two million dollars in overall programming, beating out Revue Productions, the television arm of the MCA talent agency, whose programs included *Leave It to Beaver*.

As the staff geared up for the 1958 fall season, Bob Carroll and Madelyn Pugh felt in need of a break. Madelyn by this point had married Quinn Martin, a Desilu sound editor whom Desi was grooming as a producer, and they now had a new baby. Desi understood, but he was also eager to keep the pair who had been such an integral part of *I Love Lucy* since before the beginning. So he offered to finance a sabbatical in Italy for Bob, who loved European travel, and to build an on-site nursery at the studio for Madelyn, who was at that point still one of the tiny handful of women writers in television. In the end, the two writers agreed to take an indefinite leave rather than quit altogether.

To take up the slack, Desi recruited Everett Freeman, a veteran screenwriter whom he had known at MGM and who had worked with stars like Jack Benny and Bob Hope. Freeman worked with Bob Schiller and Bob Weiskopf on a season-opening episode called "Lucy Goes to Mexico" that involved comic misadventures with a border crossing and a bullfight. Desi arranged for one of his all-time idols, Maurice Chevalier, to appear as the guest star. The scenario involves Ricky and Maurice rehearsing a show aboard the aircraft carrier USS *Yorktown* in San Diego while Lucy, Fred, and Ethel take a souvenir-hunting side trip to Tijuana. Desi and Chevalier—together with Keith Thibodeaux's Little Ricky—do a delightful dance number with straw hats and canes.

It was an unusually elaborate shoot, Jay Sandrich recalled, with high production values that were far closer to those of a feature film, using a combination of sophisticated shots on location and in the studio. When the company was on location, there was obviously no live audience to provide laughter, so a laugh track was generated later by showing the finished footage to a studio audience and recording their real-time reaction. The season premiere drew the same mix of critical doubts ("The situation isn't strong enough to sustain an hour," *Variety* said) and high ratings (it was the sixth-ranked show of the month) that the first season's efforts had, though *Variety* did allow that the show "was brought off with such skill, polish and unerring awareness of what tickles the risibilities of the average viewer that the results are frequently explosive."

But Desi was not deterred by the critics, and anyway, he acknowledged that the non-*Lucy*, dramatic anthology episodes of the *Desilu Playhouse* were his main priority for the year. He had long wanted to move into production of more serious programming, and he was determined to make good on his new venture, which CBS had accepted as the condition of keeping the *Lucy* franchise in the fold. For him, the

RKO purchase and the debut of the *Playhouse* was the logical next step in keeping the company growing, and his most important effort yet to be taken seriously as a player in a Hollywood establishment that had so long underestimated him.

"Desi was a very, very bright man," Bert Granet recalled. "His image was sorely tarnished by the role he played on *I Love Lucy*. He had a photographic memory. You couldn't shoot the breeze with him without him quoting you six months from now. He could write. He could read a script and knew everyone's part on one reading. And he was a very respectable boss, because when things went wrong Desi would say, 'Well, Amigo, I guess *we* blew it'—instead of 'Well, amigo, *you* blew it.'"

The first non-*Lucy* episode of the *Desilu Playhouse*, on October 13, 1958, was a pure bid for prestige, an adaptation of Margaret Blanton's book, now retitled "Song of Bernadette," the true story of the nineteenth-century Frenchwoman who saw visions in a grotto at Lourdes that later became a pilgrimage site for millions from all over the world. The show starred Pier Angeli, a young Italian-born film actress who had made a splash in Hollywood (she had once dated James Dean), and it drew precisely the opposite reception as the *Lucy-Desi* shows: critical praise and comparatively weak ratings. The show failed even to win its time slot, but *Variety* called it "superbly produced." Jack Gould of the *New York Times* called "Song of Bernadette" an "inherently moving" tale that "displayed good taste."

The following month, the *Playhouse* presented an even more critically praised episode, "The Time Element," written by Rod Serling, already one of the most respected writers in television. It tells the haunting story of a man, played by William Bendix, suffering recurrent dreams that he is living in Pearl Harbor on the eve of the Japanese attack and tries in vain to warn people of the impending disaster. He consults a psychiatrist about the dreams, and the episode ends with the psychiatrist suddenly staring at an empty couch. He goes to a nearby bar, where he learns by chance that the patient who just visited him had died on

December 7, 1941. Serling had originally sold his script to CBS, but it had never been produced, and Granet bought the rights for ten thousand dollars. But Westinghouse hated the story. "They didn't want to do it so bad they sent out three vice presidents who told me why they didn't want to do it," Granet recalled. "I went to Desi. Desi backed me up. We made the thing and it got big critical acclaim, enough to get Rod and his agent a series on CBS." That series was *The Twilight Zone*, which went on the air in October 1959.

Westinghouse Desilu Playhouse aspired to be a class act and would ultimately feature a raft of famous guest stars—Buddy Ebsen, George Murphy, Jane Russell, Red Skelton, Ed Wynn, and others. Its cadre of directors included Arthur Hiller, who would go on to make *Love Story*, and Ralph Nelson, who would direct Sidney Poitier's Oscar-winning performance in *Lilies of the Field*. One guest star, the Broadway and Hollywood veteran Eddie Albert, was impressed to find fresh flowers in his dressing room every day. "That's what happens," he said, "when actors own studios."

. . .

B ut Desilu's public successes could not mask the growing private unhappiness in the Arnaz household, a reality that burst into the open on November 23, 1958, at the Friars' Club roast of Desi and Lucy. A murderers' row of comedians had gathered in the ballroom of the Beverly Hilton to pay tribute to the couple through an evening of insult comedy. The Friars' modus operandi was cutting, ribald humor edging toward the blue, but Milton Berle's opening monologue cut a little too close to home. "Listen to me, Desi," said Berle, the onetime vaudeville comic who had been the most popular television performer before Lucy came along, "you don't need her. Dump her. She's nothing. Now, may I introduce Jerry Giesler?" (Giesler was a celebrated Hollywood divorce lawyer of the day.) "The marriage will not last; it will end," Berle went on, to dead silence in the room. "You can laugh, please," he

urged the uncomfortable audience of twelve hundred Hollywood no-
tables. "And when the marriage ends, what a settlement! Are you ready
for the bit? She gets Redlands"—a quiet town in the Inland Empire of
Southern California east of Los Angeles—"and he gets Olvera Street,"
the original Spanish colonial pueblo of Los Angeles. "She gets RKO, he
joins Castro," who was on the verge of revolutionary triumph in Cuba.

"This no-talent lady, sitting right here, knocking around Hollywood, drunk," Berle plunged on, "she met this poor *nebbish* here,"
using the Yiddish word for weakling, "this *farkakte* wetback"—Yiddish
for lousy—"and they laugh at him, but one of these days he may buy the
whole country, and *we'll* be the ones talking funny. When he came here,
when he came to this country, what did he come with? Three hundred
gallons of hair oil!" Berle then struck squarely at Desi's well-deserved
reputation as a womanizer with a crude joke about oral sex. "Who do
you think he has as the attendant in the men's room at Desilu?" Berle
asked. "Edith Head!" (Head was an Oscar-winning costume designer.)
Desi's hooting, musical laugh can be heard breaking through the applause on a recording of the evening.

But the surreal climax of the dinner was the appearance of Harry
Einstein, the tongue-twisting Greek-dialect comic known as Parkyakarkus (the father of the future comedian, actor, and director Albert
Brooks). "Parky" delivered a hilarious, table-pounding tribute to "my
very dear and close friends, Miss Louise Balls and Danny Arnaz"—but
as he walked back to his seat, he keeled over in Berle's arms on the dais
with a massive heart attack.

In a backstage corridor, five doctors in the house frantically mas-
saged Einstein's heart. Albert Goldman, the chief surgeon of City of
Hope hospital, slit open the comedian's chest with a scalpel and tried
to apply electric shock with a lamp cord as waiters brought in towels
from the men's room. The emcee, Art Linkletter, tried in vain to keep
the shocked crowd calm, urging the singer Tony Martin to perform.
Martin sang one of his biggest hits, which happened to be the inaptly

titled "There's No Tomorrow." Einstein was finally pronounced dead at 1:10 a.m., an hour and a quarter after being stricken.

As the doctors struggled backstage, Lucy could not bring herself to say even a few words, and Desi could barely speak. "This was an evening that comes to you once in a lifetime," he choked in a trembling voice. "It meant so much, then all at once, it doesn't mean a damn thing."

The cursed evening was a metaphor for the Arnazes' marriage. Even the biggest, happiest professional milestones and honors that came their way could not compensate for the personal sadness that seemed increasingly to haunt them.

———•❦•———

TOO MUCH AND NOT ENOUGH

A s 1958 drew to a close, Desi Arnaz was by every objective measure a true Hollywood mogul. Filming the last episode of the
1957–58 season's hour-long *Lucy-Desi* show at the Sun Valley ski resort in Idaho the previous winter, Arnaz had looked around at all the
Desilu-branded cameras and equipment perched on the mountaintop
location and marveled, "What a long way TV has come since those
early days—only about six years ago." But Hollywood still didn't quite
know what to make of him. The columnist Erskine Johnson summed
up the prevailing mix of praise and doubts by listing the varied terms
that "Desi Arnaz is called": number one, "Hollywood TV tycoon,"
number two, "TV business genius," number three, "TV film prophet,"
and number four, there "to watch Lucy pick up her Emmy." Desi himself liked to say, "There is no classification for a Cuban fellow with an
accent who plays drums and marries redheads."

That was true enough. Despite the doubters, Desi could content himself with a mogul's trappings. When Hedda Hopper visited his plush second-floor president's office at Desilu, with its big bay window overlooking a small park inside the studio grounds, she found a setting worthy of *Don Desiderio*. The spacious, airy office had mellowed wood paneling, a private dining room with a small piano, a framed front page of the *New York Herald* announcing the death of Abraham Lincoln (sent by a fan who knew of Desi's admiration for the sixteenth president), and a wood-burning fireplace with his family coat of arms hanging above it. Desi's enormous desk occupied almost the whole length of the east-facing wall and window.

When Hopper asked him how visitors could see him with the daylight flooding in behind him, he replied, "That's how I give people the tenth degree!"

"You mean third degree!" Lucy chimed in.

But as Desi's power and wealth and influence grew, he also further undermined his reputation with his increasingly public unprofessional behavior. In late October and early November 1958, he was involved in two upsetting incidents at the Riviera hotel and casino in Las Vegas. In the first, Desi got into a wee-hours argument with a fellow craps player, a woman, and when Sid Wyman, a part owner of the hotel who was presiding at the table, urged him to calm down, he threw a drink in Wyman's face. In the second, he was thrown out of the casino after making a noisy fuss. His pro forma denials were unpersuasive. "I don't *think* I threw a drink in anybody's face," he said.

"Desi could be the most charming individual who ever lived," the Hollywood columnist Dan Jenkins recalled. "He could charm needles off a pine tree. At the same time, he was chasing women all over town and drinking too much. I faced him once at a press party. I said, 'Desi, you're drinking too damned much.' He said, 'I never drink when I'm working, you know that.' I said, 'Desi, you're working right now. This party is work.' He was almost teary." Arnaz's scrapes had become quasi-public knowledge in the tight-knit world of Hollywood. The Beverly

Hills cops would routinely deposit him at the side door of the Roxbury Drive house after a bender. Desi's enthusiastic patronage of prostitutes had also become the worst-kept sort of secret.

"He was a sweetheart of a guy, with a healthy heterosexual appetite," remembered Scotty Bowers, an infamous bisexual gigolo and pimp who late in life would spill his stories of sexually servicing both genders of Hollywood's A-list. "He often called me up for girls, tipping them more generously than anyone else I knew. Instead of handing over the typical $20, which was the going gratuity at that time for a trick, he would often slip a girl as much as $200 or $300." Bowers claimed that Desi's desires were extraordinary, that he "saw at least two or three girls every few days." Though the term was not generally in use in that era, today Desi would probably be considered a sex addict. Lucy was certainly all too aware of her husband's behavior, as Bowers learned one night when he was bartending at a party, as he often did. "Lucille came striding over to me in a beautiful long evening gown, stopped in front of the bar for a second or two, and then . . . Wham! She slapped me in the face and yelled 'You! You stop pimping for my husband, y' hear?'"

Rod Erickson, a prominent advertising executive at the Young & Rubicam advertising agency, recalled going to dinner with Desi and a straitlaced agency colleague at the Luau, a Polynesian-themed celebrity hangout on Rodeo Drive in Beverly Hills. As the meal was ending, Desi summoned Erickson to join him in the men's room.

"I've got two great girls," Desi confided. "I haven't tried 'em yet. They're very highly recommended from Las Vegas." Erickson struggled to respond in a way that would not offend Desi. "He was being kind and generous, he thought. Big gift," Erickson remembered.

Finally, Erickson said, "Desi, I don't know how to tell you this . . . John and I are both married to younger women, and we come out here for a rest."

"Oh, I understand!" Desi promptly replied. "I'll take both of them!"

Still, despite these distractions, Desilu itself continued to thrive.

That fall of 1958, Desi offloaded five previously unsold Desilu pilots to NBC to fill an unexpected gap in its schedule left by the sponsor's sudden cancelation of *The Colgate Comedy Hour*. The properties included Orson Welles's "Fountain of Youth" episode, which went on to become the only rejected TV pilot ever to win the prestigious George Foster Peabody Award for excellence in broadcasting. The hour-long *Lucy-Desi* shows were still going strong. The season premiere, the Mexico episode guest-starring Maurice Chevalier, aired on October 6 and was followed on December 1 by a charming episode featuring Danny Thomas, whose show was a prime Desilu tenant. The plot involves Danny Williams, Thomas's television alter ego, and his family renting the Ricardos' Connecticut house for a country getaway while Ricky is expected to be in Hollywood filming a movie. But the project gets canceled, and the Ricardos want their house back. An epic court battle ensues, with Gale Gordon as the bewildered judge who tries to make sense of Lucy's frantically mimed testimony, acted out as if in charades, since, Ricky explains, she has "larin-yitis" after a snowball fight with the tenants. For the first time in years, the critical reception was as strong as the ratings, with the *Hollywood Reporter* pronouncing it "one of the funniest shows ever on television." Episodes with Red Skelton, Paul Douglas, and the actress-director Ida Lupino and her husband, Howard Duff, followed. But even here there were dark clouds. During the filming of the Lupino episode, there was an angry off-camera fight in which Lucy accused Desi of flirting with Lupino.

On the business side, though, all signs pointed up. The ultimate confirmation of Desilu's success came on December 3, when the once-tiny company that Desi and Lucy had started went public. The initial offering on the American Stock Exchange had a total capitalization of $5.25 million. Lucy and Desi each kept 25 percent of the company—a total of 275,000 shares—with shares also going to about twenty of their key executives and Martin Leeds having the swing vote on corporate decisions. Another 250,000 shares were offered to the public at ten dollars a share. Americans who had never invested in the stock market before stepped up to own a piece of Desilu, and much of this cash infusion would be used to pay down debt from the RKO acquisition. In his prospectus for the initial public offering, Desilu's chief financial officer, Ed Holly, summed up the company's total revenues for the previous fiscal year: $8.1 million for filming series owned by others, $6.4 million for licensing shows in which it owned an interest, and $34,153—or a mere two-tenths of 1 percent—in residuals for previously produced shows (though this last category was already the most profitable).

"The Company is engaged in a highly competitive branch of the entertainment industry," the prospectus read. "Filmed series compete with live and other filmed television programming, including motion pictures. There are approximately a half-dozen major producers of television film series and numerous smaller producers. For the current season, the Company is, for the first time, the largest producer of filmed series in this country."

This was good news indeed. But here again, Desi's growing dependence on alcohol had become an issue. Martin Leeds recalled that whereas Desi had once readily gone to New York himself to meet with advertisers and network executives, he now sent Leeds to talk up the company with the Wall Street securities analysts and investment officers. "Desi wouldn't go," Leeds said. "He said, 'You go.' I suspect he was scared."

• • •

The focus of Desi's creative energy in this period was the non-Lucy *Desilu Playhouse*. For most of the 1950s, serious, dramatic television had been the province of New York, where the industry had begun and teleplays could be produced live, featuring top Broadway actors. Young writers like Paddy Chayefsky and directors like Sidney Lumet cut their teeth creating dramas for television during these years. Westinghouse's earlier anthology program, *Studio One*, had broadcast

"Twelve Angry Men," which later became a theatrical movie starring Henry Fonda. Musical spectaculars like CBS's *Cinderella* (with a
score by Rodgers and Hammerstein) and NBC's *Peter Pan* (starring
the Broadway diva Mary Martin) had been ratings bonanzas, and CBS
itself had started *Playhouse 90* in 1956 to produce live dramas from
Television City in Hollywood. *The Miracle Worker*, William Gibson's
play about Helen Keller and Annie Sullivan, premiered there in 1957.
The *Desilu Playhouse* was Desi's bid to compete in this rarefied league.

His ambitions were high. Desi had approached top-tier talent like
the Broadway and Hollywood songwriter Frank Loesser and the playwright and director Garson Kanin to create programs for the series.
Johnny Green had written a stirring theme for the opening credits with
thrumming timpani and trumpets sounding over animated geomet-
ric shapes. The Desilu legal department was instructed to check the
availability of television rights for properties by Richard Rodgers and
Lorenz Hart, as well as Rodgers and Hammerstein, and Arnaz suggested approaching established stars like Red Skelton, Jimmy Durante,
and Jackie Gleason, who might have summertime availability between
their various network commitments. A November 11, 1958, memo
from Desi's secretary noted that there would be *Playhouse* story con-
ferences every Tuesday morning with the company's top ten executives
and added, "We need seven more stories as soon as possible"—two
musicals, three or four Westerns, and two comedies.

But from the start, these ambitious efforts ran squarely into a paradox: the decision to film the shows—the key to Desilu's initial success
and spectacular growth—now hurt the company's hopes to produce
prestigious dramatic programming. Bert Granet, the *Playhouse*'s executive producer, explained that while a live television play could
spark interest in a feature film—as had happened with "Twelve Angry
Men" and with Paddy Chayefsky's Oscar-winning best picture, *Marty*,
which began life as a live teleplay on the *Philco-Goodyear Television
Playhouse*—a TV play recorded on film seemed to torpedo a movie

deal. "We didn't quite realize at the time that on *Playhouse 90* and the others, those great names were only being kinescoped, which didn't affect their motion picture salaries," Granet recalled. By contrast, at Desilu "we were putting our shows on film, which, if we had important stars, would have affected their motion-picture salaries. The truth of it is that I don't think we ever sold it on the basis of the anthology series. It did sell on the basis of getting the *Lucy-Desi* show every four weeks." Indeed, Desi noted that the hour-long *Lucy* specials always drew the highest ratings, so they should "be followed with 'exploitation' or 'exclamation point' shows whenever possible" to try to lure viewers.

An additional complication was that the *Playhouse* was also a source of friction with Vivian Vance. She had long chafed at the limitations of the role of Ethel Mertz and had loathed being paired with the much older sourpuss Bill Frawley, who treated her with undisguised contempt offset. After having refused Desi's proposal for a Fred-and-Ethel spinoff, and having filmed an unsuccessful pilot for a series called *Guestward Ho!*, in which she would operate a New Mexico guest ranch, she was unhappy that no one had offered her a part in a *Desilu Playhouse* show. "It makes it increasingly difficult for me to negotiate with her," one Desilu executive noted, ". . . as she feels the studio has not given her any consideration in trying to use her services as an actress on its other programs."

But even in adversity, Desi was resourceful. He now pinned his hopes on a particular *Desilu Playhouse* property in the spring of 1959: *The Untouchables*, based on the memoir of an all-but-forgotten Prohibition-enforcement agent named Eliot Ness. In Depression-era Chicago, Ness had been the larger-than-life figure who helped put away the notorious Al Capone, but by the 1950s he was toiling in obscurity at a printing company in a small Pennsylvania town. He was introduced to Oscar Fraley, a veteran wire-service sportswriter, who joined him in a collaboration that mixed hard facts with some fanciful reimagining.

Desi—whose best friend in high school in Miami had, of course, been Al Capone Jr.—immediately saw Ness and Fraley's book as an exciting prospect. But the film option was owned—together with a bunch of other properties—by the talent agent and producer Ray Stark. The moment Stark's option lapsed, Desi pounced. Desilu decided to adapt the book into the most expensive television program made to date, a two-part offering budgeted at two hundred thousand dollars per part. In the process—and without fanfare or naming or promoting it as such—Desi effectively spawned a new entertainment genre, the made-for-television movie. It was yet another Desilu first.

Bert Granet commissioned a script from a writer named Paul Monash, who turned in a kind of psychological study of gangsterism, saying that was what Granet had ordered. Desi had other ideas and responded with new instructions: "I want cops and robbers." Monash went back to his typewriter and delivered a gritty, documentary-style script, notable for its frank sex and explicit violence. Over Lucy's objections, Desi once again hired Walter Winchell, who had covered the era, to narrate the show with his trademark rat-a-tat-tat delivery and snap-brim fedora.

When word of the planned project became public in the fall of 1958, Desi got a call from Sonny Capone, whom he hadn't heard from in years.

"Why you?" his old friend asked plaintively.

Desi, badly in need of a new hit, sought to couch his frankly commercial decision in congenial terms. "Sonny, if I don't do it," he said, "somebody else is going to do it, and maybe it's better that I'm going to do it."

Desi was so excited about *The Untouchables* that he at first implausibly considered playing Ness himself. His next choice was the veteran leading man Van Heflin, who turned him down. Finally, Desi's old *Too Many Girls* castmate Van Johnson agreed to play somewhat against type for ten thousand dollars—a respectable fee. But at the last minute, just as shooting was to begin on the Desilu backlot in Culver

City, Johnson's wife and agent, Evie, insisted Van should get ten thousand dollars for *each* of the two episodes. Desi refused, and on a Friday night, with production set to start Monday, Johnson dropped out. Desi turned instead to Robert Stack, a handsome stalwart who had been kicking around Hollywood since the 1930s and had recently been nominated for an Academy Award for his supporting role in the soapy melodrama *Written on the Wind*. Desi tracked Stack down at Chasen's restaurant at 2 a.m. on Sunday morning, told him that a wardrobe person would be at his house later that day to refit Johnson's period clothes, and asked him to report for work at 8 a.m. Monday.

Stack was stunned but agreed. "Desi Arnaz was the real reason I took the jump," he recalled. "I told him, 'Desi, if you promise me as an actor, not as an executive, to do a good show, I'll believe you.' He said, 'Baby, we're gonna make the best damn television show on the air.' He never let me down." It didn't hurt that Desi promised Stack an ownership interest in the show if it was picked up as its own series—a method of profit-sharing compensation that was becoming increasingly common for first-rank stars in Hollywood.

When *The Untouchables* debuted on April 20, 1959, Desi appeared on-screen to introduce the first episode. Standing against a stylized backdrop of giant beer barrels, a lit cigarette in hand, he promised "true stories, taken from the exciting autobiography of Eliot Ness." Perhaps mindful of questions about the show's fidelity to the facts, the credits billed Ness and Fraley's book as a "novel," but the show's stylish black-and-white cinematography and authentic period atmosphere imparted a newsreel quality and made it as distinctive as any old-time gangster film starring James Cagney or Edward G. Robinson. The two-part episode told the story of Ness's recruitment of an incorruptible band of investigators—the "untouchables" of the title—who finally broke Capone's hold on Chicago and sent him to prison for tax evasion. The production deployed a fleet of vintage cars and trucks, relied on expensive overtime to shoot nighttime sequences, and employed as many as

five or six cameras at once. Jack Gould in the *New York Times* praised
its "major production values" and "full motion picture proportions"
and noted that the actress Barbara Nichols, a buxom blonde in whom
Lucy suspected Desi had more than a professional interest, performed
"for TV at least a fairly sizzly striptease." In fact, Nichols, playing a mob
informant's wife, appeared obliquely topless, her breasts not fully visible but covered only by pasties—an unheard-of display for its day, in
either television or film. (Desi may have had eyes for Nichols, but the
dalliance that apparently got her in trouble was an affair with the producer Quinn Martin, which broke up his marriage to Madelyn Pugh.)

The show was a sensation, winning its time slot with a 36.1 audience share—or more than one-third of Americans who were watching television at that hour—for the first installment. In proof of the
program's cinematic ambition and quality, Arnaz subsequently joined
the two episodes together as a single film, retitled *The Scarface Mob*,
for international distribution in theaters. And then Desi stunned the
industry by selling the show as a series not to CBS, where the *Desilu
Playhouse* aired, but to ABC, the perennial third-place network. In
his memoir, Desi would claim that he did so only after Bill Paley had
passed on *The Untouchables* (because CBS had another crime drama
in the works), but at the time *Variety* reported that Desi's move had
"created hard feelings between Desilu and CBS-TV." In any case, the
sale buttressed the reality that Desilu was its own force to be reckoned
with and not merely a ward of the network where it had risen to prom-
inence.

• • •

Even with his professional successes, there wasn't much that Desi
could do to soften the hard feelings at 1000 North Roxbury
Drive. By the spring of 1959, Lucy had reluctantly concluded that she
might have to give up on the marriage in light of Desi's repeated infidelities and uncontrollable drinking. In what she would years later

concede was a last-ditch effort, she proposed a family trip to Europe—but not one likely to re-create an atmosphere conducive to a second honeymoon. The Arnazes took along Cousin Cleo and her husband Kenny Morgan, together with Lucy's maid, Harriet McCain, and the children's nanny, Willie Mae Barker. All that plus forty-eight pieces of luggage. The crew set sail on the French liner *Liberté* on May 13, bound for Paris. In a letter to Hedda Hopper from the mid-Atlantic, Lucy put a cheery face on the trip. "Weather perfect, food divine—too divine, eating ourselves out of shape," she wrote. Though she said she was unsure she could still fit into her new chiffons, Lucy added, "Everyone loves our kids—that makes us happy."

That may have been the only happy thing about the six-week trip. The troupe traveled from Paris to Rome, Capri, and London in what was by all accounts a miserable experience, thanks to Desi's by now undeniable (except by him) alcoholism. "When he wasn't drinking," Lucy recalled years later, "he spent most of his time on the phone with the studio or checking the Del Mar racetrack, where his horses were running. I was completely disenchanted, bitter, and unforgiving . . . and the kids saw and heard way too much." Indeed they did. "Those days were very intense because that was when they were really going at it," Desi Jr., who was then six, would remember. As the trip wore on, Cousin Cleo recalled, Desi was drunk a great deal of the time. "One day he fell on the cobblestones, and the next morning his face was all purple and it looked like a pomegranate." Lucie, then not quite eight, simply recalled, "It scared me to death."

In cities in Europe where *I Love Lucy* had not yet penetrated the market, Desi was once again too often dismissed as "Mr. Ball." When the Arnazes visited their former guest star Maurice Chevalier at his home outside Paris, the wise old showman sensed that their marriage might be beyond repair. With Gallic realism, he told Lucy that the ending of the relationship might seem sad, but that staying together without love would be worse.

"Desi and I came back from our trip not speaking," Lucy would recall. Desi moved into the guesthouse at Roxbury and later that year would go abroad again, this time alone.

In late June, on their return from Europe, the Arnazes shot the first episode of the 1959–60 season, with Milton Berle as guest star. The plot involves Berle, playing himself, hiding out at the Ricardos' house (without Ricky's knowledge) to finish a memoir. Lucy has offered Berle their house to lure him into appearing in the local PTA benefit, but Fred spies a mysterious stranger and alerts Ricky, who suspects Lucy of disloyally harboring another man. Uncle Miltie tries to escape the jealous Ricky in his signature drag as Mildred. More complications ensue until Berle ends up joining the Ricardos and Mertzes in a Western musical number at the PTA show. Desi himself directed the episode, and the tension with Lucy was palpable.

"What do I say here?" Lucy demanded at one point.

"You say 'I can't,'" Desi replied.

Lucy claimed not to understand whether Arnaz had said "can" or "can't," and he exploded: "I'm saying 'can't,' dammit!"

"It was sometimes a little difficult to be a twenty-four-year-old and be caught in the middle of America's sweethearts breaking up," Jay Sandrich, at the time the show's assistant director, would recall. "So I have memories of pressure rather than memories of excitement of being on the show." Still, Berle was so impressed with Desi's skills as a director that he asked him to direct one of his own shows later that year. "He's got a tremendous flair for comedy," Berle reported in a succinct summation of just what it was that Desi brought to the table in building the success of Lucy and Desilu. "There's almost nobody like him around. He's a driver, a perfectionist, and he usually knows ninety-five percent of what he wants. I think he can do more serious stuff as well. I have great respect for his ability to handle people and for his knowledge of what plays and what doesn't." He added: "Look what he did for Lucy.

She's the greatest comedienne in the world because she's one of the greatest actresses. He saw that in her and helped bring it out."

During the *Lucy-Desi* show's hiatus that summer, Lucy was, as usual, restless and at sea without work. Desi called a meeting of the Desilu department heads in his office. "Message was that something had to be done with Lucy during the summer layoff," Kenny Morgan noted. "Seems that she was playing vice president. Changing color schemes in the women's johns, repainting the reception room—*TWICE*, etc. She had been calling very expensive labor off sets to do this." So Desi approved the ninety-thousand-dollar renovation of Lela Rogers's old two-hundred-seat "Little Theatre" on the old RKO lot, where Lucy had long ago attended workshops as a young actress. Now Lucy had decided to create the "Desilu Workshop," hiring young Hollywood hopefuls— including the future Turner Classic Movies host Robert Osborne and the actress Carole Cook—to give them a chance to test their performing skills. Lucy told Hedda Hopper that her ambitions were modest. "I'm not going to teach anything," she explained, adding that the goal was to get young performers in front of an audience. "I know that constitutes acting experience—just so long as it's in front of somebody else besides your own mother."

As much as anything else, the players of the workshop ensemble came to serve as distraction—and in the case of Robert Osborne and Cook, emotional support. "She was in tears a lot of the time and in a lot of rage," Cook would recall.

. . .

As 1959 wore on, Lucy had plenty to be sad and angry about, as the gulf between Desi's professional accomplishments and his personal irresponsibility continued to widen. When the *Westinghouse Desilu Playhouse* contract was up for renewal for the 1959–60 season, the company's advertising agency, J. Walter Thompson, insisted on putting in an old-fashioned "morals clause," stipulating that the agreement could be abrogated if Desi were guilty of various sorts of misconduct—typically including alcohol and drug abuse or sexual indiscretions. Desi was outraged and refused to sign. He said he would only agree to the provision if the chairman of Westinghouse bound himself to the same commitment. "And someplace and someday, you could find a contract that now exists," Ed Holly would recall years later, in which "the chairman of the board of Westinghouse and Desi signed the contract with the morals clause against each of them."

Westinghouse's concerns proved all too well founded in the wee hours of September 19, when Desi was arrested on a charge of public drunkenness after police found him weaving down Vista Street in Hollywood, the site of a well-known strip of brothels. He was arrested after getting into a noisy argument with a plainclothesman, then booked and released an hour later after posting a twenty-one-dollar cash bond. "When booked at the station, Arnez [sic] expressed desire to phone J. Edgar Hoover and former Sheriff Eugene Biscailuz, both friends who could identify him," noted the FBI field memo recounting the local cops' arrest. "Los Angeles will endeavor to determine arrest details through established sources."

The full truth was worse. "He could have been booked *in* the whorehouse," the Desilu executive Martin Leeds recalled. "I got a call at eleven thirty from his chauffeur. He said, 'Martin, he's in the whorehouse and I think the house is on a stakeout.'" Desi was with Claudio Guzman, the Desilu art director, and Leeds told the chauffeur to tell Guzman that "if he doesn't get Desi out of there in five minutes, he'll never work in Hollywood again." Bob Osborne was with Lucy the next day when the story hit the papers. "She just went white, just white," he recalled.

In draft notes for his memoir years later, Desi was still belligerent and unrepentant about the incident, a sign of the depth of the self-destructive behavior he not only couldn't control but remained unable to acknowledge, even after it had destroyed his marriage. He claimed that he had started to talk loudly and argue with the plainclothesman on the street on purpose to alert the madam inside, who had arranged the liaisons for him and Guzman. She was one of Polly Adler's old girls, and a friend. He also complained about Lucy's failure to defend him publicly the way he had supported her through the voter registration crisis. "She knew I had been in front of the cameras until nearly 11 p.m. making commercials for the *Desilu Playhouse*," he wrote, somewhat implausibly. "I was picked up before 12 midnight and there's no way I could have gotten drunk in less than three hours."

In public Lucy kept her counsel, but she could not hide her feelings in private. At the end of September, the Arnazes filmed the next episode of the *Lucy-Desi* hour, "The Ricardos Go to Japan," with their guest star Bob Cummings. The plot called for Lucy to be disguised as a geisha, in the signature white foundation powder, and Carole Cook would never forget how forlorn Lucy looked after the shooting. "The white, white makeup," she remembered. "And she'd been crying—a lot. The eyes were extremely red. It gave her a rather—in looking at her— what I thought was a grotesque look. Because the eyes . . . and sad."

Later that fall Desi went back to Europe alone, ostensibly to scout prospects for the *Desilu Playhouse* but really just to get away. The *Lucy* writer Bob Weiskopf mordantly noted, "Desilu is a family, but Daddy's never home." Jack Aldworth, a Desilu staffer who accompanied Desi, recalled that while they were on the *Queen Mary*, Desi got a ship-to-shore call from a detective he had hired to spy on Lucy for suspected indiscretions of her own. As Desi stood at the ship's railing, Aldworth recalled, tears streamed down his face.

fifteen

————————·⊰❖⊱·————————

"THAT'S ALL"

T hursday, October 15, 1959, brought the first episode of *The Untouch-ables* on ABC. It was a smash. But the show also sparked immediate controversy on multiple fronts and drew influential adversaries—not least among them Desi's old Del Mar racetrack friend J. Edgar Hoover. Long before the two-part pilot episodes had aired back in the spring, Hoover had made it clear that he saw the show as a thorn in his side and a poten-tial risk to the FBI's carefully burnished reputation. For more than twenty-five years Hoover had chafed at the public credit that Ness—a Treasury Department agent, not an FBI man—had received for his exploits, and a flurry of never-before-published memos archived in Desi's FBI file show that the bureau was carefully monitoring the show's development. One such memo noted that Ness had applied to be an FBI agent in September 1933 but "he was not accepted because he generally did not meet the bu-reau's standards." In a letter to Desi on January 5, 1959, Hoover himself pointed out that Ness's memoir had chronicled the work of Prohibition agents, and that the official name of the FBI had not been adopted until 1935. "A direct reference to the FBI would detract from the authenticity of your presentation," he warned.

Now with the series on the air, the bureau stepped up its communication with Desilu—and its critiques. The second episode, to air on October 22, told the story of Kate Barker, alias "Ma Barker," the mother of a gang of Midwestern criminals that had been broken up by the FBI in the thirties. The best historical evidence is that Barker was not involved in her sons' crimes and that Hoover had hyped her role to justify her fatal shooting by the FBI in 1935. Now the bureau was concerned that Eliot Ness was going to get credit for an achievement that had been the FBI's to claim.

An October 17 memo from Hoover's close aide Clyde Tolson to Cartha "Deke" DeLoach, the bureau's number three official, reported that its Little Rock field office had advised that the episode—which, it should be noted, had yet to actually be aired—was going to depict Ness ("the old prohibition agent who was formerly a police officer in Cleveland") firing from behind a tree and killing Barker. Tolson wrote that the head of the Los Angeles field office had advised Desi that this would be inaccurate and that Desi had apologized for the "terrible goof." Two days later Tolson again reported to DeLoach that he had called Desi personally and told him that "although we appreciated his friendship and cooperation in the past, the Director wanted him to positively understand that we would refuse to allow usurpation of the FBI cases or perversion of FBI history." On October 21, DeLoach wrote to Tolson to report that Desi had called to promise that the FBI's name would never be used without clearance from either the Los Angeles field office or headquarters. Other memos in Desi's file show that the bureau monitored each week's episode for compliance and reported promptly back to Hoover himself.

A further controversy erupted in December, when Stack was quoted in *TV Guide* contrasting *The Untouchables'* derring-do with the contemporary FBI's elaborate bureaucracy, noting that he had a friend in the bureau and "they've got so many rules and regulations in his outfit it's all he can do to blow his nose." Hoover again wrote to Desi personally to complain about the "snide, unjustified comments" and adding, in an aside rich with hypocrisy given Hoover's own invasive methods, "While Mr. Stack may be content to revel in exploits which smack of disregard for civil liberties, I cannot with any degree of pride condone either his remarks or such actions as may be depicted on television." Desi was concerned enough that he tried to call Hoover on December 23 to plead for forgiveness but "was told that the director was in a travel status," a memo from Hoover's office noted.

And J. Edgar Hoover was far from the only one upset by the show. Desi got veiled threats (the mob hit man Jimmy Fratianno would later testify in court that there had been a contract on Desi's life), and Frank Sinatra, then a Desilu studio tenant, once nearly came to blows with Desi over the program's depiction of Italian Americans. (Sinatra reportedly carried a message to Desi from the mob reporting how unhappy the wiseguys were.) Senator John Pastore of Rhode Island, the Italian American chair of the Senate Communications Subcommittee, and Francis Cardinal Spellman of New York also complained about the portrayal of Italian Americans, while Senator Thomas Dodd of Connecticut and Newton N. Minow, chair of the Federal Communications Commission, would object to the show's unusually stark violence. Liggett & Myers, one of the program's sponsors, found cases of its cigarettes stacked up on docks by mob-friendly longshoremen who refused to move them. "Eventually, we did stop using Italian names, switching to an unrecognizable nationality which would baffle a roomful of genealogists and send a Berlitz instructor scrambling for his dictionary," Stack recalled. Finally, Desi's old friends the Capones—Al's sister Mafalda, his widow Mae, and Al Jr.—filed a multimillion-dollar lawsuit in Illinois claiming invasion of privacy and appropriation of the family name—since it was impossible to sue for libel because Capone had died in 1947. The case was eventually dismissed.

Still, *The Untouchables*, with its dramatic title theme by Nelson Riddle and Winchell's deadpan narration, swiftly became a cultural touchstone, and it helped propel ABC, the perpetual also-ran, into first place in its time slot. "We brought motion picture techniques into television for the first time," Stack recalled. "Lots of extras, lots of cars, special effects, things they never had before. . . . We shot night after night until two and three and four in the morning." The episodes featured a parade of guest stars that included such familiar or soon-to-be-familiar faces as Cloris Leachman, Peter Falk, Rip Torn, Telly Savalas, Jack Warden, Patricia Neal, Robert Redford, Carroll O'Connor, Lee Marvin, James Caan, and Elizabeth Montgomery. In Billy Wilder's 1960 film *The Apartment*, a character complains when her married boyfriend wants to move their assignations to Thursday nights: "Thursday? But that's *The Untouchables* with Bob Stack!" The show proved to be a gold mine for Stack, who owned 25 percent of the property, with ABC and Desilu dividing the rest. The night Stack won a 1960 Emmy Award for Best Actor, Desi presented him—on the spot—with the keys to a Mercedes 300 SL roadster, an elegant avocado-green sports car that Stack owned till the day he died.

And at least one distinguished critic loved the show: Ayn Rand. Writing in the *Los Angeles Times*, the objectivist philosopher and best-selling author (and onetime head of the RKO wardrobe department!) defended *The Untouchables* as "profoundly moral" and called Stack's portrayal of Eliot Ness "the most inspiring image on today's screen, the only image of a real hero."

• • •

A t the very moment that *The Untouchables* took off, the *Desilu Playhouse* that had spawned it was failing. On October 22, the *New York Times* reported that the dramatic *Playhouse* episodes, which had appeared weekly (interspersed with the less frequent *Lucy-Desi* hours), would now appear only every other week in 1960. Westinghouse was cutting back its twelve-million-dollar annual sponsorship in part to cover its expensive decision to sponsor political coverage of the party conventions and election night in the coming presidential election. "It is also no secret in trade circles that 'Desilu Playhouse' has not been as successful a venture as Westinghouse had hoped," the *Times* wrote. Under the new plan, the show—including the *Lucy-Desi* hours—would run through June, with other network specials broadcast on the off weeks.

The future of the *Lucy-Desi* show was itself in doubt as well, for one unavoidable reason: Lucy and Desi's marriage was much closer to finished than the press or the public yet knew. At various times, each would claim credit for initiating the divorce, but both agreed the end was inevitable. In Desi's telling, sometime in November 1959 Lucy had just left his office after "some other goddamn argument." She stopped in the hallway to take a drink from the water fountain outside his door, where he caught up with her and told her he wanted a divorce. She walked silently away, but back home that night she asked if he was serious. When he replied that he was, she turned on him in a rage. "By the time I get through with you you'll be as broke as when you got here," she railed. "You goddamn spic . . . you wetback!" Desi recalled thinking to himself that the Straits of Florida would have been a much longer swim than the Rio Grande. In draft notes years later for his published memoir, he wrote that in her anger and frustration Lucy had once run out of epithets and finally called him a Jew. For his part, he recalled, "I went to my dressing room, where I had a little cardboard box in my dresser in which I kept a lot of stuff like old cufflinks, chains, broken watches." He then showed her the bottom of the box. "A man's name, a telephone number, and a New York address were written on it," presumably that of a man Desi believed she'd been seeing. (Lucy never publicly acknowledged any infidelities of her own.) "Her blush must have been the blushiest blush since Fawn told Bambi she was pregnant." The two never lived together under the same roof after that moment in late 1959. Desi decamped to the Chateau Marmont hotel on the Sunset Strip.

Some of the Arnazes' friends would insist that the final straw had come when Lucy found Desi, perhaps even at home in their guesthouse, with two hookers. She told some confidants that it was she who had sought the divorce. In her own note to a ghostwriter for an abandoned attempt at a memoir a few years later, she was hard-pressed to put her tortured feelings into words. "About the breakup with Desi, I find it impossible to 'resolve' it by saying we just fell out of love or because the pace was 'too excessive,'" she wrote. "But I also find it impossible to review twenty years and to pin-point. It's too personal and what difference does it make anyway. I just suddenly realized life is too short. And life is too long for the children. So I did something about it."

It must have been excruciating to shoot the special Christmas episode of *The Desilu Revue*, which introduces Lucy's workshop class in a series of underwhelming musical numbers. The songs and dances are framed by a conceit in which Lucy is frantically nervous about her pupils' upcoming performance and gets support from such Desilu stalwarts as Vivian Vance and Bill Frawley, Spring Byington, Danny Thomas, George Murphy, Ann Sothern, and Lassie. The show begins with Lucy madly driving a golf cart through the Desilu Gower lot with a bobbling, fully decorated Christmas tree in back and Desi in the passenger seat, swamped by a stack of wrapped presents. "Seems like only *jesterday* that I made my first picture here," he says in the opening narration. That observation must have been bittersweet for the couple, who were now barely speaking and in the very spot where they had fallen for each other at first sight nearly twenty years earlier.

That December, the new issue of *Cosmopolitan* (dated January 1960) was already on the newsstands, and it contained an unusually searching and thoughtful profile of the Arnazes by Frederick Christian, who had spent time with them during the filming of the Milton Berle episode, in rehearsals for the *Revue*, and other behind-the-scenes moments. Christian noted that Bing Crosby, watching an episode of *I Love Lucy*, had once quietly murmured to one of his writers that the show had "a lot of heart." The article ended with a Desilu spokesman's not completely staunch denial that Lucy and Desi were planning to divorce, capped by a more poignant—and prescient—observation from Christian himself. "Driving back to my hotel," he wrote, "I kept seeing their faces: Desi's lined and intense, Lucy's drawn. I thought of their business-like, perfunctory conversations, with Desi hovering in the doorway of Lucy's sitting-dining room. And again I thought of Bing Crosby's comment: 'This show's got a lot of heart.' It does. And some of it may be broken."

. . .

For Desi and Lucy, the most painful task was to prepare the children for the heartbreak of the divorce to come. As Lucy later observed, they had already seen and heard too much. Lucie had an especially painful memory of a scene in the house in Rancho Mirage when she was as young as six. "The door was open to their bedroom," she recalled, "and I could see my dad sitting on a low chaise thing . . . and my mother was standing above him, and he was cowering, and she was screaming at him with these long fingernails, and she just . . . 'I wish you were dead!' She looked like a witch. And I was stunned, and then I remember that Willie Mae probably just kind of found me and took me away." Desi Jr. would recall that the problem with his parents was not that they were at work too much, though they worked fiercely hard. "They were at home," he said. "The problem was that they weren't getting along. And we knew it. And it wasn't that they weren't at home. They were home."

In the winter of early 1960, Lucy took the children—Lucie now eight and Desi Jr. about to turn seven—to Rancho Mirage, where Desi was already spending the weekends, so they could deliver the bad news together. "By way of easing them into what was ahead, we explained that there was going to be a separation, 'as of now,' and then, or a little later, there would probably be a divorce," Lucy remembered. "They would be seeing more of Daddy, Desi assured them, than they had been doing, and above all, we said in unison, we loved them very much." Lucie eventually broke a long silence to ask, "But you don't have to get a divorce, do you?" Desi Jr. said, "Can't you take it all back—and make up?"

"It wasn't good for anyone," Desi Jr. would say years later. "And we'll always remember when they sat us down and said, 'Look, you know, things aren't working.' I mean, I remember word for word." Years later, Desi Jr. would reflect: "They had it all, as Muhammad Ali said, 'I had the world,' and it was nothing."

There remained one last *Lucy-Desi* hour to be filmed—on March 2, 1960, Desi's forty-third birthday, nine years to the day after the Arnazes had shot the original tryout episode for *I Love Lucy*. The guest stars were the zany television comic Ernie Kovacs and his wife, the Broadway actress and singer Edie Adams, playing themselves in what was by now the inevitable "guest stars meet the Ricardos" conceit of the show. The plot has Ricky depressed at not getting any television or movie offers and feeling his career may be on the skids. To cheer him up, Lucy plans a cozy evening of dinner and entertainment with their new neighbors, the Kovacses, in what she hopes will amount to an audition for Ricky. Over after-dinner coffee, Adams sings the poignant— and aptly titled—ballad "That's All" to Ethel's piano accompaniment. But Ricky never gets to play his guitar, and Ernie is so impressed with Little Ricky's drum skills that he offers *him* a spot on his television show instead. The whole shoot was excruciating. An agitated Lucy made Adams do her hairstyle three different times. Desi was directing the episode, and since he and Lucy had essentially stopped speaking to each other, even the simplest stage directions were tense. "'Lucy, dear,' he'd say with elaborate politeness, 'would you please step over here when you say that line?'" Lucy recalled. "And I'd follow his directions without a word."

The last act of the show—none too plausible—has Lucy disguising herself as Kovacs's mustachioed chauffeur in an effort to make one more pitch on Ricky's behalf. But when she picks Kovacs up in his limousine, she is shocked to see that Ricky is with him and that a guest appearance is already lined up.

Lucy's cover is blown when Edie calls Ernie on his car phone, but the boys decide to torture Lucy a bit longer to teach her a lesson. When she is finally forced to reveal her identity, she plaintively explains, "Honest, honey, I was only trying to help."

"Look, Lucy," a somber Ricky says, with a long pause, his eyes downcast, "from now on, you can help me by not trying to help me, eh?"

Ernie finally leaves them alone, and they kiss. It was a moment as emotionally loaded as their kiss at the end of the first pregnancy episode nearly eight years earlier—but for the saddest of reasons. "This was not just an ordinary kiss for a scene in a show," Desi would recall. "It was a kiss that would wrap up twenty years of love and friendship, triumphs and failures, ecstasy and sex, jealousy and regrets, heartbreaks and laughter . . . and tears. The only thing we were not able to hide was the tears." In her own memoir, Lucy would simply write, "It marked the end of so many things."

The next day Lucy was in divorce court in Santa Monica, seeking a decree, in those days before no-fault divorce, on the grounds of "grievous mental suffering." The Arnazes' old friend Jim Bacon of the Associated Press told the tale in Lucy's hometown newspaper, the *Jamestown Post-Journal*: "Lucille Ball and Desi Arnaz, television's most popular married couple, are in the divorce courts today, victims of too much success. The red-haired comedienne, often called the greatest female clown, sued her Cuban tycoon in nearby Santa Monica. . . . Her charge was the usual Hollywood complaint—mental cruelty." Jack Hirshberg of the *Toronto Telegram* had a more acidic take. "Arnaz was frequently rude to her in public," he wrote, "and yesterday's trek to the divorce court was Lucille's reluctant admission that while Latins may not make lousy lovers, this one was no wow as a husband."

Rosemary Clooney, who lived just down the block from the Arnazes on Roxbury and was suffering her own marital troubles with an unfaithful José Ferrer (whom she married and divorced twice), had often commiserated with Lucy. "We'd laugh about our troubles until it got not so happy for both of us, you know," Clooney would recall years later. "I said to little Lucie once, 'There wasn't a chance on this block.' We had a Cuban on one end and a Puerto Rican on the other for God's sake."

It was the most excruciating irony that the show that Lucy and Desi had created together to save their marriage had now become the vehicle whose overwhelming success helped fuel the pressures that drove them apart. Over the years, many husbands and wives had written the Arnazes, crediting the adventures of Lucy and Ricky with making them more tolerant of each other's foibles and more forgiving. That, too, was a bittersweet irony. In a snippet of dictation for his memoir years after the breakup, Desi would recall receiving one such note: "Dear Ricky," it read. "Thank you very much for saving my marriage. I was about to leave my wife, convinced she was a nut, until I started looking at yours, which made mine look sane."

"Too bad," Desi added in rueful postscript, "I was never able to send Ricky a 'thank you note' for saving mine."

• • •

U nlike most modern long-running television series, which end with special episodes and a promotional bang, the *Lucy-Desi* show just ended. The Kovacs episode aired on April 1, and *Variety* was underwhelmed. "Miss Ball wasn't particularly up to form and Kovacs, apart from a couple of good sight gags, had to play reasonably straight," the reviewer wrote. "Even the lesser *Desi-Lucy* hours had at least one sequence in which Miss Ball turned in a show-stopping clowning routine. This one didn't."

If there was any silver lining to the divorce, it was the beginning of a much-improved relationship between Lucy and Desi, a gradually renewed warmth that would only deepen and soften for the rest of their lives. Their financial settlement was not rancorous; at first they even asked the Desilu lawyer Art Manella why he could not represent them both. In the end, he recommended an old friend of his, Milton Rudin, who would go on to represent Lucy for years to come while Manella represented Desi. And Desi and Lucy protected their business legacy by remaining very much tied together as president and vice president—and the largest stockholders—of Desilu.

That isn't to say that either one of them was cheerful. Lucy cried on the shoulders of the writer Bob Weiskopf and her workshop protégé Bob Osborne. She talked of leaving Hollywood and taking the children to live in Switzerland. Lucy took the houses in Beverly Hills and Rancho Mirage, while Desi divided his time between a penthouse at the Chateau Marmont and a forty-acre horse ranch he had bought in December 1959. In the short term, Lucy made a movie, *The Facts of Life*, her first since *Forever, Darling*, with her old friend and costar Bob Hope. It was a half-serious comedy about a topic perhaps too close to home—adultery. Stepping into a rowboat in one scene, Lucy gashed her leg and banged up her face. Desi rushed to Del Mar to be with her during her recuperation, sparking rumors of a reconciliation. Walter Winchell's column reported that he hoped "to keep two of my best friends from making what would be—in my opinion—a terrible mistake." The brief reunion only confirmed the Arnazes' conviction that the marriage was really over, and yet they could not quit each other. In September, Lucy and the kids headed to New York as she prepared to make her Broadway debut in a play with Desi as its uncredited producer.

The vehicle was *Wildcat*, a slender story about oil drillers in turn-of-the-century Texas, and its entire three-hundred-thousand-dollar capitalization was provided by Desilu. The score, by Cy Coleman and Carolyn Leigh, produced one enduring standard, "Hey, Look Me Over!," which was sung repeatedly in the show to make up for the rest of an underwhelming evening. *Wildcat* opened on December 16, 1960, but Lucy, brilliant as she was, was really neither a singer nor a dancer, and the critics were lukewarm at best. "Miss Ball is pouring her whole heart into a stencil," the respected Walter Kerr wrote in the *New York Herald Tribune*, while Richard Watts in the *New York Post* called the show "a tremendous disappointment." It ran for 171 performances but ultimately closed in May.

Before *Wildcat* opened, Ball had met a struggling nightclub comedian named Gary Morton at dinner with a mutual acquaintance and soon began dating him regularly. He was tall, ruggedly handsome, and despite the difference in their ages (he was at least a decade younger) and status (he had never played the big time) Lucy told friends that he made her laugh. Desi, affecting unconcern but actually resentful, would forever refer to Gary as "Barry Norton." And meantime, Lucy and Desi were still talking virtually every day, even after he went back to Los Angeles after the opening of *Wildcat*. In the winter of 1961, they actually considered remarriage—he had apparently proposed. But ultimately Lucy found herself remembering not the happy times with Desi but the bad ones.

Still, Lucie and Desi Jr. had not given up on a reconciliation. Over and over again during the summer and fall of 1961 they made their parents watch *The Parent Trap*, the new Walt Disney movie that starred Hayley Mills as twin sisters who were separated as babies but meet at summer camp and arrange the reunion of their long-divorced parents. But the lobbying was in vain. On November 19, just about eighteen months after her divorce, Lucy married Gary in a ceremony performed by her old spiritual counselor, the Reverend Norman Vincent Peale, at New York's Marble Collegiate Church.

. . .

Meantime, Desi continued running Desilu, with renewed pressures. In the summer of 1960 he had fired Martin Leeds. Tensions had been building for years, with Leeds increasingly resenting having to cover for Desi's erratic behavior and Desi resenting Leeds for gossiping too openly all over town about his drinking. "He phoned me at three o'clock in the morning, dead drunk," Leeds would recall. "I could have turned it around. I always had before whenever we had a fight." But Leeds's wife had recently died, and he was exhausted. Desi had come to have a jaundiced view of Leeds, describing him years later as "a man who could argue with you—underwater. He was always sincere—whether he meant it or not." Arnaz bought back Leeds's 35,000 shares of Desilu stock, valued at around $367,000, and bought out his $135,000-a-year contract.

Leeds's departure was a loss for the company, since he had enforced order and brought discipline to the studio's decision-making. Desilu now needed such qualities more than ever. The company's gross income for the fiscal year that ended in April 1961 had fallen to $19.8 million, compared to $23.4 million the prior year, and profits had shrunk by more than half, to $319,146, down from $811,000 in 1960. Desi's letter to shareholders that accompanied the 1961 annual report attributed the decline to a Writers Guild strike, write-offs for pilots that had not yet been picked up by the networks, and a reduction in production of Desilu's own shows, with the *Lucy-Desi* show and the *Desilu Playhouse* now off the air. The body of the annual report touted the company's deployment of a new Univac computer to analyze ratings and produce new pilots and programming that would draw maximum viewer and advertiser interest. But the report's tone had the air of protesting too much. "Desi Arnaz is the studio's top salesman as well as its chief executive officer and programming director," the report claimed. "With the comprehensive survey, he calls on the networks, the ad agencies, sometimes even a potential sponsor to discuss ratings and shows." An interim report to shareholders in November 1961 acknowledged that *The Untouchables* was now the only Desilu-owned program on the air, but insisted, "Your management is confident that success in the television industry is engendered through initiative, leadership, new ideas and top-quality management. With these concepts in mind, Desilu is on the threshold of a most prosperous future."

As 1962 approached, it was becoming increasingly apparent that such a future would depend on another series starring Lucille Ball. Since 1960, Desilu had managed to produce a few short-lived series: *Guestward Ho!*, the failed Vivian Vance vehicle, reworked for Joanne Dru; *Harrigan and Son*, a show about a father-and-son law firm starring Pat O'Brien; and a raft of pilots that either wound up not making it onto network schedules or never being produced at all. Desilu was still renting production facilities and services, or simply soundstage space, to *The Andy Griffith Show*, *My Three Sons*, *The Danny Thomas Show*, and *The Dick Van Dyke Show*, but the studio had nothing in its lineup remotely equal to the proven drawing power of Lucy.

Desi had bought the rights to a gently comic novel *Life Without George* by Irene Kampen, about a widowed single mother. He recruited Madelyn Pugh and the three Bobs—Carroll, Schiller, and Weiskopf— to come up with a scenario about a character named Lucille Carmichael, who was raising her two children in the fictional town of Danfield, New York. Bill Frawley was unavailable, having taken a part on *My Three Sons*, but Lucy persuaded a reluctant Vivian Vance to play her best friend, a divorcée named Vivian Bagley with a young son of her own. Jess Oppenheimer let it be known that the new character sounded a lot like the Lucy Ricardo he had registered as his own creation with the Writers Guild, and indeed it was. Oppenheimer eventually successfully sued to force a financial settlement. But for now the Arnazes quietly ignored him, and filming began at Desilu Gower in the summer of 1962, with Desi as executive producer.

When Vance arrived to start production, she found a dozen familiar faces but a very different feeling. Early in the shooting, she saw Desi high on a catwalk above the soundstage, looking down in tears. "Oh, Desi," she murmured as she embraced him, "it isn't the same, is it?" Years later, she summed up the change: "Here we were, starting again, only this time he was on the outside looking in, and it wasn't fun anymore. So much had happened to so many people, but most of all to Desi, leaving him alone, and a little sad, though he had tried to hide it."

The Lucy Show, as it was eventually titled (the original working title had been *We Love Lucy*), debuted on October 1, 1962, again on Monday nights, just a half hour earlier, at 8:30. Its rhythms were familiar to anyone who had watched television over the past decade. "So far, we have five scripts done, and already need a trampoline, two fencing masks, a do-it-yourself plywood paneling kit, the interior of a space capsule, and a sheep who likes to be sung to," Madelyn Pugh had written to Hedda Hopper. "So we are hopeful that it will have some of the old Lucy flavor." That it did. By the end of the first season's thirty episodes, the show ranked number five in the Nielsen ratings and had drawn overwhelmingly positive feedback from the critics.

Desi was responsible for conceiving the show, assuring its quality, and running it day-to-day. But it was Gary Morton who now warmed up the studio audience before filming, and Desi could not hide his disappointment. Desi was often drunk on the set, sometimes actually falling asleep in his director's chair until Lucy would contrive to have someone trip over his extended feet on purpose to wake him up without embarrassing him. "There was a part of him that wasn't there anymore," said the actress Candy Moore, who played Lucy's daughter. "Maybe his heart wasn't totally in it. He seemed chronically distracted. Although he never really did anything, he seemed like he was seething and almost about to explode. He had a drinking problem. He was hungover."

Even so, Desi remained belligerent—and in control—enough to

lower the boom on Lucy's brother, Fred Ball, who had been deputized
to confront him about his lapses.

"We're concerned that you're not running the studio," Fred told him.

"I'll tell you who's running the studio," Desi replied. "You're fired."

But in fact control was slipping away. Desi's own executives were
warning Lucy that she would have to assume greater responsibility
for business affairs, in which she had always deferred to her husband.
And despite the success of the new *Lucy Show*, Desilu's fortunes were
also floundering. For the fiscal year that ended April 1962, revenues
were down to $14.2 million from $19.8 million the year before, and net
earnings were just $611,921—a figure boosted by the onetime $340,000
sale to CBS of the company's residual interest in the thirteen *Lucy-Desi*
hours, part of the deal for the new *Lucy Show*. Even the strong ratings
for *The Untouchables* had at last declined, after its violence was toned
down and Desilu moved to save money on overtime for the crews by
using black muslin over the cameras to shoot night scenes during the
less costly daytime hours. "You can't please everyone," Robert Stack
complained, "and if you try, by doing something for a sponsor each
week and the network the next, you soon end up with nothing." Stack
believed the show's writing had begun to decline by the second year,
"and the third year, it became a copy of a copy, and the fourth year, it
didn't work at all." Early projections for the 1963–64 season showed
that Desilu would have just two hours of shows on the air, far behind
its rivals MCA (nine and a half hours) and Screen Gems (four hours).

There were structural and industrywide reasons for these changes.
Hour-long shows were becoming more popular and were too expensive for single sponsors, so multiple sponsors divided the cost of the
programs, which gave the networks the upper hand, since they negotiated the sponsorships. Moreover, except for *The Untouchables* and
the *Lucy-Desi* hours, Desilu had never had a solid hit with an hour-
long show.

But the indisputable factor in the company's decline was Desi's collapse as an effective steward of its fortunes. "Over a period of time, he assumed he didn't have to work hard to keep it together," Fred Ball would recall. "As a result of that, his life deteriorated and the studio itself deteriorated. He figured he had other interests that were more important than keeping a tight rein on the studio." It fell to Ed Holly, the company's low-key financial expert, to tell Desi that Lucy was invoking the long-standing buy-sell agreement they had signed before taking the company public. One of them would have to buy out the other's ownership interest. The plain truth was, Desi was in deep enough personal debt with activities like his Thoroughbred breeding farm that he could not have afforded to buy Lucy out even if he had wanted to. And he didn't seem to want to. "He rather readily agreed that he had lost the drive or the punch or the interest to continue," Holly remembered years later. And so Desi would have to sell his shares to Lucy.

Lucy offered more than generous terms. She paid Desi ten dollars a share at a time when the stock was publicly trading around seven dollars, down from its high of twenty dollars a share, making his total payout roughly three million dollars (more than thirty million in 2024 dollars). On November 9, 1962, his last day in the office, Desi sat at his desk in front of the big mullioned window overlooking his domain and gazed around at the shelves with their expensive leather-bound volumes of *Lucy* scripts and scores of awards and mementos. "After sitting there in my big chair, looking around for quite a while," he would recall, "I picked up an old octagonal leather piece, two inches high, with eight pictures of Lucie and Desi, which was always on my desk, and that's all I took and left."

Though it could not have been a complete surprise, his sudden departure nevertheless came as a shock to the industry—and to the hundreds of workers at the company he had built. He left behind only a short memo: "All Desilu employees: I just want to thank all of you for your cooperation, trust and loyalty. Also, I want to wish each one of you the best of luck in the future. Sincerely, Desi."

In her interim report to shareholders a month later, her first as company president, Lucy wrote, "I am sure you will join the board of directors, your officers and your employees in extending our appreciation and gratitude to Desi Arnaz for his contribution to the growth of your company from its inception in 1951 until his resignation as president last month."

A better indication of her deepest feelings was this: She never let anyone else occupy Desi's office but moved into it herself.

sixteen

Slow Fade

With his Desilu windfall—three million dollars, at a time when a new Rolls-Royce cost about eight thousand—Desi made good on his intention to take it easy. In December 1959, before the divorce, he had bought a horse ranch in Corona, in northwestern Riverside County, about fifty miles east of Los Angeles, where he raised Thoroughbreds. He took pleasure in reliving the life of a *ranchero* that he had first known as a kid on the family's land in El Cobre. In 1961 he had purchased an oceanfront house in Del Mar, where the family had long rented and spent summers with Marcus and Marcella Rabwin. And in Rancho Las Cruces, a beachfront club and community in Baja California started by his old friend Rod Rodriguez, the son of a former Mexican president, he would build an elegant white stucco house with a guitar-shaped swimming pool, where he could relive something akin to his youth on Cayo Smith. Baja—on roughly the same meridian as Cuba—became his place of refuge, where he could fish and drink and escape, remembering the triumphs of the past while facing a future that loomed as uncertain. "He also put into the Bank of Mexico enough money to pay all expenses of the home from the accrued interest," Marcella Rabwin recalled. That last move was a smart, but ultimately unsuccessful, idea, since by 1961 Desi's annual expenditures of about $175,000 were already exceeding his estimated after-tax income of $150,000. For the rest of his life, he would increasingly invade his principal to live on, and while his children still own the house in Mexico, Desi's planned nest egg for its maintenance ran out before he died.

Most important, on his forty-sixth birthday, March 2, 1963, Desi remarried, to Edith Eyre McSkimming Hirsch, an attractive, lively, five-foot-four-inch redhead whom he had first met when she was a cigarette girl at the Santa Anita racetrack. Edie and her former husband, Clement Hirsch, a wealthy horseman and proprietor of the Kal Kan pet food empire, had been friends with Lucy and Desi in the Del Mar social circle that included the Rabwins and Jimmy and Marge Durante, who witnessed Desi and Edie's wedding, along with Van Johnson, at the Sands Hotel in Las Vegas. Desi and Edie's relationship had begun while she was still married, and at one point the once and future husbands each had private detectives tailing the other. The whole thing got "kind of silly," in Desi's words, and they agreed to call off the dogs—but not before Desi's visiting father, with whom he had gradually developed warm relations in his last years with Lucy, crouched protectively in the bushes outside Clement Hirsch's house with a .38 in case the negotiations went south. Edie got a quickie Mexican divorce, and Lucy sent a horseshoe-shaped congratulatory arrangement of flowers with the message YOU BOTH PICKED A WINNER.

Edie was easygoing, or at least forbearing, in ways that Lucy was not. "If I blow my top she will pay absolutely no attention to me whatsoever," Desi would recall. "She will start doing the dishes or finding something else to do, and sometimes I get so goddamn mad at her, I say, 'Why won't you argue with me?' You know, I'm so used to Lucy and

I arguing and Lucy throwing coffee pots or chairs or something, you know . . . that this is kind of a switch."

Lucie and Desi Jr. had always felt warmly about Edie, who brought her own six-year-old son, Greg Hirsch, to the blended family. Greg found in Desi a warm and loving stepfather. "You couldn't help but be in awe of Desi whenever he entered the room," he recalled. "We fished with Durante on the beach at night. They'd be there every night at ten thirty with an empty bucket of salt water, waiting for the first fish." When Greg got older, he would go out fishing with his mother, Desi, Desi Jr., and Lucie on Desi's latest boat, a forty-eight-footer christened *Mi Querida*, "My Darling." On one trip, Lucie caught the first fish—a marlin—and Desi raised a blue flag on the boat's angled flagpole. Then Desi Jr. caught a sailfish and his father hoisted a red flag. Finally, Greg caught a ninety-five-pound wahoo, a member of the tuna family, so heavy that it broke his rod in half. Desi helped reel in the catch, but there was no flag for it, and Greg began to cry. "He takes my mother down in the bow, and he tells her to take off her brassiere and he runs it up the pole next to the other flags," Hirsch remembered years later, adding Desi's words: "Okay, amigo, there's no flag for a wahoo, but when we go into the beach, all the people are gonna say, *Okay, blue flag for the marlin, red flag for the sailfish*, and they're gonna go *Wahoo!* for the brassiere, okay?"

Lucie would recall that her father was "more fun" than her mother in those days but added: "In all fairness, he had us on weekends and summers. My mother was working really, really hard, and then she'd come home and the guilt of not having been there all day, the first thing she'd go was, 'Did you do this, did you do that, did you get that done?' So Mrs. Responsibility you know, Madame Responsible. And my dad would be like, 'You wanna go horseback riding or do you wanna go fishing?' So how can you compare the two?"

Desi would ultimately have a total of four kitchens in the Del Mar house—one on the beachfront porch, one on the main floor, one in an

apartment over the garage, and one on a second-floor lanai he built
when he added a top story so he could install Lolita in residence downstairs. "And sometimes he would use all four kitchens if he was cooking
for a lot of people," Lucie recalled.

But Desi's personality could shift dramatically when he was drinking. "He had a real marshmallow streak," recalled Paul Rabwin, Marc
and Marcella's son, noting that when he grew up he sometimes thought
his name was "Amigo," because that's what Desi always called him. At
the same time, Rabwin acknowledged, "I saw him throw more than
one babysitter down the stairs." Desi Jr. acknowledged his father's
"Latin emotion." "Right out in front," he remembered. "He wore his
heart on his sleeve—which was good at times, maybe not so good at
other times." As Lucie grew into her teenage years, she became more
disturbed by Desi's drinking and eventually stopped going down to the
beach.

• • •

After three years of fishing, horse breeding, and general loafing—
and, one suspects, a combination of boredom and a dwindling
bank balance—Desi decided to get back in the game. As 1966 dawned,
the entertainment press announced his comeback: A DIFFERENT DESI
RETURNS TO FILMLAND was the headline on an Associated Press story.
Desi had formed a new company, Desi Arnaz Productions Incorporated (DAPI), for which he rented space at Desilu Culver, taking David
Selznick's plush former quarters as his own office and pronouncing
Lucy "the prettiest landlady in the world." Still, the Hollywood press
continued to present Desi to the world in stereotype. Hal Humphrey,
the *Los Angeles Times*'s syndicated television columnist, published an
interview that rendered Desi's comments in accented dialect. "The
thins that got me where I was were the thins I couldn't do when I got
there," Humphrey reported. "Thins got too big before. There'll be no
more studio and I'm very happy just paying rent to Lucy."

Desi's passion project at this crossroads was a strange one, an obscure novel called *Without Consent* by Theodore Pratt. *Without Consent* was a dark tale about an otherwise ordinary nineteen-year-old college boy who is overcome with carnal urges and rapes a teenage girl in a Florida swamp town. The novel—creepy for its time and repugnant six decades later—recounts how the boy's defense attorney consults a supposedly pathbreaking sexologist, who theorizes that "to rape and be raped is one of the primal urges of man." The book advocates the natural health benefits of masturbation, praises the public licensing of bordellos in "Latin countries," and generally asserts that women are raped because they ask for it by wearing provocative clothing in an increasingly permissive society; men can't be expected to help themselves. Desi envisioned Spencer Tracy as the crusading lawyer, and he put more than fifty thousand dollars of his own money (ten times that in 2020s currency) into buying the rights and commissioning a screenplay from Ben Maddow, the respected author of *The Asphalt Jungle*.

Years later, Desi would describe the project as "a very touching love story," explaining his view that it reflected "a peculiar period of American society's attitude toward sex—confusing and hypocritical" in which "our young people were pretty messed up. It had to deal with increasing nudity, masturbation and, of course, rape—subjects which were then tabu [*sic*] for a film. Even the mention of the word masturbation was forbidden. So not thinking that I could possibly fail in treating these subjects honestly, in good taste, and successfully, I went ahead and rented studio space."

At one point, Desi tried to rewrite the script himself and enlisted Marcella Rabwin as his secretary. "I kept saying, 'Desi, it's such a repulsive subject,'" she would remember. He called her after writing fifteen or twenty pages and asked for help, and she was surprised to find that "he had written it quite well. . . . He had tremendous enthusiasm for it. A large part of what I did was to put down his thoughts and rearrange them as scenes." When their effort ended, he sent her an effusive letter of thanks, along with a fur coat. But *Without Consent* was no *To Kill a Mockingbird*, and the script was never completed. "He never could sell it," Rabwin said.

That was surely a blessing, for Desi and for the wider world. But his intense interest in the project—and his empathy for the protagonist— offers a window into his views about sexuality, which were, to put it mildly, a strange mixture of free-thinking, sexist, misogynistic, and tortured. In unpublished draft notes for his memoir years later, he made a stab at explaining himself. "I have always needed lots of sex and have been promiscuous," he wrote. "While confessing this to a brilliant and modern priest friend of mine, he suggested that perhaps I was really afraid of women and unable to relate to them in a continuing and meaningful way and that my sexual exploitation and promiscuity was to convince myself of my 'machismo' (masculinity) and to disguise my fear." In a frustrated moment, Lucy herself once reflected on a similar theme. When Bob Schiller asked her why she thought Desi, six years younger, had married her when her busy Hollywood career so dwarfed his nascent one, her answer was flip. "She says, 'I know all about that mother figure crap,'" Schiller recalled. "'But why didn't somebody tell me that he hated his mother?'"

On the other side of the parent-child dynamic, Desi was "ridiculously protective" of his daughter. "I couldn't go to a bonfire on the beach with twenty other kids and stay out past nine o'clock in the summer," Lucie remembered. "You know, he'd come up on the porch with a gun, a rifle, 'It's nine o'clock, get up here!' Jesus. I mean the boys don't come back after that, I want you to know. They don't want to have bonfires with girls whose fathers carry rifles. . . . And when he was drinking, it got worse, and then he would imagine things and accuse me of stuff that I was even too young to understand what he was saying." In late August 1966, Desi chased some teenage boys away from the Del Mar house by firing a gun into the air. He said he'd fired blanks, but the gun's chamber was empty, and he couldn't prove it. The police held him for a few hours before releasing him on bail.

After realizing that *Without Consent* wasn't going anywhere, Desi recalled, "It became necessary to get involved in some network financed television projects to help pay the rent to Lucy and the salaries to those I had already hired." One idea seemed particularly promising. In the fall of 1966, he developed a pilot for Carol Channing, the croaky-voiced, saucer-eyed Broadway star fresh from her triumph in *Hello, Dolly!* Bob and Madelyn wrote the episode, which introduces a ditzy small-town girl, no longer exactly young, who comes to Manhattan to try to make it in show business and causes chaos for the friends who put her up. Desi directed what amounted to a Lucy-less version of *I Love Lucy*, sometimes with leering close-ups of Channing's face that were too big and too intense for the small screen.

But the network balked, and Channing went off to make the film *Thoroughly Modern Millie*, which won her an Oscar nomination for Best Supporting Actress. Desi was crushed, as he said in a letter to Abe Lastfogel, the powerful head of the William Morris Agency. "I'm still in a state of shock as a result of our conversation last night," he wrote. "I cannot overemphasize how important the success or failure of these shows are, not only to my career but to my personal life and future plans. In other words, Amigo, if anyone ever really needed you before, your Cuban friend sure needs you now. Please try as best as you can. Hopefully and affectionately."

Desi did produce one series in the late sixties that clicked. That was *The Mothers-in-Law*, a comedy about a quartet of less-than-friendly next-door neighbors in Los Angeles whose children marry each other, forcing a tense bonhomie and all manner of misadventures. It starred the Desilu stalwart Eve Arden and Kaye Ballard in the title roles and premiered on NBC on Sunday, September 10, 1967, sandwiched between *Walt Disney's Wonderful World of Color* and *Bonanza* and competing with CBS's still-popular *Ed Sullivan Show*. Bob and Madelyn were the series' creators and principal writers, and it featured guest appearances by a roster of established and future TV mainstays, including Ozzie Nelson, Jimmy Durante, Paul Lynde, Larry Storch, Alice Ghostley, and a young actor named Rob Reiner, the son of the comedian Carl Reiner, the man who had created *The Dick Van Dyke Show*.

In contrast to the single-camera method that had by then become more typical for sitcoms, the show was filmed the old Desilu way, with three cameras before a live audience—at least part of the time on the old General Services lot where *I Love Lucy* had begun. During the week, Desi and Edie lived in a two-bedroom bungalow on the lot so Greg could go to school in Beverly Hills. "For me, it was cool," he recalled—especially since *Batman* was being filmed on the same lot.

The Mothers-in-Law's opening credits ("Desi Arnaz Presents") featured hipster Day-Glo colors and cartoonish typefaces, but its plotlines were non-topical throwbacks to Lucy-esque situations: neighborly arguments, domestic crises, physical slapstick. It was funny enough (and would develop a minor cult following in the era of home video), but it broke no new ground at a time when broader society was changing dramatically. "There is nothing 'new' or 'different' about *The Mothers-in-Law*, any more than there is anything new or different about the circus or the way people laugh," Desi told *Variety* somewhat defensively after the show premiered. "People laugh at something funny and *The Mothers-in-Law* is funny. That's all it is. It doesn't pretend to be anything else."

Desi directed most of the shows and made four guest appearances himself as a Spanish bullfighter, Rafael Del Gado, starting in a special two-part episode titled "The Hombre Who Came to Dinner." In a Latin twist on the old Kaufman and Hart play about a demanding houseguest who has an accident that forces him to stay underfoot for weeks, Señor Del Gado is gored by a Viking helmet in an attempt to demonstrate his bullfighting technique (don't ask) and utterly disrupts his hosts' daily routine: eating dinner at 11 p.m.; ordering up roast suckling pig (which turns out to be a live little porker named Bright Eyes that no one can bear to kill); and importing all seven of Snow White's dwarves after a manic day of sightseeing that ends in Disneyland. Sidelined from bullfighting by his injury, Del Gado agrees to perform in a talent show instead and hires his hosts' drum-crazy grocery delivery boy, Tommy, played by Desi Jr.

When Tommy comes through the hosts' door to audition, beating a conga drum and wailing a plaintive song, Del Gado (who seems about half-crocked) demands, "What's the name of that thing you singing there?"

" 'Babalú,' " Tommy answers.

"Never heard of it!" Del Gado rejoins as the studio audience explodes in appreciative laughter.

The show lasted two seasons (NBC renewed it only after the sponsor, Procter & Gamble, threatened to take it to a rival network), wound up at fortieth place in the weekly ratings, and was surely not helped by Desi's ongoing personal struggles. As had become his pattern, he alternated on the set between warm avuncularity and volcanic outbursts.

"I was in the middle of a scene and I improvised, I started improvising," Rob Reiner would recall of his second guest appearance. "And Desi just blew his stack. I mean, he says, 'I pay ten thousand dollars a script! What are you doing? You cannot improvise. I don't like these improvisational actors!' And he starts screaming at me, screaming like this, and he says, you know, and he walked off the stage, and I thought 'Oh, my God, what have I done here?' you know, and then everybody said, 'Don't go out there, don't talk to this guy, he's crazy.'

"I went out there and said, 'Listen, Desi,' . . . and he said, 'Don't talk to me like this. . . . Maybe that's the way they do it on the Van Dyke show,' he was talking about my father . . . 'but we don't do that on this show' . . . and he's pushing me, literally pushing me up against a soundstage."

Desi eventually apologized, saying, "No, no, Amigo, that's all right. Amigo, you got talent," but Reiner told him he'd better find another actor.

Arnaz found himself having a harder and harder time getting projects on the air. A worksheet in his files from this era lists ten abandoned projects, with losses from Desi's personal outlays totaling $189,548 (about $1.5 million in 2024). In 1968, he made appearances for Richard Nixon's presidential campaign, making a swing through Texas wearing a "Nixon Numero Uno" button, composing a campaign song to the tune of one of his father's old melodies, and insisting that the nation needed "two Ricardos."

"There is nothing in it for me" if Nixon wins, Desi said. "I'm not going to become the ambassador to Cuba or Mexico," though Nixon did eventually appoint him as the nation's unpaid goodwill liaison to Latin America.

. . .

In 1967, Lucy had sold Desilu to the Gulf & Western conglomerate, which already owned the Paramount Pictures studio next door on Melrose Avenue. The price was $17 million, of which her personal share was about $10 million (or nearly $100 million in 2024). She had never liked dealing with the business aspects of the company and was often insecure without Desi's advice, which she still routinely sought. "She said, 'You know, when I was married to the Cuban, Desi did everything,'" the actress Carol Burnett recalled. "'Then all I had to do was come in on a Monday and be crazy little Lucy.'" As an executive, Lucy suddenly had to make tough decisions, Burnett went on. "And she said, 'Kid, that's when they put the s on the end of my last name.'" Lucy did make one very tough business decision that would influence pop culture for decades to come. In her last year running the company, Desilu was offered two pilots for dramatic series that would be so expensive in the short term—and demand such cash flow—that the company's top

...

executives told Lucy she would have to sell Desilu if she green-lit them. The executives told her that any profits from these series would be far in the future, but Lucy believed in both projects and approved them. The series were *Star Trek* and *Mission: Impossible*, both of which would eventually reap billions of dollars in earnings for Paramount.

In the fall of 1968, Lucy began production on a third comedy series for CBS, *Here's Lucy*, in which she portrayed yet another variation on the indelible character—this time with Lucie and Desi Jr. playing her children. Desi and Edie would come for the tapings, and Gary continued to do warm-ups, introducing Desi as "my ex-husband-in-law." Dorothy Aldworth, a script supervisor, said that the chemistry was still obvious between Lucy and Desi. "There was a tremendous pull between the two of them, even though she tried not to show it," she said. "Lucy was very nice to him, but she found other things to do while he was there or would go to her dressing room. The people who knew him would surround him so she wouldn't have to be face to face with him." When the new show debuted in September, Desi took out full-page ads in *Variety* and the *Hollywood Reporter*: "LUCIE AND DESI: I AM SO PROUD. LOVE, DAD. P.S.—THAT RED-HEADED GAL PLAYING YOUR MOTHER IS THE GREATEST."

Desi had tried to be a good father. "I never thought they did anything but love us with all their hearts," Desi Jr. remembered. But the younger Desi, especially, struggled. As a little boy he often had trouble sleeping, sometimes, he would recall, on account of nightmares prompted by Disney movies screened in the family's projection room. More than once he left penciled notes for Lucy begging to "sleep on the little thin bed in your room" signed "Desi Arnaz IV." Barely into his teens, he had become the drummer in a band with his friends Dean Paul "Dino" Martin and Billy Hinsche, and they were pulling in four thousand dollars for weekend gigs, going on tour with the Beach Boys, and opening for the Mamas & the Papas on breaks from school. He was growing up too fast in ways that would lead to years of drug and alcohol abuse. Desi had told his son the band was all right only if he kept his grades up. "I don't want a stupid drummer around the house," he said, his intensity surely reflecting his abiding regret about the limits of his own formal education. When Desi Jr. turned sixteen, Desi wrote him a letter echoing almost word for word the advice his own father had given him at the same age. He warned his son that he would surely face a tight spot someday, and when he did, he should do nothing until thinking the situation through. Then, when he set course, he should let nothing stop him. That's certainly how Desi himself had lived. "Remember, good things do not come easy, and you will have your share of woe," he wrote. "The road is lined with pitfalls. But, you will make it, if when you fail, you try and try again." He urged him not to forget that "the Man upstairs" is always there to offer help—and not to be afraid to ask for it.

By this point Desi's own failures had become more common than his successes. For some years, his Thoroughbred operation in Corona had been profitable—producing some winning horses, including Amerigo's Fancy, winner of the 1968 Santa Barbara handicap—and eventually a lucrative breeding operation. "It was a going business until it wasn't," Lucie Arnaz recalled. In October 1968, Desi advertised in the *Hollywood Reporter* for a "100% sale" of his stock. "The value of the land has become so attractive that I can no longer make long range plans for our current operation," he wrote. "Thus I feel, after much thought and many considerations, that I am forced to curtail my thoroughbred activities."

At the end of 1968, Desi's years of abusing his body caught up with him, and he was rushed to Cedars of Lebanon for emergency diverticulitis surgery that resulted in a temporary colostomy. But he did not change his habits.

In the summer of 1970, after the cancelation of *The Mothers-in-Law*, Desi took a guest-starring role in the Western television series *The Men from Shiloh*. "The simple truth is I was getting tired of seeing Ricardo Montalban and Fernando Lamas in all these Mexican roles," he told the press. Not long after, Lew Wasserman, the chairman of MCA, which owned Universal Studios, gave Desi office space and a development deal. Desi proposed a comeback vehicle for himself, *Chairman of the Board*, in which the commonsensical proprietor of a New York bar and grill becomes the head of a large corporation, but it never got even to the stage of producing a pilot. He appeared in a 1974 episode of the popular *Ironside* crime drama as Juan Domingo, a Cuban refugee physician and amateur detective. The role was envisioned for a possible spinoff, but Desi was often simply too drunk to function.

"I don't think Desi wanted to leave the industry," the former Desilu executive Bernie Weitzman said. "I think the industry left him."

seventeen

Sunset

From a desire to take stock, claim overdue credit, make money, or—most likely—some combination of all these motives, Desi resolved to write his memoirs. In the fall of 1973, he signed with William Morrow for a substantial advance of $125,000 (more than $800,000 in 2020s dollars) and agreed to work with the veteran editor Howard Cady, who had been in the trade since Desi was drumming with Cugat and who had published the memoirs of Bette Davis and Errol Flynn, among others. Desi set out to collaborate on the drafting with Kenny Morgan, by now divorced from Cousin Cleo, and from the start the process was fraught. For one thing, Morgan was also a bad drinker and enabler who brought out Desi's worst behavior. Reliving his life also proved painful for Desi.

At fifty-six, Desi was not anywhere near what Winston Churchill had called "the broad, sunlit uplands" of life, and the stock-taking was frightening. His second marriage was not going well—he had come to a kind of armed truce with Edie and a grim view of himself. An early note for the book—in the form of an apparently unsent letter to Edie—makes that clear.

"In the last few years I have gone from the guy who you seemed to be madly in love with, respected, admired, understood and loved to have sex with, to a guy whom you told you didn't love anymore, had no respect for, were ashamed of, did not understand and only occasionally submitted to have limited versions of sex with," he wrote with raw candor. "Once it was, 'Your life is my life—anything you want to do is what I want to do.' Now it is, 'I have my own life to live.' You were either wrong then or you are wrong now. Whichever it is, it is more than I can handle. Many things have happened in the last few years. I have gone from the Penthouse at the Chateau Marmont to the cellar of your sister's house—from a guy who never thought about the cost of anything to one who has to count pennies—from the plushest office in my business to a closet at Universal. The change has not been easy for me and probably it was not easy for you either. I am 56 years old and trying to do something I never thought I would have to do—make a comeback. God knows, I am trying hard. Whether I should keep on trying or give up and adjust to a new way of life—whether I should stay with you or not—are things that I do not know at this moment and so in all honesty, I cannot tell you what it will be. That is the problem. Maybe time will bring a solution and I hope that when it does, it is the right one. In the meantime, let's try to be civilized enough to make it easy on each other. I will deposit $5,000 in your checking account at Del Mar today, so that you, at least, will not have to worry about your needs for the time being."

In March 1974, Cady wrote to Desi's agent, Marvin Moss, summing up a recent trip to Del Mar to work on the manuscript. He explained why he was willing to come to Los Angeles for another session but was resisting Desi's invitation to visit the Baja house at Rancho Los Cruces. "If I am a guest in his home, if I cannot walk out when the stuff gets too rough or too deep, if we are too near the bar, if he brings in local entertainment"—an apparent euphemism for hookers—"(and I can think of many more ifs), the author-editor relationship will go right down the drain," Cady wrote. He said that Desi had been conscientious and productive in their previous session. "He absolutely amazed me last September, but he was tired after four or five hours of taping," he wrote. "Thinking about his life reminded him of all kinds of things that troubled him. He had been on the wagon for a long while and he needed to get drunk. When he did, however, he came damn near blowing the whole deal on two different occasions. Not even Rex Harrison has talked to me the way he did." He added: "I am very fond of Desi and I have no intention of taking any crap from him."

Desi dictated his recollections to Morgan or Cady, with the manuscript having to be pulled out of him a page at a time. By June, Cady was reacting to early drafts, urging Desi to cut lengthy sections about Cuban politics from the beginning of the story. He also recommended trimming several passages of "schoolboy boasting of sexual contests" that made Desi "much less a man of the world who has been properly trained in the best whorehouse in Santiago, Cuba." A week later Cady wrote again, noting that Kenny Morgan had communicated Desi's anger at his editorial suggestions. "Frankly, I don't know what to do. You want my help and advice and the benefit of the experience I have gained during the past 37 years of editing books. At the same time, however, you want to oversee the operation more or less in the role that you had at Desilu Productions. In a sense, I find myself working for you. The trouble is, however, I have to account to my leaders here." At the same time, Cady praised Desi's skills as a storyteller and urged him to provide more atmospheric details about "a typical visit up to Polly Adler's" bordello and about the personalities of Rodgers and Hart and George Abbott. "Face the fact that I want more for you out of this book than you do," he advised. "Don't think of me as sitting here trying to make trouble for you."

Voluminous drafts of the manuscript suggest that Desi ultimately took most of Cady's suggestions. For better and worse, the book is authentically in Desi's voice, full of good humor, enthusiasm, and at times a wry self-awareness. But in his telling, he is also perennially the hero of his own life, sometimes to the extent of taking credit for the contributions of others. For example, a reader of the book would not know that Jess Oppenheimer was the producer of I Love Lucy or that Al Simon was a crucial link in the development of the three-camera filming method. Desi may have felt resentful of Hollywood having taken for granted his contributions to the creation and success of I Love Lucy, but now he was swinging the pendulum too far in the other direction in a bid to make certain that posterity would credit him. The narrative stops with the end of I Love Lucy and his divorce from Lucy, concluding on a bittersweet note. "If we hadn't done anything else but bring that half-hour of fun, pleasure and relaxation to most of the world, a world in such dire need of even that short time-out from its sorrows and problems, we should be content," Desi wrote.

A Book ("What a weak and uninteresting title!" Marcella Rabwin would sniff) was published at the start of 1976, to modest fanfare. Its cover billed the book as "The outspoken memoirs of 'Ricky Ricardo'— the man who loved Lucy," effectively selling Desi as the second-billed character in his own life. A publicity tour sent him to The Tonight Show with Johnny Carson and also onto a new late-night program called simply NBC's Saturday Night, where Desi appeared with Desi Jr. as a musical guest in a series of only-sort-of-funny sketches that uncomfortably straddled the line between fond homage and campy send-up. One bit purported to have uncovered a lost pilot episode of I Love Lucy, with Desi Jr. playing Ricky and Gilda Radner playing Lucy in I Loathed Lucy, a tale of spousal abuse. Another prolonged riff on The Untouchables had Desi playing a gangster with drugs hidden in a conga drum. Finally, Desi played a doctor specializing in "Cuban ack-a-puncture" who treats John Belushi with cigars, not needles, in his ears and nostrils before giving him a therapeutic hotfoot. The show concluded with a rousing rendition of "Babalú."

"I remember him yelling at the crew," *Saturday Night* writer Al Franken recalled. "He referred to them by their union number—local 554 or something like that. He was the only host who ever did that. I also remember that we had awfully long goodnights that night—the show was a little short—and he was leading a conga line, playing his drum, and it went on and on and we were worried that he'd have a heart attack."

A Book was serialized in the *National Enquirer*, far from the most prestigious outlet, and drew mostly brief reviews of a few paragraphs in the major newspapers. *Variety* complained that Desi had overshared about his sex life in a narrative with "a great deal of vulgarity," while the *San Diego Union* judged: "He likes wine, women and song . . . not necessarily in that order. And who will say nay to him on that score?" Still, the book rose to number nine on the *New York Times* bestseller list, though sales would slow by the end of April. In early May, Cady wrote to Marvin Moss that there was no competition for paperback rights and no interest from the major book clubs. He also said that the publisher was already spending more than one dollar in promotion for every book shipped and was unwilling to do more unless sales picked up. Ultimately, *A Book* sold about thirty thousand copies in hardcover, a respectable showing, but it failed to earn back its advance. Eventually, the publisher would write to Moss, insisting that Desi surrender the last $1,532.61 of the payment that had been held in escrow from the first serial sale to the *Enquirer*.

Desi did not give up. At the end of 1976 he wrote to Moss, outlining his ideas for a sequel, to be called *Another Book*, in a six-page, single-spaced book proposal. Picking up his life story from the sale of his half of Desilu to Lucy, he tried to explain his decision to quit the business. "For now, just the essence of it—once you arrive at the plateau of success we were at, you find yourself in a whole new ballgame where the players are engaged in fierce competition for more and more success and more and more money and more and more power, and which strains and tensions are such that the only relief they find is in pills, alcohol and sex which enables them, for at least a short time, to continue in this seemingly endless contest," he wrote. "A merry-go-round you wonder how you got on and how in hell you can get off! Most people never get off for fear of losing it all." He promised to explain "How do you at 42 years of age, much too young to retire and too old to begin college, go about searching for a new life?"

But just as the starch had gone out of him in life, so the conviction was lacking in the book proposal. It amounted to one long unintentional admission that since 1962, and *The Lucy Show*, he really hadn't accomplished enough professionally to interest a broad readership. William Morrow passed on the idea of any sequel. Desi never followed through on a suggestion from Howard Cady that might actually have made a compelling book: an account of his encounters with the great and good of show business, in the mold of David Niven's charming, episodic 1975 portrait of his famous Hollywood friends, *Bring on the Empty Horses*.

The roster of those famous friends was dwindling for Desi. In January 1980, his longtime pal and neighbor Jimmy Durante, who had suffered a debilitating stroke in 1972, died, and his widow, Marge, asked Desi to organize the funeral. Mrs. Durante asked the actress and singer Constance Towers to sing Gounod's "Ave Maria." As Towers recalled, "She told me that Desi was producing the funeral and I thought, 'Oh, boy, this is going to be interesting,' because my only experience with Desi was when he was drinking, and it was chaotic. So when we sat down to plan the funeral, the thing that was so extraordinary to me was that he had just—either by a doctor's directive or his own volition or whatever, he had totally dried out. He was completely, totally sober, and I had the opportunity, the privilege, of working with the brilliant, clearheaded Desi Arnaz. I was so impressed. I saw the genius in the way he organized the whole funeral. He had to decide who goes on first—Bob Hope or Danny Thomas—and they were both being very temperamental about it. I'd heard all these stories about how he was responsible for *I Love Lucy* and so on, and I could see it all."

Over the following months, Desi was restless and once again suffering a variety of ailments. In March 1980 he was treated at Scripps Memorial Hospital in La Jolla for an ulcer and arthritis, prescribed Percocet for pain, and advised to hew to a daily diet of no more than twelve hundred calories. In an exercise log he kept that summer, he recorded, "The problem is the legs, due to my knees, can't take much. Swimming is not bad but ocean water is too cold. I am going to try a wet suit . . . I am hungry most all the time."

He scratched out ideas for civic improvement in Del Mar, an acting school or theater club, a cable TV or radio station; ideas for tours, concerts, or Las Vegas club dates; television commercials; notions for short stories or novels—one called "Lulu and Dario." He made notes of a telephone conversation with CBS's Bill Paley in which he proposed a special to commemorate the thirtieth anniversary of *I Love Lucy.* On bits of various hotel stationery he jotted other ideas in illegible, evidently drunken handwriting. On the cardboard back of a yellow legal pad he recorded a grid of $100 and $150 bets on the Angels, Chargers, Rams, Padres, and Dodgers—together with phone numbers, presumably of bookies—and in the far-right column the repeated notation "lost, lost, lost."

· · ·

Around this time Desi took one last shot at performing. The director Francis Ford Coppola had recently launched Zoetrope Studios, his bid to replicate the story-to-screen-style atelier of the old studio system—with writers, directors, and cameramen all working under one sheltering roof. Working with his longtime producing associate Fred Roos, Coppola bought the old General Service Studios, and one of his first projects was *The Escape Artist,* a quirky film to be directed by the cinematographer Caleb Deschanel. Based on a novel by David Wagoner, the movie tells the story of an orphaned teenager, a would-be magician out to redeem the reputation of his late father, once known as an escape artist second only to Houdini. When the film was released in 1982, the *New York Times*'s Vincent Canby pronounced it "not quite a fantasy, not quite an adventure, not quite a comedy, not quite coherent on any level."

The film stars Griffin O'Neal, the son of Ryan and brother of Tatum, and a virtual Who's Who of Hollywood veterans like Jackie Coogan and newcomers like Raul Julia, who plays the slightly menacing son of a corrupt mayor. The mayor is played by Desi, who chose to be billed for the first and only time as "Desiderio Arnaz" in deference to Desi Jr., whose own screen career had by now made him perhaps better known to a new generation. On-screen Desi looks cadaverous, his character appearing with long white hair, blue lips, and a volcanic temper. A key element of the plot turns on the mayor's purloined wallet, filled with marked bills, and at one point, Julia plops down in Desi's lap like a naughty little boy, and there is a physical struggle as Desi's office chair flips over, landing him flat on his back.

"When we did that scene, and I'm really not sure where it came from, but Desi and Raul Julia got into the most heated screaming confrontation with each other over it," Deschanel remembered. "And I have no idea what they were saying because it was all in Spanish. It was really kind of fascinating because it was sort of this wonderful moment and it kind of ended up petering out and defusing, and they went back to work without ninety percent of people on the set having any idea what it was about. But I suspect it had a lot to do with the fact that Raul was very much a really wonderful, imaginative actor, and he would come up with ideas as he was going, and he would always have an idea that he wanted to try, and I would almost always let him try it. But I think it was something that sort of threw Desi off, who was used to everything going by the script, you know."

In private notes for a telephone conversation with Deschanel, Desi revealed his excitement about being back in harness, along with some ambivalence about the project. "It is not an important part," he wrote to himself. "The money is nothing, but the association might be worthwhile. . . . I like Francis, and Roos and you—the whole company, in fact—and the idea of working with you is very appealing." But in scattered notes on yellow legal paper, Desi also questioned the characterization, lines, and various plot points regarding his character.

Most of the film was shot on location in Cleveland, but interiors were filmed on the old General Service lot. That was like old home week for Desi. Lucy Fisher, then the studio's young head of production and later herself a successful film and television producer, cherished Desi's ritual at the end of each day's shooting: He would drop by her office bungalow—it might once have been his—and call out, "Luu-ucy! I'm home!"

• • •

On June 22, 1980, Lucie Arnaz married the actor Laurence Luckinbill. Her previous marriage, nine years earlier, to Phil Vandervort, had been brief. In the six years since the final episode of *Here's Lucy* in 1974, Lucie had forged a successful acting career of her own; she and Luckinbill had met while they were both appearing on Broadway—she in Neil Simon's *They're Playing Our Song* and he in the same playwright's *Chapter Two*. Their wedding took place on a farm in Upstate New York, and Desi, accompanied by an accordionist, sang "Forever, Darling" as Lucy, a nosegay in one hand and a cigarette and handkerchief in the other, teared up and wiped her eyes.

Desi Jr. was more settled in his life as well. After his tempestuous teen years, and his well-publicized romances with Patty Duke and Liza Minnelli, among others, Desi Jr. had experienced his own serious troubles with alcohol and drugs. He would get sober in 1981 at the Scripps Clinic near San Diego and then lived for a time with his father, though Desi Sr. was unwilling to join the rest of the family in group therapy sessions, resisting the airing of private troubles in public. Desi Jr. became an adherent of Vernon Howard's New Life Foundation, a spiritual movement drawing on various faith traditions aimed at self-understanding, and would grow closer to his dad. After a brief marriage to the actress Linda Purl, Desi Jr. would eventually marry Amy Bargiel, a dancer, and they settled in Boulder City, Nevada, creating a ballet company there.

Desi took great pride in both children and in the arrival of his first grandson, Simon Luckinbill, Lucie and Larry's son. The last time he and Lucy were photographed together is preserved in a poignant home video clip from the spring of 1981, in which the long-divorced grandparents paddle around with little Simon in the Luckinbills' swimming pool. Lucy chides Desi for not having taught their own children Spanish, while he drums the water and sings "Ba-ba-luuuu." Lucy tenderly brushes Desi's wet white hair off his forehead in a gesture of old intimacy. In March 1982, Desi appeared with both his kids in Florida at the annual Carnival Miami celebration of Cuban culture, with Desi as grand marshal. He sang "Cuban Pete," and Lucie re-created her mother's "Sally Sweet" role, with Desi Jr. on drums in a grand closing performance at the Orange Bowl.

In the wee hours one night before the show, Desi pulled out his guitar in his hotel suite and waxed nostalgic with his old friend and accompanist Marco Rizo on the piano, just the two of them. "And it was so beautiful that night, everything came out just great," Rizo would recall. "No one there, just Desi, his guitar, and the piano." The two shared a Cuban coffee, and "at the end, he said, 'Marco, this has been one of my happiest nights that I ever have.' It was very emotional. I cried, so he did, too."

But that was a rare moment of pleasure for Desi in what had become a grim forced retirement. He still felt pressure to present himself a certain way on the rare occasions when he had to appear in public.

"Whenever he would go out, he would have to, in effect, put on a show, using the limousine or whatever," his accountant Howard Sheppard recalled. By this point, Desi's capital had dwindled, and Sheppard was reduced to writing letters to the Directors Guild, seeking an accounting of whatever pension Desi might be owed.

Desi's generosity had always been extravagant, and he had never lost his sense of *cubanidad*, the intense native feeling of national identity and ego. Over the years, he had contributed to the support of his extended Cuban émigré family members. But he never again went back to his beloved island home and seemingly never wanted to, so changed did he feel the country had become under Fidel Castro, its bushy-bearded Communist leader. Appearing in 1983 on *Late Night with David Letterman*, Desi performed Irving Berlin's "I'll See You in C-U-B-A," which he described as "a song about my country, many, many years ago, before they stopped shaving down there, if you know what I mean." Mayor Arnaz had died in 1973, having been supported in part till the end by Desi, who was also still responsible for Lolita, now approaching ninety. Only the Bacardí stock that the de Acha family had owned for decades enabled Arnaz to continue to care for his mother, and even then he was forced to carve out a small apartment for her in his own beach house at Del Mar. (She would ultimately outlive Desi by almost two years, dying at ninety-two in October 1988, after Lucie had assumed responsibility for her care.)

"Nobody could stop him," Marcella Rabwin recalled. "He said, 'I'm not going to live so long I'll outlive the money.' It wound up that they couldn't pay their bills some of the time. Edie always said, 'If worse comes to worst, we'll get out of here and go live in Mexico.' It was so idiotic, because he'd been such a smart businessman."

At one point Edie had temporarily left him. "Edie loved Desi as much as Lucy did, and she suffered as much from him," their friend, the actress and comedienne Kaye Ballard, recalled. Desi shut himself off and seemed determined to drink himself to death, but the couple reconciled.

In March 1985, Edie died of uterine cancer at sixty-seven, and that October, with Desi Jr.'s loving encouragement and help, Desi was finally willing to address his own addiction. He sought Desi Jr.'s guidance and entered the Scripps McDonald Center's alcohol rehabilitation program in La Jolla, registering as "Bill Sanchez" to protect his privacy.

"Edie died, he was totally alone, drinking himself to death, and he finally picked up the phone and said to Desi, 'I need help. I don't want to die,'" Lucie recalled. For the previous couple of years, Desi (who also struggled with painkillers and sedatives) had been exploring Desi Jr.'s own sobriety with him. His son had assured him—in the time-tested terms of A.A.—that nothing would change until he acknowledged that he was powerless over alcohol, that his life had become unmanageable, and he became willing to surrender to a power greater than himself. "It was really nice," Desi Jr. said, "because whatever I was going through, it was paying off. I said, 'I can't do anything for you, but there's a place that can.' He understood that." For her part, Lucie remembered: "And so Desi goes, 'Okay, this is the call I've been waiting for,' because Desi had been through it several times himself. And he checked him into Scripps, and we all went to family week with Dad, and he got the little marble at the end. He thought it was a crock of shit, most of it, but he did it." Indeed, Desi at first resisted treatment, going so far as to leave the hospital after a few days, but he returned and persisted.

She added, "We were there for him, proudest moment of my life . . . when he stood up and said, 'My name is Desi, and I'm an alcoholic.' I cried my eyes out. I was so proud of him." In his post-discharge worksheet, published here for the first time, he cataloged the "tools" that could maintain his sobriety—"Reading the Big Book," "Going to meetings"—and he listed "Mother's Health" and "My health" as potential "stressors and situational factors" that could lead to relapse. In another worksheet he pledged "to stop being such a loner, to try to socialize more, to go back to work . . . to stop feeling sorry for myself."

"I am trying to change my way of life," he concluded.

"And then," Lucie said, "minutes after he got home from that, he got sick." The doctors diagnosed lung cancer, the result of all those years of cigarillos. Desi never drank again but spent most of 1986 on morphine and other painkillers. "He still felt he had something to give," Marcella Rabwin recalled. "But he was despondent. He did a lot of reading. Eventually, instead of sitting, he'd go to bed and read. Then, toward the end, he was in bed all the time."

For both Desi and Lucy, the fall of 1986 was misery. The previous spring, the producer Aaron Spelling, the onetime Desilu actor who had become the leading television producer of the late 1970s and early 1980s, had enticed Lucy back into a weekly sitcom for ABC. It was to be called *Life with Lucy* and would costar her old friend and foil Gale Gordon. To give herself confidence after a decade more or less out of harness, Lucy recruited Marc Daniels, *I Love Lucy*'s original director, to direct the new show, and Bob Carroll and Madelyn Pugh to write it. She and Gordon played in-law grandparents who ran a hardware store.

In March, Madelyn had written to Desi, "As you undoubtedly know, Lucy is going to do another series. Bob and I have been asked to go along on the voyage, and of course we couldn't say no. We're not sure if it will be lots of fun or if we have lost our minds." Madelyn told Desi that she and Bob Carroll often remarked how much they'd appreciated him—and felt she ought now to say so out loud. "What a joy it was to work with somebody with your enthusiasm, your showmanship, and your instinctive feeling for what was good. We were so young and green that we took this kind of thing for granted. When we got out in the real world, we realized how lucky we were to work with you, with your great gift for bringing out the best in us."

Yet the old gang was no longer young, and at seventy-five, Lucy could not be expected to turn the same slapstick somersaults as she had done thirty-five years earlier—too often, they prompted viewers' fears she would hurt herself. Spelling, and Bob and Madelyn, had envisioned a show that might deal honestly with the realities of an aging grandmother, but Lucy was reluctant to change the formula that had worked. Shooting live on the old Goldwyn soundstages where she'd begun her Hollywood career, Lucy was greeted with rapture by the studio audience, and ABC was so confident about the show that it guaranteed payment for twenty-two episodes and scheduled it for Saturday nights, then dominated by NBC's popular sitcoms *The Golden Girls* and *The Facts of Life*. But critical reaction was brutal. "She gamely attempted her old style of slapstick, but her impeccable timing had fled" was the verdict in *Channels* magazine. ABC pulled the plug in November, after taping thirteen episodes and airing just nine—a public humiliation. "ABC's let me go," Lucy told her old friend the actress Ann Sothern. "They don't want to see an old grandma."

By now, Desi was dying in Del Mar. The cancer had left him in great pain, but he soldiered on, proud and defiant. At Scripps, he had to have fluid drained from his lungs. One day, as he lay on an inclined table, Lucie reached for his hand. But Desi couldn't bring himself to be vulnerable enough to really squeeze it back. At night he took to wandering the house and rearranging the furniture, so private-duty nurses eventually had to take turns in round-the-clock twelve-hour shifts.

As his health failed completely, Desi was reluctant for Lucy to see him. The chemotherapy had taken much of his hair and he was all skin and bones, looking almost as old as his mother, who was virtually bedridden in her own room downstairs. But Lucy came anyway. On the second of two visits, Lucie put on some videotapes of old *I Love Lucy* episodes and left her parents alone—laughing, she said, as if on their first date. When Lucy finally got up to return to Beverly Hills, Desi asked, "Where are you going?" "I'm going home," she said. "You *are* home," he replied. The two spoke one last time, by phone, each simply repeating, "I love you. I love you. I love you." Only later did Lucie realize that the date was November 30, the forty-sixth anniversary of their wedding. Two days later, with Lucie holding him close, Desi died. He was sixty-nine years old.

Lucy was told the news during a taping of the television quiz show *Super Password*. "She turned to me and said, 'You know, it's the damnedest thing,'" the other guest, Betty White, recalled. "'Goddamn it, I didn't think I'd get this upset. There he goes.'"

The obituaries gave Desi his due. The *New York Times* pronounced him "an important figure in the history of television" and noted that the success of *I Love Lucy*'s live, three-camera system had "led eventually to a seismic shift in television production from New York to Hollywood." Cecil Smith, the emeritus television critic of the *Los Angeles Times* (and by now married to Lucy's cousin Cleo), wrote that Desi was not just a beloved performer. "It's also well to be reminded that every evening you spend watching television, you are exposed to Desi Arnaz." Smith added: "He was a strong man, a powerful man, an oak. He took a long time dying. His timing, so precise on stage, wasn't so good off. He'd outlived his fame. Yet I think the passing of Desi Arnaz should be marked by more than silence."

• • •

Condolences came from all over. "When you have watched and loved someone all these years, you get to believing you're a part of their lives," the humor columnist Erma Bombeck wrote to Lucy. Van Johnson, Desi's long-ago castmate, sent a note to Marcella Rabwin, asking her to forward it to Lucie: "Please accept my deepest sympathy. They don't make 'em like that one anymore." Carol Burnett, Tommy Tune, Henry Winkler, Steve Lawrence, and Eydie Gormé all wrote to Lucie and her husband.

But Desi's funeral was not well attended. Of the television establishment that Desilu once dominated, only Danny Thomas, a former studio tenant, attended the small memorial service at St. James's Roman Catholic Church in nearby Solana Beach, within earshot of the track at Del Mar. Thomas had called Lucie insisting he would deliver a eulogy, and she felt powerless to resist. "I will never, ever forget his tremendous help to me," Thomas told the congregation, "and I speak not only about what he did for me but what he has done for the entire industry. Television owes him a tremendous debt of gratitude and no one, but no one, has ever come close to the kind of TV Desi brought with Lucy to this industry."

The band of a hundred-odd mourners included Bill Asher, Keith Thibodeaux, and Dino Martin Jr., along with a line of parochial schoolchildren who stood sentinel on the sloping grounds of the modern glass, wood, and buff-brick church. Poignantly nestled among the signatures in the little guest book that Lucie kept was that of Desi's old friend and first costar, Diosa Costello, whose fiery, oscillating dance moves he had so admired nearly a half century before. A visibly emotional Lucy sat in a front pew with Gary Morton and left the hour-long service clutching a wilted pink rose. Lucie, in her own tearful eulogy, thanked the doctors and nurses who had cared for her father in his final illness and recalled that as the end neared, Desi "took a long look at me and said, 'I did the best I could.'"

Three days later, in Washington, D.C., the cream of the political and entertainment world gathered for the annual black-tie Kennedy Center Honors, where Lucille Ball (but *not* Desi Arnaz) was celebrated along with Ray Charles; the violinist Yehudi Menuhin; the choreographer Antony Tudor; and another famous husband-and-wife performing team, Hume Cronyn and Jessica Tandy. Perched in the plush red boxes of the Center's Opera House, three seats away from President Ronald Reagan, Lucy covered her mouth with a manicured hand and struggled to control her emotions at the evening's sentimental high point, a tribute from Robert Stack, *The Untouchables'* Eliot Ness, who read a few words from Desi. "He wanted to be here tonight," Stack told the glittering assembly. "I'd like to read something that he wrote: '*I Love Lucy* had just one mission: To make people laugh. Lucy gave it a rare quality. She can perform the wildest, even the messiest physical comedy, without losing her feminine appeal. The *New York Times* asked me to divide the credit for its success between the writers, directors, and the cast. I told them give Lucy ninety percent of the credit, and divide the other ten percent among the rest of us.'" Blending the real and fictional names of their costars, Desi's message continued, "'Lucy was the show. Viv, Fred and I were just props—damn good props, but props nevertheless.

"'P.S. *I Love Lucy* was never just a title.'"

EPILOGUE

Lucille Ball lived another two years after Desi's death. Though she had had steadier work than he did, and much greater financial stability, that did not necessarily translate into more happiness. In the spring of 1974 she had ended the run of *Here's Lucy*, which was by then no longer among the top twenty-five prime-time programs on the air, and CBS proved unwilling to renew it. That same year, the disastrous critical reception to her starring role in the film version of the Broadway musical *Mame*—which Desi had counseled her not to take—scotched any hope of resuming a career in feature films. After more than twenty years as a top-rated performer, and forty years as a working actress, she was effectively put out to pasture except for an occasional special or television movie. *Life with Lucy* on ABC was her last chance to reestablish herself in television. When it, too, failed, there was nothing left but to collect more lifetime achievement awards like the Kennedy Center Honors in 1986. Though these tributes were gratifying in their way, they were no substitute for the only activity that had ever brought her real satisfaction: plain, hard work.

In May 1988 Lucy suffered a stroke, but she worked hard to re-cover her speech and movement on her partially paralyzed right side. Not quite a year later, she underwent emergency open-heart surgery to repair a torn aorta and weakened valve. She seemed to be making a good recovery when, on the morning of April 26, 1989, she woke with a sharp pain in her back, and the repaired aorta burst. She died instantly. Her death at age seventy-seven was front-page news all over the world, her legacy timeless, her achievements indelible and indisputable. The obituaries gave her everything she was due. But they underplayed Desi's essential contributions to her success—something she herself had never done. A few years earlier, Fred Bernstein, then a young writer for *People* magazine, had come to interview Lucy for a cover story on the Golden Age of Television. Lucy's handlers instructed him not to mention Desi, but for two hours Desi was the only thing she wanted to talk about.

· · ·

The simple truth is that neither Lucy nor Desi ever achieved any-thing alone that approached the artistic achievement they enjoyed together. Their collaboration was lightning in a bottle, a once-in-a-lifetime combination that could never be recaptured but has been pre-served forever, thanks to Desi's insistence on putting *I Love Lucy* on film. "It was a piece in time, with just the right chemistry all the way around—from the writing, the casting, the two of them, what nerve they had to jump into that and somehow make it fly," Lucie Arnaz says. "The excitement of what that felt like had to be like the Wright Brothers, you know, like what's fun after that? You just created flying, you know. You just invented an airplane, what're you going to do next, Wilbur?"

Late in life, Lucy, in an atypically bitter moment, assessed Desi's achievements—and his undoing. "He could win, win, high, high, high stakes," she told Barbara Walters in a television interview as Gary Morton sat awkwardly beside her, trying to smooth things over. "He could work very hard. He was brilliant." As if suddenly realizing how unflattering such praise must have seemed to Gary by comparison, she added, "But he had to lose . . . he had to fail at everything that he built up. Everything he built up, he had to break down." In fact, Desi had reinvented himself so often since he was forced to flee Cuba in his teens—and taken so many risks—that he gambled that he could always start over again. In his last decades, diminished by drink and depression, he had finally gambled wrong.

And yet Desi Arnaz's legacy lives on. It endures in the long line of successful Latin performers, the crossover artists who have come after him, from George Lopez to John Leguizamo, from Ritchie Valens to Ricky Martin, from Gloria Estefan to Jennifer Lopez to the Cuban-born rapper Mellow Man Ace—who calls himself the Ricky Ricardo of Rap, named his son Desi, and whose signature song is "Babalu Bad Boy." Poignantly, though, Desi's legacy lives on as well in the struggles of many of those artists for full acceptance and respect in the entertainment world. "You can be as talented as Marlon Brando or Ingrid Bergman, you can write like William Shakespeare, you can have the screen presence of Ryan Gosling or Jennifer Lawrence," Leguizamo wrote in 2022. "But if you look Latino, or if you have a Latino last name, the odds are against you in Hollywood." Indeed, while performers like J-Lo, Jessica Alba, and Selena Gomez have built formidable business brand empires, to this day it is Desi Arnaz who remains not only the first but also arguably the most prominent Latino studio executive in Hollywood history, more than sixty years after he left Desilu.

Desi's cultural impact lives on in other ways. In Oscar Hijuelos's haunting 1989 Pulitzer Prize–winning novel, *The Mambo Kings Play Songs of Love*, the Cain-and-Abel story of two Cuban musician brothers, Desi Arnaz appears as a mythic, talismanic character. (Desi Jr. played his father in the film version of the book.) The emotional high point of the story is an encounter with Desi in a New York club that leads to a sentimental, rum-soaked dinner and the brothers' guest appearance on an episode of *I Love Lucy*. Lucille Ball, perhaps for the first time in popular culture, is relegated to the status of dutiful wife and demure supporting player. In 2021, the Oscar-winning screenwriter and director Aaron Sorkin dramatized the *I Love Lucy* story in *Being the Ricardos*, a feature film that condensed the Red Scare episode and Lucy's pregnancy into a single frantic week in the life of the show, with Javier Bardem bringing Desi vividly to life. The following year Amy Poehler directed *Lucy and Desi*, a thoughtful documentary that came much closer to capturing the Arnazes' real lives.

But Desi's impact persists most powerfully in the way that so much of television entertainment—especially situation comedies—is still made: live, on film (or, more recently, videotape and digital recording), playable and saleable over and over and over again. The innovations born of necessity in 1951 have lasted for almost three-quarters of a century. Though Desi was not solely responsible for those innovations, he played a crucial, courageous—even daring—role in their creation. "If you're going to do a drama, fine, use one camera," the actor Gale Gordon, Ball's costar in the two later *Lucy* series, once said. "Use half a camera. It doesn't matter. But when you're going to do comedy, you've got to have something to time the laughs with, or you've got nothing." In the 1960s, bland, middle-of-the-road shows like *My Three Sons* and *Bewitched* were filmed with a single camera and a tacked-on laugh track (sometimes for the convenience of their stars, like Fred MacMurray, whose contract stipulated that his scenes for the whole season had to be shot in a condensed period, allowing more time for golf). But as the seventies and eighties brought a revolution in edgier, more topical humor to TV, such iconic programs as *All in the Family*, *The Mary Tyler Moore Show*, *Cheers*, and *Seinfeld* were all filmed in front of a live audience, with multiple cameras.

In the 1970s, the director Garry Marshall produced the nostalgic 1950s sitcom *Happy Days*, which started out as a single-camera show, but the energy was lacking. "When they changed to live audience, three-camera," the actor Anson Williams told the *New York Times* on the show's fiftieth anniversary, "that's when the chemistry really came in, when we could work together as a team every day." Robin Williams's madcap improvisations on *Mork & Mindy* led Marshall, who also produced it, to add a fourth camera to capture the antics. James Burrows, who helped create *Cheers* and directed early episodes of *Friends*, *Will & Grace*, and *Taxi*, insists that there is no substitute for a live audience. "There are a lot of single-camera comedies that get chuckles," he says. "They don't get guffaws." Peter Roth, the longtime Warner Bros. television executive, agrees. "I would put any episode of *Big Bang Theory*," shot live, "against any episode of *Modern Family*," made with one camera, he said. "There's just something about that live audience." With *Friends*, he recalled, "We never had to sweeten the track. The laughs were so hot because the audiences that were there were so glad to be there, they were screaming with laughter."

Even today, Paul Feig, the director of hit feature film comedies like *Bridesmaids*, insists on using a multicamera technique in his movies, despite the extra complications it requires. "Every cinematographer just hates it," he has said, "but I can't do this kind of comedy without cross-shooting. Amazing improv happens. And I got one side of it, and trying to re-create it? It's never the same."

• • •

The legacy of *I Love Lucy* is so ubiquitous as to need almost no elaboration. Martina Navratilova taught herself English by watching its reruns. Pee-Wee Herman was inspired to become a performer by watching the same shows. The Tony Award–winning actor Jonathan Groff performed old episodes for his tenth birthday party. At the seventy-fifth anniversary of the Emmy Awards in 2024, Tracee Ellis Ross presented the trophy for Best Comedy Series with a reenactment of the chocolate factory skit. The opening episode of *Saturday Night Live*'s fiftieth season featured the reigning television comedienne of the moment, the seventy-three-year-old Jean Smart—who was born just a month before *Lucy* went on the air—in a sketch that reimagined Lucy Ricardo as a drunken Joan Crawford–style diva. All these homages tend to focus on Lucille Ball. But Desi Arnaz's contributions were just as crucial to the success of the show.

The straight man is the essential, undercelebrated spark of any comedy duo—the person who sets the trap that snaps satisfyingly closed in the joke. Gracie Allen would not have been half as funny without George Burns. Jerry Lewis forged a successful solo career but never recaptured the special charm of his partnership with Dean Martin. Lucy had a skilled foil in Gale Gordon but never the same spark as she had with Desi. "We never saw that level of comedy again" in the subsequent *Lucy* shows, says Kate Flannery, who played Meredith Palmer in *The Office*, a redheaded comic heir to the Lucy tradition. "It just never played out as well." To be an effective straight man, Flannery explains, "you have to be willing to *not* be the person who speaks last before the laugh comes. You're just as important, but you have to accept that you're part of this system, this setup, this team."

Desi was always that—and so much more, because the straight man is also the eyes and ears of the audience. For all her brilliant clowning and quicksilver spirit, it isn't Lucy Ricardo with whom the viewer most identifies. It is her solid, steady, sometimes-exasperated partner who stands in for the rest of us. It is Ricky. It is Desi. "Essential as she is, the secret to 'I Love Lucy' is not Lucy, but the I who loved Lucy before any of us knew that we should," the playwright, director, and actor Douglas McGrath wrote in the *New York Times* on the show's fiftieth anniversary in 2001. "As Ball's onscreen partner—and the success of the show relies on this partnership—he gave 'I Love Lucy' both a comic balance and an emotional base that are at the heart of its longevity." McGrath noted that Desi was never so much as nominated for an Emmy for his performance as Ricky, though he did win an Emmy as a producer. "Yet what he created in Ricky Ricardo was infinitely more advanced and complicated than William Frawley's cheap grump. He has to play the full range of feelings a man has for his wife: love, desire, frustration, fury, forgiveness, delight, amusement."

In that small apartment at 623 East 68th Street in Manhattan, love ultimately reigns supreme. Lucy and Ricky endure their ups and downs, as in the rarely heard lyrics of the show's theme song: "We have our quarrels but then . . . how we love making up again." But it is the making up that counts most. Desi Jr. insists that this tension was an essential dynamic of the show. "What was it about?" he asks. "Tensions. Only they made up. Every twenty-four minutes. They didn't hurt each other. But they *almost* hurt each other, every Monday night." The longtime Desilu executive Martin Leeds may have explained it best. "You believed inside of you, and you still do," he once said, "that there wasn't anything that she could do he wouldn't love her." So we loved her, too, and it seems we always will.

Desi Arnaz could be harder to love in real life than Ricky Ricardo. His self-destructiveness deeply hurt not just him but those who cared for him most, undermined his spectacular successes, and contributed to the diminishment of his reputation in the last years of his life and in the decades since his death. But his talents were remarkable, his achievements deserve to be remembered and celebrated, and his charms are ultimately irresistible. In unpublished notes for his memoir, Desi wrote, "Whatever my indiscretions—my mistakes—they were never evil. They might have shown a weakness in certain areas—a not-too-stable character, but never evil. I was always frank, simple, sensitive and warm. To be evil you must have a much more complex makeup."

To the end Desi kept up a brave front, but he was not without regrets. He was capable of self-reflection, and of sorrow at what he had made of his life, and—at the end—of confronting some of his demons. But as with most people—and certainly so many high-achieving people—his strengths were bound up with his weaknesses. It was the youthful trauma of losing everything that made him willing to risk anything. The upside of his profligacy was his generosity; the flipside of his restlessness was his creativity; the corollary of his addictions was his drive. Asking what he might yet have achieved if he had stopped drinking earlier is like asking him to have been a different person. In the end, the professional achievements he built have endured despite the personal bonds he strained or broke. He was a genuine original, and for better and worse, he knew it.

"With all his genius," his friend Rod Rodriguez once said, "he possessed an honest heart, honest manners, good sense, and good humor. Yet, as a romanticist, he was one of the most incorrigible human beings that ever lived. If I reminded him of his follies, intending to induce a useful lesson, he would light up at the recollection, retrieving the experience with a fondness that showed he would want nothing better than to do it again."

ACKNOWLEDGMENTS

This book would have been impossible without the unstinting trust, generosity, and kindness of Lucie Arnaz. She and her husband, Laurence Luckinbill, welcomed me into their home and to her meticulously maintained family archive. She is a conscientious, clear-eyed steward of her parents' legacies and answered endless questions, corrected factual errors (and spelling, punctuation, and pagination), while never seeking any control or approval over what I wrote. Of priceless help were the transcripts of dozens of interviews (from her Emmy-winning documentary, *Lucy and Desi: A Home Movie*) that she conducted with key participants in this story who are no longer alive. Lucie's brother, Desi Arnaz IV, spent many patient, vulnerable hours on the telephone sharing his own invaluable perspectives on their father. My gratitude to both of them is deep. Any mistakes are mine.

I thank my old friend Allen Sviridoff for connecting me with Lucie, the redoubtable Ted Chapin for vouching for my bona fides, and Warren Dern for slicing through a legal thicket that might have derailed the whole project without his help. Cullen Murphy read and improved the proposal with his usual skill and kindness, and my lawyer Bob Barnett made the proposal a reality. My editor, Mindy Marques at Simon & Schuster, showed early and enthusiastic faith in this idea when others did not and went on to shepherd the book to completion with grace, good humor, and a demon eye for the dread passive voice. She is a calm anchor for writerly anxieties, and I am so grateful to her. My gratitude also to Jon Karp and Priscilla Painton and Johanna

Lee at S&S, and the entire team there: Morgan Hart, Gregory Lauzon, Richard Willett, Jamie Selzer, Lewelin Polanco, Math Monahan (for the beautiful jacket design), Omesha Edwards, and Ingrid Carabulea. Paul Golob, a trusted friend and matchless editor, scrubbed the first-draft manuscript as only he could, raising good questions, weeding out excess enthusiasms, and making the book better in every way. The brilliant Melissa Goldstein once again unearthed just the perfect pictures, including the striking image on the cover, and navigated the thickets of reproduction rights.

Yet again, my debt to the Music Division of the Library of Congress is incalculable. Ray White, in charge of the Ball-Arnaz collection there, and his colleague, my friend Mark Eden Horowitz, were unfailingly helpful in giving me access to the fragile collection of Ball-Arnaz family scrapbooks in their care. C. C. Mesa carefully researched the Spanish-language scrapbooks, compiled by Desi's father, that are part of the library's collection. Archivists, curators, and administrators at other libraries also provided crucial assistance, including Meg de Waal of the Margaret Herrick Library of the Academy of Motion Picture Arts and Sciences in Beverly Hills; Sarah Conner at Cal State San Diego; Terre Heydari at the DeGolyer Library at Southern Methodist University in Dallas; Ryan Lintelman and Dwight Blocker Bowers of the Smithsonian Institution's National Museum of American History; and Laura LaPlaca and Gary Hahn of the National Comedy Center in Jamestown, New York.

Desi's stepsister, Connie Arnaz, and his cousin George Rodon both generously shared family memories of life in Cuba and Miami. Gregg Oppenheimer not only took time for a long interview but provided unpublished materials related to his father Jess's career and then carefully read the chapters recounting his father's role in creating *I Love Lucy*, saving me from embarrassing errors. Lucille Ball's longtime secretary Wanda Clark, who compiled many of the family scrapbooks now at the Library of Congress, kindly took time to answer my questions. Bill

Rapaport, who with his wife, Mary, owns and has restored Lucille Ball's childhood home in Celoron, New York, gave me a detailed private tour on a rainy autumn day. Wendy Coleman, Anne Mehrtens, and JuJuan Bolding of Sunset Studios made it possible for me to see the original Hollywood soundstages on which *I Love Lucy* was first filmed, while Randall Throop of the Paramount Pictures archives patiently squired me around the parts of that venerable studio that once belonged to Desilu.

Ana Maria and Rob Fielding of the travel company Inbound Cuba—and Tania Vivar and Alicia Howland, the superb guide and researcher they found—made it possible for me to spend a fascinating week exploring Desi's childhood haunts in Santiago de Cuba. I thank the travel planner Wendy Perrin for sending me their way. And to my welcoming hosts at La Hiedra, an elegant *casa particular* in Santiago— Reinaldo Suarez Suarez, Sheila Beatriz Nunez Castro, and Caridad Castro Valiente—I send my deepest thanks for wonderful meals and warm hospitality.

My old Washington journalism colleague Kevin Bohn, a one-man *Lucy-Desi* fan club, plied me with YouTube clips and support. Coyne Steven Sanders and Tom Gilbert's 1993 book *Desilu: The Story of Lucille Ball and Desi Arnaz* is a pioneering and deeply researched work, and I'm in its debt.

For manifold kindnesses, including bed and board, research help, and forgiving friendship, I thank Betsey Apple, Ann Louise Bardach, A. Scott Berg, Lara Bergthold, Fred Bernstein, Matthew Broderick, Susan Brophy and Gerald McGowan, John Burnham, Tita Cahn, Bill Carrick and Beegie Truesdale, the late Rosemary Clooney, Catherine and Grant Collins, Sean Daniel and Ruthie Hunter, Anthony de Palma, Caleb Deschanel, Lucy Fisher, Kate Flannery, Friends at Moorpark, Linda Greenhouse, David Hoffman, Mitchell Kaplan, Betsy Kolbert, Sherry Lansing (and the late William Friedkin), the late Norman Lear, Eduardo Machado, Thomas Mallon, Steve and Judy Myers, Adam

Nagourney and Ben Kushner, Michele Norris, Steve Oney and Madeline Stuart, David Philp, Charles Pignone, Jennifer Preston, Paul and Karen Rabwin, Clay Risen, Mo Rocca, the late Fred Roos, Margot Roosevelt, Jamie Rose, Kevin Sack, Lee Satterfield and Patrick Steel, George Stevens Jr., Tina Sinatra, Evan Thomas, Constance Towers, Tom Troupe, Matt Tyrnauer, Don van Natta and Lizette Alvarez, and Thomas Watson.

Much of this story takes place within fifteen or twenty blocks of our house in Los Angeles, where the loving and patient Rosa Barraza keeps things in order and to which our daughter, Kate, and son, Stephen, still seem to like to come home. They remain our best productions and our pride and joy. To their mother, Dee Dee Myers, I have long since owed everything, especially the courage to change. I don't need a keyboard to send her a message.

This book's dedication reflects the debt I owe to Douglas McGrath. I met him at Princeton when the world was still young, and forty years later, at the lowest moment of my career, he suggested a way forward. I am so sorry he did not live to see the result of his inspiration, and only hope he would approve.

Todd S. Purdum
Los Angeles
New York
Washington, D.C.
Jamestown, New York
Palm Springs
Del Mar
Santiago de Cuba

NOTES

abbreviations

AMPAS: Academy of Motion Picture Arts and Sciences, Margaret Herrick
              Library
B-AS: Ball-Arnaz Scrapbooks
DA: Desi Arnaz
DAP: Desi Arnaz Papers
LAL: Lucie Arnaz Luckinbill Family Archive
LB: Lucille Ball
LOC: Library of Congress
NYPL: New York Public Library for the Performing Arts
OH: Oral History
SDS: San Diego State University
SMU: Southern Methodist University, Ronald L. Davis Oral History
            Collection

Note: When not otherwise specifically cited, quotations and actions attributed in this book to Desi Arnaz come from his memoir, *A Book* (New York: William Morrow and Company, 1976), and can most often readily be found in chronological order in its text.

prologue

1   *At a V-shaped banquet table bedecked with flowers*: "Lucille Ball & Desi Arnaz Receive Tribute on Ed Sullivan Show 1954," posted December 10, 2019, by Chronic Nostalgia, https://www.youtube.com/watch?v=qNRRCE -nWmM.

4   *He was, as NPR's* Planet Money *once put it*: Sonari Gointon and Robert Smith, hosts, *Planet Money*, podcast, "How Desi Invented Television," January 22, 2021, https://www.npr.org/transcripts/959609533.

4   *"There's a misconception that we"*: Madelyn Davis OH, LAL.

4   *Today, nearly four decades after his death*: Ann Miller OH, LAL.

5   *"I Love Lucy was a crucial part"*: Norman Lear, author telephone interview, September 30, 2022.

5   *"In real life or fiction"*: Miguel Perez column, New York *Daily News*, December 1986, B-AS, LOC.

6   *"If you feel betrayed by your own country"*: Eduardo Machado, author telephone interview, September 12, 2023.

7   *"Yes, he's the wetback they all waited for"*: Folder 973, Sammy Cahn papers, AMPAS.

7   *"My God, I can get to the president"*: Johnny Aitchison OH, LAL.

7   *"He spoke no known language"*: George Schlatter, author interview, August 2023.

7   *"Everybody thinks of Desi as flamboyant"*: Marcella Rabwin OH, LAL.

8   *"How do you like that?"*: Lloyd Shearer, "Desilu: The Story of an Empire," *Parade*, October 13, 1957.

8   *"I think TV is still a child"*: Earl Wilson column, scrapbook 45, B-AS, LOC.

8   *"They kind of kicked him to the curb"*: Lucie Arnaz, email to author, summer 2021.

8   *"I had this feeling"*: Gladys Hall papers, AMPAS.

8   *"He made it all happen"*: Cleo Smith OH, LAL.

9   *Arnaz himself acknowledged*: *Lucy and Desi*, directed by Amy Poehler (2022, Amazon Studios).

9   *"You know me, pardner"*: Madelyn Pugh Davis and Bob Carroll Jr., *Laughing with Lucy: My Life with America's Leading Lady of Comedy* (Cincinnati, OH: Clerisy Press, 2007), 142.

10   *At the beginning of the twenty-first century*: Ibid., 263.

10   *"Because he was an outsider"*: Jude Dry, "How Amy Poehler Brought the Love to Documentary 'Lucy and Desi,'" *IndieWire*, March 5, 2022, https://www.in diewire.com/features/general/amy-poehler-lucy-and-desi-interview-i-love-lucy -documentary-1234704706/.

chapter one: Once on an Island

11   *Not twenty years earlier*: Theodore Roosevelt, *The Rough Riders* (Las Vegas: Public Domain On-Demand Reproduction, 2024), 76.

12   *"Something about* Oriente": Patrick Symmes, *The Boys from Dolores: Fidel Castro's Schoolmates from Revolution to Exile* (New York: Pantheon, 2007), 41–42.

13   *By the time of Desi's birth*: Undated memo, LAL.

15   *Arnaz family lore*: *La Independencia*, November 19, 1929, scrapbook 42, B-AS, LOC.

NOTES   313

15   *So his parents sent him off*: Connie Arnaz, author telephone interview, April
     2023.

16   *He later wound up as a vice president*: Tom Gjelten, *Bacardi and the Long Fight
     for Cuba* (New York: Penguin, 2008), 106, 122.

16   *He built parks*: Various contemporary Cuban newspaper articles, compiled and
     translated for author by Alicia Howland.

16   *The alameda opened in 1928*: Ned Sublette, *Cuba and Its Music: From the First
     Drums to the Mambo* (Chicago: Chicago Review Press, 2004), 372.

19   *"I don't rest"*: Undated clipping, LAL.

17   *"Desi, always social"*: Mayor Arnaz notes on photo, scrapbook 43, B-AS, LOC.

18   *The bullet struck*: Draft manuscript, box 1, DAP, SDS.

18   *Old-fashioned brass lamps*: Series V, writings (digitized), Marco Rizo papers,
     NYPL.

18   *"Music was something"*: Series V, writings, Rizo papers, NYPL.

19   *"a little mountain coming out"*: Draft manuscript, Desi Arnaz, *A Book*, box 1,
     DAP, SDS.

19   *"After locking the door"*: Desi Arnaz, *A Book* (New York: William Morrow and
     Company, 1976), 14.

20   *"Have you ever seen me insult"*: Arnaz, *A Book*, 17.

20   *In an unpublished draft*: Draft manuscript, Desi Arnaz, *A Book*, box 1, DAP, SDS.

20   *"I learned the whole deal"*: Arnaz, *A Book*, 1.

21   *Marco Rizo recalled*: Series V, writings, Rizo papers.

21   *When Desi's grandfather*: Arnaz, *A Book*, 10.

21   *"I got very mad at my father"*: Draft manuscript, Arnaz, *A Book*, box 1, DAP, SDS.

21   *Indeed, by all accounts*: Cleo Smith OH and Marcella Rabwin OH, LAL.

22   *Of Mayor Arnaz himself*: Connie Arnaz, author telephone interview, April 2023.

22   *Rabwin would remember*: Rabwin OH, LAL.

22   *Decades later, Desi's daughter*: Lucie Arnaz, author interview, Palm Springs, CA,
     August 2023.

22   *"Neither an overt rebel nor a dreamer"*: Series V, writings, Rizo papers.

22   *In his junior year of high school*: Arnaz, *A Book*, 22–23.

23   *In March 1933*: Arnaz, *A Book*, 313.

24   *He undertook an ambitious plan of public works*: David E. Hoffman, *Give Me
     Liberty: The Story of Oswaldo Payá and His Daring Quest for a Free Cuba* (New
     York: Simon & Schuster, 2022), 22.

24   *"Machado was the cleverest politician ever produced"*: R. Hart Phillips, *Cuba: Is-
     land of Paradox* (New York: McDowell, Oblensky, 1959), 4.

25   *On the eve of Santiago's carnival*: Sublette, *Cuba and Its Music*, 370–71.

25   *In his memoir decades later*: Arnaz, *A Book*, 61.

26   *"Race mattered in Santiago, deeply"*: Symmes, *The Boys from Dolores*, 42, 43, 62.

26 *"We had that town pretty well wrapped up"*: "Desi Arnaz Sits Down with Bob Hope and Don Rickles/Carson Tonight Show," posted August 16, 2022, by Johnny Carson, https://www.youtube.com/watch?v=AkjoMbf7vRg.

26 *His nephew George Rodon*: George Rodon, author telephone interview, August 2023.

27 *In an unpublished draft*: Draft manuscript, Arnaz, A Book, box 1, DAP, SDS.

27 *"the big beams in the open ceiling"*: Arnaz, A Book, 18.

27 *By the summer of 1933*: Phillips, *Cuba*, 34.

28 *In Santiago, Desi was*: Arnaz, A Book, 24.

28 *Machado had taken a plane*: Arnaz, A Book, 30.

28 *"Just as I hung up"*: Arnaz, A Book, 25.

29 *Desi's mother's rosewood piano*: manuscript article, Gladys Hall papers, AMPAS.

29 *"Civilization was stripped away"*: Phillips, *Cuba*, 40.

29 *"For the next few days"*: Arnaz, A Book, 29.

29 *"There was one sight"*: Arnaz, A Book, 32.

chapter two: La Conga!

31 *"In my opinion as a lawyer"*: Antonio Bravo Correoso letter to Desi Arnaz, scrapbook 42, B-AS, LOC.

32 *"Money means nothing"*: Draft manuscript, Desi Arnaz, A Book, box 1, DAP, SDS.

32 *When Desi at last made it*: Desi Arnaz, A Book (New York: William Morrow and Company, 1976), 32–33.

33 *A building boom in the 1920s*: Ned Sublette, *Cuba and Its Music: From the First Drums to the Mambo* (Chicago: Chicago Review Press, 2004), 452.

33 *This occasionally led to trouble*: Arnaz, A Book, 36.

34 *The mayor just stared at Desi*: Arnaz, A Book, 37.

34 *"We were finally making enough money"*: Arnaz, A Book, 40.

35 *He didn't want his new schoolmates*: Arnaz, A Book, 42.

35 *"Oh, he was very polite"*: John Ingraham OH, LAL.

36 *"The real Miami Beach"*: Howard Kleinberg, *Miami Beach* (Miami: Centennial Press, 2014), 133.

36 *Desi had scraped together*: Arnaz, A Book, 42.

37 *Desi auditioned and was offered*: Arnaz, A Book, 43–44.

37 *She was a young widow named Ann Wilson*: Connie Arnaz, author telephone interview, April 2023.

38 *Desi's childhood Cuban friend*: Marco Rizo OH, LAL.

38 *"He was really the only father"*: Connie Arnaz, author telephone interview.

38 *In his St. Patrick's 1937 senior class*: St. Patrick Junior-Senior High School 1937 yearbook, Miami Beach, FL, LAL.

39 *Years later, Desi would recall*: Arnaz, A Book, 45; Xavier Cugat, *Rumba Is My Life* (New York: Didier, 1948), 118.

39   *"Showgirls, swimmers, fantastic costumes"*: Arnaz, *A Book*, 47.

40   *The guest turned out to be Bing Crosby*: Arnaz, *A Book*, 48–49.

41   *When Desi assembled the sorry-looking group*: Arnaz, *A Book*, 61–62.

42   *And while it is true*: Sublette, *Cuba and Its Music*, 406–8, 452–54.

43   *The act of* arrollando: Lani Milstein, "La Conga: Santiago de Cuba's Badge of Honor," *ReVista: Harvard Review of Latin America* XIII, no. 3 (Spring 2014): https://revista.drclas.harvard.edu/la-conga/.

43   *The local press took appreciative note*: Desi Arnaz: Florida Historic Marker Project, http://thankyoudesiarnaz.com.

43   *"Bobby Kelly was ecstatic"*: Arnaz, *A Book*, 62.

44   *"I read it," he told Desi*: Arnaz, *A Book*, 66.

44   *The 1939* WPA Guide to New York City: *WPA Guide to New York City* (New York: Pantheon, 1982), 27.

44   *Desi found a home*: Arnaz, *A Book*, 67–73.

45   *As it happened, sitting out there*: Arnaz, *A Book*, 63, 77.

chapter three: Too Many Girls

47   *Desi recalled that Torsatti*: Desi Arnaz, *A Book* (New York: William Morrow and Company, 1976), 73.

48   *In the fall of 1938*: "A Conversation with Diosa Costello," posted July 18, 2013, by National Museum of American History, https://www.youtube.com/watch?v=yT2QKAWnT8Y.

49   *Dorothy Kilgallen, who wrote*: Dorothy Kilgallen, "Voice of Broadway," newspaper column (publication unclear), August 24, 1939, scrapbook 31, B-AS, LOC.

49   *La Conga had timbered ceilings*: Wolfsonian Collection, Florida International University, https://wolfsonian.org/_assets/docs/2024_menus_qr_labels_ramp1.pdf.

49   *Adler was a celebrity in her own right*: Polly Adler, *A House Is Not a Home* (Amherst: University of Massachusetts Press, 2006), 328, 241.

50   *Desi became a customer*: Arnaz, *A Book*, 74–75.

50   *"A man's visit to Polly's"*: Adler, *A House Is Not a Home*, 320–21.

50   *Desi's summary of the experience*: Arnaz, *A Book*, 76.

51   *But in the short term*: Arnaz, *A Book*, 74–76.

51   *One night after the first show*: Arnaz, *A Book*, 76.

51   *"I don't know," Desi answered*: Arnaz, *A Book*, 77.

52   *"How much of an actor he was"*: George Abbott OH, LAL.

52   *Diosa Costello had already been cast*: "A Conversation with Diosa Costello."

53   *In a pattern that would persist*: Arnaz, *A Book*, 85, 86.

54   *The dancer Margaret Little Durante*: Marge Durante OH, LAL.

55   *Still, he managed*: Draft manuscript, Desi Arnaz, *A Book*, box 1, DAP, SDS; Arnaz, *A Book*, 104.

55   *The* Boston Post's *esteemed drama critic*: Scrapbook 31, B-AS, LOC.

55   *Dorothy Kilgallen allowed*: Scrapbook 31.

58   *"Man, that is a hunk of a woman"*: Arnaz, *A Book*, 109.

chapter four: Enter Lucy

59   *"I wasn't an unloved or an unwanted child"*: Lucille Ball, *Love, Lucy* (New York: G. P. Putnam's Sons, 1996), 26.

60   *"I think that people who have known her"*: Pauline Lopus OH, LAL.

60   *"Ed was never mean"*: Ball, *Love, Lucy*, 9.

61   *"Wintertime was Currier and Ives"*: Cleo Smith OH, LAL.

61   *"Probably the most important thing"*: Fred Ball OH, LAL.

62   *"All I learned in drama school"*: Kathleen Brady, *Lucille: The Life of Lucille Ball* (New York: Hyperion, 1994), 24.

63   *Joanna Ottinger, a friend of Fred's*: Smith OH and Ball OH, LAL.

63   *"It ruined Celoron for us"*: Ball, *Love, Lucy*, 42.

63   *Lucille played Agnes Lynch*: Brady, *Lucille*, 33.

64   *The studio was a graduate school for Lucille*: *Lucille*, 69, 78.

65   *She had a tempestuous romance*: various newspaper clippings, scrapbook 47, B-AS, LOC.

65   *"She wouldn't be specific"*: Lucie Arnaz, author interview, Palm Springs, CA, August 2023.

66   *"I think that he was a very important source"*: Marcella Rabwin OH, LAL.

66   *"I couldn't take my eyes off this Desi"*: Ball, *Love, Lucy*, 116.

66   *"And when they got there"*: George Abbott OH, LAL.

67   *"I sat down and never went back"*: Desi Arnaz, *A Book* (New York: William Morrow and Company, 1976), 110.

67   *"When you fall in love immediately"*: manuscript, Gladys Hall papers, AMPAS.

67   *"That's no good," he would say*: Undated *Boston Globe* clipping, scrapbook 31, B-AS, LOC.

68   *Once, after filming a close-up shot*: Lucille Ball OH, SMU.

68   *Abbott himself would confess*: Abbot OH, LAL; Arnaz, *A Book*, 111.

68   *"I don't remember a time"*: Rabwin OH, LAL.

68   *In an infamous 1936* Esquire *article*: Gustavo Pérez Firmat, *Life on the Hyphen: The Cuban-American Way* (Austin: University of Texas Press, 1994), 62–63.

69   *Lucille was not naive*: Stefan Kanfer, *Ball of Fire: The Tumultuous Life and Comic Art of Lucille Ball* (New York: Alfred A. Knopf, 2003), 100.

69   *"I had flipped"*: Ball, *Love, Lucy*, 122.

69   *The reviews were not*: Ball, *Love, Lucy*, 129.

70   *Decades later, in unpublished notes*: Notes, box 1, DAP, SDS.

70   *She accused him*: Brady, *Lucille*, 114–15.

71   *"We really all of us were taken"*: Smith OH, LAL.

71   *For her part, Lucille would recall*: Ball, *Love, Lucy*, 134.

71   *Desi was so happy*: Scrapbook 42, B-AS, LOC.

chapter five: Desílu

75   *To be sure, Hollywood's welcome*: Undated clipping, scrapbook 45, B-AS, LOC.

77   *Restrictive real estate covenants*: Kevin Starr, *The Dream Endures: California Enters the 1940s* (New York: Oxford, 1997), 172.

79   *Eventually, the* ranchito: Undated clipping, scrapbook 45, B-AS, LOC.

79   *"He felt very obligated"*: Marge Durante OH, LAL.

80   *"It was the most hospitable"*: Van Johnson OH, LAL.

80   *He loved cooking his Cuban specialties*: Lucille Ball, *Love, Lucy* (New York: G. P. Putnam's Sons, 1996), 146.

80   *"He had a magic touch"*: Marcella Rabwin OH, LAL.

80   *"It meant," the actor Jackie Cooper*: Jackie Cooper OH, LAL.

81   *She called Desi "the* mañana *boy"*: Undated clipping, scrapbook 45, B-AS, LOC.

81   *For his part, Desi would call*: Ball, *Love, Lucy*, 144; Rabwin OH, LAL.

81   *Years later, in dictated notes*: Draft notes, Desi Arnaz, *A Book*, box 1, DAP, SDS.

81   *And yet, as Lucy would recall*: Ball, *Love, Lucy*, 144.

81   *Marcella Rabwin would recall* : Rabwin OH, LAL.

81   *Jackie Cooper said*: Cooper OH, LAL.

82   *The previous January*: Undated clipping, scrapbook 45, B-AS, LOC.

82   *"Desi was a little concerned"*: Cooper OH, LAL.

83   *Eleanor Roosevelt hosted*: *Washington Post* clipping, scrapbook 16, B-AS, LOC.

83   *The revue was staged*: William Robert Faith, *Bob Hope: A Life in Comedy* (New York: Da Capo, 2003), 136.

83   *"I think there has never been"*: Draft manuscript, Arnaz, *A Book*, box 1, DAP, SDS.

83   *"Crosby came in"*: Bob Hope OH, LAL.

83   *Crosby, a punctilious performer*: Gary Giddins, *Bing Crosby: Swinging on a Star: The War Years, 1940–1946* (New York: Little, Brown, 2018), 197.

84   *Bert Lahr, the blustery Cowardly Lion*: Faith, *Bob Hope*, 137.

84   *"Only one passenger sparked real enmity"*: Giddins, *Bing Crosby*, 200.

84   *The critics took note*: Kathleen Brady, *Lucille: The Life of Lucille Ball* (New York: Hyperion, 1994), 128.

85   *The* New York Times *judged*: "At Loew's Criterion," *New York Times*, November 12, 1942.

87   *The* New York Times' *Bosley Crowther*: "'Bataan' Film of Historic Defense of Peninsula, Starring Robert Taylor, Robert Walker and Thomas Mitchell, at Capitol," Bosley Crowther, *New York Times*, June 4, 1943.

87   *"Desi is doing a big job"*: Undated clipping, scrapbook 45, B-AS, LOC.

88   *In the scrapbooks she kept faithfully*: Scrapbook 50, B-AS, LOC.

88   *Both Desi and Lucy were jealous*: Brady, *Lucille*, 14.

88   *His solo nightlife also had Hollywood*: Stefan Kanfer, *Ball of Fire: The Tumultuous Life and Comic Art of Lucille Ball* (New York: Alfred A. Knopf, 2003), 94.

88   *"I closed my eyes"*: Ball, *Love, Lucy*, 170–71.

89   *After filing for the divorce*: Danton Walker column, Los Angeles *Daily Mirror*, September 30, 1944.

89   *That November, the day before*: Desi Arnaz, *A Book* (New York: William Morrow and Company, 1976), 154–55; Brady, *Lucille*, 145–46.

chapter six: Necessity's Invention

91   *"When Desi comes back"*: Undated clipping, scrapbook 45, D-AP, LOC.

92   *"When she arrived at MGM"*: Kathleen Brady, *Lucille: The Life of Lucille Ball* (New York: Hyperion, 1994), 133.

92   *"actually it was as orange"*: Lucille Ball, *Love, Lucy* (New York: G. P. Putnam's Sons, 1996), 156.

93   *He now discerned in her*: Ball, *Love, Lucy*, 172.

93   *He had first met Lucy*: Brady, *Lucille*, 49.

94   *But if she picked up*: Brady, *Lucille*, 162.

94   *Lucy needed*: Ball, *Love, Lucy*, 165.

94   *But the studio often shunted*: Ball, *Love, Lucy*, 166.

94   *Lucy has a bravura, eye-rolling drunk scene*: *New York Times*, July 12, 1946.

94   *"Whatever they had in mind"*: Lucille Ball OH, SMU, AMPAS.

95   *This lapse, presumably a result*: Brady, *Lucille*, 152.

96   *The number was written in the 1930s*: Ned Sublette, *Cuba and Its Music: From the First Drums to the Mambo* (Chicago: Chicago Review Press, 2004), 534.

97   *George Schlatter, who booked the acts*: Brady, *Lucille*, 153.

97   *Desi's appearance featured the comedian*: Undated newspaper clipping, scrapbook 32, B-AS, LOC.

97   *It opened that July*: Hollywood Reporter, July 19, 1946.

98   *"I'd say, 'Give him a line'"*: "Desi Arnaz Sits Down with Bob Hope and Don Rickles/Carson Tonight Show," posted August 16, 2022, by Johnny Carson, https://www.youtube.com/watch?v=AkjoMbf7vRg.

98   *In a way that makes for cringeworthy listening*: "Desi Arnaz," Old Time Radio Downloads, https://www.oldtimeradiodownloads.com/actors/desi-arnaz.

99   *Early in their time together*: Undated clipping, scrapbook 32, B-AS, LOC.

99   *To the end of her life*: Unpublished notes, box 1, DAP, SDS; Brady, *Lucille*, 155.

100   *"She has efficiency as a comedienne"*: Brady, *Lucille*, 157.

100   *In Chicago, the columnist Irv Kupcinet*: Scrapbook 32, B-AS, LOC.

101   *"He couldn't be awakened"*: Fred Ball OH, LAL.

101   *"In spite of his limited musical training"*: Series V, writings (digitized), Marco Rizo papers, NYPL.

102   *As Ball's biographer Kathleen Brady wrote*: Brady, *Lucille*, 164.

104   *"She would be a stage-struck schemer"*: Jess Oppenheimer and Gregg Oppenheimer, *Laughs, Luck . . . and Lucy: How I Came to Create the Most Popular Sitcom of All Time* (Syracuse, NY: Syracuse University Press, 1996), 115.

104   *"Oh, my God, Jess"*: Oppenheimer, *Laughs, Luck . . . and Lucy*, 126.

104   *Lucy plays the dimmest graduate*: David C. Tucker: *S. Sylvan Simon, Moviemaker: Adventures with Lucy, Red Skelton, and Harry Cohn in the Golden Age of Hollywood* (Jefferson, NC: McFarland & Company, 2021), 182.

106   *"It was a beautiful ceremony"*: Ball, *Love, Lucy*, 192.

106   *The coolness with Mayor Arnaz*: Scrapbook 50, B-AS, LOC.

106   *He reversed this procedure*: Brady, *Lucille*, 173.

106   *"He is a comic caballero"*: Pérez Firmat, *Life on the Hyphen*, 61.

107   *"There was no way I could play that guy"*: "Desi Arnaz Sits Down with Bob Hope and Don Rickles/Carson Tonight Show."

108   *The Arnazes' act opened*: all the following clippings cited here, Weiler, etc., scrapbook 53, B-AS, LOC.

chapter seven: Getting Airborne

112   *The production values were sketchy*: "Lucille Ball and Desi Arnaz - The Ed Wynn Show - December 24, 1949," posted November 29, 2020, by Finding by W.D.F, https://www.youtube.com/watch?v=2_vk1pbCtnI.

113   *Mayor Arnaz was now involved*: Letter from Desiderio Arnaz II to Lucille Ball, July 27, 1950, scrapbook 42, B-AS, LOC.

113   *"It meant . . . you were washed up"*: Jackie Cooper OH, LAL.

113   *"So terrified was Hollywood"*: Lucille Ball, *Love, Lucy* (New York: G. P. Putnam's Sons, 1996), 204.

114   *Desi had made a few commercials*: Coyne Steven Sanders and Tom Gilbert, *Desilu: The Story of Lucille Ball and Desi Arnaz* (New York: William Morrow and Company, 1993), 33.

114   *That idea did pique the interest of NBC*: Jess Oppenheimer and Gregg Oppenheimer, *Laughs, Luck . . . and Lucy: How I Came to Create the Most Popular Sitcom of All Time* (Syracuse, NY: Syracuse University Press, 1996), 133.

115   *"Bill said he was completely opposed"*: Draft manuscript, Harry Ackerman memoir, Gregg Oppeheimer private collection, Santa Monica, California.

115   *Opening a typical show*: "Desi Arnaz Your Tropical Trip Radio Show 3-25-51 Pre 'I Love Lucy,'" posted March 2, 2022, by hans Jeff Borger, https://www.youtube.com/watch?v=-v7XYEW9bFY.

116 *"Lucy had that kind of power"*: Sanders and Gilbert, *Desilu*, 33.

116 *"I'm proud to be called Mrs. Arnaz"*: Undated clipping, unknown publication, scrapbook 51, B-AS, LOC.

116 *In Ackerman's memory*: Draft manuscript, Harry Ackerman memoir.

116 *Brainstorming together one day*: Oppenheimer, *Laughs, Luck . . . and Lucy*, 134.

118 *Still, the performance almost did not happen*: Oppenheimer, *Laughs, Luck . . . and Lucy*, 140.

118 *That same day, Oppenheimer*: Oppenheimer, *Laughs, Luck . . . and Lucy*, 139.

120 *There was clearly lingering skepticism*: Bart Andrews, *The "I Love Lucy" Book* (New York: Doubleday, 1985), 25.

121 *There was one adman*: Oppenheimer, *Laughs, Luck . . . and Lucy*, 172.

121 *In his own memoir*: Milton H. Biow, *Butting In: An Adman Speaks Out* (Garden City, NY: Doubleday & Company, 1964), 155–57.

122 *In the end, Philip Morris*: Sanders and Gilbert, *Desilu*, 37.

122 *The contract with Philip Morris*: Oppenheimer, *Laughs, Luck . . . and Lucy*, 172–73.

123 *But Biow was adamant*: Oppenheimer, *Laughs, Luck . . . and Lucy*, 142.

123 *"There are only two shades"*: *New York Herald Tribune*, October 25, 1949.

123 *The Hollywood trade papers*: Sanders and Gilbert, *Desilu*, 38.

123 *On top of everything else*: Desi Arnaz, *A Book* (New York: William Morrow and Company, 1976), 202–3.

124 *The best evidence suggests*: Oppenheimer, *Laughs, Luck . . . and Lucy*, 143.

chapter eight: Lightning in a Bottle

125 *If recorded broadcasts were permitted*: Stanley Cloud and Lynne Olson, *Murrow Boys: Pioneers on the Front Lines of Broadcast Journalism* (Boston: Houghton Mifflin Harcourt, 1996), 60.

126 *"It is only a network"*: James L. Baughman, *Same Time, Same Station: Creating American Television, 1948–1961* (Baltimore, MD: Johns Hopkins University Press, 2007), 129.

127 *Ackerman, especially, feared*: "Letters" column, letter from Martin N. Leeds, *Emmy* magazine, November–December 1989.

129 *Jess Oppenheimer called Freund*: Jess Oppenheimer and Gregg Oppenheimer, *Laughs, Luck . . . and Lucy: How I Came to Create the Most Popular Sitcom of All Time* (Syracuse, NY: Syracuse University Press, 1996), 151.

129 *Freund had photographed*: Peter J. Patrick, "Oscar Profile #570: Karl Freund," *Cinema Sight*, October 21, 2021, https://www.cinemasight.com/oscar-profile -570-karl-freund/.

130 *Brooks was stunned*: Jeanine Basinger and Sam Wasson, *Hollywood: The Oral History* (New York: Harper Collins, 2022), 332–33.

131   *"There are no rules"*: Lucille Ball, *Love, Lucy* (New York: G. P. Putnam's Sons, 1996), 210.

131   *In 1947 and 1948, Jerry Fairbanks*: "Myths and Mysteries Surround Pioneering of 3-Camera TV," Jon Krampner, *Los Angeles Times*, July 29, 1991.

132   *But in a draft manuscript*: Draft manuscript, Desi Arnaz, *A Book*, LAL.

132   *"Desi quickly proved"*: Draft manuscript, Harry Ackerman memoir, Gregg Oppeheimer private collection, Santa Monica, California; Oppenheimer, *Laughs, Luck . . . and Lucy*, 145.

133   *"I turned it down"*: Edward Buzzell OH, SMU, AMPAS.

134   *In June, CBS screened*: Coyne Sanders and Tom Gilbert, *Desilu: The Story of Lucille Ball and Desi Arnaz* (New York: William Morrow and Company, 1993), 37, 47.

134   *Oppenheimer then told Desi*: Oppenheimer, *Laughs, Luck . . . and Lucy*, 148.

136   *"I've never in my life"*: Rob Edelman and Audrey Kupferberg, *Meet the Mertzes: The Secret Stories of* I Love Lucy's *Other Couple* (Los Angeles: Renaissance Books, 1999), 42.

136   *Frawley agreed*: Desi Arnaz, *A Book* (New York: William Morrow and Company, 1976), 215.

136   *She would later recall*: Frank Castelluccio and Alvin Walker, *The Other Side of Ethel Mertz: The Life Story of Vivian Vance* (New York: Berkley Boulevard, 2000), 150.

137   *Lucy had spent the final weeks*: Ball, *Love, Lucy*, 186–87, 196.

137   *"This was the way"*: Ball, *Love, Lucy*, 203–4.

138   *"This is our baby"*: Kathleen Brady, *Lucille: The Life of Lucille Ball* (New York: Hyperion, 1994), 187.

138   *Lucie's own first memory*: Lucie Arnaz, author interview, Palm Springs, CA, August 2023.

139   *She insisted from the start*: Brady, *Lucille*, 204.

139   *Leeds advanced sixty thousand dollars*: Sanders and Gilbert, *Desilu*, 40.

139   *At this point, Desi's to-do list*: Arnaz, *A Book*, 219.

140   *The floor crew and CBS executives*: Sanders and Gilbert, *Desilu*, 59–60.

143   *"That change in plans"*: Oppenheimer, *Laughs, Luck . . . and Lucy*, 161.

143   *"I was adaptable"*: Oppenheimer, *Laughs, Luck . . . and Lucy*, 155–57; "Dann Cahn," The Interviews, Television Academy Foundation, https://interviews.televisionacademy.com/interviews/dann-cahn.

chapter nine: It's a Hit!

147   *He pronounced it "unfunny"*: Stefan Kanfer, *Ball of Fire: The Tumultuous Life and Comic Art of Lucille Ball* (New York: Alfred A. Knopf, 2003), 139.

147   *"For here is a film"*: *Variety*, October 17, 1951.

148 *"Every once in a rare great while"*: Hollywood Reporter, October 16, 1951.

149 *"When we started* I Love Lucy*"*: Jess Oppenheimer and Gregg Oppenheimer, *Laughs, Luck . . . and Lucy: How I Came to Create the Most Popular Sitcom of All Time* (Syracuse, NY: Syracuse University Press, 1996), 172.

149 *"Desi accidentally slipped"*: Madelyn Pugh Davis and Bob Carroll Jr., *Laughing with Lucy: My Life with America's Leading Lady of Comedy* (Cincinnati, OH: Clerisy Press, 2007), 61.

150 *"The audience had to believe"*: Lucille Ball, *Love, Lucy* (New York: G. P. Putnam's Sons, 1996), 207.

150 *"The captivating thing about Lucy"*: American Magazine, September 1952, 27–28.

151 *"It's dazzling to find one TV show"*: Laura Bergquist, "Desi and Lucy: The Love Story Behind Their Six Years at the Top," Look, December 25, 1956.

151 *"The revelation of* I Love Lucy*"*: Kathleen Brady, *Lucille: The Life of Lucille Ball* (New York: Hyperion, 1994), 204–5.

152 *"The audience resented it"*: Davis, *Laughing with Lucy*, 62.

152 *Desi's real accent*: Davis, *Laughing with Lucy*, 141–42.

153 *At least one critic*: Oakland Tribune, November 2, 1951.

154 *"Desi was always much better"*: Oppenheimer, *Laughs, Luck . . . and Lucy*, 174.

154 *Her first reactions were often negative*: Madelyn Pugh Davis OH, LAL.

155 *"At the readings, Desi would"*: "William Asher," The Interviews, Television Academy Foundation, https://interviews.televisionacademy.com/interviews/william-asher.

155 *Bill Frawley was notorious*: Brady, *Lucille*, 199.

156 *"We usually tried"*: Davis, *Laughing with Lucy*, 81.

156 *Once, after he gave them*: Oppenheimer, *Laughs, Luck . . . and Lucy*, 191.

156 *Once the three-headed monster*: Bart Andrews, *The "I Love Lucy" Book* (New York: Doubleday, 1985), 75.

156 *Madelyn would recall*: Davis, *Laughing with Lucy*, 68.

156 *By the end of 1951*: Coyne Steven Sanders and Tom Gilbert, *Desilu: The Story of Lucille Ball and Desi Arnaz* (New York: William Morrow and Company, 1993), 57–58, 60.

157 *For Desi, the show*: Desi Arnaz, *A Book* (New York: William Morrow and Company, 1976), 230.

158 *But the company's chairman*: Arnaz, *A Book*, 272–73.

158 *"We were the first company"*: Ed Holly OH, LAL.

159 *"If a retake with dialogue"*: Undated clipping, scrapbook no. uncertain, B-AS, LOC.

159 *The reality was slightly more complicated*: Brady, *Lucille*, 205.

chapter ten: Baby Mogul

162 But a few days later Jess was shocked: Jess Oppenheimer and Gregg Oppenheimer, Laughs, Luck . . . and Lucy: How I Came to Create the Most Popular Sitcom of All Time (Syracuse, NY: Syracuse University Press, 1996), 194.

163 "He started to get into the various areas": "Dann Cahn," The Interviews, Television Academy Foundation, https://interviews.televisionacademy.com/interviews/dann-cahn.

163 "It kind of became a wedge": "William Asher," The Interviews, Television Academy Foundation, https://interviews.televisionacademy.com/interviews/william-asher.

163 "Bob and I have always attributed": Madelyn Pugh Davis and Bob Carroll Jr., Laughing with Lucy: My Life with America's Leading Lady of Comedy (Cincinnati, OH: Clerisy Press, 2007), 127.

164 A much more credible account: Oppenheimer, Luck, Laughs . . . and Lucy, 5.

165 Mr. Lyon, I guess it all: Desi Arnaz, A Book (New York: William Morrow and Company, 1976), 234.

166 He had served as an adviser: Gary Giddins, Bing Crosby: Swinging on a Star: The War Years, 1940–1946 (New York: Little, Brown, 2018), 515.

170 John Crosby in the New York Herald Tribune: "Radio and Television: The Unborn Celebrity," John Crosby, New York Herald Tribune, December 21, 1952.

170 The combined pregnancies: Charles Pomerantz memo, scrapbook 54, B-AS, LOC.

170 "Well, don't just lie there, do something!": Lucille Ball, Love, Lucy (New York: G. P. Putnam's Sons, 1996), 222.

170 "It's a boy!": James Bacon, Hollywood Is a Four Letter Town (Chicago: Henry Regnery Company, 1976), 309.

170 Desi went to the Brown Derby: Ball, Love, Lucy, 222.

171 "To Lucy, to Ricky": Kathleen Brady, Lucille: The Life of Lucille Ball (New York: Hyperion, 1994), 213.

171 "Is this the little fellow": Arnaz, A Book, 239.

171 "I conceived the idea": Pandro Berman OH, SMU, AMPAS.

172 At the film's first preview: Howard Strickling memo, Vincente Minnelli papers, AMPAS.

173 In the 1952–53 season: Variety, September 12, 1952.

173 Lucy, listening at home: Ball, Love, Lucy, 227.

174 "In those days that was not a big, terrible thing": Arnaz, A Book, 248.

175 His first move was to call: Arnaz, A Book, 249; "The Press: City Editor," Time, June 30, 1947.

176 Moments before Desi headed out: Coyne Steven Sanders and Tom Gilbert, Desilu: The Story of Lucille Ball and Desi Arnaz (New York: William Morrow and Company, 1993), 83.

176   *"Lucy is as American as Bernard Baruch"*: Newspaper clipping, source unclear, scrapbook 57, B-AS, LOC.

177   *At the end of the session*: Arnaz, *A Book*, 255.

177   *"One cannot help but wonder"*: Brady, *Lucille*, 221.

177   *And feelings still ran high*: Various correspondence, folder 667, Hedda Hopper papers, AMPAS.

178   *"If we are going to continue"*: Todd S. Purdum, *Something Wonderful: Rodgers and Hammerstein's Broadway Revolution* (New York: Henry Holt & Company, 2018), 225.

chapter eleven: "It's Only a Show"

179   *"You will still get home in time"*: Scrapbook no. unknown, B-AS, LOC.

180   *Now, in the fall of 1953*: Valerie J. Nelson and Kenneth Reich, "Roz Wyman, City's Youngest Council Member Who Helped Bring Dodgers to L.A., Dies at 92," *Los Angeles Times*, October 10, 2022, https://www.latimes.com/obituaries/story/2022-10-27/rosalind-wyman-los-angeles-city-council-dodgers-dead.

180   *The products ranged*: *Dayton Daily News*, November 17, 1952; Jack Hirschberg papers, AMPAS.

180   *Executives of the American Character Doll Company*: *Toys and Novelties*, November 1952.

180   *Jack Gould, the* New York Times's: Jack Gould, "Why Millions Love Lucy," *New York Times Magazine*, March 1, 1953.

182   *The couple exhibited real wedded bliss*: Madelyn Pugh Davis and Bob Carroll Jr., *Laughing with Lucy: My Life with America's Leading Lady of Comedy* (Cincinnati, OH: Clerisy Press, 2007), 84.

182   *As for* The Long, Long Trailer: Minnelli papers, AMPAS.

182   *"any resemblance to human beings"*: Bosley Crowther, "Lucille Ball and Desi Arnaz Bring 'Long, Long Trailer' to Music Hall," *New York Times*, February 28, 1954.

183   *"Lucy used to phone Desi"*: "Dann Cahn," The Interviews, Television Academy Foundation, https://interviews.televisionacademy.com/interviews/dann-cahn.

183   *"If you're trying to create"*: Martin Leeds OH, LAL.

183   *"The problem we had with Desi"*: Kathleen Brady, *Lucille: The Life of Lucille Ball* (New York: Hyperion, 1994), 223–23.

183   *"As a calming wifely stratagem"*: Laura Bergquist, "Desi and Lucy: The Love Story Behind Their Six Years at the Top," *Look*, December 25, 1956.

183   *When Desi's mother showed up*: Coyne Steven Sanders and Tom Gilbert, *Desilu: The Story of Lucille Ball and Desi Arnaz* (New York: William Morrow and Company, 1993), 89.

184   *"What is she excited about?"*: Brady, *Lucille*, 224.

184   *"I have come to the terrible realization"*: Sanders and Gilbert, *Desilu*, 92.

184 *"In my judgment, God"*: Family letters, LAL.

184 *"At the present time we are very busy"*: Scrapbook no. unclear, B-AS, LOC.

185 *On the same night that Desi defused*: Sanders and Gilbert, *Desilu*, 76.

185 *Desi then promptly parlayed*: Desi Arnaz, *A Book* (New York: William Morrow and Company, 1976), 276–78.

186 *"It was a Camelot"*: Leeds OH, LAL.

186 *Desi's secretary, Johnny Aitchison*: Johnny Aitchison OH, LAL.

187 *"You just bought yourself another coffin"*: Brady, *Lucille*, 230.

187 *"Miss Ball is always trying"*: Sanders and Gilbert, *Desilu*, 85.

189 *The Desilu film editor Dann Cahn*: "Dann Cahn," The Interviews, Television Academy Foundation, https://interviews.televisionacademy.com/interviews /dann-cahn.

189 *As part of its promotional deal*: Davis, *Laughing with Lucy*, 90.

189 *But it turned out*: Lucie Arnaz email to author, July 28, 2024.

190 *In December 1954, he became the target*: Brad Shortell, "Does Desi Really Love Lucy?," *Confidential*, January 1955, https://media.wnyc.org/media/resources /2010/Oct/07/Confidential_Lucy__Desi.pdf.

190 *As Leeds would later recall*: Martin Leeds OH, LAL.

191 *"I thought she was very domineering"*: Marge Durante OH, LAL.

191 *Martin Leeds saw her*: Leeds OH, LAL.

191 *When he surprised her*: Lucie Arnaz, author interview, Palm Springs, CA, August 2023.

191 *"Within the home, Desi"*: Marcella Rabwin OH, LAL.

191 *Lucy had become a mother*: Kathleen Brady, *Lucille: The Life of Lucille Ball* (New York: Hyperion, 1994), 203.

192 *"DeDe was the real linchpin"*: Coyne Steven Sanders and Tom Gilbert, *Desilu: The Story of Lucille Ball and Desi Arnaz* (New York: William Morrow and Company, 1993), 113.

192 *"We were raised by a Black woman"*: Desi Arnaz Jr. OH, LAL.

192 *Lucie's lasting impression*: Lucie Arnaz, author interview.

192 *"My father had this amazing sense"*: Desi Arnaz Jr. OH.

192 *By contrast, Lucie remembered*: Lucie Arnaz, author interview.

193 *"I thought she was a loving parent"*: Rabwin OH, LAL.

193 *The children attended*: Lucie Arnaz, author interview.

193 *"I was very much embracing"*: Desi Arnaz Jr., author telephone interview, July 2024.

194 *"She didn't have much time"*: "Maury Thompson," from *Lucille Ball: Finding Lucy*, American Masters Digital Archive, WNET, December 3, 2000, https://www.pbs .org/wnet/americanmasters/archive/interview/maury-thompson/.

194 *"And it was the most natural thing"*: Johnny Aitchison OH, LAL.

194 *"You got kids?"*: William Friedkin, author interview, circa 2023.

chapter twelve: *An Empire of Their Own*

195   *As early as 1952*: Hal Humphrey column, *Los Angeles Times*, September 17, 1952, scrapbook no. unknown, B-AS, LOC.

197   *"It is overwhelming"*: Port Huron *Times Herald*, March 16, 1956, scrapbook no. unknown, B-AS, LOC.

197   *"They came by Ciro's"*: George Schlatter, author interview, August 2023.

198   *Manufacturers provided*: Folder of family papers, re: Roxbury house, LAL.

198   *"Desi really flipped"*: Lucille Ball, *Love, Lucy* (New York: G. P. Putnam's Sons, 1996), 244–47.

198   *"Desi would want 7-Up"*: Johnny Aitchison OH and Martin Leeds OH, LAL.

199   *"We knew that if he asked"*: Coyne Steven Sanders and Tom Gilbert, *Desilu: The Story of Lucille Ball and Desi Arnaz* (New York: William Morrow and Company, 1993), 156.

199   *Martin Leeds recalled*: Martin Leeds, unpublished manuscript, LAL.

201   Variety *reported an unspecified "conflict"*: Sanders and Gilbert, *Desilu*, 102.

201   *In fact, Philip Morris's sales*: Bart Andrews, *The "I Love Lucy" Book* (New York: Doubleday, 1985), 156; Richard Kluger, *Ashes to Ashes: America's Hundred Year Cigarette War, the Public Health, and the Unabashed Triumph of Philip Morris* (New York: Vintage, 1997), 173.

201   *"I left the show because"*: Andrews, *The "I Love Lucy" Book*.

202   *"You god-damned, redhead sonofabitch"*: Kathleen Brady, *Lucille: The Life of Lucille Ball* (New York: Hyperion, 1994), 229.

202   *He said that Lucy*: "Maury Thompson," from *Lucille Ball: Finding Lucy*, American Masters Digital Archive, WNET, December 3, 2000, https://www.pbs.org /wnet/americanmasters/archive/interview/maury-thompson/.

203   *Desi dispatched Ed Hamilton*: Sanders and Gilbert, *Desilu*, 169.

204   *The critics were brutal*: William K. Zinsser, "Screen: Forever Darling," *New York Herald Tribune*, February 10, 1956, scrapbook no. unknown, B-AS, LOC.

204   *"I haven't been in many flops"*: Ball, *Love, Lucy*, 247.

205   *"We had already taken them to Hollywood"*: Jess Oppenheimer and Gregg Oppenheimer, *Laughs, Luck . . . and Lucy: How I Came to Create the Most Popular Sitcom of All Time* (Syracuse, NY: Syracuse University Press, 1996), 213.

206   *he would ultimately leave NBC*: Sanders and Gilbert, *Desilu*, 108.

208   *"Dear Lucy: I tuned in"*: J. Edgar Hoover letter to Lucille Ball, October 2, 1956, family files, LAL.

208   *The language of the sale agreement*: Desilu sale agreement with CBS, October 1, 1956, family files, LAL.

209   *"We extrapolated out the number of shows"*: Ed Holly OH, LAL.

209   *"So when CBS offered to buy"*: Oppenheimer, *Laughs, Luck . . . and Lucy*, 216.

210   *The set for the new Connecticut house*: Andrews, *The "I Love Lucy" Book*, 373.

210   *Jay Sandrich recalled*: Brady, *Lucille*, 235.

211   *Desi Jr. played a child*: Andrews, *The "I Love Lucy" Book*, 379.

211   *"I was working much too hard"*: Desi Arnaz, *A Book* (New York: William Morrow and Company, 1976), 286.

211   *"And he was doing it"*: Holly OH, LAL.

chapter thirteen: Catastrophic Success

213   *"When I turned that down"*: Bart Andrews, *The "I Love Lucy" Book* (New York: Doubleday, 1985), 196.

213   *"You can't afford to sit still"*: Coyne Steven Sanders and Tom Gilbert, *Desilu: The Story of Lucille Ball and Desi Arnaz* (New York: William Morrow and Company, 1993), 142.

214   *"We'll be able to move around more"*: Andrews, *The "I Love Lucy" Book*, 198.

215   *It would be managed by Frank Bogert*: "Desi's Hotel Opens Saturday," *Daily Enterprise*, March 29, 1957, scrapbook no. unknown, B-AS, LOC.

215   *"We won't discriminate"*: Andrews, *The "I Love Lucy" Book*, 245.

215   *A fourth camera was added*: Andrews, *The "I Love Lucy" Book*, 197.

217   *She described herself*: Tallulah Bankhead, *Tallulah: My Autobiography* (New York: Harper & Brothers, 1952), 308.

218   *"Tallulah was half-crocked"*: Desi Arnaz, *A Book* (New York: William Morrow and Company, 1976), 294.

218   *"They had this plot"*: Gilbert and Sanders, *Desilu*, 134.

218   *"We all assembled"*: Madelyn Pugh Davis and Bob Carroll Jr., *Laughing with Lucy: My Life with America's Leading Lady of Comedy* (Cincinnati, OH: Clerisy Press, 2007), 145.

220   *Holly took her aside*: Ed Holly OH, LAL.

220   *"Her reaction was pretty much"*: Kathleen Brady, *Lucille: The Life of Lucille Ball* (New York: Hyperion, 1994), 238.

220   *"Lucy was stunned"*: Holly OH, LAL.

220   *In the filming that night*: Andrews, *The "I Love Lucy" Book*, 199.

221   *"Desi was a delight"*: Sanders and Gilbert, *Desilu*, 148.

221   *Lucy was daunted*: Lucille Ball, *Love, Lucy* (New York: G. P. Putnam's Sons, 1996), 253.

221   *"Amigos, if anything happens"*: Sanders and Gilbert, *Desilu*, 139.

221   *The* Hollywood Reporter *summed up*: Sanders and Gilbert, *Desilu*, 140.

222   *"Might it not be better"*: Sanders and Gilbert, *Desilu*, 142.

222   *"Every office needed refurbishing"*: Sanders and Gilbert, *Desilu*, 146.

222   *In December, Mayor Arnaz*: Desi Arnaz II to Lucille Ball, scrapbook no. unknown, B-AS, LOC.

223   *In their 1940 book*: Smiley Blanton and Norman Vincent Peale, *Faith Is*

the Answer: A Psychiatrist and a Pastor Discuss Your Problems (New York: Abingdon-Cokesbury Press, 1940), 184.

223   *For his part, Peale advised*: Blanton and Peale, *Faith Is the Answer*, 193.

223   *Blanton wrote to Desi*: Smiley Blanton letter, LAL.

224   *"I was grateful that Desi"*: Ball, *Love, Lucy*, 252.

224   *On October 13, Blanton wrote*: Blanton letter, LAL.

225   *"Desi saw Dr. Blanton a few times"*: Ball, *Love, Lucy*, 253.

225   *What is worse*: Draft manuscript, Desi Arnaz, *A Book*, box 1, DAP, SDS.

226   *The new contract*: Andrews, *The "I Love Lucy" Book*, 204.

226   *"all without a single test"*: Andrews, *The "I Love Lucy" Book*, 204.

227   *"We want our stories"*: undated memo, no author noted, Business files, LAL.

228   *The season premiere drew the same mix*: Sanders and Gilbert, *Desilu*, 161.

229   *"Desi was a very, very bright man"*: Sanders and Gilbert, *Desilu*, 147.

229   *Jack Gould of the* New York Times: Jack Gould, *New York Times*, October 13, 1958.

230   *"They didn't want to do it so bad"*: Sanders and Gilbert, *Desilu*, 151.

230   *"That's what happens"*: Kenny Morgan career chronology, LAL.

230   *But Desilu's public successes*: This account is taken from various sources, including a souvenir privately printed LP record album, "The Friars Club Present the Lucille Ball and Desi Arnaz Testimonial Dinner," of the evening's entertainment purchased by the author on eBay. See also: "'Parkyakarkus' Dies After Giving Monologue at Comedy Roast," *New York Times*, November 25, 1958.

232   *"This was an evening"*: Sanders and Gilbert, *Desilu*, 165.

chapter fourteen: Too Much and Not Enough

233   *"Desi Arnaz is called"* . . . *"There is no classification for a Cuban fellow"*: Kenny Morgan career chronology, LAL.

234   *When Hedda Hopper visited*: Hedda Hopper radio script or column, September 22, 1958, Hedda Hopper papers, AMPAS.

234   *His pro forma denials were unpersuasive*: Coyne Steven Sanders and Tom Gilbert, *Desilu: The Story of Lucille Ball and Desi Arnaz* (New York: William Morrow and Company, 1993), 163.

234   *"Desi could be the most charming"*: Sanders and Gilbert, *Desilu*, 157.

234   *The Beverly Hills cops*: Kathleen Brady, *Lucille: The Life of Lucille Ball* (New York: Hyperion, 1994), 248.

235   *"He was a sweetheart of a guy"*: Scotty Bowers with Lionel Friedberg, *Full Service: My Adventures in Hollywood and the Secret Sex Lives of the Stars* (New York: Grove Press, 2012), 191–92.

235   *"I've got two great girls"*: "Rod Erickson," part 7, The Interviews, Television

Academy Foundation, https://interviews.televisionacademy.com/interviews/rod-erickson#interview-clips.

236 *For the first time in years*: Bart Andrews, *The "I Love Lucy" Book* (New York: Doubleday, 1985), 166.

237 *"The Company is engaged"*: Desilu Initial Public Offer Prospectus, December 3, 1958, Ed Holly papers, AMPAS.

237 *"Desi wouldn't go"*: Sanders and Gilbert, *Desilu*, 156.

238 *"We need seven more stories"*: Bernie Weitzman to Bert Granet, undated "Inter-Department Communication," Bert Granet papers, AMPAS.

238 *Bert Granet, the* Playhouse's *executive producer*: March 9, 1959, Granet papers, AMPAS.

239 *"We didn't quite realize"*: Sanders and Gilbert, *Desilu*, 149.

239 *"It makes it increasingly difficult"*: Undated memo, Granet papers, AMPAS.

241 *Stack was stunned but agreed*: Robert Stack with Mark Evans, *Straight Shooting* (New York: Berkley, 1981), 254.

242 *In his memoir, Desi would claim*: Sanders and Gilbert, *Desilu*, 176.

243 *"Weather perfect, food divine"*: Lucille Ball to Hedda Hopper, May 24, 1959, Hopper papers, AMPAS.

243 *"When he wasn't drinking"*: Lucille Ball, *Love, Lucy* (New York: G. P. Putnam's Sons, 1996), 257.

243 *"Those days were very intense"*: Desi Arnaz Jr. OH, Cleo Smith OH, Lucie Arnaz OH, LAL.

243 *With Gallic realism, he told Lucy*: Brady, *Lucille*, 255.

244 *"Desi and I came back from our trip not speaking"*: Ball, *Love, Lucy*, 257.

244 *"What do I say here?"*: Andrews, *The "I Love Lucy" Book*, 208.

244 *"It was sometimes a little difficult"*: Jay Sandrich OH, SMU, AMPAS.

244 *"Look what he did for Lucy"*: Andrews, *The "I Love Lucy" Book*, 209.

245 *"Message was that something had to be done"*: Kenny Morgan career chronology, LAL.

245 *"I'm not going to teach anything"*: Hedda Hopper radio script or column, September 22, 1958 Hopper papers, AMPAS.

246 *"And someplace and someday"*: Holly OH, LAL.

246 *"When booked at the station"*: Desi Arnaz FBI file, LAL.

246 *The full truth was worse*: Sanders and Gilbert, *Desilu*, 189.

246 *"She just went white"*: Sanders and Gilbert, *Desilu*, 189.

246 *In draft notes for his memoir*: Draft manuscript, Desi Arnaz, *A Book*, box 1, DAP, SDS.

247 *"The white, white makeup"*: Carole Cook OH, LAL.

247 *Bob Weiskopf mordantly noted*: Brady, *Lucille*, 251.

247 *As Desi stood at the ship's railing*: Brady, *Lucille*, 257.

chapter fifteen: "That's All"

249   *One such memo noted*: January 2, 1959 memo from "Mr. Nease" to M.A. Jones, Desi Arnaz FBI files, LAL.

250   *An October 17 memo*: Arnaz FBI files. The episode, as aired, obscures the shooter.

251   *"While Mr. Stack may be content"*: J. Edgar Hoover to Desi Arnaz, December 11, 1959, Arnaz FBI files.

251   *Frank Sinatra, then a Desilu studio tenant*: Matthew Pearl, "Behind *The Untouchables*: The Making of the Memoir That Reclaimed a Prohibition-Era Legend," *Vanity Fair*, December 27, 2017, https://www.vanityfair.com/hollywood/2017/12/the-untouchables-the-making-of-the-memoir-prohibition-era-legend.

251   *Sinatra reportedly carried a message to Desi from the mob*: Aleesha Lange, "Paramount Plus Series 'Mafia Spies' Analyzes Frank Sinatra's Mobster Past," *Palm Springs Life*, July 22, 2024, https://www.palmspringslife.com/paramount-plus-series-mafia-spies-analyzes-frank-sinatras-mobster-past/.

251   *"Eventually, we did stop using Italian names"*: Robert Stack with Mark Evans, *Straight Shooting* (New York: Berkley, 1981), 271.

251   *Finally, Desi's old friends*: Maritote v. Desilu Productions, Inc., 230 F. Supp. 721 (N.D. Ill. 1964), https://law.justia.com/cases/federal/district-courts/FSupp/230/721/1413083/.

252   *"We brought motion picture techniques into television"*: Robert Stack OH, SMU, AMPAS.

252   *And at least one distinguished critic loved the show*: J. Hoberman, "The Untouchables TV Series: Old-School Gangster Trapping," *New York Times*, August 5, 2016.

253   *In draft notes years later*: Box 1, DAP, SDS.

254   *Some of the Arnazes' friends*: Kathleen Brady, *Lucille: The Life of Lucille Ball* (New York: Hyperion, 1994), 257.

254   *"But I also find it impossible"*: Gladys Hall papers, AMPAS.

254   *That December, the new issue of* Cosmopolitan: Frederick Christian, "Lucille Ball's Serious Life with Desi Arnaz," *Cosmopolitan*, January 1960.

255   *"The door was open to their bedroom"*: Lucie Arnaz, author interview, Palm Springs, CA, August 2023.

255   *Desi Jr. would recall*: Desi Arnaz Jr. OH, LAL.

256   *"It wasn't good for anyone"*: Arnaz Jr. OH; Desi Arnaz Jr., author telephone interview 2024.

256   *"'Lucy, dear,' he'd say"*: Lucille Ball, *Love, Lucy* (New York: G. P. Putnam's Sons, 1996), 259.

257   *"It marked the end of so many things"*: Ball, *Love, Lucy*, 260.

257   *Jim Bacon of the Associated Press*: "Jim Bacon from Hollywood," *Jamestown Post-Journal*, March 4, 1960, scrapbook 7, B-AS, LOC.

257   *Jack Hirshberg of the* Toronto Telegram: Jack Hirschberg papers, AMPAS.

258   *"We'd laugh about our troubles"*: Rosemary Clooney, author interview, 1999.

258   *"Too bad," Desi added*: Draft manuscript, Desi Arnaz, *A Book*, box 1, DAP, SDS.

259   *"Even the lesser Desi-Lucy hours"*: Coyne Steven Sanders and Tom Gilbert, *Desilu: The Story of Lucille Ball and Desi Arnaz* (New York: William Morrow and Company, 1993), 197.

259   *Walter Winchell's column reported*: Brady, *Lucille*, 262.

260   *"Miss Ball is pouring her whole heart"*: Steven Suskin, *Opening Night on Broadway: A Critical Quotebook of the Golden Age of Musical Theatre*, Oklahoma! *(1943) to* Fiddler on the Roof *(1964)* (New York: Schirmer, 1990), 711–13.

261   *"He phoned me a three o'clock in the morning"*: Martin Leeds OH, LAL.

261   *Desi had come to have a jaundiced view*: Draft manuscript, Desi Arnaz, *A Book*.

261   *Arnaz bought back*: Sanders and Gilbert, *Desilu*, 207.

261   *"Desi Arnaz is the studio's top salesman"*: Undated public relations brochure, circa 1961, prepared by Wolcott & Associates, Ed Holly papers, AMPAS.

263   *"Here we were, starting again"*: Frank Castelluccio and Alvin Walker, *The Other Side of Ethel Mertz: The Life Story of Vivian Vance* (New York: Berkley Boulevard, 2000), 245.

263   *"So far, we have five scripts done"*: Hedda Hopper papers, AMPAS.

263   *"There was a part of him that wasn't there"*: Sanders and Gilbert, *Desilu*, 234.

264   *"You can't please everyone"*: Sanders and Gilbert, *Desilu*, 230.

264   *Stack believed the show's writing*: Robert Stack OH, SMU, AMPAS.

265   *"Over a period of time"*: Sanders and Gilbert, *Desilu*, 246.

265   *"He rather readily agreed"*: Sanders and Gilbert, *Desilu*, 246.

265   *"After sitting there in my big chair"*: Draft manuscript, *A Book*.

266   *"I am sure you will join"*: Holly papers, AMPAS.

chapter sixteen: Slow Fade

268   *"He also put into the Bank of Mexico"*: Marcella Rabwin, *Yes, Mr. Selznick: Recollections of Hollywood's Golden Era* (Pittsburgh: Dorrance Publishing Co., 1999), 104.

268   *The whole thing got "kind of silly"*: Draft manuscript, Desi Arnaz, *A Book*, box 1, DAP, SDS.

268   *Lucy sent a horseshoe-shaped congratulatory arrangement*: Kathleen Brady, *Lucille: The Life of Lucille Ball* (New York: Hyperion, 1994), 249.

268   *"If I blow my top"*: Draft manuscript, *A Book*.

269   *"You couldn't help but be in awe"*: Greg Hirsch, author telephone interview, 2023.

269   *Lucie would recall*: Lucie Arnaz, author interview, Palm Springs, CA, August 2023.

270   *"He had a real marshmallow streak"*: Paul Rabwin OH, LAL.

270 *Desi Jr. acknowledged*: Desi Arnaz Jr., author telephone interview, summer 2024.

270 *Desi had formed a new company*: "A Different Desi Returns to Filmland," Bob Thomas Hollywood column, 1966, scrapbook 8, B-AS, LOC.

270 *Hal Humphrey, the* Los Angeles Times's *syndicated television columnist*: "Desi's Return is a Special Thin," Hal Humphrey, March 31, 1966, *Los Angeles Times*, scrapbook 8, B-AS, LOC.

271 *Desi's passion project*: Theodore Pratt, *Without Consent* (London: Arthur Barker Limited, 1963), 102.

271 *Years later, Desi would describe*: Desi Arnaz letter to Marvin Moss, December 8, 1976, family papers, LAL.

271 *"I kept saying, 'Desi, it's such a repulsive subject'"*: Marcella Rabwin OH, LAL.

272 *"He never could sell it"*: Coyne Steven Sanders and Tom Gilbert, *Desilu: The Story of Lucille Ball and Desi Arnaz* (New York: William Morrow and Company, 1993), 298.

272 *"I have always needed lots of sex"*: Draft manuscript, *A Book*.

272 *In a frustrated moment, Lucy herself*: Bob Schiller OH, LAL.

272 *On the other side of the parent-child dynamic*: Lucie Arnaz, author interview.

272 *In late August 1966*: Brady, *Lucille*, 289.

273 *"I'm still in a state of shock"*: Desi Arnaz letter to Abe Lastfogel, February 22, 1967, box 24, DAP, SDS.

274 *"People laugh at something funny"*: Richard Irvin, *The Forgotten Desi and Lucy TV Projects: The Desilu Series and Specials That Might Have Been* (Orlando, FL: BearManor Media, 2020), 159.

275 *"I was in the middle of a scene"*: "Rewind: Rob Reiner Remembers Being Screamed at by Desi Arnaz," posted December 18, 2021, by take2markTV, https://www .youtube.com/watch?v=X25bkNJkJpM.

276 *"There is nothing in it for me"*: Mary Alice Evans, "'I Love Nixon,' Warbles Desi," *Corpus Christi Caller*, October 25, 1968, scrapbook unknown no., B-AS, LOC.

276 *"Then all I had to do was come in"*: Carol Burnett in *Lucy and Desi*, directed by Amy Poehler (2022, Amazon Studios).

277 *Desi and Edie would come for tapings*: Brady, *Lucille*, 313.

277 *"There was a tremendous pull"*: Brady, *Lucille*, 313.

277 *"I never thought they did anything but love us"*: Desi Arnaz Jr. OH, LAL.

278 *"I don't want a stupid drummer"*: Sanders and Gilbert, *Desilu*, 317.

278 *By this point Desi's own failures*: "Desi Arnaz Announces 100 Percent Sale of Corona Breeding Farm Brood Mares," etc. advertisement, *Hollywood Reporter*, October 9, 1968, scrapbook 8, B-AS, LOC.

278 *"It was a going business until it wasn't"*: Lucie Arnaz, author telephone interview, 2024.

279 *The role was envisioned for a possible spinoff*: Marge Durante OH, LAL.

279 *"I don't think Desi wanted to leave"*: Sanders and Gilbert, *Desilu*, 334.

chapter seventeen: Sunset

282   *"In the last few years I have gone"*: Unpublished letter, box 1, DAP, SDS.

282   *In March 1974, Cady wrote*: Howard Cady letter to Marvin Moss, March 8, 1974, LAL.

283   *He also recommended trimming*: Howard Cady letter to Desi Arnaz, June 18, 1974, LAL.

283   *"Face the fact that I want more for you"*: Howard Cady letter to Desi Arnaz, June 25, 1974, LAL.

284   *"What a weak and uninteresting title!"*: Marcella Rabwin, *Yes, Mr. Selznick: Recollections of Hollywood's Golden Era* (Pittsburgh: Dorrance Publishing Co., 1999), 105.

285   *"I remember him yelling at the crew"*: Al Franken, email to author, December 1, 2022.

285   *A Book was serialized*: Various newspaper clippings, family papers, LAL.

285   *In early May, Cady wrote*: Cady letters, LAL.

285   *Desi did not give up*: Arnaz files, LAL.

286   *As Towers recalled*: Constance Towers, author telephone interview, December 2, 2022.

287   *"The problem is the legs"*: Arnaz notes to self, LAL.

287   *He scratched out ideas*: Arnaz notes to self.

288   *When the film was released*: Vincent Canby, "Griffin O'Neal (Tatum's Brother) in 'The Escape Artist,'" *New York Times*, May 28, 1982.

288   *"When we did that scene"*: Caleb Deschanel, author telephone interview.

289   *"It is not an important part"*: Arnaz notes to self.

289   *"Luu-ucy! I'm home!"*: Lucy Fisher, interview and emails with author, various dates 2022, 2023, 2024.

290   *Desi took great pride*: *Lucy and Desi: A Home Movie*, directed by Lucie Arnaz (1993, Arluck Entertainment).

290   *"And it was so beautiful that night"*: Marco Rizo OH, LAL.

291   *"Whenever he would go out"*: Howard Sheppard OH, LAL.

291   *Appearing in 1983 on* Late Night: "Desi Arnaz, Sr. (& Jack Paar) on Letterman, May 23, 1983," posted April 30, 2016, by Don Giller, https://www.youtube.com/watch?v=5u6-LgExBjQ.

291   *"Nobody could stop him"*: Coyne Steven Sanders and Tom Gilbert, *Desilu: The Story of Lucille Ball and Desi Arnaz* (New York: William Morrow and Company, 1993), 249.

291   *"Edie loved Desi as much as Lucy"*: Kathleen Brady, *Lucille: The Life of Lucille Ball* (New York: Hyperion, 1994), 290.

292   *"Edie died, he was totally alone"*: Lucie Arnaz, author interview, Palm Springs, CA, August 2023.

292 *For her part, Lucie remembered*: Lucie Arnaz, author interview.

292 *"It was really nice"*: Desi Arnaz Jr., author telephone interview, 2024.

292 *In his post-discharge worksheet*: Desi Arnaz rehabilitation records, LAL.

293 *"He still felt he had something to give"*: Sanders and Gilbert, *Desilu*, 348.

293 *In March, Madelyn had written to Desi*: Madelyn Pugh Davis and Bob Carroll Jr., *Laughing with Lucy: My Life with America's Leading Lady of Comedy* (Cincinnati, OH: Clerisy Press, 2007), 260.

294 *"She gamely attempted her old style"*: Stefan Kanfer, *Ball of Fire: The Tumultuous Life and Comic Art of Lucille Ball* (New York: Alfred A. Knopf, 2003), 292.

294 *By now, Desi was dying*: Lucie Arnaz, Laurence Luckinbill, author interviews, April 2022; family papers, LAL.

294 *"Where are you going?"*: Kanfer, *Ball of Fire*, 293.

295 *Lucy was told the news*: Kanfer, *Ball of Fire*, 293.

295 *The obituaries gave Desi his due*: Tim Page, "Desi Arnaz, TV Pioneer, Is Dead at 69," *New York Times*, December 3, 1986; Cecil Smith, "More to Remember than 'Babaloo,'" *Los Angeles Times*, December 4, 1986,

295 *Condolences came from all over*: Letter from Erma Bombeck to Lucille Ball, December 10, 1986; Marcella Rabwin to Ball, December 9, 1986, scrapbook 1, B-AS, LOC. Letter from Van Johnson, funeral folder, LAL.

295 *But Desi's funeral was not well attended*: Kathleen Brady, *Lucille: The Life of Lucille Ball* (New York: Hyperion, 1994), 337.

296 *The band of a hundred-odd mourners*: Memorial guest book, December 4, 1986, LAL.

296 *Lucie, in her own tearful eulogy*: Susan Shroder-Murray, "Family, Friends Mourn Desi Arnaz," UPI, December 4, 1986, https://www.upi.com/Archives/1986/12/04/Family-friends-mourn-Desi-Arnaz/5244534056400/.

296 *"He wanted to be here tonight"*: "Lucille Ball Kennedy Center Honors 1986—Walter Matthau, Robert Stack, Bea Arthur, Valerie Harper," posted December 23, 2020, by John Flanagan, https://www.youtube.com/watch?v=vNBWBO1svBk.

epilogue

300 *A few years earlier, Fred Bernstein*: Fred Bernstein, author telephone interview, August 2022.

300 *"It was a piece in time"*: Lucie Arnaz, author interview, Palm Springs, CA, August 2023.

300 *"He could win, win"*: "Lucille Ball & Barbara Walters: An Interview of a LifeTime (FULL)," posted August 12, 2012, by HNRY LMR, https://www.youtube.com/watch?v=xQR5BzN4EKg.

301 *"You can be as talented"*: John Leguizamo, "An Open Letter to Hollywood," *Los Angeles Times*, November 6, 2022, E5.

302   *"If you're going to do a drama, fine"*: Gale Gordon OH, SMU, AMPAS.

303   *"When they changed to live audience, three-camera"*: Michael Arkush, "'Happy Days' at 50: 'The Fonz Bought Me a House,'" *New York Times*, January 15, 2024, https://www.nytimes.com/2024/01/15/arts/television/happy-days-50-anniver sary.html.

303   *James Burrows, who helped create*: Alexis Soloski, "On a New 'Frasier,' James Burrows Has a Joke for You," *New York Times*, October 10, 2023, https://www.ny times.com/2023/10/10/arts/television/frasier-paramount-james-burrows.html.

303   *Peter Roth, the longtime Warner Bros. television executive*: Peter Roth, author telephone interview, June 13, 2023.

303   *Even today, Paul Feig*: Jeanine Basinger and Sam Wasson, *Hollywood: The Oral History* (New York: Harper Collins, 2022), 721.

304   *"We never saw that level of comedy again"*: Kate Flannery, author telephone interview.

304   *"Essential as she is"*: Douglas McGrath, "Television/Radio: The Good, the Bad, the Lucy: A Legacy of Laughs; The Man Behind the Throne: Making the Case for Desi," October 14, 2001, *New York Times*, https://www.nytimes.com/2001/10/14 /arts/television-radio-good-bad-lucy-legacy-laughs-man-behind-throne-mak ing-case-for.html.

305   *Desi Jr. insists*: Desi Arnaz Jr., author telephone interview, June 2024.

305   *"You believed inside of you"*: Martin Leeds OH, LAL.

305   *"Whatever my indiscretions"*: Draft manuscript, Desi Arnaz, *A Book*, box 1, DAP, SDS.

306   *"With all his genius"*: Rod Rodriguez OH, LAL.

BIBLIOGRAPHY

Abbott, George. *"Mr. Abbott."* New York: Random House, 1963.

Adler, Polly. *A House Is Not a Home.* Amherst: University of Massachusetts Press, 2006.

Aguilar, Luis E. *Cuba 1933: Prologue to Revolution.* New York: W. W. Norton & Company, 1972.

Andrews, Bart. *The "I Love Lucy" Book.* New York: Doubleday, 1985.

Applegate, Debby. *Madam: The Biography of Polly Adler, Icon of the Jazz Age.* New York: Anchor Books, 2022.

Armstrong, Jennifer Keishin. *When Women Invented Television.* New York: Harper Collins, 2021.

Arnaz, Desi. *A Book.* New York: William Morrow and Company, 1976.

Bacon, James. *Hollywood Is a Four-Letter Town.* Chicago: Henry Regnery Company, 1976.

Bair, Deirdre. *Capone: His Life, Legacy and Legend.* New York: Doubleday, 2016.

Ball, Lucille. *Love, Lucy.* New York: G. P. Putnam's Sons, 1996.

Ballard, Kaye, with Jim Hesselman. *How I Lost 10 Pounds in 53 Years: A Memoir.* New York: Backstage Books, 2006.

Bankhead, Tallulah. *Tallulah: My Autobiography.* New York: Harper & Brothers, 1952.

Barmash, Isadore. *"Always Live Better Than Your Clients": The Fabulous Life and Times of Benjamin Sonnenberg, America's Greatest Publicist.* New York: Dodd, Mead & Company, 1983.

Barnouw, Erik. *The Golden Web: A History of Broadcasting in the United States 1933–1953.* New York: Oxford University Press, 1968.

Barnouw, Erik. *Tube of Plenty: The Evolution of American Television.* New York: Oxford University Press, 1990.

Basinger, Jeanine, and Sam Wasson. *Hollywood: The Oral History.* New York: Harper Collins, 2022.

Baughman, James L. *Same Time, Same Station: Creating American Television: 1948–1961.* Baltimore: The Johns Hopkins University Press, 2007.

Beidler, Philip D. *The Island Called Paradise: Cuba in History, Literature, and the Arts.* Tuscaloosa: The University of Alabama Press, 2014.

Beltran, Mary. *Latino TV: A History*. New York: New York University Press, 2021.

Biow, Milton H. *Butting In: An Adman Speaks Out*. Garden City: Doubleday & Company, 1964.

Blanton, Margaret Gray. *The Miracle of Bernadette*. Englewood Cliffs: Prentice-Hall, 1958.

Blanton, Smiley, and Norman Vincent Peale. *Faith Is the Answer: A Psychiatrist and a Pastor Discuss Your Problems*. New York: Abingdon-Cokesbury Press, 1940.

Bowers, Scotty, with Lionel Friedberg. *Full Service: My Adventures in Hollywood and the Secret Sex Lives of the Stars*. New York: Grove Press, 2012.

Brady, Kathleen. *Lucille: The Life of Lucille Ball*. New York: Hyperion, 1994.

Bramson, Seth. *Lost Restaurants of Miami*. Charleston: The History Press, 2020.

———. *Miami Beach*. Charleston: Arcadia Publishing, 2005.

Brochu, Jim. *Lucy in the Afternoon: An Intimate Memoir of Lucille Ball*. New York: William Morrow and Company, 1990

Capone, Deirdre Marie. *Uncle Al Capone*. Recap Publishing, 2011.

Castellucio, Frank, and Alvin Walker. *The Other Side of Ethel Mertz: The Life Story of Vivian Vance*. New York: Berkley Boulevard Books, 2000.

Cloud, Stanley, and Lynn Olson. *Murrow Boys: Pioneers on the Front Lines of Broadcast Journalism*. Boston: Houghton Mifflin Harcourt, 1996.

Cooper, Jackie, with Dick Kleiner. *Please Don't Shoot My Dog: The Autobiography of Jackie Cooper*. New York: Berkley Books, 1982.

Cugat, Xavier. *Rumba Is My Life*. New York: Didier, 1948.

Dalton, Mary M., and Laura R. Linder, eds. *The Sitcom Reader: America Re-viewed, Still Skewed*. Albany: State University of New York Press, 2016.

Dann, Mike (as told to Paul Berger). *As I Saw It: The Inside Story of the Golden Years of Television*. El Prado, NM: Levine Mesa Press, 2009.

Davis, Bette. *The Lonely Life*. New York: Berkley Books, 1990.

Davis, Madelyn Pugh (with Bob Carroll, Jr.). *Laughing with Lucy: My Life with America's Leading Lady of Comedy*. Cincinnati: Clerisy Press, 2007.

Davis, Ronald L. *Van Johnson: MGM's Golden Boy*. Jackson: University Press of Mississippi, 2001.

DePalma, Anthony. *The Cubans: Ordinary Lives in Extraordinary Times*. New York: Viking, 2020.

Diliberto, Gioia. *Debutante: The Story of Brenda Frazier*. New York: Alfred A. Knopf, 1987.

Duke, Patty, with Kenneth Turan. *Call Me Anna: The Autobiography of Patty Duke*. New York: Bantam Books, 1987.

Edelman, Rob, and Audrey Kupferberg. *Meet the Mertzes: The Life Stories of* I Love Lucy's *Other Couple*. Los Angeles: Renaissance Books, 1999.

Edgerton, Gary R. *The Columbia History of American Television*. New York: Columbia University Press, 2007.

Edwards, Elisabeth, ed. *Lucy and Desi: A Real-Life Scrapbook of America's Favorite TV Couple*. Philadelphia: Running Press, 2004.

Eig, Jonathan. *Get Capone: The Secret Plot That Captured America's Most Wanted Gangster*. New York: Simon & Shuster, 2010.

Epstein, Edward Jay. *The Hollywood Economist: The Hidden Financial Reality Behind the Movies*. Brooklyn: Melville House, 2012.

Etter, Jonathan. *Quinn Martin, Producer: A Behind the Scenes History of QM Productions and Its Founder*. Jefferson, NC: McFarland & Company, 2003.

Faith, William. *Bob Hope: A Life in Comedy*. New York: Da Capo Press, 2003.

Federal Writers' Project. *WPA Guide to New York City*. New York: Pantheon, 1982.

Ferrer, Ada. *Cuba: An American History*. New York: Scribner, 2022.

Ferrer, Ada. *Insurgent Cuba: Race, Nation and Revolution, 1868–1898*. Chapel Hill: University of North Carolina Press, 1999.

Freeland, David. *American Hotel: The Waldorf Astoria and the Making of a Century*. New Brunswick: Rutgers University Press, 2021.

Giddins, Gary. *Bing Crosby: The War Years, Swinging on a Star, The War Years, 1940–1946*. New York: Little, Brown and Company, 2018.

Gjelten, Tom. *Bacardi and the Long Fight for Cuba*. New York: Penguin, 2008.

Gonzales, Juan. *Harvest of Empire: A History of Latinos in America*. New York: Penguin, 2022.

Goodwin, Betty. *Hollywood du Jour: Lost Recipes of Legendary Hollywood Haunts*. Los Angeles: Angel City Press, 1993.

Graham, Sheilah. *The Rest of the Story*. New York: Coward-McCann, 1964.

Green, Abel, and Joe Laurie Jr. *Show Biz: Variety from Vaude to Video*. New York: Henry Holt and Company, 1951.

Halberstam, David. *The Fifties*. New York: Random House, 1993.

Harris, Eleanor. *The Real Story of Lucille Ball*. Chosho Publishing, 2022.

Harris, Warren G. *Lucy & Desi: The Legendary Love Story of Television's Most Famous Couple*. New York: Simon & Schuster, 1991.

Higham, Charles. *Lucy: The Real Life of Lucille Ball*. New York: St. Martin's Press, 1986.

Hijuelos, Oscar. *The Mambo Kings Play Songs of Love*. New York: Farrar Straus Giroux, 2015.

Hoffman, David E. *Give Me Liberty: The True Story of Oswaldo Paya and His Daring Quest for a Free Cuba*. New York: Simon & Schuster, 2022.

Irvin, Richard. *The Forgotten Desi and Lucy TV Projects: The Desilu Series and Specials That Might Have Been*. Orlando: Bear Manor Media, 2020.

Jewell, Richard B. *Slow Fade to Black: The Decline of RKO Radio Pictures*. Oakland: University of California Press, 2016.

Kanfer, Stefan. *Ball of Fire: The Tumultuous Life and Comic Art of Lucille Ball*. New York: Alfred A. Knopf, 2003.

Kelley, Kitty. *His Way: The Unauthorized Biography of Frank Sinatra*. New York: Bantam Books, 1986.

Kleinberg, Howard. *Miami Beach*. Miami: Centennial Press, 1994.

Klepser, Carolyn. *Lost Miami Beach*. Charleston: The History Press, 2014.

Kluger, Richard. *Ashes to Ashes: America's Hundred Year Cigarette War, the Public Health, and the Unabashed Triumph of Philip Morris*. New York: Vintage Books, 1997.

Lapidus, Benjamin. *New York and the International Sound of Latin Music, 1940–1990*. Jackson: University Press of Mississippi, 2021.

Leamer, Laurence. *King of the Night: The Life of Johnny Carson*. New York: William Morrow and Company, 1989.

Leonard, Sheldon. *And the Show Goes On: Broadway and Hollywood Adventures*. New York: Limelight Editions, 1995.

Maier, Thomas. *Mafia Spies: The Inside Story of the CIA, Gangsters, JFK, and Castro*. New York: Skyhorse Publishing, 2024.

Mallon, Thomas. *Up with the Sun*. New York: Alfred A. Knopf, 2023.

Maslin, Michael. *Peter Arno: The Mad, Mad World of* The New Yorker's *Greatest Cartoonist*. New York: Regan Arts, 2016.

McGee, Tom. *Betty Grable: The Girl with the Million Dollar Legs*. New York: Welcome Rain Publishers, 2010.

McWilliams, Carey. *Southern California Country: An Island on the Land*. New York: Duell, Sloan & Pearce, 1946.

Milland, Ray. *Wide-Eyed in Babylon*. London: The Bodley Head, 1974.

Morehouse, Ward III. *The Waldorf-Astoria: America's Gilded Dream*. New York: M. Evans and Company, Inc., 1991.

Navasky, Victor S. *Naming Names*. New York: Penguin Books, 1981.

Ness, Eliot, with Oscar Fraley. *The Untouchables: The Real Story*. New York: Pocket Books, 1985.

Nesteroff, Kliph. *The Comedians: Drunks, Thieves, Scoundrels and the History of American Comedy*. New York: Grove Press, 2015.

Olsen, Christopher T. *Lucy Comes Home: A Photographic Journey*. New York: G Arts, 2017.

Oppenheimer, Jess, with Gregg Oppenheimer. *Laughs, Luck . . . and Lucy: How I Came to Create the Most Popular Sitcom of All Time*. Syracuse: Syracuse University Press, 1996.

Perez Firmat, Gustavo. *Life on the Hyphen: The Cuban-American Way*. Austin: University of Texas Press, 1994.

Phillips, R. Hart. *Cuba: Island of Paradox*. New York: McDowell, Obolensky, 1959.

_____. *The Cuban Dilemma*. New York: Ivan Obolensky, Inc., 1962.

Pomeroy, Lynn, and Carolee Pomeroy. *Rancho Las Cruces: The Place, The People, The Flavors*. Foothill Partners, 2017.

Pratt, Theodore. *Without Consent*. London: Arthur Barker Limited, 1963.

Rabwin, Marcella. *Yes, Mr. Selznick: Recollections of Hollywood's Golden Era*. Pittsburgh: Dorrance Publishing Co., 1999.

Rayfiel, Howard. *Where the Hell Is Desilu: How to Fail in Hollywood Without Really Trying*. New Canaan: Paribus Press, 2007.

Rice, Elmer. *Dream Girl*. New York: Coward-McCann, 1946.

Rodon, George A. *George's Story: The Early Life and Times of George Rodon: One Man's Story*. Privately published, 2011.

Rodriguez, Clara E. *Heroes, Lovers, and Others: The Story of Latinos in Hollywood*. Washington: Smithsonian Books, 2004.

Roosevelt, Theodore. *The Rough Riders*. Las Vegas: Public Domain On-Demand Reproduction, 2024.

Rorick, Isabel Scott. *Mr. and Mrs. Cugat: The Record of a Happy Marriage*. Cleveland: The World Publishing Company, 1946.

Royal, Sarah. *A.K.A. Lucy: The Dynamic and Determined Life of Lucille Ball*. Philadelphia: Running Press, 2023.

Sanders, Coyne Steven, and Tom Gilbert. *Desilu: The Story of Lucille Ball and Desi Arnaz*. New York: William Morrow and Company, 1993.

Schlatter, George (as told to Jon Macks). *Still Laughing: A Life in Comedy*. Los Angeles: The Unnamed Press, 2023.

Sonnenberg, Ben. *Lost Property: Memoirs and Confessions of a Bad Boy*. New York: Summit Books, 1991.

Stack, Robert, with Mark Evans. *Straight Shooting*. New York: Berkley Books, 1981.

Starr, Kevin. *The Dream Endures: California Enters the 1940s*. New York: Oxford, 1997.

Storm, Howard, and Steve Stoliar. *The Imperfect Storm: From Henry Street to Hollywood*. Orlando: Bear Manor Media, 2019.

Sublette, Ned. *Cuba and Its Music: From the First Drums to the Mambo*. Chicago: Chicago Review Press, 2004.

Suskin, Steven. *Opening Night on Broadway: A Critical Quotebook of the Golden Age of Musical Theatre*, Oklahoma! *(1943)* to Fiddler on the Roof *(1964)*. New York: Schirmer, Macmillan, 1990.

Symmes, Patrick. *The Boys from Dolores: Fidel Castro's Classmates from Revolution to Exile*. New York: Pantheon Books, 2007.

Tannen, Lee. *I Loved Lucy: My Friendship with Lucille Ball*. New York: St. Martin's Press, 2001.

Thomas, Danny, with Bill Davidson. *Make Room for Danny*. New York: G.P. Putnam's Sons, 1991.

Thomas, Evan. *The War Lovers: Roosevelt, Lodge, Hearst, and the Rush to Empire, 1898*. New York: Back Bay Books, 2011.

Tucker, David C. *S. Sylvan Simon, Moviemaker: Adventures with Lucy, Red Skelton and*

Harry Cohn in the Golden Age of Hollywood. Jefferson, NC: McFarland & Company, 2021.

Twiss, Clinton. *The Long, Long Trailer*. New York: Thomas Y. Crowell Company, 1954.

Van Druten, John. *The Voice of the Turtle*. New York: Dramatists Play Service, 1944.

Vaughn, Robert. *Only Victims: A Study of Show Business Blacklisting*. New York: G.P. Putnam's Sons, 1972.

Watson, Tom. I Love Lucy: *The Classic Moments*. Philadelphia: Courage Books, 1999.

Weller, Sheila. *Dancing at Ciro's: A Family's Love, Loss and Scandal on the Sunset Strip*. New York: St. Martin's Griffin, 2004.

INDEX